DATE DUE

MAR 1 8 1996	
MAY 2 4 2005	

BRODART

Cat. No. 23-221

TAKING ROOT

THE BRANDEIS SERIES
IN AMERICAN JEWISH HISTORY,
CULTURE, AND LIFE
Jonathan D. Sarna, Editor

Leon A. Jick, 1992
*The Americanization of the Synagogue,
1820-1870*

Sylvia Barack Fishman, 1992
*Follow My Footprints: Changing Images of
Women in American Jewish Fiction*

Gerald Tulchinsky, 1993
*Taking Root: The Origins of the
Canadian Jewish Community*

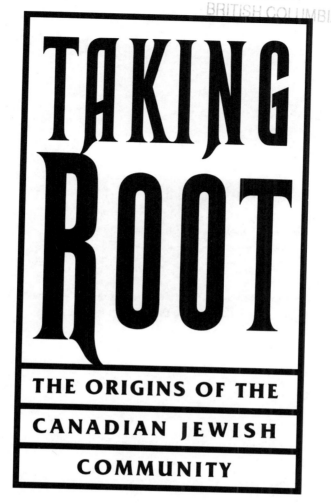

TAKING ROOT

THE ORIGINS OF THE
CANADIAN JEWISH
COMMUNITY

GERALD TULCHINSKY

BRANDEIS UNIVERSITY PRESS
PUBLISHED BY UNIVERSITY PRESS OF NEW ENGLAND
HANOVER AND LONDON

BRANDEIS UNIVERSITY PRESS
Published by University Press of New England,
Hanover, NH 03755

"Of Remembrance" and "Autobiographical" by A. M. Klein.
Used by permission of the University of Toronto Press.
"Strange" and "A Jew" by J. I. Segal. Used by permission.
Jacket image: detail of Torah valance, Austrian Empire, early
19th century. Used by permission of the State Jewish Museum
in Prague, Czechoslovakia.

Every reasonable effort has been made to trace ownership of
copyright materials. Information enabling the Publisher to rectify
any reference or credit in future printings will be welcomed.

Library of Congress Cataloging-in-Publication Data

Tulchinsky, Gerald J. J., 1933-
   Taking root: the origins of the Canadian Jewish community/
Gerald J. J. Tulchinsky.
      p. cm. – (The Brandeis series in American Jewish history,
     culture, and life)
   Includes bibliographical references.
   ISBN 0-87451-609-9
    1. Jews – Canada – History.   2. Canada – Ethnic relations.
I. Title. II. Series

F1035.J5T85 1993   92-28210
971'.004924 – dc20

Printed and bound in Canada.

5 4 3 2 1

In the days to come shall Jacob take root,
Israel shall blossom and bud;
And the face of the world shall be filled
with fruitage.

Isaiah 27:6

——

This book is dedicated to the
memory of the six million Jews
who were murdered by the German
Nazis and their collaborators in
Europe between 1933 and 1945.

Contents

Acknowledgements

This work was initially undertaken as part of the "Generations" project with the sponsorship of the Multiculturalism Branch of the Department of the Secretary of State whose officers, Myron Momryk and Yok Leng Chang among others, provided advice and encouragement throughout. The editorial committee members were of great assistance, especially the editors of this series, Jean Burnet and the late Howard Palmer. I wish to pay tribute to the memory of Louis Rosenberg, whose outstanding work on Canadian Jewish history provided me with a standard I have tried to match. David Rome, while serving as a director of the Jewish Public Library of Montreal, offered a wealth of rich insights into this subject during lengthy discussions many years ago. I am happy to pay a special tribute to him and to the many other librarians and archivists who gave me such generous assistance during my years of research on this project. At the National Archives of Canada enthusiastic, kind, and helpful assistance was freely given by Lawrence Tapper, Barbara Wilson, Glen Wright, James Whalen, Terry Cook, and others who were always ready to answer my requests for help. In Jerusalem, the Central Zionist Archives' rich source of primary Zionist materials was opened to me by Dr. Michael Heymann, Dr. Philip, and Yoram Mayorek, while the State of Israel Archives' materials were made available by Dr. Alsberg and Dr. Moshe Moussek. At the archives of the Canadian Jewish Congress in Montreal, I was assisted by Mr. Rome and by his successors, Judith Nefsky and Janice Rosen. At the archives of the Canadian Jewish Congress, Central Region, in Toronto, Dr. Stephen Speisman provided useful advice and assistance. Barry Hyman of the Provincial

Archives of Manitoba greatly facilitated my research there. I am also grateful to research assistants who helped me over many years: Peter Freedman, Michelle Sherwood, Wolfgang Gomille, Ken Wise, Lisa Talesnick, Catherine Sykes, and Jillann Rothwell who were employed with funds provided by the Multiculturalism Branch, the Social Sciences and Humanities Research Council of Canada, and the Queen's University Advisory Research Committee.

I wish to extend warm thanks to the entire staff at the Douglas Library at Queen's, especially to those working in the Reference Room, Marcia Sweet, Melanie Harris, and Elizabeth Gibson, to Bonnie Brooks and Lorraine Helsby in Interlibrary Loans, and to William Morley and Barbara St. Remy in Special Collections. The late Dr. Nathan Kaganoff at the Archives of the American Jewish Historical Society in Waltham, Massachusetts, generously answered all of my requests.

I am happy to acknowledge also the encouragement and assistance provided by a number of my colleagues, at Queen's and elsewhere, who read early drafts of parts of this manuscript and offered me their helpful comments: Lucien Karchmar, George Rawlyk, the late Roger Graham, and Donald Swainson. Lucien Karchmar also read chapter six and saved me from making several errors. Special thanks are due to Stephen Speisman, Ian McKay, Ramsay Cook, James Pritchard, Maurice Careless, Louis Greenspan, Paul-André Linteau, David Bercuson, Harry Gutkin, and Jonathan Sarna, all of whom read the entire manuscript and rescued me from many factual errors and inconsistencies. I extend special thanks to Ian McKay for giving me several illuminating references, to Roland Tinline of the Queen's Department of Geography for timely advice, as well as to Annette Hayward of the Queen's Department of French, who helped with the translations in chapter two. To all of them and to many others who encouraged me in this work I am profoundly thankful. I also am happy to acknowledge the advice and assistance of my publisher, Malcolm Lester, and the superb editorial work of Gena Gorrell. Jack Granatstein gave me very helpful advice in the final stages of this project.

I feel deep gratitude to my many teachers, especially to my late father, Harry Tulchinsky, the late Rabbi (Rav) Gedaliah Felder, Maurice Careless, and Ze'ev Mankowitz for their wisdom, patience, inspiration, intellectual rigour, and *menschlichkeit*. I owe a very special debt to Alan Cruess, MD FRCSC, head of Queen's University's Department of Ophthalmology, for his surgical skills and continuing attention. To my wife, Ruth, and my children, Steve, Ellen, and Laura, I owe more than words can express.

Kingston, Ontario, August 1992

Preface

"Go Catch the Echoes of the Ticks of Time"

The history of Canadian Jewry has received surprisingly little attention from historians, given that the Jewish communal experience began in 1768, when the first synagogue was organized in Montreal. Benjamin Sack, a professional journalist, made the first attempt to write a comprehensive history of the Jews in Canada during the 1920s, with his articles in the *Keneder Adler*, his survey of early Canadian Jewish history to the 1880s in A.D. Hart's *The Jew in Canada*, published in 1926, and his 1948 book *Geschichte fun Yidn in Kanada*.[1] It was pioneering work that was based largely on original sources, sound judgement, and clear insight into some of the distinctive features of the Jewish experience in this country. This book was intended to be the first of a multi-volume work. But Sack, who worked alone, without grants, and in his spare time, was not able to finish it. Of his contemporaries, Abraham Rhinewine, editor of Toronto's *Yiddisher Zhournal*, and Simon Belkin, manager of the Jewish Colonization Association, also wrote on Canadian Jewish history: Rhinewine a survey and a 1932 book commemorating the hundredth anniversary of Jewish political emancipation, and Belkin a study of the Labour Zionist movement in Canada.[2]

Belkin's book – a detailed and comprehensive examination of Zionist leftist culture and politics – was a most significant contribution to the historiography of Canadian Jewry, while his scholarly study of Jewish immigration and settlement, published in 1961, put him among the first rank of historians of this community.[3]

But it was Louis Rosenberg – another civil servant of Canadian Jewry, as

Regina agent of the JCA and research director of the Canadian Jewish Congress – who emerged by 1939 as his generation's premier scholar of Canadian Jewry. In that year he published an important statistical study which not only was the indispensable source for understanding the sociology of the contemporary community, but also supplied enormously valuable data on the growth of the Canadian Jewish population.[4] His approach was impeccably scholarly; he set for himself the task of collecting and compiling the evidence of Jewish migration patterns, geographical distribution, economic structure, occupational trends, life cycles, ages, and other aspects of the community's social evolution. In time, Rosenberg might have produced the definitive history of Canadian Jewry, so sensitive was he to the central issues of the Canadian Jewish experience. As research director for the Congress, he collected documents and published many of them in the series *Canadian Jewish Archives* published during the early 1960s, and it seems that he rightly regarded this vital task as preliminary to any serious effort at synthesis and analysis.

His successor at the Congress, David Rome, had been for many years previously the director of the Jewish Public Library in Montreal, since 1914 a most significant institution in the intellectual and cultural life of that community. Rome's studies of Canadian Jewish literature and his contribution to the collaborative work (with Bernard Figler) on Hananiah Meir Caiserman – the founder of the Congress in 1919 – are noteworthy for their insights into the rich dimensions of Yiddish culture,[5] while his many volumes of commentary on documents dealing with Canadian Jewish history constitute a unique resource that could be profitably exploited by future generations of historians.[6] The research of Abraham Arnold and Cyril Leonoff on western Canadian history, Arnold's on the prairie farm settlements and Leonoff's on early British Columbia settlements and pioneering figures, have added greatly to our understanding of those vital communities.[7]

Of the post-1960 attempts at writing a comprehensive Canadian Jewish history, Rabbi Stuart Rosenberg's was probably the most ambitious, wide-ranging, well illustrated, and readable, until Irving Abella's recent *A Coat of Many Colours* was published.[8] A notable survey, Professor Abella's work includes valuable observations based upon years of intensive research. The brief survey by the late Professor Bernard L. Vigod effectively summarizes the main themes of Canadian Jewish history.[9] Michael Brown's *Jew or Juif? Jews, French Canadians, and Anglo-Canadians 1789-1914* is a substantial and exceptionally well documented study, in many ways the first of its kind, both in depth of research in original sources and in its central thesis, which contends that the Canadian Jewish community before 1914 "saw in American-Jewish society a paradigm of all that was dynamic, liberal, and progressive."[10] Arguing further that "in general, Jews had an easier life with Protestants than with Catholics – especially since Catholics felt obliged to preserve the Catholic nature of society," Brown contends that the "presence of Jews and the toleration of Judaism presented a threat to Catholic hegemony". Thus, while emphasizing the attraction of both British and American models, Brown stresses the rejection by Catholic Quebec as a major conditioning factor in the Canadian Jewish experience – all the more vivid in recent times, he avers, with the advent of militant and increasingly exclusionist French Canadian nationalism. The work is a significant contribution to Canadian Jewish studies and will remain an important point of departure for students in this field for years to come. The same can be said of Stephen Speisman's fine scholarly study of the institutional evolution of Toronto Jewry before 1937, of David Bercuson's excellent analysis of Canadian policy towards the State of Israel, and of Pierre Anctil's significant work on the interface of Jews and Québécois in the interwar period.[11] Besides these, the work of several younger scholars – like Ruth Frager on Jewish women and women's issues, Henry Trachtenberg on the social politics of Winnipeg Jewry, Richard Menkis on aspects of cultural development, and Phyllis Senese on antisemitism in French Canada – are already coming to fruition, with enormous benefit to those interested in a deeper understanding of Canadian Jewish social history.

Quite clearly, Canadian Jewish history is a subject in its own right, not a branch or pale reflection of the Jewish experience in the United States. Its contours were shaped by Canadian conditions, not necessarily reflecting occurrences and trends taking place first in the American mainstream and then, years later, happening to the northern cousins. The Americanization of the Jews – their gradual or rapid adaptation to and acceptance in the mainstream of American culture, and the development of what might be called the American Jewish symbiosis – was not necessarily mirrored in Canada. The Canadian Jew who becomes Chief Justice of the Supreme Court of Canada, or Governor of the Bank of Canada, or a member of a federal Cabinet, or a senior officer in the Royal Canadian Air Force, or a leading literary figure, is not simply the northern equivalent of an American Jew like Justice Brandeis, Henry Morgenthau, Bernard Baruch, Admiral Rickover, or Philip Roth.

To be sure, there are many significant – almost overpowering – resemblances between the American and Canadian Jewish historical experiences, and in certain respects the communities are so similar as to be indistinguishable. Without doubt, the more numerous and more highly developed American

Jewish communities exercised strong and continuing influences on Canadian Jewry. After all, in both cases most of their people came from Eastern Europe in sudden and vast immigration waves before 1914. And of course the cultural baggage they brought with them was identical in both countries: deeply pious, rigid Orthodoxy in many, and a complex mix of philosophies such as Marxism, socialism, anarchism, zionism, bundism, and other ideals among many of the young, who had been exposed to the intellectual transformations outside their own narrow world. The historical developments of both American and Canadian Jewries were also highly similar, particularly in such things as post-1900 settlement patterns, cultural life (including the use of Yiddish in newspapers, theatres, and schools), and the economic struggle, especially in the clothing industry. These and other similarities, interchanges, and influences must be acknowledged.

What should not be conceded, however, is that all of the major forces that shaped the Jewish experience in Canada were the same as, or even similar to, those in the United States. Jonathan Sarna suggested, in a brief 1981 paper in the *Canadian Jewish Historical Society Journal*, where some important differences might lie.[12] Notwithstanding the many strong similarities, Canadian Jewry experienced a significantly different evolution as a result of the national context in which it was situated. It is not enough to say that Canada was a different country; after all, Canada's proximity to the American giant, and the similarity of peoples and outlook, inevitably resulted in very strong American influences affecting all aspects of Canadian life, including the evolution of the Jewish community. It is important to understand that at the same time there were different co-ordinates to the Canadian constitutional structure, political life, national composition, urban patterns, and economic development, which all directly affected the evolution of Jewish life in Canada. Some of the most significant factors influencing the Jewish community in this country had no counterparts in the United States. Consequently, if Canadian and American Jewry have now in certain respects become indistinguishable from one another, they reached this commonality by different routes.

The duality of Canada's national personality posed particularly acute problems for that very large part of Canadian Jewry – until recently it was nearly half – living in the province of Quebec. There the confessional school system established at Confederation put the Jewish community at a serious disadvantage, because there was no legal provision for Jewish children in either the Catholic or the Protestant system of schooling. Whether these children had a right to go to school was a testy legal and political question which was resolved in stages over nearly thirty years of struggle, between 1903 and 1930.[13] It was a battle for fundamental civil rights that were being denied them by the Protestant school commissioners of Montreal and the Quebec provincial government. Minor victories in the courts and in the legislative assembly after 1903 were the result of a galvanization of the Jewish community on a massive scale, which led to the emergence of a collective consciousness noteworthy for its major spokesmen, newspaper development, intense intracommunal debate, and greatly heightened awareness of the Jewish place in the legal, political, and social context of the province of Quebec.[14] Nothing like this kind of Jewish civil rights fight occurred in the United States, because nowhere in the republic did the same kind of co-ordinates exist to bar the Jewish advance to social equality.

This crucial contest, with its ramifications through all sectors of life in a community that included almost half of the Jews in the Dominion, was only one feature of Canadian Jewish history that grew out of Canada's duality. In fact, Quebec's rapidly expanding Jewish community ran directly afoul of French Canadian nationalism at its beginnings in the early 1800s, and during its efflorescence in the late nineteenth and early twentieth centuries. In this era such nationalism, with its blend of what the French Canadian historian Michel Brunet calls agriculturalism, anti-statism, and messianism, where, Denis Monière asserts, the Church regarded "the opposition forces . . . as the fiends of hell," combined a militant ultramontane Catholic faith with the national rebirth of an agricultural, French-speaking republic on the St. Lawrence.[15] Amongst those who believed in this visionary frame of reference the Jew was a standing affront, a force fostering morals which threatened French Canada's survival.[16] Among other things, the Jew was the infidel, the Christ-killer whose continuing rejection of Christianity constituted an insult to the faith and whose rapidly increasing presence in Montreal was seen as a dire threat to the purity of the French Canadian ideal. He was also viewed by certain segments of French Canadian society as the arch-traitor, the perfidious betrayer of France's honour, as was proven beyond a shadow of doubt in the conviction of Captain Alfred Dreyfus in 1894 for treason.[17] The Jew came to be regarded as an economic threat as well – both as an unscrupulous exploiter in the clothing industry, where Jewish contractors worked the piecing-out system using Jewish and French Canadian sweated labour in home or attic shops where eighty-hour weeks were not uncommon, and as a competitor in the market for unskilled and semiskilled jobs.[18] The Jew was also perceived as the political and social radical and trade-unionist activist, the purveyor of insidious socialist and anarchist ideas which some French Canadian clerical and lay leaders saw as infectious and corrosive poisons in the pure springs of their people's religious and social life.[19] Thus, paradoxically, in the clothing industry the Jew was seen at one and the same time as exploiter and radical. In all, then, the Jew was included among those who constituted a threat to the destiny of the Québécois to survive and thrive as a distinctive Catholic and French agrarian polity in Quebec.

That the Jews attracted such animosity, which welled up repeatedly in some newspapers, pamphlets, and church sermons, should not surprise us. Jews were the largest minority in the province, outside of the old-stock English-speaking groups, who – though separated by class and religious issues – nevertheless maintained a certain transcendent coherence and unity, and were headed by a tight, tough, wealthy, and influential elite. Montreal's Jewish quarter, which stretched north from the docks along St. Lawrence Street to Dorchester by about 1900, had mushroomed in size with the pre-1914 infusions of immigrants.[20] By 1920 virtually the entire city section from the waterfront north, in a belt a few blocks wide on either side of St. Lawrence–Main to the lower reaches of Outremont, constituted a huge, predominantly Jewish enclave of factories, shops, synagogues, and tightly packed housing. Although it was not the only sector of Montreal in which Jews lived, the fact that this "Jewish quarter" was at the geographical centre of the city and divided the French from the English sections of Montreal was also symbolic of the precarious marginality of the Jewish presence to both communities. Insofar as the Anglophones were concerned, the Jews were not particularly welcome, as indicated by the treatment which Jewish pupils and teachers received from the Protestant Board of school commissioners after 1900.[21] The Francophones, because of their closer physical proximity, far greater numbers, and political prowess, were able to manifest their antisemitism both on the street and in the political arena. However, the antisemitism of Montreal's Anglo-Protestants, who made Jews unwelcome in their schools and severely restricted their entry into McGill University, was much more damaging to Jews. French and Anglo-Canadian antisemitism was a very serious business, and it had a long-lasting effect on the political and social well-being of the large Jewish population of Quebec.

Although these incidents – with the exception of the Plamondon case of 1910, when Jews were publicly accused of practising abominations allegedly stemming from the Talmud – were in themselves relatively harmless, they did underscore the fact that antisemitism in Quebec seemed to possess a special force, a greater depth and virulence, than anywhere else in North America. After 1920 this antisemitism welled up time and again, not only to remind Jews of their inferior position in the eyes of some French Canadian nationalist and ultramontane clerics, but also to reduce their presence in sectors where they had achieved some prominence.

Of course, antisemitism was not unique to Canada. The phenomenon is deeply rooted in Western Christian culture, and stems largely from religious sources. Antisemitism has found frequent expression in America in various forms reflecting these religious origins since colonial times. Although there are, as yet, no scholarly surveys of antisemitism in Canada, evidence suggests that the same could be said of English Canada, where such sentiments also received widespread expression, most notably from the pen of Toronto's leading late-nineteenth-century intellectual, Goldwin Smith. Still, it appears that anti-semitism outside Quebec was not nearly as strong as the anti-Oriental feelings on the Canadian west coast, or the anti-Slavic attitudes on the Prairies.[22] The special character, dimensions, and persistence of the French Canadian variety from the 1920s onwards helped to shape the community-consciousness of about half of Canada's Jews – and indirectly, through national organizations dominated by Montreal, of a significant portion of the remainder. If the Canadian Jewish community has been much more effectively governed in national organizations than American Jewry, this is largely attributable to the fact that Canadian Jewry has felt more threatened. A leading reason for the reactivation of the Canadian Jewish Congress after 1933 was the need to counter the increasingly virulent antisemitism in Quebec and elsewhere in Canada.

Governance through national organizations like the Congress, which was originally established in 1919, was also facilitated by another peculiar feature of Canadian Jewry: its overwhelming concentration in a few metropolitan centres, after the 1880s. In contrast to the Jews in the United States, where, by the 1840s, significant Jewish communities existed in all major cities up and down the eastern seaboard, in the mid-West, and on the Gulf coast, Canada's Jews before 1900 overwhelmingly chose Montreal and Toronto. Later, Win-nipeg became a third centre. The Trois-Rivières community declined, the one in Quebec city withered, that of Victoria stagnated and dwindled, and the Maritime centres had barely begun in the nineteenth century.[23] In the United States, even before the Civil War, there were about 200 congregations in exis-tence across the country, some of them in major Southern cities.[24] In the 1870s, Cincinnati emerged as a leading centre of Jewish religious life, and Philadel-phia as a major educational and cultural hub, while Chicago attracted a huge Jewish population after the 1880s. All of these communities were independent of New York, a city one-quarter Jewish by 1914 and the residence of about half of all America's Jews. In Canada there were no counterparts to Cincinnati,

Philadelphia, Chicago, Boston, or the other Jewish centres, which so diffused power and influence in American Jewry that national organizations have always been relatively weak. With a high concentration of Canadian Jews in two or three cities, and about half of them in one preeminent metropolis, countervailing influences did not develop here on anything like the scale that they did in the United States. Hence, Jewish national organizations were apparently able to establish themselves more effectively than their American counterparts.

After 1898, for example, the Federation of Canadian Zionist Societies was greatly envied by the Americans because of its impressive national structure, active branches, and tight organization, controlled from Montreal by the patrician Clarence de Sola.[25] After its reestablishment in 1933, the Canadian Jewish Congress, which was also based in Montreal, served as a forum for all shades of political, religious, and cultural expression. As a spokesman for Canadian Jewry on major issues it was far more effective than the American Jewish Congress, which suffered from the rivalry of a number of competing national organizations.[26] This is not to say that the Canadian Jewish community was more politically or intellectually homogeneous than the American, or always unified, or that, notwithstanding Montreal's obvious importance, there were not competing regional and other interests. The leadership of Toronto's Jewish community came to resent strongly the control of national organizations by the Montreal patricians, while in Winnipeg and elsewhere on the Prairies an independent spirit emerged early and persisted for many years.[27] Yet virtually all elements agreed on the need for strong national organizations.

Certain factors help to explain this broad commonality of purpose. The most important one is the comparatively strong religious homogeneity of Canadian Jewry. This is the third major point of difference between the two North American communities, and it constitutes an essential ingredient in any understanding of the contours of Canadian Jewish history. American Jewry was shaped and, until at least 1900, was dominated by the German immigrants who arrived in the United States during the 1840s and 1850s.[28] The cultural baggage of some German Jews included fragments of the Enlightenment philosophy of Moses Mendelssohn and some of the influences of the new scientific study of Jewish culture, *Wissenschaft des Judentums*.[29] From this early nineteenth-century German-Jewish Reformation a new synagogue, theology, and liturgy had emerged, in which virtually all elements of Jewish particularism were expunged and Jewish universalism was celebrated; thus many Jews were transformed into Germans of the Mosaic persuasion. Jewish religious beliefs were reinterpreted and reformulated root and branch by the rabbis of the new

Judaism. In their transposition to America these Germans erected their Reform synagogues, established Cincinnati as their centre, and virtually dominated American Jewish religious life, so that by 1880, one authority claims, most of the 270 synagogues in the United States were Reform.[30] Furthermore, they now became Americans of the Mosaic persuasion. Acquiring wealth, influence, power, and social prestige, the Loebs, Kuhns, Gimbels, Guggenheims, and others of "Our Crowd" began a process of merging into the American mainstream, while still others made significant contributions to American progressivism.[31] Not only did they imprint upon American Jewish life a strong Reform synagogue, they also implanted a dominant philosophy or mystique of Americanness, as in Germany many had come to believe in their Germanness. The fact that this mystique meshed with one important aspect of the American ethos – outspoken patriotism – served only to accentuate this identity. Is it just coincidence that Jews wrote some of the most patriotic American popular songs, including "God Bless America" and "White Christmas"? Indeed, American Jewish songwriters like Hart, Hammerstein, Rodgers, Berlin, Kern, and the Gershwin brothers may be among the most rhapsodic celebrants of American life.

North of the 49th parallel, the Jewish community developed in a much different way. Canada did not receive significant numbers of German Jewish immigrants with Reform impulses to overwhelm the existing institutions, and thus it escaped being heavily influenced by the Reform movement and its accompanying philosophy of emancipation. Not that Canadian Jews, small in numbers and concentrated in very few centres, refrained from trying to adjust economically, politically, and in every other way. But most of them had not been exposed to either the German Jewish Reform synthesis or to the Enlightenment-influenced Orthodoxy of Samson Raphael Hirsch. Indeed, the most influential element culturally in Montreal until the 1880s was the "Spanish and Portuguese," while in Toronto British and Lithuanians outnumbered all other elements.[32] These dominant groups in Toronto and Montreal were essentially conservative and observantly Orthodox in religious practice. The historian of Toronto Jewry, Stephen Speisman, points out that until the early twentieth century "the division between the traditional and liberal wings of the [Holy Blossom] congregation appear to have been minor. . . . There were no major departures from orthodoxy while the congregation remained [without its own premises]."[33] And while certain Reform influences began to affect the main group in Toronto in the 1880s, the Montrealers remained adamantly, almost pugnaciously Orthodox. Reverend Abraham de Sola and his son Meldola, who held the pulpit of the Shearith Israel synagogue in succession for about seventy years, acted as stout defenders of the old faith in Montreal, and successfully kept the tiny Reform group out of the mainstream of religious life in the community.[34]

The absence of a German migration to Canada large enough to over-whelm or replace the traditional communities is thus highly significant. For while American Jewry was greatly influenced by the Reform philosophy, Canada was affected to a much lesser degree, and in Montreal a certain counter-reformation spirit prevailed. Most of Canadian Jewry remained pre-dominantly tied to the old faith, even though some assimilation was already under way. This outlook may also have reflected the comparatively conserv-ative ethos of nineteenth-century Canada, where traditional values prevailed of Crown, established churches, and certain quasi-aristocratic trappings related to the British connection. Canadian Jews like the influential de Sola family saw themselves as defenders of the British tradition as well as of Jewish Orthodoxy. Although this outlook never had the philosophical respectability of the ideal German- or American-Jewish symbiosis, it did establish a certain British tone or shading for the community. In Canada, especially in Quebec, Jews knew that they were different and would remain so, equal in law perhaps but distinct, whereas in the United States there was a belief – especially among the second generation – in a larger degree of inte-gration into a culture which, because it was by definition republican, demo-cratic, and libertarian, would allow the Jewish admixture.[35]

With Orthodoxy and tradition still firmly in place and centred in a very much smaller, more concentrated group of communities, by the 1880s and 1890s Canadian Jewry faced the hordes of immigrants who continued to arrive until the First World War. During the 1920s many of these dissimilarities between the two North American communities began to diminish. But not entirely: In both Canada and the United States the Eastern European Jews, whether traditional or radical, came increasingly into communal prominence. They thronged into the clothing factories and concentrated themselves in urban ghettos, and in Canada a small but symbolically important group moved out to settle on the Prairies. Yet previously developed national differences in the two Jewries nevertheless continued to influence the ways in which certain institutions and organizations evolved, while the timing of national economic development somewhat affected the subsequent demographic distribution of Jews.[36] Thus differences, some subtle and some blatant, continued. For example, Zionism has been, from the 1890s until the present, a continuous and dominant part of the Canadian Jewish identity. This is not to say that a majority of Canadian Jews have been openly Zionist – but significant segments of the old patrician and *nouveaux riches* elites have been so.[37] American Jewry, or at least its leadership and moneyed elite, on the other hand, either held back from Zionism or actively opposed it.[38] For many American Jews – especially those who shared the ideal of symbiosis, that goal implanted by the mid-nineteenth-century German immigrants – Zionism was a threat, because it raised the problem of dual loyalty. The nagging question of how one could become a Zionist – that is, one who believed in the return of Jews to the ancient homeland – while still being a loyal American dedicated to the achievement of cultural integration in the United States, could not be easily answered. Even after Louis D. Brandeis, the famous justice of the U.S. Supreme Court, developed a partially satisfying answer to this dilemma, most of the old German community – now America's Jewish elite – continued in a steadily militant anti-Zionist stance.[39] And it is interesting to note that the Reform synagogue – the quintessential expression of the German-American-Jewish quest for symbiosis – was a major vehicle for opposition to Zionism, although there were a few significant Reform leaders who actively espoused it. At the Cincinnati seminary, rabbinical students were taught by outspoken opponents of the idea of a Jewish homeland in Palestine; consequently this message was heard from many American Reform pulpits.[40] When one American rabbi, Maurice Eisendrath, tried to bring this anti-Zionism into his Toronto Reform congregation in the late 1920s, the community was outraged and a sizeable secession from the synagogue took place, although the unrepentant rabbi continued his attack.[41] He only ceased his opposition in the late 1930s, as did most of the rest of Reform Jewry – for one principal, terrible reason.

The explanation of the more favourable attitude towards Zionism among Canadians brings us to another point, which has already to some extent been anticipated. Jews in Canada did not understand that there were any tests of Canadian nationalism they had to meet. In Montreal, insofar as both French and English were concerned, Jews were pariahs, and barely tolerated. But the predominant strain of pre-1914 Canadian nationalist thought, that of the imperial federationists, though expressing a narrowly British view of history, national character, and Canada's mission, also indirectly implied an integration into British imperialism, a toleration, an openness, a liberality towards racial and cultural diversity, and a grudging acceptance in this polity in which freedom is said to wear a crown.[42] From the standpoint of James S. Woodsworth's Social Gospel outlook, Jews – like Galicians and Chinese – were communities which could be absorbed.[43] It may be that the origins of the idea of the Canadian mosaic lie somewhere in these attitudes, and in the fact that there appears to have been no public ethos in English Canada which necessarily overrode all other loyalties. In any event, Canada was without the intellectual influences of the German Jews, who might have been inclined to think their way into a Canadian Jewish loyalty conundrum.

In these circumstances of no competing nationalism and no opposing Reformation ideology, the Zionist movement in Canada thrived. Under the leadership of Clarence de Sola, a member of the Spanish-Portuguese "aristocracy" of Montreal Jewry who headed the Canadian Zionist Federation from 1898 to 1919, the movement grew. It spread quickly through the metropolitan centres, into small communities across the country and even into the few scattered farming colonies on the Prairies.[44] So successful was this organization that de Sola proudly held it up as a model for Zionists in other countries to follow — especially for the Americans, who were grappling with a multitude of problems, the most serious being an intellectual justification of the movement's first principles. No such problems bothered de Sola. His followers included many of the Russian, Polish, and Romanian Jews who were pouring into the country in the early 1900s, outnumbering all previous Jewish immigration. After 1901, when the nation's Jewish population stood at about 16,000, an average of 6,000 Jews arrived every year. By 1911, the Jewish population had reached 75,681, an increase of almost 370 per cent over just one decade.[45] In 1913–14 alone over 18,000 Jews reached Canada.[46] Even during the First World War, an annual average of 4,000 Jews arrived. The resurgence of Jewish immigration in the 1920s brought additional, though smaller, waves from the Ukraine, Poland, and Lithuania. To most of these Eastern European Jews, modern political Zionism came as one major vehicle of redemption from a hateful and oppressive czarist regime which was also, semi-officially, antisemitic. Consequently they arrived in Canada with no predispositions towards symbiosis. Perhaps Zionism thrived also because some Canadian Jewish leaders like Clarence de Sola and Rabbi Ashinsky, of Montreal's Sha'ar Hashomayim synagogue, saw the movement as potentially an integral part of British imperialism.[47] De Sola waxed eloquent on this theory, and claimed later to have broached the idea of a British pro-Zionist declaration several months before the famous Balfour Declaration of November 1917.

The Canadian Zionist Federation became a kind of national Jewish congress because of its countrywide support – though, even among both religious and secular Russian immigrants, this was not unanimous. It was followed by the Canadian Jewish Congress, a fundamentally Zionist organization, after the war. Zionism thus went deeper into the Canadian Jewish context than into the

American one, because of the conjuncture of separate and distinctive cultural, demographic, and political factors, and because of the unique constitutional and racial structure of Canada. Perhaps Canadian Jews, in reaction to French Canadian antisemitism and nationalism, may even have absorbed some nationalistic influences from the French Canadians in Montreal. At any event, Zionism's greater strength and support from Canadian Jewry was noted by the world leaders of the movement, and was expressed by higher per capita financial contributions and emigration to Palestine both before and after the proclamation of the state of Israel in 1948.

A further determining factor in Canadian Jewish history is the fact Canada continued to receive substantial Jewish immigration through the 1920s, while the tide to the U.S., though numerically larger, was relatively far less significant.[48] The typical immigrants of 1924 were probably somewhat different from their counterparts of 1914 or earlier. They had experienced first-hand the European turmoil of 1914–18, the massive upheaval of the Russian Revolution, the ensuing devastating civil war, and the terrible Ukrainian pogroms. Recent East European history and the modernization of Russia before 1914, as well as the resonances of the Old World (through the arrival of nearly 50,000 Jewish immigrants during the 1920s), probably had a deeper, more pervasive, and more lasting effect on the Canadian community, because of its relative size, than on the American one.[49] Moreover, this immigration of the 1920s included a small number of young intellectuals, and likely had a strong enriching influence on Jewish cultural life in Canada.

Thus the contours of Canadian Jewish history were determined by a set of co-ordinates which were unique to the northern half of this continent, and which resulted in the evolution of a community with a personality different from American Jewry's. Canada had a different history, polity, and culture, and different immigration, economic, and urban-growth patterns. Not surprisingly, there evolved here a community that was more traditional, more superficially unified, and more culturally homogeneous than that of our U.S. cousins. While American Jewry yearned for integration into the mainstream of the great republic, Canadians strove to express their Jewishness in a country that had no coherent self-definition – except perhaps the solitudes of duality, isolation, northernness, and borrowed glory. In the United States, Irving Berlin wrote "God Bless America"; in Canada the quintessential Jewish literary figure, who is probably this country's greatest twentieth-century poet – Abraham Moses Klein – wrote poems of anguish expressing longing for redemption of the Jewish soul lost in a sea of modernity. "Go catch the echoes of the ticks of time;

Spy the interstices between its sands," he tells us in "Of Remembrance".[50] And while he was able, in his collection of poems *The Rocking Chair*, to capture the culture of French Canada better than any Anglophone has done in recent times, he reiterated throughout his career his Jewish frame of reference. Towards the end his thoughts returned to "the ghetto streets where a Jewboy dreamed pavement into pleasant Bible-land":

> It is a fabled city that I seek;
> It stands in Space's vapours and Time's haze;
> Thence comes my sadness in remembered joy
> Constrictive of the throat;
> Thence do I hear, as heard by a Jewboy,
> The Hebrew violins,
> Delighting in the sobbed Oriental note.[51]

We have seen some of the features that make Canadian Jewish history a separate study. To be sure, they are not entirely distinct from the American Jewish experience, as a reading of Henry Feingold's superb survey, *Zion in America*, demonstrates.[52] Many similarities exist, and as Canadian history is in certain respects both different from and similar to American, the historical experience of at least one ethnic group in this country is a reflection of that reality. Can one perhaps generalize from this Jewish history to the history of other ethnic groups in Canada? It is not easy to answer this question. But if the Jewish experience is in any way representative, the peculiarities of this country's history, culture, and pace of evolution must be considered in understanding the development of Ukrainian, Polish, or Hungarian communities as well.[53] In this way we explain not only ethnic history but also some of the only partially explored dimensions of Canada's past and present personality. Perhaps this will help us understand how we got to where we are now.

Introduction

Long into the night the sounds of muffled conversations could be heard in our house. It was the winter of 1942–43, and the fate of the world was being decided at the Battle of Stalingrad. So was the fate of the Jewish people of Europe. If the details of their destruction were not then fully known – except by the free world's leaders – Jews like my father, who had lived through the Ukrainian pogroms of 1918 and 1919, understood instinctively that a cataclysmic disaster was in the making. And long into the night he, my mother, and their friends would discuss the information they read in the Canadian press, and in the Yiddish newspapers and magazines that arrived every week at our house.

My father and other Eastern European immigrant Jews of his generation understood that the German Nazis were obliterating the Jews of Europe. They also knew that they could do nothing about this mass murder. But they could and did discuss their fears, as their hopes waned of saving even some Jews, possibly their families, from that charnel house. And so I, a boy of nine who slept lightly, would sometimes be woken up by excited discussions taking place in the rooms below. The sound of Yiddish resonated throughout the house as my father recounted to the family, his local cronies, and the numerous visitors – usually representatives of Zionist organizations – his analysis of the news, fragmentary though it was. He tried to suck from it such meaning as it had concerning the fate of the Jewish people.

I sensed too, vaguely and certainly uncomprehendingly, that the world of European Jewry my father talked about was at an end. Not just the huge clan of my uncles, aunts, and cousins living in Moldavia and the eastern Ukraine, but the entire civilization of which they were a part was gone. The thousand-year-old heartland of the Jewish world was being destroyed. Only later did I begin to understand, slowly, weakly, and incompletely, what this Jewish civilization comprised. Through the media, history, music, liturgy, legends, photographs, and art, I tried to learn something – it amounted to no more than tiny fragments – about the ruined garden of a culture and a people that are no more. They had no future, only a history, most of which is as yet undiscovered – though, as reform sweeps Eastern Europe, it may in time produce researchers dedicated to the scholarly rediscovery of the Jewish civilization in these countries.

Jews like my grandparents were at one time part of that world. They were human fragments of a civilization so complex, so nuanced, and so diversified that only now can those who did not experience that world begin to learn of its richness. The knowledge comes from historians, who publish the vast array of their learning in books and journal articles that indicate the dawning of a golden age of Jewish historiography. Between 1904, when my maternal grandparents reached North America, and 1924, when my father landed at Halifax, the world they came from experienced the most profound changes that modernization, failed revolution, education, enlightenment, Zionism, world war, successful revolution, civil war, and mass murder could bring. They came not from the tragi-comic *shtetl* (small-town) world of *Fiddler on the Roof* (which was immortalized in the wonderful stories of the great Yiddish writer Sholem Aleichem) but from a real world of political upheaval, ethnic and ideological turmoil, massive destruction, social revolution, and widespread death by famine and pogrom. And to this country, then the Dominion of Canada, in 1904 enjoying the sunny age of Wilfrid Laurier and in 1924 experiencing the crusading opportunism of Mackenzie King, they brought some of the shards of that world.

They and the many other immigrants, Jewish or otherwise, may not have fully comprehended the fact that they had come to a country that was in many important ways distinct from the United States. As part of the British Empire, Canada was governed by political institutions that emerged from the venerable tradition of Crown, Parliament, Cabinet, and responsible government. The United States, on the other hand, was born in revolution, and its constitution set out a clear separation of powers between executive, legislative, and judicial branches of government. Canada was a nation of two nations, or "races," as André Siegfried – an astute French observer – stated early this century, that had established a delicate equilibrium between French and English "rights" between the 1840s and the 1860s, when Confederation brought the Province of Canada into union with two Maritime colonies and, less than a decade later, with the rest of British North America (except Newfoundland) as well. If America was different from Europe, then Canada was different, though not so much, from the United States.

Although it is one of the oldest ethnic groups in Canada, the Canadian Jewish community is small in comparison to many others in the world, being only sixth in size, while its influence on world Jewish affairs was not, until recently, significant. But the community is marked by some unique features. Now numbering more than 300,000 people, the Canadian Jewish community is highly concentrated in major cities and towns, and includes a number of the nation's leading business people, scientists, jurists, intellectuals, artists, and academics. Jews have made notable contributions to virtually every major sector of Canadian life, from agriculture to literature.

To recount fully those achievements would require a multi-volume work. Fortunately, it is not my task to assemble that record, but rather to write a history of the Jewish experience in Canada, and an assessment of the community's evolution from its modest beginnings in the eighteenth century until its maturation by 1920. Like most other historians of Jewish life, I am torn between noting the importance of its unique features, and stressing the universality of its experiences. The historian of modern Jewish life is confronted by the momentous events affecting Jews in modern times: the Holocaust – their worst tragedy; and the rise of the state of Israel – their greatest triumph. The historian must examine the importance of these themes. For example, we might ask: To what extent is the history of Jews in Canada unlike that of other ethnic groups, or unlike the Jewish experience in other countries?

As the late Robert Harney pointed out in a brilliant analysis of the state of Canadian ethnic historical writing, the multiculturalists' efforts in recent years may well have helped to perpetuate certain myths of immigration history.[1] Moreover, putting immigrants at the centre of Canadian history, and thereby depicting Canada as a country built by successive waves of immigrants, robs the history of its complexity and subtlety. These myths portray the various migrations as due to political or religious persecution, declare that Canada is the sum of all its ethnic groups' cultures and that the immigrants moved up social, economic, and political ladders to success by self-sacrifice and hard work, and claim that immigrants formed cohesive self-supporting communities to assist themselves to move forward and upward through adversity.

Such myths are especially prevalent in some of the popular perceptions of

Canadian Jewish history: Jews fled from the persecutions of the Russian-Polish pogroms; Jews adapted themselves readily to the new environment and became one of Canada's great success stories; Jews moved quickly up the social and economic ladders and established a well-organized communal life marked by cohesion and self-help, except for certain minor divisions between the earlier and later arrivals. The trouble with myths is that they usually contain a certain amount of truth, and the difficulty lies in distinguishing between the times and places when they are and are not true. To apply them as universal truths denies the validity of the special and unique.

In the study of Canadian Jewish history, certain questions present themselves, some of them addressing those myths, others raising different issues concerning Jewish immigration, settlement, and adjustment in Canada. As the process began in the old country itself, we must ask why Jews left, and from which elements or classes they were drawn. How were they received in Canada, by Jews and non-Jews, and how did they adjust to their new lives in the urban environment? What types of institutions emerged within the Jewish communities of those cities, and how did these structures change over time as newcomers came to outnumber their forerunners? As these transformations occurred, what kinds of economic, social, and political relationships emerged among different groups or classes within the communities: i.e., how sharply did uptown and downtown Jews (or east-end and west-end, or north-end and south-end) differ from each other? Through what channels did Jews achieve upward economic mobility? Was it principally by means of schooling, or through business? How effective was the Jewish labour movement (which was focused on the clothing-trade unions) in representing those class differences, and in marshalling the intellectual and political resources of the Jewish working class in a sustained manner to effect change?

What was the source of Jewish workers' social consciousness? Was it Russian socialism, as was the case among many Finns in Canada, or was it some hybrid which also included other admixtures, such as Jewish ethical culture? What explains the early emergence of an unusually strong Zionist movement in Canada? Was it perhaps the existence of a divided Canadian nationalism, or the British imperial relationship, which encouraged the rise of this form of Jewish nationalism? Or was Zionism essentially a combination of philanthropy and cynical self-interest which sent Jews to rebuild Palestine? What distinguishes the history of the Canadian Jewish community from that of American Jewry, with which it has had so much in common? Why has Canadian Jewry been able to organize and sustain strong national organizations and cultural institutions?

What explains the promising growth of Jewish agricultural settlements on the Canadian Prairies during the early 1900s, a feature which suggests a commonality with Argentinian Jewish history?

An attempt will be made to answer these and other questions in the pages that follow. What I hope will emerge is a history of a most interesting community, which derives its uniqueness largely from the Canadian context. While some features of Jewish history are universal, in the sense that Jews underwent the same or similar experiences wherever they lived, it is important to understand those that are not. In Canada, these distinct historical features produced an identity that reflects the political, social, and economic evolution of the Dominion of Canada – for it was that evolution that shaped the destiny of the Jews who – like so many other ethnic groups – arrived on these shores expectant and astonished.

The period of Canadian Jewish history treated in this volume covers the 160 years from the beginnings of the community in the 1760s down to the end of the First World War, and of the European upheavals that transformed the lives of the Jews of Eastern Europe, and thus of the massive migrations from those countries to the Dominion of Canada. Within a few years the government would begin to impose new policies restricting Jewish immigration. The year 1920 also marks, therefore, the termination of the long formative period of Canadian Jewish history, when the community's social politics witnessed the passage of the old Zionist leadership and the emergence of the short-lived Canadian Jewish Congress, an organization which represented the claims of the immigrants to a share in the formation of the communal agenda for Canadian Jewry.

During the 160 years when the Canadian Jewish identity was being forged, and its distinctiveness within North America was slowly being defined, the Canadian polity underwent the transforming experiences of separating itself from the mother country and distinguishing itself from the United States. The Canadian Jewish identity was formulated within the parameters of the emerging Canadian national personality, however vague, inchoate, tenuous, and divided that remained.

The Canadian Jewish community was formed out of the human material that emigrated from Europe to British North America, which became the Dominion of Canada in 1867. But while the institutional structure of this community was based on experiences and ideals emanating from the immigrants' old homes, and in response to exigencies and opportunities found in the New World, they did not attempt to re-create the world from which they had come.

Therefore, this community was not a fragment of the Old World, a particle flung off and intellectually or in any other way congealed. The Canadian Jewish community grew in every dimension during these sixteen decades, from a tiny group of transplanted British American Jews professing a Sephardic connection in the 1760s to a fully articulated, diversified, and dynamic national community that defined itself as Canadian while expressing itself in the varied political and social contexts of the Dominion. At the same time it was a part of a world of political and social change that rendered insignificant the physical distances separating Odessa, Warsaw, and other European sources of inspiration from Montreal, Toronto, Winnipeg – and all the secondary cities and towns where Canadian Jews lived – as letters, books, journals, newspapers, and people crossed and sometimes recrossed the Atlantic. The golden chain of Jewish tradition, religion, language, economy, and history was set down and renewed many times in these northern lands, to take root and flourish in rough symbiosis with a new society that was distinctively North American: overwhelmingly British and French, conservative, traditional, precarious, and defensive.

PART I

OLD SUBJECTS IN

THE NEW PROVINCE

1760–1846

1

Beginnings in Quebec

When fifteen Jews forgathered to form Canada's first congregation, in Montreal on December 30 of 1768, they were continuing a North American Jewish communal tradition that had begun in New Amsterdam a hundred and fourteen years earlier, when a handful of their co-religionists fleeing Portuguese persecution in Brazil had come together to worship in a small loft on the town's waterfront. Nor was even this the first Jewish congregation to be established in the New World. A generation before, Jewish traders had arrived in the Dutch colonies of Recife and Curaçao, in South America and the Caribbean.[1] And still earlier, Jews had reached the Americas with Spanish and Portuguese explorers and settlers. There is no doubt that among Columbus' crewmen in 1492 there were several Jews – his interpreter, Luis de Torres, and doctors Maestre Bernal and Marco – while speculation still lives that the great discoverer was himself a secret Jew, a Marrano.[2] Later, the Spanish clerical authorities were so worried about the religious authenticity of some of New Spain's Catholics of Jewish descent that the Inquisition was established in the colonies in 1570, to ferret out and destroy these hated and feared Marranos, nominal Catholics who practised Jewish rites in secret. Some were discovered and subjected to the famous *auto-da-fé*, like the eleven Marranos who were burned at the stake in Lima, Peru, in January of 1639. But not all were found, and there is evidence that, throughout the seventeenth and eighteenth centuries, thousands of Spanish and Portuguese Marranos found refuge in the colonies of the New World.

And so, long before Montreal's Jews organized themselves as congregation Shearith Israel, "the remnant of Israel," on that winter day in 1768, Jews in the Americas had organized synagogues. Jews must pray in a congregation of at least ten men, circumcise their sons eight days after birth, marry only other Jews, partake of meat and fowl only if they have been slaughtered according to a rigorous code, and refrain from eating forbidden food. They are required to bury their dead in separate ground, support the sick, aid the poor, and protect the orphaned. They are enjoined by their holy books and hallowed tradition to observe all of those and many other religious and social practices that cumulatively decree and prescribe in minute detail the order of their lives from birth to death, from their waking in the morning to the waning of their consciousness at night. Thus, in the farthest reaches of the Brazilian jungle or the Canadian interior, wherever Jewish traders might reach, they carried – to a greater or lesser extent, depending on their inclination to observe and their knowledge of the practices – a tradition that stretched back to the covenant established on Mount Moriah between Abraham and the Almighty himself.

In the British colonies south-east of Montreal, Jewish communities had existed in a number of cities. Before the American Revolution, congregations were formed in New York, Philadelphia, Baltimore, Newport, Charleston, and Savannah. To these centres of colonial commerce, Jews came from various countries. The original settlers were mostly Sephardim, whose ancestors originated in Spain and Portugal. Expelled from those countries in 1492 and 1497, they moved to The Netherlands, a more tolerant region, and later to England, where in 1655 they were admitted by the Protector, Oliver Cromwell.

In colonial America, Jews were accorded a degree of toleration seldom granted them in all the countries of their previous sojournings, Moorish Spain being the exception. By the mid-eighteenth century they faced no major religious restrictions, and those lesser restrictions that remained were rapidly falling under the impact of a toleration that arose from the very diversity of religious expression in the British American colonies. Most Jews were merchants – notably in shipping, importing, or trading in staples like fish, indigo, tobacco, and furs – while others worked as artisans in New York and Philadelphia.[3] Newport, a flourishing seaport noted for its trade to the West Indies, was home to such a large Jewish population – numbering nearly a thousand at mid-century – that its prosperous citizens were able to build a majestic synagogue in 1763. Charleston, Savannah, and Richmond also had small but thriving Jewish communities which built synagogues in the same period.

By the 1780s, the Jews of the former thirteen colonies, numbering about three thousand out of more than three million, were an accepted minority in a new nation whose very identity was already being shaped by a variety of peoples and religions, among whom Jews might find peace, toleration, and prosperity. By then, however, the composition of the Jewish population had changed considerably. While the first Jews to settle in the colonial towns had been Sephardim from Holland or England, those who followed them were largely of Ashkenazi background, mostly from Germany. By mid-century, it is estimated, the Ashkenazi comprised about half of all Jews in British America. But they conformed to the Sephardic order of prayer in existing synagogues, often intermarrying into the older families and ultimately adopting the Sephardic identity, which emphasized the Spanish and Portuguese heritage in a distinctive order of prayers and cantorial singing in the synagogue.

Thus, while most of Canada's first Jewish settlers who formed Shearith Israel – Chapman Abraham, the brothers Gerson, Simon and Isaac Levy, Benjamin Lyons, the cousins Ezekiel and Levy Solomons, David Lazarus, the brothers John and David Salisbury Franks, the brothers Samuel and Isaac Judah, and Andrew Hays – were Ashkenazim, they identified themselves as Sephardim, not just because of the implicit cachet but because the Sephardic order of prayer was an integral part of the American Jewish culture they shared before moving to Quebec.[4] Even though the handful of Sephardim in the congregation in 1768 had largely disappeared within a decade, the congregation retained that identity. Its members took its name from that of New York City's major synagogue and, though oriented to London for religious personnel and guidance, the Montreal congregation continued its strong connection to the Jewish communities in New York and Philadelphia.[5] "An additional reason for retaining the Sephardic ritual was in order to obtain money from wealthier Sephardic congregations throughout the new world. By affiliating itself with Shearith Israel in New York, the [Montreal] congregation was able to feel it had a 'mother' in the new world, and lots of other 'relatives' besides. Had the congregation been Ashkenazic, it would have been an orphan."[6] Indeed, some Montreal Jews sought refuge and help from the New York Jewish community.[7] For business and family reasons, the ties between the Montreal and New York Jewries remained strong through the eighteenth century. There were many instances of continuing business relationships between American and Canadian Jews.[8] As British citizens they enjoyed contacts throughout the British North American colonies.

Given their orientation to trade and commerce, it is not surprising that some Jews were among those who accompanied or followed the British army that captured Quebec in 1759 and Montreal in 1760. There were many Jews among the merchants operating on the American frontier as fur traders or purveyors to the scattered army garrisons. The forces of General Amherst, Commander-in-Chief of the British army in North America, included a considerable number of Jewish suppliers, or sutlers, as well as several officers in the colonial militia regiments that formed part of his army.[9] While some moved in from Halifax, Albany, New York, and Philadelphia, most of these early Jewish arrivals in Montreal probably came from London.[10]

Because they had enjoyed a British identity before arriving in what would later be the Province of Quebec, Jews benefited from all of the rights of "old subjects," and the economic advantages that went with them. British merchants gradually came to dominate the economic life of Quebec by pushing aside the French bourgeois who remained following the Cession of 1763, using their superior political connections and commercial ties to the metropolis of London.[11] Economically aggressive, these newcomers induced a reluctant governor, James Murray, to open the interior fur-trading posts, and they rushed upcountry to the *pays d'en haut* in the late 1760s to trade their goods with Indians who had several years' worth of rich pelts to barter, held back by war.

Situated at the farthest point of deep-water navigation on the St. Lawrence river, Montreal was the entrepôt for the western trade. From nearby Lachine the fur traders set out each spring in convoys in dozens of big freight canoes – *canots du maître*, which carried up to three tons of men and supplies – on voyages to the fur-trading posts at Detroit, Michilimackinac, Green Bay, and the Wisconsin country. By the 1770s some of the most aggressive Montrealers were pushing farther westward into the north-west, to the Peace River and Athabasca districts. By the end of the next decade Alexander Mackenzie had reached the Arctic Ocean, and a few years later he stood on the shores of the Pacific at the mouth of the Thompson River. In search of the richest fur-bearing regions of the continent, the Montreal fur traders now organized into loose but competitive associations and co-partnerships that later merged into the North West Company, and mastered the rivers and portages of the northern interior and the Pacific slope.

Montreal, then, was the town with the most promising commercial future in the new British colony of Quebec. But the town enjoyed this advantage not only because of its importance to the fur trade. It was also the principal centre for the lucrative provisioning trade to the British naval and military forces that were stationed there, at nearby forts like St. John on the Richelieu, and in the interior at Niagara and Detroit. When numbers in these garrison troops increased during crises like the American Revolution and the War of 1812–14, this business thrived.

By the 1780s a third (and eventually more important) element was added to Montreal's commercial trade: the supply of goods to new settlers in the western regions of the province, where the Loyalists and later immigrants from the United States who sought refuge and free land under the British flag were beginning to settle. Only about six thousand in number in 1784, these Loyalists and later immigrants into what became the Province of Upper Canada in 1791 were to raise its population to almost one hundred thousand in 1812. Quebec, still vibrant and indeed larger than Montreal, had a very busy port, while Trois-Rivières was the economic fulcrum of the middle St. Lawrence and St-Maurice river commerce. But near Montreal, at the top of Mount Royal, one looked out west to the Ottawa River, to the Lachine Rapids, which barred shipping from entering the interior, to the upper St. Lawrence, which drained the Great Lakes, and to the vast, commercially lucrative regions of the interior. Montreal was rapidly becoming the commercial hub of the north, and it was here that the future seemed most promising.

The experiences of some of the earliest Jewish traders are instructive. In the hope of profiting from the fur trade, Lucius Levy Solomons, who came from Albany, went upcountry from Montreal in 1761. In partnership with his cousin Ezekiel Solomons, and several other New York Jews, he reached Michilimackinac with a huge load of trade goods even before the British troops took over from the French. But he lost the entire stake, worth an estimated £18,000, when he was captured by Indians during Pontiac's rebellion of 1763.[12] Solomons and some of his partners got back into business a few years later, however, and by 1770 he was again a big player in the fur trade. In the Detroit region, Chapman Abraham, a German-born Jew from Montreal, traded in wine and brandy, and supplied muskets, gunpowder, ball, and shot to the British forces there until he was captured during Pontiac's uprising in 1763 (he was later released).[13]

There were so many Jews operating out of Montreal, in the fur trade in the interior and in importing, that "at least ten percent of the Montreal merchants in the 1760s were Jews."[14] They were not just involved in the fur traffic: Jews acted in virtually all commercial capacities served by eighteenth-century merchants, who diversified in order to protect themselves and to exploit the opportunities present in a thriving commercial centre; Levy Solomons, for example, dealt in hogs.[15]

Not all of Quebec's earliest Jewish settlers lived in Montreal. Samuel Jacobs, an Alsatian Jew who came to Quebec by way of Nova Scotia and lived in

St-Denis on the Richelieu, had a store that sold a wide variety of foods and goods to local French Canadian farmers in return for wheat, while British soldiers from nearby garrison posts bought liquor. With branch stores at St-Charles and St-Ours and with shares in a distillery and a potashery, Jacobs diversified his investments; and he remained a major commercial figure in the region until his death in 1786.[16]

One of Jacobs' many business contacts was Aaron Hart, who was, without doubt, the most successful of Canada's first Jewish settlers. He established a family that became famous and acquired great wealth and influence in Trois-Rivières, where he lived from 1762 until his death in 1800.[17] Like both the Jacobses and the Solomonses, Hart came up to Quebec by way of New York in 1759 as a sutler to the British army. Following the troops northwards, he became a purveyor to the forces stationed at Trois-Rivières. Hart ventured into the fur trade in 1763 and shortly thereafter, often in conjunction with his brother Moses of Montreal, into many real estate transactions, including his acquisition of the fief of Bruyères and the seigneuries of Sainte-Marguerite and Bécancour, as well as the marquisate of Le Sable and numerous plots of land in and around Trois-Rivières. Having established a strong business presence and a lengthy dynasty in the Trifluvien region, Aaron Hart has attracted some attention from historians. The first historical account was hardly flattering. It depicted Hart as a shrewd, oversharp Jew, *"égoïste et mystérieux dans ses desseins,"* with an *"ambition dévoratrice."* [18]

Hart also operated a store in Trois-Rivières, where he conducted a diverse wholesale and retail business, and he extended commercial and real estate loans throughout a wide area around the town. Prospering by these diverse operations, he bequeathed a huge legacy to his eight surviving children; sons Moses, Ezekiel, Benjamin, and Alexander inherited the vast bulk of his estate, while daughters Catherine, Charlotte, Elizabeth, and Sarah received £1,000 each. Hart's sons did not fulfil their father's hopes of establishing a dynasty in Trois-Rivières, however. All of them except Moses eventually left the town, as did most of the daughters. Those who remained gradually blended into the local French Canadian community and, as Jews, eventually disappeared.

The Harts were not the only Jewish family to conduct business in rural areas, though they are the most famous. Other Jews lived in Sorel, Verchères, St-Antoine-de-Padone, Rivière-du-Loup, Yamachiche, and Berthierville for varying lengths of time, ultimately leaving those places or in some cases, like Samuel Jacobs, intermarrying and assimilating. The few families that established themselves at Quebec founded a community which flourished for many years. For a few years at least, Jews in Quebec City were probably numerous enough to hold religious services, and they likely had a cemetery before the Jews of Montreal.[19] But the largest Jewish congregation was located at Montreal.

To be sure, the small group that came together there in 1768 to constitute the beginning of an organized Jewish life were not the first Jews to reach these shores, or to have important contact with Canada. Joseph de la Penha, a Dutch Jewish merchant of Spanish and Portuguese descent, was granted the territory of Labrador by England's King William III in 1697, possibly because one of de la Penha's captains had discovered the area.[20] In 1732 a young Jew named Ferdinande Jacobs was employed as an apprentice by the Hudson's Bay Company.[21] Jacobs became chief factor at Fort Prince of Wales and at York Factory before returning to England in 1775. Like many other white traders, he took an Indian "wife" and fathered a number of children. Aside from the probably apocryphal story of the famous stowaway to New France, Esther Brandeau, in 1738, and the Dutch Jew who converted upon reaching Louisbourg, there is evidence that Jews traded to the French colonies in the Americas, including New France and Acadia, and there may even have been a few Marranos among the French merchants living in Quebec during the French regime.[22] Between 1744 and 1759, Abraham Gradis of Bordeaux conducted a huge trade with New France, much of it in conjunction with the intendant, François Bigot, whose corrupt practices were exposed in the investigations known as *l'affaire du Canada*, which also implicated Gradis.[23] And there was a small group of Sephardic Jews who had come north with invading British troops in 1759 and 1760 but had soon disappeared.[24] Their names, Moresca, Fonseca, Cordova, and Miranda, were to be found among Jews in Curaçao, Barbados, and London. Some of them apparently married Christian women. Jacob de Maurera is one example; he had been a sergeant-major in the commissariat branch of the British army and was given a grant of land after reaching Canada about 1760. Changing his name to Jacob Maurer after marrying a local woman, Josette Coyteaux, in 1768 in Montreal's Christ Church, he became fully integrated in the French Canadian community.[25] Other early Sephardim returned to New York or Philadelphia after only brief sojourns.

Indeed the Montreal congregation's first years were difficult because many of its founders were also transitory. Most moved away, like other traders who came north looking, perhaps, for quick gains on this commercial frontier and, finding little, drifted elsewhere. Some may have despaired at the distance from family and the lack of a Jewish community, or realized the unlikelihood of finding Jewish wives there.

Within the decade, therefore, the membership of the congregation had almost completely changed. By 1778 it included Levy Solomons, Uriah Judah, Samuel Judah, Andrew Hays, David bar Abram, Myer Michaels, Abraham Franks, Myer Myers, David David, Heineman Pines, Barnet Lions, Abraham Judah, and Samuel David. They had erected a small synagogue on Little St. James Street on land owned by David David. Though they apparently used the building for services, the acquisition of its religious accoutrements, notably the *sefer torah*s (scrolls of the Pentateuch), was not completed until about three years later.

As important as these acquisitions was the development over the next two or three years of a strict code of synagogue governance. The minutes of the congregation of 1778 record that "the synagogue as we all comprehend is meant for the use of all Israelites who conform to our Laws and our Regulation and under the management of a Parnass [President], Gabay [Functionary], and a Junto [committee] of three of the Elders . . . "[26] Levy Solomons was elected *parnass* and Uriah Judah *gabay*, while Ezekiel Solomons, Samuel Judah, and Andrew Hays constituted the first *junto*. Some of these positions were not easy to fill and, in order to discourage members from declining office, a system of stiff fines (£2 10s per refusal) was instituted for those who demurred. Two other honorary positions were established, that of *hatan torah*, the man called up to the reading of the last portion of Devarim, Deuteronomy, and *hatan Bereshit*, the man called up to the reading of the first portion of Bereshit, Genesis. Both took place on Simchat Torah, the Rejoicing of the Torah, which ends the festival of Succoth, the feast of Tabernacles. These honours were usually a prelude to synagogue office. The *junto* was delegated to formulate "a proper Code of Laws for the better Regulating of this *Kahal* [congregation]." These statutes were modelled on those in effect in the New York synagogue and they, in turn, were based on those governing London's venerable Sephardic , or Spanish and Portuguese, synagogue in Bevis Marks.[27]

That the congregation's minutes were kept in English suggests that most members recognized it as their common language. But the use of Hebrew dates in the minutes indicates a considerable degree of Jewish knowledge on the part of some members. Services were conducted according to the Sephardic ritual. Within a year two Torahs and a *shofar*, a ram's horn, were acquired from sources in London. There was also a punctilious regard for observance of Jewish laws and traditions. For example, early minutes include a reference to a decision not to bury uncircumcised male babies in the congregational cemetery, to prevent a recurrence of such a burial as that of the child of Ezekiel Solomons, who had married a French Canadian woman.[28]

To retain tight control over the congregation, the *junto* decided to give themselves and their sons a double vote at congregational meetings. They also decided to allow new members to vote only after two years and to assume executive office only after three – provided they paid a stiff entry fee of £10 "to preserve to those Present Subscribers the Founders of this Congregation which have been so far Established at an expense beyond the Bounds of our Circumstances, that we may enjoy certain Privileges beyond any Stranger that may hereafter Settle here."[29] In order to recruit all the newcomers to join, however, they stipulated also that any Montreal "Israelite" who did not join the congregation within twenty days of coming to town, "and those out of the Town within Six Months," would not even be allowed to do so. The constitution also levied certain fines for members who caused a disturbance, refused office, failed to perform a *mitzvah* (duty), or missed a meeting. "Severe penalties," moreover, would be imposed "on those who shall be the Means of giving a bad Name to any of the Congregation, by which a Disgrace may be brought on any of the Israelites," a provision against slandering fellow members.[30]

Such regulations, if enforced, were bound to cause problems. At least one dispute erupted within the first year, between Jacob Franks and the *parnass*, Levy Solomons, who allegedly had "made use of expressions to the Manifest Injury of the Congregation." The affair was taken seriously by the *junto* because "it appeared to us of the Greatest Consequence to ourselves and the future Welfare of our Religion in this Province." Found guilty of the infraction, Solomons was immediately replaced as *parnass*.[31]

While the status of the Jewish religion in Quebec does not seem to have met with any public challenge, Jews nevertheless may have felt themselves exposed to the possibility of disapproval, if not outright antisemitism. Of this, as in other British North American colonies, however, there is little evidence. On the other hand, because most of them were in some form of business, Jews were in daily contact with their fellow traders and merchants throughout the province and neighbouring parts of the United States, in ways that suggest the existence of few if any commercial restrictions on them. They bought, leased, and sold property, traded in commodities, imported manufactured goods, participated in joint ventures to own ships, dispatched fur-trading brigades to Michilimackinac and other interior posts, traded with Indians, contracted to provision and supply British garrisons, signed apprenticeship agreements, joined with other merchants in petitions for liberalization of trade, redress of grievances, and the establishment of a legislative assembly, and supported each other, as well as their non-Jewish colleagues, in meeting their financial obligations in times of economic distress.[32] And the fact that a tiny community of no more than a score of families was able to finance the construction and fitting out of a synagogue is evidence not just of their prosperity, but also of their confidence in the possibilities of Jewish continuity in Montreal.

The congregation's minutes indicate that their members' formal commitment to Jewish observance was serious. In 1779, two Torahs were purchased in London and brought over to Montreal by a special emissary, an English Jew, Jacob Raphael Cohen, who was employed by the congregation as a combined cantor, teacher, circumcisor, and ritual slaughterer.[33] In 1782 Cohen was succeeded by Hazan de Lara, who remained until 1810. He was assisted by several members of the congregation, including Myer Levy and Isaac Valentine, who also were able to conduct religious services.[34] But, like his counterparts in the thirteen colonies, the colonial Canadian Jew "lived in a Gentile world without a ghetto and without a rabbinate." [35] Religious observance was bound to suffer in a context where business was conducted on the Jewish Sabbath and holidays, forcing Jews to neglect certain major religious obligations and prohibitions. In a free society where there were no communal religious practices, a decline in formal religiosity was in evidence.[36]

The effects on Quebec's Jewish community of the American Revolution and the invasion of Quebec by General Montgomery's forces in 1775 have been treated in Jacob Marcus' *Colonial American Jew*, where he points out that only a few of the colony's Jews – like David Salisbury Franks and Levy Solomons – were so sympathetic and helpful to the invaders that they were forced to leave the colony when the Americans retreated south in the spring of 1776.[37] Though actively supporting the establishment of a legislative assembly, along with a majority of their fellow merchants in Quebec, most Jews were not prepared to side openly with the Americans, even though Aaron Hart and Samuel Jacobs – among others – sold goods to the American army. Like most other Canadians, "new subjects" or "old subjects," Jews preferred to remain neutral.[38]

While less is known of the lives of Jewish women and children than of men, certain facts are clear. Most of the earliest settlers were unmarried when they arrived and, as there were practically no Jewish women in the colony, went abroad to marry – like Aaron Hart, who brought his cousin Dorothea back as his bride from London in 1778 – or married non-Jewish women. In all probability, fur traders who spent lengthy periods at posts in the interior took Indian "wives" *au coutume du pays;* traders recognized the economic utility of these alliances, as well as the need for emotional and sexual comfort.[39] There is little reason to believe, therefore, that Jewish contemporary intermarriage rates in

Quebec were much less than the 28 per cent for American Jewry in the Federal period.[40] The shortage of marriageable Jewish women in eighteenth-century Quebec could well have been an important factor in the fairly high rates of migration in the first wave of Jewish merchants to the larger communities in the United States. Several members were forced to go abroad for wives, but most found wives in New York, Newport, or Philadelphia, while others married daughters of community members, like the Hart sisters.

Most married women bore large numbers of children. Dorothea Hart had eight surviving children and her days must have been filled with caring for them. The Harts were observant Jews – in 1778 Aaron admonished his son Moses to keep the dietary laws and to return home to Trois-Rivières for the Passover holiday – and Dorothea would have had a heavy schedule to ensure strict attention to the code. Meat and fowl had to be ritually slaughtered, and dairy and meat foods had to be kept apart and eaten only with separate dishes and cutlery. Even though servants might do much of the real work of the kitchen, constant surveillance by the mistress of the house was necessary to ensure that the separation was rigidly adhered to. Sons were circumcised and given the rudiments of Jewish education by their father, or by itinerant teachers who may also have worked in one of Aaron's businesses. Sons were expected to enter the business, usually after serving an apprenticeship, and daughters to be married off at an early age. Sarah Hart married Samuel David, Charlotte married his brother Moses David, while Catherine married Bernard Judah.[41] A noted American historian observed that "It was not unusual for a woman to step into her husband's shoes after his death." Phoebe David, a widow and the sole support for five children, carried on her husband's business after he died in 1776.[42] But it is unlikely that many other Canadian Jewish women entered business affairs in those early days. Home and childbearing were their destiny. Average family size is unknown, but it was likely very similar to those prevailing among Jews in eighteenth-century American cities. Recent studies of Jewish demographic patterns before 1820 in New York, Newport, Philadelphia, Charleston, and Savannah reveal that the average Jewish family had 5.9 children.[43]

Virtually all of these Jews were middle-class and, as property holders, importers, wholesalers, and retailers, were inevitably drawn into social, economic, and political relationships with non-Jews. Business dealings meant the sharing of certain interests in the creation of a favourable environment for commerce; thus many of the earliest settlers supported petitions for the establishment of English commercial law, and other changes that would facilitate the improvement of the local business climate. As essentially middle-class urbanites,

Canadian Jews were in the same economic and political camp as the Anglo-Saxon elites that governed the colony and dominated its commerce.

Between 1760 and the early 1780s, therefore, the Canadian Jewish experience began with small but firmly committed steps towards the establishment of a permanent community. In Montreal, a synagogue was built, a cemetery acquired, a code of governance drawn up, a small group of families established, and an identity affirmed. Among the noteworthy characteristics of the community is that, despite the American origins of many of these Jews, they were now forced to come to terms with a new political and social environment that was significantly different from the one they had left behind. The Quebec Act of 1774 confirmed the already well recognized uniqueness of the province by allowing the continuation of the Roman Catholic faith and religious hierarchy, the French laws of real property and inheritance, and the seigneurial land-holding system. The Act also implied the official abandonment of attempts to anglicize the French population of Quebec and the prospect of establishing representative government institutions like a legislative assembly. The governing Executive Council of Quebec was to contain eight French Canadians among its twenty-two members, thus giving it a "preponderantly French Canadian . . . tone."[44] Although the British government later made a few concessions to Quebec's English-speaking merchants by allowing the application of English law for the collection of debts and the enforcement of contracts and agreements and suits for damages, these provisions were not enforced and such matters remained a sore spot for years.

Though under the British flag, then, Quebec seemed to many contemporaries to be recognized officially by the mother country as a "distinct society," while under the Quebec Act the French Canadians became beneficiaries of wide liberties in law, religion, and custom. Though modifications were made through instructions to governors that confirmed a policy of "gentle but steady and determined anglicization,"[45] the Quebec Act and the failure of the Americans to capture the province by force during the Revolution confirmed that Quebec would retain its uniqueness in North America, at least for some time to come.

The extent to which Jews – as distinct from other "old subjects" who had immigrated to Quebec from different parts of British North America before the American Revolution – were apprehensive about their status and prospects in such an environment is not clear. In view of the serious disabilities Jews still suffered in contemporary France, even aside from the reservations they held about the Quebec Act, Jews may well have been concerned about their future in a society that was predominantly Catholic and French.[46] It was true that they conducted business among French Canadians without apparent difficulty, and Quebec was, after all, a British possession, in which their personal liberties were protected and Jewish communities were not subjected to disabilities of any kind. Because they were "close to that [Protestant] clique and sided with it, literate and with some wealth, the Jews were obviously an important part of the Canadian power structure."[47] But while these realities were undoubtedly apparent to all Jews in Quebec, the possibility existed that the province might again be acquired by France, which still claimed ownership of vast territories in North America. Jews were not unused to dealing with political uncertainties such as these, and the possibility – however remote – of falling under the dominion of a nation where Jews did not yet enjoy equal status must have given Quebec's Jews additional reason to be uneasy.

Finally, there is little doubt that the majority of Quebec's Jews behaved as if they were part of the new British community of administrators and business-men. Their language was English, many had been born in the thirteen colonies or in England, and virtually all of them were traders whose ultimate political allegiance during the Revolution was to Britain, even though – like most of their business confrères – they were essentially neutral during the early stages of the conflict. Once the Americans abandoned serious attempts to invade Quebec, after the disaster of 1775–76, British residents in the province professed their loyalty to the king, while continuing to petition for the establishment of a legislative assembly that would allow them to participate in the governance of the colony. Many of Quebec's Jews signed the petitions that were produced by agitators among the "old subjects" periodically between the Conquest and the Constitutional Act of 1791, for an assembly and other "reforms."[48] Thus, while they recognized their Britishness in ways common to the Anglophone community to which they belonged, they also expressed their desire to enjoy the institutions of self-government that were prominent features of the American colonies from which many of them came.

The completion of a synagogue constitutes a statement – a declaration, indeed – that the Jew has arrived and may well stay on. But it is much more than that. It denotes, as well, a commitment by its people – in Montreal there were a bare fifteen men – to define a separate community and to continue their own personal lives as Jews. The proclamation, in other words, is as much to themselves as to the non-Jewish society. In contrast to Europe, where the syn-agogue "was only one agency of the Jewish community," in America it "became *the* community."[49] By building a synagogue and acquiring a cemetery, they did more than create a vehicle for observing religious rites; they bound themselves to submit to a discipline, to pay fines, to obey, and to pursue God's will through observance. By the waters of the St. Lawrence, as it were, the "old subject" Jews awesomely and solemnly reaffirmed the old covenant. They were on the way to formulating a distinctive Jewish identity in a new and somewhat disquieting political and social context – and in a great raw land.

2

Social and Political Transformations

The revolution that created the United States of America also drew a border between what remained of British North America and the new republic. British sovereignty over Quebec and the Maritime colonies of Nova Scotia, Prince Edward Island, and Newfoundland, as well as the vast western domains of Rupert's Land and the Northwest Territories, was confirmed by the Treaty of Versailles of 1783. Though that authority would be challenged by the United States during the War of 1812–14 and by Canadian insurrectionists during the rebellions of 1837, it stayed in place, mainly because the Canadian people desired to remain British. And that was a fact of the most far-reaching importance in the lives of all the people of British North America, including the Jews.

Being British meant many things in the late eighteenth century: the sovereignty of the Crown, the rule of common law and the governance of the British Parliament. For Canadians it meant, above all, colonial rule, which, though usually benign, was not always attuned to the vagaries of frontier public opinion, or sensitive to the multifaceted population with its religious rivalries and disputes, land questions, and other testy issues that would emerge over the next forty to fifty years. British law applied in Canada in all matters pertaining to criminal law, trade, external relations – in particular, those with the United States – and a variety of other matters.

British rule brought in numerous officials, manners, and social contacts which contributed in many ways to setting the tone of society in these northern colonies during the late eighteenth and early nineteenth century. Army and navy officers, besides rank-and-file soldiers and sailors, were living representatives of the colonial tie and symbols of dependency on the mother country for protection during British North America's not infrequent problems with the United States.

Economic activity in these northern colonies was also heavily dependent on the British connection. The Parliament in London appropriated huge sums of money annually to maintain military and naval garrisons at strongpoints like Quebec, Montreal, Crown Point, Prescott, Kingston, Niagara, and Detroit, as well as at Halifax, to defend against attack from the United States and to maintain British dominion over trade routes to North America and the West Indies. These heavy military and naval expenditures, which assumed enormous proportions during the periodic crises that might lead to war, were important mainstays of the colonial economy and provided considerable business for merchants who secured army or navy contracts. The imperial authorities also stimulated the Canadian staples trade during and after the Napoleonic Wars by favouring Canadian timber, wheat, and flour in the British market.

Most important of all the factors making Canadian society increasingly British was the flood of immigrants from England, Scotland, and Ireland who began arriving following the Napoleonic Wars. They overwhelmed the existing population of Upper Canada, which was largely American in origin, streamed into the towns and cities of Lower Canada, and inflated the population of the Maritimes as well. To be sure, American influences were also significant in British North America. Immigrants, trade, and ideas inevitably found their way into the Canadas and the Maritimes across the guarded frontier. Newspapers, songs, literature, and political and religious ideas of the new republic entered the northern colonies and indubitably influenced the culture of British North Americans; tastes, thought, customs, and habits both social and political, were in part "Yankee."[1] Therefore, while the official tone of society in the colonies north of the American boundary was in many ways British, and while most people – notably the immigrants – approved of its Britishness with varying degrees of enthusiasm, there was still an American spirit about the place. This spirit was actively discouraged by officials after the War of 1812–14, but Yankee attitudes were present to some extent throughout the colonies in the early decades of the nineteenth century.

These factors helped to shape the political, social, and economic environment in which Canadian Jews lived. Being British in the North American continent meant for them, as it did for everyone else, balancing two traditions that, despite certain similarities, pulled in different directions. Had the

British–American tension been the only element of insecurity, Jews would have been no more affected than other Canadians. But for the Jews of Lower Canada, serious problems arose from the fact that they were living in a province where newly emergent French Canadian nationalism challenged the special status and interests enjoyed by the elite British appointed officials in Quebec and the mainly Anglophone merchants of Montreal.

Thus caught between two conflicting sets of ideas about the future of Lower Canada, the Jews became involved in a fascinating and dramatic battle for their civil rights. It began in 1805, when British officials and merchants attempted to create an infrastructure for economic development, including the erection of jails to enforce the collection of debts, by introducing a tax on land. The French Canadian majority of the Legislative Assembly (created by the 1791 Constitutional Act) argued that the vast bulk of the population would be adversely affected by such levies and not benefited by the public works created by them. The Assembly raised import duties instead, in an effort to put the financial burden on the English commercial sector, where, in their view, these expenditures should be met.[2] The ensuing Assembly debate was marked by rising acrimony on both sides, and sparked the emergence of the Parti Canadien, a group of intellectuals and members of the Assembly who insisted on the principle of the "supremacy of the legislative branch over the executive authority"[3], while voicing increasingly assertive expressions of French Canadian nationalism as well. The newspaper *Le Canadien* was founded in 1806 to counter the aggressive attacks by their English opponents in the Quebec *Mercury* and the *Montreal Gazette*. The new governor, Sir James Craig, who had arrived in 1807, was alarmed by the rising acrimony and by the uproar that now emerged over the eligibility of judges and Jews to sit in the Assembly.

It fell to Ezekiel Hart, the second son of Aaron Hart, to be a casualty in this clash. Born in May of 1770, Ezekiel Hart had lived briefly in Albany, New York, before returning to Trois-Rivières to enter the family business.[4] Ezekiel, like his brothers Moses and Benjamin, took an interest in politics; in 1804 he was a candidate for one of the local seats in the Assembly. He lost that contest, but ran again in a by-election on April 11, 1807, when he won the seat over three other candidates. This was a significant victory for Hart. For one thing, he had pitted himself against powerful men: Matthew Bell, owner of the nearby St. Maurice iron works, a former member of the Assembly, and a person of considerable local influence;[5] Thomas Coffin, a colonel in the local militia, son of a United Empire Loyalist, justice of the peace, coroner, and former Assembly member; and Pierre Vézina, a rising lawyer and militia officer.

Hart's second major hurdle was his Jewishness. The electoral officer, Judge Louis Foucher, a strong supporter of the government, was not troubled by scruples of impartiality.[6] Not only did he favour the candidature of Thomas Coffin but, in the words of the *Mercury*, he also "cast . . . many aspersions on the situation of Mr. Hart and his brothers . . . " and pointedly "adverted to the religion of Mr. Hart."[7] His attack was so hostile that "no Spanish Monk, in the height of ascetic zeal, could have poured on this subject, more bitter invective or intolerant warmth." Judge Foucher also ridiculed Hart's short stature. Nevertheless, of the 116 ballots cast, Hart won 59, just over 50 per cent – a convincing victory in a field of three candidates (Vézina had withdrawn in favour of Coffin). What forces carried Hart to victory are not known, though his brother Benjamin's spirited response to Judge Foucher's overt antisemitism may have helped. It was a Saturday, the Sabbath, and though Hart demurred at signing various electoral documents, he complied when pressed. He presented himself at Quebec on January 29, 1808, at the opening of the Assembly's next session, ready to be sworn in and take his seat.

In the meantime, his election had already become a minor *cause célèbre* in Lower Canada. Since the ballot, two of his defeated opponents had publicly asserted that Hart could not be sworn in on the grounds that he was a Jew.[8] The week following voting day, *Le Canadien* had published a letter from "Christianus" accusing Hart of "having employed the most vile and corrupt methods,"[9] while another letter held that "the election of a Jew to represent Trois-Rivières . . . must be regarded as proof of the existence of an influence among the electorate that is stronger than their sense of duty to their country." What this letter-writer, who, in the contemporary custom, remained anonymous, wanted *Le Canadien's* readers to know was that "Everywhere the Jews [are] a people apart from the main body of the nation in which they live," and that "A Jew never joins any other race." Warming to his subject, the writer continued:

> The Jews are united among themselves, however spread out among all countries, forming an entity that has no other centre than itself. If such a confederation, united by a continuous correspondence, does not provoke the jealousy of other people, neither does it merit their encouragement.[10]

No member of this people had a right to represent Trois-Rivières: "By what right can a Jew who is only worried about himself and his sect expect to look after the interests of the whole nation? And what reason is there to expect that such a man would work in the interests of the common good?" Having elected Hart, the people of Trois-Rivières, the writer stated ominously, should expect "no indulgence after [making] such an extraordinary choice." The 1807 election also produced this impromptu, an extemporaneous composition sung to the tune of a popular song and comparing Hart's election – unfavourably – to Caligula's decision to appoint his horse as consul of Rome:

Si Caligula l'Empéreur
Fit son Cheval Consul à Rome,
Ici notre peuple Électeur
Surpasse beaucoup ce grand homme;
Il prend par un choix surprenant,
Un Juif pour son représentant.[11]

The Quebec *Mercury* meekly expressed the hope that Hart would not be "regard[ed] as less capable of serving his country, because he differs in religious ceremony."[12]

When presented with the oath, Hart put his hand on his head as a substitute for the Jewish traditional covering, and replaced the word "Jewish" for "Christian" at an appropriate point in the recitation. This was not the prescribed oath, however, and Thomas Coffin, along with various members of the Assembly, seized on that fact to try to prevent Hart from taking his seat.[13] This move was supported by the provincial attorney-general, Jonathan Sewell, by Pierre-Amable de Bonne, a judge and a sitting member of the Assembly, and by several other English-speaking members. Hart attempted to explain himself. On February 15, 1808 the Assembly agreed to form a committee to consider his petition.

It met the following day and, after lengthy debate, recommended that Hart be allowed to sit pending the outcome of an inquiry as to why he had not taken the usual oath.[14] The following day, however, this recommendation was rescinded and Hart was ordered to appear at the bar of the House – a serious measure – to debate the legality of his sitting in the Assembly as a Jew who had not taken the proper oath.[15] Hart appeared on Friday the 19th, presented his case, and presumably was questioned on it. The next day the Assembly formed a special committee to consider the matter and recommended against him: *"Ezekiel Hart, Ecuyer, professant la Religion Juive, ne peut siéger ni voter dans cette chambre."*[16] This resolution was passed by the Assembly and Ezekiel Hart was thereby banned. By implication, so too, were all other Jews. Though Hart protested, "praying the oath might again be administered to him in due form," he was not successful in overturning the measure.[17] Because the Assembly had been dissolved, he had to wait a year before trying to get himself re-elected. Writing in the *Mercury*, one commentator pointed out, "The Jews, in the United States, are eligible to any place and hard then would be their lot, if they were denied that privilege in this frigid wilderness."[18]

The debate in the Assembly on this issue, according to a lengthy report carried in *Le Canadien*, had been a spirited one. Pierre-Stanislas Bédard, leader of the Parti Canadien, argued strenuously for a narrow definition of naturalization laws that others believed would allow Jews to sit in the Assembly of a British dependancy. As *Le Canadien* informed its readers in March 1808,

> He says that he sees it as a certainty that Jews born in His Majesty's domain could not be admitted to sit in the parliament of this province nor any parliament within the British Empire [and] that the honourable members are convinced of this. They would not use this statute unless they were convinced that under it no Jew would have this right.[19]

Bédard pointed out that before the Jews were expelled from England in the thirteenth century, they did not enjoy the rights of citizens; moreover, they were regarded as the property of the king who had the right to imprison or buy and sell them wholesale or retail. When Jews were readmitted to England by Cromwell, Bédard continued, "he did not grant them any new rights." In any case, the condition of the Jews, he asserted, "was no better in other Christian countries, [for] nowhere were they allowed the right of citizenship, and that this was not an injustice, because they themselves did not wish to be citizens of any country." Spread out over all countries, Jews "did not regard any [country] as theirs; they stayed in the country where they could do good business, and they did not give this country any title other than their country of residence." His explanation for this was that "they were led by their beliefs to act this way, that they were waiting for the Messiah, their prince, and that while awaiting him they could not give their allegiance to any other prince than the one for whom they waited." Bédard and his allies were attempting to use a petty legal technicality to keep Hart, whom they correctly perceived to be one of the British merchants they so feared and hated, out of the Assembly. John Richardson, a Montreal merchant who delighted in challenging Bédard and his associates, responded that he thought these arguments were the kind of pure sophistry which could reduce Jewish rights to absolutely nothing.

In the next provincial election, in a field of four contestants for two seats, Hart stood in second place.[20] Having thus been re-elected, he appeared at Quebec when the Assembly convened on April 10, 1809, and took the required oath, this time without covering his head or hedging on the oath's

Christian character. Nine days later, he was nevertheless ousted, this time simply because he was a Jew. The Jews of Lower Canada, already alarmed by these events, had petitioned the Assembly for redress in March, but their appeal was rejected.[21] During the debate on Hart's eligibility on May 5, 1808, Jean-Marie Mondelet, member for Montreal East, asked that the Assembly be informed of the manner in which Hart had taken the oath. When told that he had done so *"sur les Saints Evangiles,"* Mondelet moved that Mr. Hart, being a Jew and unable to bind himself by this oath, could not claim his seat.[22] Joseph-Bernard Planté, member for Kent – presumably not wishing to lose an opportunity for some drollery in this tedious business – proposed an amendment "that Mr. Hart should abstain until it was verified that he was a Christian when he was elected."

No one would second this amendment and the original motion was then debated, apparently amid some hilarity, for James Cuthbert, member for Warwick, proposed a delay until May 15 "that Mr. Hart might be officially notified [that] if he had become a Christian since last year he would not have neglected to inform the Chamber." The vote was seventeen to seven in favour of the motion. The Assembly again resolved "Que c'est l'opinion de ce comité que Ezechiel Hart, Ecr., professant la réligion judaïque, ne peut prendre place, siéger, ni voter dans ce chambre."[23] This decision was upheld by the colonial secretary, Lord Castlereagh, on the grounds that a Jew could not sit in the Assembly "as he could not take the oath upon the Gospels."[24] Having been expelled a second time, Hart made no further attempts to enter the Assembly. His brother, Moses, ran for one of the Trois-Rivières seats in the next elections, in November of 1809, and was defeated. The Harts did not accept the Assembly's rejection for membership with resignation. Following Ezekiel's second expulsion, he presented a bill intended to "raise all doubts concerning the eligibility of persons professing the Jewish Religion to sit or vote in the House of Assembly."[25] But, by a vote of sixteen to eleven, the house rejected a motion to appoint a special committee to consider the bill.[26]

Several aspects of the affair need to be clarified, argues historian Jean-Pierre Wallot.[27] He contends that this clash occurred in the context of heated passions over the broad question of who might be eligible for membership in the House of Assembly. The principal conflict was over the suitability of judges, several of whom had attempted to take their seats following their election. Behind that was "the political struggle of two ethnic groups, social and religious antisemitism, personal animosities, and weaknesses in the law."[28] The concern of the Parti Canadien in the Assembly was political, not religious.

While keeping Hart out, it was attempting also to expel two French Canadians who happened to be judges and were suspected of harbouring sympathies for the ruling English party.

These observations are undoubtedly valid, as is the fact that antisemitism was not restricted to the French Canadians. Governor Craig did not come to the defence of Hart; instead he exploited the issue to try to teach the Parti Canadien a "lesson" because of its obstreporousness on several other matters. He dissolved the Assembly after administering a severe tongue-lashing on these issues.[29] Nevertheless, Jews were now officially second-class citizens. They were ineligible for membership in the Assembly and legally unfit to hold any other office, civil, judicial, or military, because they could not be bound by the required oath of office. Except for the Assembly, however, this ban seems not to have been enforced.

There is no record of any other Jew attempting to gain membership in the legislature of Lower Canada, though several joined the militia, which required a similar oath, and became officers. Others took up minor appointments which likewise demanded swearing-in ceremonies and oaths of office. But the contest of 1808 compelled them to take an oath which included the phrase "on the true faith of a Christian." This requirement rankled in the Jewish community, especially in the Hart family, which had been so powerfully affected by the expulsions of Ezekiel in 1808 and 1809. Ezekiel's son Adolphus Mordecai, and his nephew Aaron Philip, attempted to make possible an oath that did not include this phrase, thereby eliminating the disqualification.[30]

The eventual result of this agitation was the passing of an act by the legislature in March of 1831 declaring that all persons professing the Jewish religion being natural born British subjects inhabiting and residing in this Province, are entitled and shall be deemed, adjudged and taken to be entitled to the full rights and privileges of other subjects of His Majesty . . . to all intents, constructions and purposes whatsoever, and capable of taking, having or enjoying any office or place of trust whatsoever, within this Province.[31]

Introduced by John Neilson, it had the support of Louis-Joseph Papineau, the leader of the Parti Patriote (as the Parti Canadien had been renamed) in the Assembly and by Denis-Benjamin Viger, who presented petitions to the Legislative Council.[32] While Papineau's motives might have been essentially political,[33]

"the virulent character of the earlier controversy found no echo in 1832 in the legislative assembly, the council or the press; it was simply treated in a factual manner by both English and French." [34]

Even though the measure passed in the House and became law on June 5, 1832, it was challenged on technical grounds; it was considered by a special committee of the Assembly in 1834 and confirmed.[35]

While the affirmation of Jewish political rights in Lower Canada, and by implication in the rest of British North America, was not achieved until the early 1830s, it must be emphasized that, like their co-religionists in England, Quebec's Jews enjoyed a highly emancipated state.[36] Their status was not defined by special laws; they enjoyed freedom of movement, freedom of occupation, and freedom of owning real estate.

Jews were deeply involved in the major economic transformations of that era. The Hart family's enterprises in Trois-Rivières were thriving in the early decades of the nineteenth century. Aaron was growing older, and his son Moses, among all of his eight children, seems to have been the firm's principal businessman. The Hart papers at the Seminary of Trois-Rivières constitute an enormous record of Moses' remarkable business activities – of his many transactions in both urban and rural real estate, of his extensive local trade in virtually all commodities, including furs, and of his importation and distribution of manufactured goods, which he sold wholesale and retail over the entire Trifluvien region.[37]

One of the Harts' most important real estate acquisitions was the seigneury of Bécancour, a feudal grant located across the St. Lawrence from Trois-Rivières. Purchased in sections between 1791 and 1817, the Bécancour seigneury gave them ownership of nearly 5,500 arpents, from which they would derive an annual revenue of cens et rentes and lods et ventes of $4,031.17 by 1858.[38] This, however, was just the beginning. After Aaron died in 1800, Moses acquired even more land. His enormous holdings included many properties in the Eastern Townships, and parts or all of the seigneuries of Grondines, Belair, Gaspé, Sainte-Marguerite, Carufel and Godefroy, Dutort and Courval, besides the marquisate of Le Sable and the Vieuxpont fief. With considerable investments also in Canada's earliest banks and in the development of the St. Lawrence River steamboat business,[39] Moses Hart became an important figure in Lower Canada's economic life.

In Montreal, new economic opportunities opened up with the beginnings of settlement in Upper Canada. By the early 1800s the city's merchants – many still supplying the fur traders of the pays d'en haut – also exploited the demand for goods and supplies from settlers, as well as the need for steamboats and other improved transportation services, and for more efficient banking services. Montreal's population grew from 22,540 in 1825 to 44,591 in 1845. In

Quebec, still the larger centre and the entrepôt of the square timber trade – which had boomed since 1809 under tariff protection provided by Great Britain – shipping activity expanded enormously, while shipbuilding and ancillary business sparked considerable urban growth. Quebec's military and governmental establishments also provided big local markets for imports and commodities.

In Montreal, David David was perhaps the major Jewish participant in this transforming economy.[40] Starting off as a "winterer" in the north-west fur trade, he linked up with the North West Company and was admitted in 1817 to Montreal's prestigious Beaver Club. While operating a store in Montreal and dabbling in the wheat trade he did business with the military. Like his fellow merchants who were interested in fostering the city's economic growth, David – now a prosperous man – supported formation of the Committee of Trade in 1822 to give the Montreal business community a stronger voice on trade matters with local and imperial authorities. From 1818 to 1824, he served as a director of the Bank of Montreal and acted as one of the promoters of a company to build a canal between Montreal's port and Lachine to improve communications with Upper Canada.[41]

By the time he died in 1825, David was a rich man. His holdings of Bank of Montreal stock were worth nearly £7,000, and his personal account had a balance of £1,575; his portfolio included over £3,300 in Bank of England annuities and about £24,000 in mortgages, promissory notes, and other assets.[42] He also did business with many of the city's biggest import–export houses, and he owned some four thousand acres of rural land in Lower Canada, besides a great deal of urban real estate. Altogether his estate was worth nearly £70,000.

Moses Judah Hayes was another Jew who actively fostered Montreal's economic development. He helped to promote one of the city's early gas companies, and a bank, and in 1832 he bought Montreal's waterworks, which he sold to the municipality in 1845.[43] He then built a four-storey hotel and theatre called Hayes House, an elegant establishment that became a favourite of Montreal's *nouveaux riches* – the merchants, bankers, ship owners, and entrepreneurs and their families who prospered from the city's impressive economic growth as the commercial, financial, and transportation hub of the St. Lawrence economy.

Though it would be risky to generalize too boldly about the role played by Jews in Lower Canadian society, it is clear that many of them were deeply involved in the new economic activity dominated by the Scots, English, and Americans in Montreal. And yet David, Hayes, and several members of the Hart family who lived in Montreal and Trois-Rivières did business with French

Canadians as well. Import and export listings record that Benjamin Hart of Montreal exported some of the largest consignments of pot and pearl ash to British ports, while he imported cargoes of iron bars, tin plate, boiler plate, lead sheets, and nails. Levy and Benjamin Solomons ran a prosperous tobacco and snuff importing business where they also employed journeymen to manufacture some of their stock-in-trade. Meanwhile, their relation Henry Solomon, a Montreal furrier, required his journeymen to work twelve-hour days, "sabbath and other holidays of the Jewish religion excepted."[44]

Business had crossed ethnic, national, and language lines in Lower Canada since the Conquest, even though, by mid-nineteenth century, some economic sub-specialization by ethnic groups had begun to emerge in Montreal. "La bourgeoisie Canadienne-française," while participating in a small way in financial, commercial, and industrial capital, had its real strength in the real-estate sector," and that while French Canadian businessmen were not alone in investing in this sector, *"leur présence est beaucoup plus forte qu'ailleurs."*[45] Jews who bought and sold real estate, therefore, likely would have done business with French Canadians, while those who sold to country traders, peddled goods in the timber camps, or toured the countryside to purchase commodities probably encountered French Canadian businessmen at all levels of their operations. And so did most businessmen in Montreal, this city of increasingly mixed cultures and nationalities. In this respect, then, Jews appear to have been no different from most others.

A few Jews could indeed make the transition to full membership in one of the two major surrounding cultures, as Samuel Jacobs had done earlier. Levi Koopman, who was born in Amsterdam, came to Montreal in 1826, adopted the name of Louis Marchand, and joined a French Canadian merchant in business in the Chambly River area; he converted to Roman Catholicism in 1828 and married a local French Canadian woman two years later.[46]

Others adapted in different ways. The norms of propriety observed among Montreal's Jews were shattered with dramatic panache in May of 1840 by Eleazar David.[47] The eldest son of Samuel David and his wife, Sarah Hart, Eleazar was a lawyer who joined the Royal Montreal Cavalry in the 1820s and served during the Rebellion of 1837 as a senior captain in command of a reconnaissance and dispatch-rider unit at the battle of St-Charles-sur-Richelieu. He was "mentioned in dispatches," an honour signifying better than average service under fire, and was promoted to major. He fought at the battle of St-Eustache as commander of a large unit. Rising up the ranks of the militia after the Rebellion, David saw his promising military, legal, and personal career shattered by his decision to elope with a British army captain's wife, Eliza Harris, with whom Eleazar had been conducting an illicit relationship. (The elopement was perhaps precipitated by the birth of their child the month before.) They spent the next ten years in exile in the United States, France, Italy, and the West Indies. When they returned to Montreal in 1850, with their five children, David resumed his activity in the militia and in the legal profession, although he was to attract more notoriety some twenty years later.

Yet there was another dimension of the lives of most Jews – an important one to many – that was enclosed and in a way unreachable by those outside the Jewish community. Their religion and culture separated them from their fellows by an invisible fence of laws, traditions, language, and history – not to mention fears and suspicions. In Montreal in the early nineteenth century a strict degree of observance was difficult, if not impossible, to achieve. Surviving records of the synagogue and its members indicate how serious those problems were.

The most pressing of these was the synagogue itself. Situated on Little St. James Street, not far from Nelson's Column at the top of Place Royale, the small stone structure that had been standing since 1778 was probably still adequate for the community's needs. According to a register of 1832 kept in the Montreal prothonotary's office, there were only fifteen males over the age of twenty-one identifying themselves as Jews. There seem to have been a few more by the end of the 1830s, but the total was still very small.[48] Therefore, the problem was not the size of the synagogue, but its location and ownership. It had been built on land donated by David David, who, it appears, owned only a life interest. On his death in 1824, the property reverted to his heirs.[49] The congregation was forced to abandon the building and services were held in the homes of members, often at Benjamin Hart's. But without a proper religious centre, there was no specific focus for observances and festivities. Though Benjamin Hart attempted, from 1826 on, to galvanize the community to build a new synagogue, the project dragged on for another decade.

In the fall of 1832, efforts were made to erect a building. A meeting was held at the courthouse, chaired by the Honourable Augustin Cuvillier, but little was accomplished until 1838,[50] when a large donation of £575 started off a fundraising campaign which extended as far as England – without any success, except for a contribution of £5 from the philanthropist Sir Moses Montefiore. A reason for the poor showing, in the opinion of Abraham Hart, was "the complaint . . . that you have no Killer [*schochet*, or ritual slaughterer], and so are not living as Jews."[51] But enough money came in to get the project started, and a new structure was planned by a local architect. In March of 1835 the trustees – Isaac

Aaron, Benjamin Hart, Moses Judah Hayes, and Isaac Valentine – commissioned the carpentry work at a cost of £166 and the masonry for £483.[52] By September of 1838 the impressive structure – described as "a fine specimen of the Egyptian style of architecture" – was ready for use.[53] "Also in the Egyptian style," the description continued, "is a very beautiful mahogany Ark, over which are placed the Ten Commandments, in Hebrew characters, cut in white marble."

Now the search began for a religious functionary. The congregation even advertised in England and the United States for a person who would serve as *hazan* and *mohel*. (A *hazan* is a non-ordained reader or leader in the Sephardic tradition; a *mohel* is a ritual circumcisor.) Abraham Hart, who acted as the congregation's agent in London, was pessimistic about finding one because "were he to be met with twould not be necessary for him to go to America for a situation [because] his services would be too eagerly sought on this side of the Atlantic."[54] He pointed out, moreover, that

> you could never expect that Five Hundred Dollars would be any induce-ment for a Man possessing the qualifications you require to leave his Home & Country. . . . I do tho think . . . that you will succeed in procur-ing from the London Portuguese Community a competent person to administer in your Synagogue.

Within a year or two, David Piza, from London, was employed as *hazan, mohel, schochet*, and teacher.

But the major achievements of erecting a new synagogue and employing David Piza (who was soon succeeded by another individual) contrasted sharply with the continuing tensions over the vital question of which order of service, the Portuguese or the Dutch-German (Sephardic or Ashkenazic) should be fol-lowed. Benjamin Hart referred to these controversies in a letter to his fellow congregant Isaac Valentine, in October of 1833. "Provided we have a Por-tuguese Shool," he pointed out, "impressive financial support could be secured from even local Jews and strangers [who] . . . have all told me they prefer our [Sephardi] Ceremonies to their own."[55] But as a safeguard against interlopers who might try to change the synagogue's ceremonies, Hart asked Valentine for the names of those who would vote to retain the established order so that "we are perfectly secure from the Dutch, German . . . ." "No Dutch will ever have our Shool for their own," he snorted, "[because] they are themselves ashamed of their ceremonies." Hart appended several proposed changes to the syna-gogue's by-laws to strengthen the grip of the old guard and ensure victory for his side. They provided "that all youths brought up to the Portug. mode of worship, or brought up in this congregation shall at the age of 21 become members – provided they have been seat holders three years."[56] These provisions also stipulated that, although sermons might be given in English, "the fixed Prayers shall be read in the *Hebrew Language* according to the custom of the Spanish and Portuguese Jews and no other."[57]

But other complications soon arose, and the joy attending the opening of a new synagogue, and the apparent settlement of the ceremonies issue, did not solve the many difficulties of keeping together this tiny diverse congregation. There was still the question of raising enough money to finance all the services, and the problem of finding a religious leader who could provide them. Even with the community's new building and its willingness to pay its necessary religious functionary up to five hundred dollars a year, there were no candidates. Sadly for the community, Abraham Hart's dour warnings now proved to be correct. Consequently, several members refused to pay their dues. Isaac Aarons held back on the grounds

> that the regular fixed Prayers have not for eleven months past been read in the said synagogue and that during the said eleven months, no regular performance of divine service according to the portuguese custom (or any other custom of the Jews) have [*sic*] been performed in the . . . synagogue . . . for the want of a Hazan or reader.[58]

He also pointed out that even the by-laws calling for fixed prayers to be read in Hebrew "according to the custom of the Spanish & Portuguese Jews and no other" were being violated. Over nearly a year of close observation, he reported indignantly, "a part of the fixed prayers have been twice or thrice publicly read in the english language in the . . . Synagogue." Clearly, both religious education and religious enthusiasm were at a low ebb among Montreal's Sephardim.

The worst difficulty of all was the fact that there was no *schochet* in Montreal. Aarons complained that

> A Shochet or Killer of the meat is indispensable in a Congregation of Jews, as it is the first Pillar, No congregation of Jews can be or is ever formed without a Shochet, and although where a number of Jews are congregated they can dispence with a Hazan or reader and even a Public Synagogue, they can not according to our fundamental rites of religion dispence [*sic*] with the Shochet or Killer.[59]

By the late 1830s, then, there were at least two serious problems: the division over the *minhag* (customary practice) to be observed in the prayers, and the absence of religious leadership and of such fundamentals as kosher meat. A building, however beautiful, was simply no substitute for observance. But while there was no one able to conduct services according to the Portuguese *minhag*, there existed a tiny group of members – many of them recent arrivals – prepared to conduct services in the German, or Ashkenazic, style. This group was apparently able to provide kosher meat – likely through one of their number who was familiar with the rites of *schechita*. By the early 1840s these dissenters had decided to separate and form their own congregation, and in early June of 1845 they began by meeting to conduct prayers.[60] In 1846 they sought and received legal status, through an act of the legislature which authorized "the diverse persons of the Jewish faith calling themselves German and Polish Jews" to form a separate congregation with the same rights and privileges as the Shearith Israel.[61]

The split was inevitable, though it had taken some time for the break to occur. There had been a slow influx of German and Polish Jews to Montreal for a number of years, and though some were prepared to adhere to the religious norms already established by the existing congregation, others were not willing to accept its limitations. In religious life, in family formation, and in the flow of ideas, Lower Canada's Jews were thus able to draw on both the Sephardic and the Ashkenazic heritage. Religious guidance, marriage partners, news, and ideas were sought from both sources, and neither was more important than the other. Several Montreal Jews were among the earliest subscribers to *The Occident*, a Philadelphia weekly devoted to Jewish news and opinion, when it began to appear in 1843.[62]

However loyal the Montreal congregants may have been to their tradition, not every Jew in Lower Canada was a strong adherent of the religion. Influenced by the writings of eighteenth-century deists – and possibly also by reflection upon the religious intolerance that had kept his brother Ezekiel out of the Legislative Assembly – Moses Hart devoted much thought to religous questions. In a small book entitled *Modern Religion*, which he published in New York in 1816, Hart urged Jews and deists to adopt what he called a "universal religious system" in order to "harmonize the religious contentions of mankind."[63] While Hart's system proclaimed a belief in a supreme being, or benevolent Creator, he eschewed established religious observances. In their place he proposed a set of three public festivals and "duties obligatory," which included prayers, rites, and blessings on special occasions. Influenced, according to Jacob Marcus, by eighteenth-century ideas of reason and the "trinity" of God, immortality, and ethics, Hart based his revolutionary new religion on his belief in the general need for a liberal religious faith.[64] But the fact that Jews were among his primary targets for conversion to this "modern religion" suggests that he was deeply uncomfortable with Judaism.[65] The work was reprinted in the United States, where it had aroused interest among members of Jewish communities contemplating "Americanizing" their religious practices.[66]

For over fifty years the Jewish community of Lower Canada had thus undergone enormous pressures. The most important of these was the confrontation with the political reality of the French–English conflict in Lower Canada, and the exposure of Jewish vulnerability in the struggle between French Canada's pursuit of cultural distinctiveness, and the Anglo-Saxon forces of economic progress. Jews were squeezed between the upper and nether millstones of nationalism and continentalism, between French rejection of attempts to force them into a new mould and British disdain for a way of life and institutions which appeared to bar the door to economic growth. This was surely the crux of the Hart crisis of 1808 and 1809 – not antisemitism, which was a minor, though ugly, addendum. Had antisemitism been the main issue, then it would have resurfaced when the 1831 bill giving Jews full entitlement was passed in a Legislative Assembly dominated by a strongly nationalistic French Canadian majority led by Louis-Joseph Papineau.

It is important to note that this "Jew bill" was the first of its kind in the British Empire, preceding by a generation the extension of full civil rights to Jews in Britain. In Europe, full Jewish civil rights were accessible only in France, and even there Napoleon had seen fit to convoke a special meeting of Jewish notables in 1809 to discuss Jewish loyalty to the state and establish limits for Jewish uniqueness in a secular society. All the same, the vital comparison is with the United States, where Jews had enjoyed full civil rights for almost a century. In the North American context, the political discrimination in Lower Canada was a glaring anomaly. And antisemitism surfaced once again in the 1830s. In the aftermath of the failed rebellions of 1837, a number of rebels organized Hunters' Lodges (Frères Chasseurs) which recruited members in both Upper and Lower Canada, but many more in the United States.[67] Before launching an invasion of Lower Canada, they announced a program which called for the strangling of all Jews and the confiscation of their property.

For the majority of Jews in British North America, the cultural conflict in Lower Canada was a political reality that seriously affected their civil status.

Official limitations of political rights not only set up barriers, but also established a principle that could have manifested itself in further refinements. Ezekiel Hart was rejected even after swearing an oath of office which included a reference to Christ – thus even a Jew who publicly abjured his Jewishness (in this one matter, at least) was still unacceptable. What else might Jews be prevented by law from doing?

PART II

FOUNDATIONS

1847–1882

CHAPTER

3

Montreal Jewry in the Era
of the de Solas

When Abraham de Sola, the newly appointed spiritual leader of Shearith
Israel congregation, reached Montreal in January of 1847, he had come, of
necessity, through the port of New York. There he would have observed first-
hand what he must already have read concerning the condition of Jewry in the
United States. Enervated by growing indifference, drained by alarmingly high
rates of intermarriage, impoverished by ignorance of Jewish religion and
culture, reduced by weak leadership, and threatened by the far-reaching revi-
sionism proposed by the Reform movement, traditional Judaism in America
was undergoing significant challenges and transformations that reflected the
relative openness of American society and the powerful influences of American
Protestant culture.[1] But, after what must have been a physically laborious and
unpleasant winter trip from New York to Montreal, de Sola soon would have
realized that British North America was a somewhat different society. Its northern cold was a matter for his mordant comment, and he could hardly have
missed the vital fact that half the population of the city, and most of the surrounding countryside's, was French and Catholic. De Sola's intellectual world
seems to have been largely limited to Jewish learning and the tensions that gal-
vanized those concerned with the survival of traditional Judaism in the modern
world. The tiny community of Montreal's Shearith Israel was to be his realm for
the next thirty-five years, and because he saw his chief role as that of the community's religious leader – its rabbi in all but name – he devoted himself to it.
At the same time he enjoyed the rewards of teaching at McGill College, and

participating in local numismatic and scientific societies. But because the leading item on his agenda was his role at Shearith Israel, he existed essentially in a Jewish intellectual and social environment that stretched from London to Philadelphia, to persecuted Jews in Persia, to the needs of charities in Palestine, to the threats from reformers in Germany and America, to the tensions within Montreal Jewry itself.

By the early 1840s the community had come through a significant decade. Their full civil and political rights had been recognized by the Lower Canadian legislature, their synagogue had been erected on Chenneville Street, and they were finding wealth and respectability in Anglophone Montreal. As well, they had attained modest but noteworthy levels in the civic administration, the officer corps of the militia, certain Masonic lodges, and various professions.[2] Small in numbers, closely related, and culturally homogeneous, the Jewish community had reached a comfortable equilibrium by about 1840.

Yet there was unease in this Zion by the St. Lawrence. Though still tiny in size, the community was growing through immigration. Previously dominated by the older interconnected families like the Harts, Davids, and Josephs, it now included Mosses, Silvermans, and Aschers; while officially Sephardic in its religious rites and English in language and associations, it now encompassed increasing numbers of English, German, Alsatian, and Polish Jews used to the Ashkenazic traditions common throughout Central and Eastern Europe. In the 1840s the conjuncture of these elements precipitated changes, and the accompanying tensions would alter the community beyond all recognition over the next forty years. The three major developments that embodied those changes were: the formation of a second congregation in 1846; the appointment of Abraham de Sola as *hazan* of the Spanish and Portuguese synagogue in 1847; and the establishment of a Hebrew Benevolent Society that same year.

The scion of a London rabbinical family, Abraham de Sola had received his education from his scholarly father, David Aaron de Sola, and from Louis Loewe, an orientalist.[3] On his arrival in January of 1847, he at once began to invest his considerable learning, boundless energy, and humanitarian sympathies in the community. That his arrival was noticed in Philadelphia's *The Occident* underlines the continuing importance of Montreal Jewry's American linkages.[4]

De Sola's immediate concern was the revitalization of Shearith Israel's educational, fraternal, and benevolent activities, which had been faltering since the completion of the synagogue in 1838. He accomplished veritable prodigies in all of these areas. Within a year he had started a congregational Sunday school to expose children to the basic elements of Judaism, including prayer,

Hebrew, Bible, and Jewish history; he drew his inspiration from the work of Rebecca Gratz, who had begun a Hebrew Sunday school at Philadelphia's congregation Mikveh Israel in the 1830s.[5] He organized the Hebrew Philanthropic Society to assist Jewish indigents, and took on duties as lecturer in Hebrew and oriental languages at McGill College.[6] All within one year! It was because de Sola continued to invest such effort in his work that his congregation remained such a vital and significant sector of the larger Montreal Jewish community.

De Sola also became recognized as one of Montreal's leading intellectual figures. Not only did he join many English-language cultural organizations, including the Mercantile Library, Mechanics Institute, Numismatic and Antiquarian Society, and Natural History Society, but he also delivered learned papers which won him local renown as a scholar of Judaica. In recognition of these achievements, McGill awarded him an honorary doctor of laws degree in 1858, and in 1872 he opened the United States House of Representatives with prayer, the first Jew and the first British subject to do so. As well, he enjoyed prominence among some of the leading Jewish religious leaders – they were not ordained rabbis – in North America, two of whom, *reverends* Jacques J. Lyons of New York and Isaac Leeser of Philadelphia, collaborated with him in several publishing ventures.[7]

It is noteworthy that, as far as surviving evidence indicates, in his Montreal career lasting 35 years de Sola had virtually nothing to do with the city's growing French-Canadian communities. In all of his voluminous correspondence with Leeser and in his other papers, there is not a single reflection of the French fact in the metropolis. And while he sought out liberally-minded intellectuals, mainly Protestant clergy and McGill academics, in the English community, de Sola seems to have made no effort to make the acquaintance of the many French-Canadian liberals in the *Institut Canadien*, which became a thriving body in Montreal during the 1860s and 1870s. In all likelihood, some members of the *Institut* would have extended to de Sola a cordial welcome – he was, after all, a man of scholarly attainments and intellectual interests, and there is no evidence of antisemitic expression among *Instituteurs* who "conducted and organized programs of debates and lectures on all the intellectual, economic and political issues of the day."[8] However, de Sola probably had no verbal French and he was inclined towards the English-speaking community because of his background and existing social and economic affiliations of the vast majority of the Jewish community of Montreal – in which he was, after all, a paid employee. In Montreal of that day, French and English cultures were largely separate; they included many distinct issues; their agendas were different – sometimes at odds. De Sola probably understood instinctively that his interests and those of his community lay with the English. Yet he missed what might have been a golden opportunity as a major leader of Montreal Jewry in these formative years to make contact and possibly establish a useful meeting of minds with those elements of French Canadian society who, like Wilfred Laurier and many others, were attempting to create a genuinely liberal Quebec.[9]

His research and writing covered a number of aspects of Judaic law and history, and included articles on the history of the Jews in France, Persia, and England, as well as on various Jewish holidays and festivals for American Jewish publications like Philadelphia's *The Occident*, New York's *Jewish Messenger*, and London's *Jewish Chronicle*. He collaborated with the minister of New York's Shearith Israel, Jacques Judah Lyons in 1854 in publishing *A Jewish Calendar for Fifty Years, from A.M. 5614 to A.M. 5664*.[10] He also took an interest in natural science, probably influenced by his McGill colleagues William Dawson and William Logan, who were leading geologists at the forefront of the Canadian fascination with science and natural history.[11] His first publication in this field, an 1849 article entitled "Critical examination of Genesis III. 16; having reference to the employment of anaesthetics in cases of labour," was published for the *British American Journal of Medical and Physical Science*, and manifested his concern for reconciling religion and science.[12] This was followed by "Observations on the sanatory institutions of the Hebrews as bearing upon modern sanatory regulations[sic]" in 1852–53, for the *Canada Medical Journal and Monthly Record of Medical and Surgical Science*,[13] which was later published as a book.

Young, well grounded, and enormously self-confident, Abraham de Sola was a one-man whirlwind of activity from the moment he reached Montreal. As if his philanthropic efforts with the Benevolent Society, running of the Sunday school, and articles for *The Occident* were not enough to keep him fully occupied, he kept up an active correspondence with at least one of the major leaders of American Jewry, Isaac Leeser, minister at Philadelphia's Mikveh Israel synagogue. Until his death in 1868, Leeser remained a close contact of de Sola's, who confided to him that he had arrived in Montreal with burning evangelical zeal. "Nothing would give me greater pleasure than to participate in a movement which might (and doubtless would) tend to promote the awfully neglected interests of our much prized faith," he wrote to Leeser in December of 1848. "Anything that would agitate, awake, our community from the *tardema* [deep sleep] which enwraps and paralyses them, should be encouraged by every lover of God's people."[14] He was referring, of course, not just to Montreal but to the whole Jewish community in America, which he knew suffered from an indifference bred by affluence and smugness. Despite his most earnest hard work to ignite a spirit of true Judaism in Montreal – or at least in his own congregation – de Sola realized how difficult it would be. Responding in May 1856 to Leeser's request that he encourage more of his congregants to subscribe to *The Occident*, de Sola lamented, "my people are very like their brethren t'other side the line; *the Journal*, Ledger + Cash Book have great interest as serious reading while for lighter moments the Book of Kings (+ aces) obtain their share of attention".[15]

In October 1848 de Sola organized the Montreal Committee for the Relief of the Persecuted Persian Jews, to lead Montreal's Jewish and Christian communities into protesting against the persecution – including many forced conversions – of Jews in Persia.[16] Aroused to this action by the visit to Montreal of Rabbi Nissim ben Solomon, a refugee from those persecutions, de Sola delivered public lectures on the subject, arousing interest and sympathy for Persia's persecuted Jews. "There was an unusually large audience to hear me," he reported to Leeser in April 1849, "since they came numerously to hear about the countrymen of R[abbi] Nissim, notwithstanding that lectures so late in the season are . . . rather thinly attended."[17] De Sola supported Leeser's attempts in 1848 to convene delegates from all of America's Jewish communities to a conference on Jewish concerns. "God grant that the movement, provided it indeed takes place, may prove an important one and beneficial to this and other generations 'yet unborn'," he prayed.[18]

At McGill, de Sola found a congenial and collegial intellectual climate. Here he encountered William Dawson, who, as principal, encouraged the study of Hebrew.[19] In a letter to Isaac Leeser in January 1860, de Sola wrote:

> Dr. D has a claim on Jews. . . . He respects Hebrew learning and the Hebrew language. . . . I do thank him that he has invariably in his published writings shown how important is the study of Hebrew to all. But Dr. D has this special claim on us just now. He is a man of depth, and he is out on *our* side. . . ."[20]

Dawson encouraged de Sola to write a review essay countering some of Ernest Renan's assertions concerning the similarities between Hebrew and the Iroquois and Algonquin languages. "My answer," de Sola confided to Leeser in April of 1864, "is to N.O., a priest of the Seminary here . . . a fellow student of Renan. I write . . . at the request of Dr. Dawson who is not 'up' on the Semitic languages – and the part he has already seen of the manner I handle the priest has given him not a little amusement."[21]

De Sola regarded his position at McGill as a distinct honour. He was promoted to professor – an unpaid position, however – in 1853, awarded the honorary LL D in 1858, and delivered the convocation address in the spring of 1864.[22] "It was gratifying to me," he informed Leeser, "the occasion being an unusual one, and evincing the liberality of the College authorities, for tho' there are Jewish professors, I believe no one has ever yet been entrusted with giving parting moral advice to graduates."[23] Indeed his position at McGill and in Montreal society seems at times to have been as important to him as his work for the Jewish community. When Leeser asked in the spring of 1865 why sales of *The Occident* were not increasing in Montreal, de Sola replied:

> If you have no field here, be comforted with the reflection that neither have I nor anyone else. It is because I have as good a position as a Jew could obtain among Xians [Christians] and that my position at College has greatly improved that I am satisfied with the extent of my Jewish field.[24]

In his contacts at the Presbyterian College, where he lectured on Hebrew, de Sola was associated with its principal, Daniel MacVicar, and other leaders of that communion. He may well have rubbed shoulders with the noted Montreal Christian free-thought advocate Robert Chambliss Adams, and was undoubtedly aware of his preaching.[25] De Sola's associations with Montreal intellectual circles are reflected also in the acknowledgement to him by Ellen Ross, in her novel *The Legend of the Holy Stone*, which was published in Montreal in 1878.

For all his involvement in Montreal's Anglophone intellectual life, however, there is no evidence that de Sola was influenced by the currents of religious renewal or regeneration that were beginning among many intellectuals in English Canada during the 1870s and 1880s. Clearly he was too strongly committed to Orthodox Judaism to be swayed by reformist or regenerative ideas, from outside or inside the Jewish community. Though firmly opposed to Reform Judaism, he was, however, influenced by that stream of thought that employed modern scientific knowledge to understand and explain religious beliefs and practices. Like Isaac Leeser, he was influenced by the Jewish enlightenment pioneered in Germany by Samson Raphael Hirsch, which stressed the importance of rationalism and modern secular knowledge among Orthodox Jews for a comprehensive understanding of the place of Judaism in the modern world.[26] While Leeser envisaged a unique American role in the achievement of Jewish redemption,[27] de Sola's vision was similar in regarding British North America as holding out great promise for the renewal of faith in a land of British liberty.

Although modern in his respect for some of the new scholarship on aspects of religious practices, and in his use of English in sermons and of modern Hebrew-English books in the congregation's Sunday school, de Sola nevertheless was an unrelenting enemy of the Reform movement. "I too am a reformer as far as endeavours which I believe to be consistent and legal in the manner of synagogue worship are concerned," he confided to Leeser in 1847.[28] "I don't think the cause of orthodoxy would suffer much did conservative Synagogues introduce quiet and respectability in their services." "Orthodoxy by nature, by age and by character is respectable," he continued, "[but] absurd and inconsistent novelty in the Synagogue is disreputable in its very essence. . . ." In 1855 he advised Leeser not to "attach too much importance to . . . the doings of our ultra reformers,"[29] suggesting instead that he expose "the extreme ugliness of their deformities [to] better serve the cause of historical Judaism than by creating into heroes a few men who have more philosophy than religion."

De Sola even had a grudging respect for some of Reform's leaders. In the same letter he informed Leeser that "the talent and activity of these ultras cannot but be admired and movement and life are always better than drowsiness and stagnation." In fact he was more worried about the weakness of traditional Judaism in America than he was about the activities of the Reform movement:

> Perhaps if it were not for the doings of some of these mischievous demagogues, a long *tardema* would fall upon the people – awakening from which we should find the fabric of Judaism had so suffered that most laborious efforts persevered in for many years must be resorted to, to restore it to its pristine excellence.

Still, he preserved an abiding disdain for the reformers, whom he described as "flippant [and] shallow German rationalists – who have influence enough to spare."[30] Some Reform leaders were, in his opinion, less dangerous than others.

Four years later de Sola was worried about the threats which Gustav Poznanski, preacher and reader of Charleston's Beth Elohim (House of the Lord) congregation, posed to Orthodoxy. "Can't you get a good man for Charleston," he wrote to Leeser in June 1866, "a proper, strong man would now check [the] Reform movement of the old stamp for the next quarter of a century."[31] So strong was his fear of Reform that he was even prepared to swallow his abhorrence of B'nai B'rith "for since this organization, which I view with anything but favour, has assumed its present proportions, I suppose we *must* look after it, lest our humble modest pious etc. reform brethren use it as a tool – a terrible one too – against orthodoxy."[32]

For the same reason, no doubt, de Sola himself became the leading

Canadian officer of the Kesher Shel Barzel (Links of Iron), an American Jewish organization founded in the 1860s to promote fraternal bonds and good works. He was deeply involved in its activities in Montreal, Toronto, and Hamilton, and visited those lodges occasionally to address meetings and install officers.[33] But in doing so he had to overcome his earlier reservations, which he expressed to Leeser in August 1865: "I hate the very idea of a Jewish secret society – No Roman Catholic prelate ever hated Masonry[,] Orangeism[,] Ribbonism or any other secret ism more than I abhor such an organization among us – or one at all approaching these Christian religious or political secret societies."[34]

De Sola was enraged at the popularity of certain books that improperly shortened the traditional canons of worship in many synagogues, and fulminated to Leeser that:

> The Synagogue in America is fast approaching the state of the Protestant Church there. Presumably there will be "no prayer book," "no ritual at all". . . . Extempore prayer being so superior, as they will assert. Indeed I should not be at all surprised to find the doctrines of Mormonism advocated by some Drs – at least polygamy. . . . The truth is we have too many "carnal minded Jews" in our midst. Is it the peoples fault as much as the Doctors or could the latter play the antics they do? – eating on a Ta'anit tsibur [public fast day] – smoking on a shabbat [Sabbath].[35]

With firm belief in the final religious outcome, he asserted that he had "too much confidence in the divine strength of our holy faith to suppose that such a set [of reformers] can . . . injure it permanently. We may have to witness some 'sorry sights' but they will not remain to blast out vision longer than Banquo's ghost."

Given his origins in London's Spanish and Portuguese community, he was also a devotee of the Portuguese *minhag* within traditional Orthodox Judaism. Writing to Leeser in 1854 about the formation of another synagogue in Philadelphia, he observed, "there is plenty of room for two or even three for the Portuguese minhag in these days of minhag America."[36] Indeed he viewed the Portuguese tradition as both superior to the Ashkenazic and a possible counterpoise to the worrisome advance of Reform. "When hundreds of German & Polish Congregations are formed under the most unpromising auspices, why in the name of religion should we not multiply – or attempt to multiply – congregations having so superior a ritual as the Portuguese?" he wrote in June 1857.

De Sola's relations with Montreal's growing congregation of Germans, English, and Polish were coloured by these kinds of prejudices against the Ashkenazi manner of prayer, as well as by his disdain for its "Pollack" members.

His relations with its religious leaders were not always friendly. "Entre nous, Mr. Fass is at present too much engaged with manufacturing vinegar, to cultivate pulpit eloquence," he wrote to Leeser in August 1865.[37] His own congregation's Polish and German members he was prepared to regard as "brethren." "I don't know what I should do without them," he once told Leeser. "I sometimes think I am as much a *Pollack* as any of them."[38] He was not above private expressions of contempt for such people, however. "The German [synagogue] . . . that formerly existed," he confided in the mid-1850s, "is on its last legs. They were but a poor and troublesome set who lately [are] . . . neither ornamental nor useful in a Synagogue above all in a Portuguese Synagogue the [*minhag*] of which they 'tont untershtant'."

Leeser was editor of *The Occident* from its founding in 1843 until his death in 1868. De Sola contributed news items, sermons, and extracts from his writings over many years, and he often purchased books from Leeser at the same time as he sought support for the publication of some of his own works. While Leeser was his senior by some twenty years, and one of America's leading rabbis — founder of America's first Hebrew high school, of the Board of Delegates of American Israelites, of Maimonides College, and of the first American Jewish rabbinical school — de Sola regarded him with a breezy though respectful collegiality. Even at the start of his Montreal career, at the age of twenty-three, de Sola had possessed considerable self-confidence. "I am not too proud," he wrote in February 1848, "to receive suggestions from *you*, though I might be from others. I don't mind the stroke of the lion, but I don't like the kick of the ass."[39]

De Sola devoted much of his energy to encouraging Montrealers to subscribe to *The Occident*. This was, perhaps, one way of boosting his income, which remained precarious for many years. "The claims of my avocation are pressing," he confided to Leeser in November 1862:

> you do not know how many extra dollars — good Canadian dollars and none of your Yankee shin-plasters — it requires to provide for all the wants of a little family — but I can assure you it makes a tight squeeze on the purse of a Fortunatus. So I have to develop myself to that which brings in a more immediate return.[40]

However, there is no indication in their correspondence that Leeser would not publish de Sola's contributions unless he boosted sales. On the contrary, Leeser seemed to be constantly in need of copy, and de Sola believed that almost any piece he sent to *The Occident* would be published there. His motives for encouraging subscriptions to *The Occident*, and for distributing prayer books, seem to

have been largely based on the hope of preserving Jewish learning and observance in his congregation. He believed in *The Occident's* philosophy of traditional orthodoxy.[41] However, there was too much competition from other
Jewish papers. "It is true," he wrote consolingly to Leeser, "your number is
here small . . . many . . . subscribe to papers here . . . but they nearly all prefer the
'weaklies'. The Messenger, the Israelite, & particularly the Chronicle which is
popular here, have their subscribers and there is no increase in our reading
population." The popularity of the *Jewish Chronicle*, he suggested, was largely
attributable to the fact that, because it was published in London, many Montrealers believed that its news of British and European Jewry was more comprehensive and up to date than that of New York or Philadelphia journals.

Recognizing the need for a more systematic structure for *tsedakah* (charity)
in Montreal, de Sola established the Hebrew Philanthropic Society in 1847,
shortly after his arrival. Its most pressing task was to raise money and dole it
out to needy German Jewish immigrants who had just arrived in the city.[42]
Besides de Sola, the society's relief committee included Moses Hayes, the
police chief of Montreal, as well as Simon Hart, David Moses, and Joseph
Lyons.[43] They received requests for help, while Dr. David Hart ministered to
their health.[44] These German Jews, most of them in transit to the United
States, apparently posed an unusual burden for the Montreal congregations. In
a letter to Leeser in late November 1847, de Sola wrote:

> during the whole summer an unprecedented number of German Jewish
> Emigrants visited Canada. Indigent and in many cases sick, they proved
> a most serious drain on the funds of our Infant Philanthropic Society.
> About thirty persons many with families besides, mostly pensioners, were
> recipients.[45]

But the crisis passed quickly. As the immigrants departed or settled in, the
society was left to assist only a few local and transient indigent Jews; for these
purposes an occasional passing of the hat seems to have sufficed, and the
society ceased to exist.[46]

By 1863, however, the situation had changed. More Jewish immigrants had
begun arriving, many of them from the United States, while local indigency was
also increasing.[47] The previous pattern of informal collection and handouts was
not working, and a new, larger, and stronger organization was needed, to draw
more effectively on the combined resources of both congregations.

In July of 1863, about thirty men met "to consider the desirability of forming
some association to assist our needy or unfortunate co-religionists."[48] The

result, the Young Men's Hebrew Benevolent Society, was limited at first to bachelors, but the membership was enlarged in 1869 to include married men.[49] Its founders were drawn from both of the city's congregations, and membership was more or less evenly balanced between them.[50] The operative body of the organization was the Relief Committee, which included both religious leaders, de Sola and Fass (of the English, German, and Polish congregation), along with three or four others.[51] Even though the differing synagogue affiliations resulted in some friction, there were never any suggestions that this rivalry affected the dispensation of charity. In fact, though members of the Spanish and Portuguese synagogue filled the presidency for some years and made the largest contributions until the early 1890s, the executive positions were pretty evenly divided between the two congregations, indicating a general willingness to share authority and responsibility.

During its first decade the relief work of the YMHBS was limited. Although the Jewish population of Canada East (which became the Province of Quebec in 1867) had grown by 1861 to 572 people, with all but a few dozen of them living in Montreal,[52] over the next ten years the community actually declined in size as many immigrants and some established residents left the city. An upswing in immigration to Canada during the 1870s increased the Montreal Jewish population to about 950 by 1881, and over the next ten years the city's Jewry grew to 2,473 people. Many of the new arrivals came from Central and Eastern Europe in impoverished condition and needed considerable help.

The immigration of the 1870s was barely under way when strains started appearing. At its meeting in October 1874, society members complained that they had to bear heavy financial burdens due to "many families having arrived here from Germany and other adjoining countries in a state of utter destitution."[53] Helping some forty-two families had cost $542 and depleted the society's resources; the society had even been forced to resort to deficit financing. But the strain was brief and by no means overwhelming.

Except for two years in the mid-1870s, the sums of money raised and spent on relief were in fact very small, usually between two and five hundred dollars annually. The funds came almost entirely from the members' annual fees, or from special contributions raised whenever the treasury was especially low. Collection committees were struck to encourage members to pay their dues and to collect from other local Jews.[54] Occasionally, contributions were received from non-Jewish donors, including an annual grant from the Montreal City and District Savings Bank.[55] The society attempted to augment its finances by holding theatricals and dances.[56]

Although most expenditures went to alleviate distress among resident and transient Jews, by providing necessities such as food, clothing, coal, and medicines, money was also spent on assisting transients to move on. The committee that handled these cases reported at quarterly or semi-annual meetings and at the annual general meeting, where full reports of all cases were provided. A visiting committee determined the needs of applicants and provided some follow-up, while medical assistance was provided by Dr. Aaron Hart David, a prominent local doctor, and hospital care was arranged at the Montreal General Hospital.[57]

The heaviness of these obligations became an issue at one of the society's earliest meetings. Reflecting the prevailing Victorian ideas of charity — and, perhaps, some dilatoriness in the payment of annual dues — one prominent member argued in 1863 that the society "is not based on the principle of granting permanent relief" and that therefore "no application [should] receive assistance oftener than once in three months."[58] He suggested that relief payments be limited to an annual maximum of ten dollars for any single applicant or family group. Recognizing that providing permanent relief would necessitate the raising of much larger amounts of money, members reiterated their commitment to provide only "temporary" relief.[59]

Abraham de Sola was not happy with this decision, and he raised the issue again, in open disagreement with these views. "In view of the desirableness of affording permanent relief required by the parties hitherto receiving the same from the Society," he urged the society to form a special committee to increase its revenue accordingly. The society could not confine itself to alleviating immediate distress because there were growing numbers of indigents whose rehabilitation would take much longer. A decision was made to extend permanent relief to "selected applicants" but it was reversed a short time later "in view of this Society not having been sufficiently supported by some of our co-religionists."[60] Thus the decision to keep its commitments to the bare minimum was reasserted.

Over the next decade, the problem of long-lasting poverty in the Montreal community became serious. In 1876, Moses Gutman called attention to several families who were annually dependent upon the society during "our long winters" because of their inability to find employment.[61] He felt that these families should be denied relief altogether if they refused to move "to some other place where they might perhaps find friends or relations to assist them or constant work and pay the year round."[62] This view was supported by E.M. Myers, the new minister of the English, German, and Polish congregation, who even suggested that these families were "unable to support themselves any longer and should be forced to go away." Precisely how many families were regularly imposing on the society is not clear, nor was either Gutman or Reverend Myers prepared to say where these families would be able to make a more regular income. But their protest against being permanently imposed upon by indigents suggests that the spirit of *tsedakah* had limits.

In an effort to improve its efficiency in helping immigrants, and to lessen its own obligations, the society attempted also to establish co-operative contact with other philanthropic organizations in Montreal, not all of whom were friendly towards these overtures.[63] In 1874, Mona Lesser recommended that they participate, with "all the National and Charitable Societies in this City," in the formation of a "Colonization Society," to try to secure a grant from the Dominion government for relieving immigrants landing in Montreal. No encouragement was received from Ottawa, while local national or ethnic societies like the St. Andrew's, the Irish Benevolent, and the German were also apparently not interested.

The society also made an effort to limit demands upon it by stemming the flow to Canada of what it called "too many destitute and helpless Israelites."[64] In 1875, alarmed by the rumours of a large Jewish migration on its way to Canada, the executive dispatched strong protests to the London newspapers the *Jewish World* and the *Jewish Chronicle*, in the hopes of preventing various Jewish organizations, such as London's Ladies Emigration Society, from shunting too many of the European Jews arriving in England out to North America. These protests elicited favourable editorial response from the *Jewish Chronicle* in October 1875: "Our transatlantic brethren object – and we confess, very properly so . . . to being burdened with the poor and unskillful Jews who are assisted to emigrate from Europe to the United States and Canada."[65] But such sympathetic comments did not stop the London agencies from continuing to export their problems. Two years later the Montrealers found it necessary to complain again to the London organizations that they were sending too many Jews "in a state of destitution and generally incapable of self help."[66] Besides writing hostile letters to the London papers, the society sent de Sola on a mission to protest in person to the Jewish Emigration Society, which was chiefly responsible for sending poor Jews to Canada.[67] While there, he was partly persuaded that "the statements of the immigrants that they had been sent by the Jewish Emigration Society should not always be accepted." In any event, his protests seem to have had the desired effect, and for the time being, anyway, the export of poor Jews from London ceased abruptly.[68]

During the influx of the mid-1870s, the formation of other Jewish charities in Montreal resulted in some duplication of relief efforts. The most important of these organizations, the Ladies' Hebrew Benevolent Society – concerned with the welfare of women and children since its formation in 1877 – had exchanged information with the Young Men's Hebrew Benevolent Society on those people seeking help. However, similar co-operation or sharing of responsibility had apparently not been established with any of the other newer charities, most of them self-help associations formed by the immigrants themselves. This resulted in considerable confusion and animosity because of the increasing numbers of overlapping appeals to the Jews of Montreal.

Observing this proliferation of effort, and perhaps influenced by the success of New York's recently formed United Hebrew Charities, one of the society's most active early members, Moses Gutman, suggested in 1874 that a similar body be established in Montreal. In his view, he said, "the interest of charity will be best served by this Society merging itself into a more general organization, embracing all the Jews of Montreal as its members."[69] Few of his associates were ready for that. Some of them claimed that such action should be taken "only after mature deliberation," since it would "threaten . . . the very existence of the Society." The objections suggest that the officers of the society preferred to retain control and to limit the extent of their obligations. The transformation of the society into a mass charity organization was an unwelcome prospect at a time when immigrants were beginning to outnumber residents. These newcomers were more likely to be receivers than givers of philanthropy, and they might well have more generous, and costly, concepts of what Jewish charity should be.

The society's directors and a good number of the members were either Canadian-born or long-time residents; some were making a living while others were well-to-do. In this period there was still considerable common ground on which the immigrants met the established group. While they were not likely to meet socially, and some contacts were probably on an employer–employee basis, they might well meet in either of the two synagogues which competed for the newcomers' membership.[70] Some of the immigrants tended to keep shy of the older congregations, however, with their imposing buildings and dignified services that included sermons in English. Both Shearith Israel and the English, German, and Polish congregation completed impressive new edifices during the mid-1880s, while a small Reform group calling itself Temple Emanu-el was formed a few years later.[71] The East European immigrant favoured the small congregations – often no more than a mere *minyan* (quorum) of ten or more men who met in an empty store or apartment – springing up in his own district in the lower east-central part of the city, where he and his countrymen lived. Here they could worship in the manner in which they always had.

The benefit of new religious leadership, the growth of a new congregation, and the establishment of a philanthropic society reflected commitment and involvement by Montreal Jewry in the social and economic life of this burgeoning city. As it grew after the 1840s, members of Montreal's Jewish community were attracted into a variety of new ventures associated with that diversification.

The history of Montreal Jewry from the mid-1840s to the early 1880s thus encompassed many significant transformations. While de Sola's arrival in 1847 coincided with the beginnings of a second congregation and with the establishment of the first philanthropic organization in the community, it also marked the beginning of stronger connections with the Jewish world outside Montreal. De Sola's correspondence with Moses Montefiore and the London rabbinate, and his involvement in its scholarly interests, as well as his growing associations with American religious figures like Isaac Leeser, put Montreal closer to the contemporary currents of Jewish life than it had been previously. Montreal Jewry in the mid-Victorian age enjoyed a period of relative tranquillity and internal harmony, notwithstanding its gradual growth and accompanying diversity. The Young Men's Hebrew Benevolent Society fairly effectively brought both congregations together in the cause of *tsedakah*, as did the Ladies' Hebrew Benevolent Society. In this way the community responded to the immigrants who came from the world beyond.

The division of the community into two congregations in 1846 did not eliminate tensions within Shearith Israel. Although it had never been entirely, or even largely, composed of Spanish and Portuguese Jews, the synagogue that bore that name did follow the Sephardic order of prayer and traditional melodies, as well as holiday and many other religious customs. These practices were distinguished from those of the Ashkenazic rite, and, like doctrinal differences about aspects of Christian belief among ardent members of Protestant sects, these divisions aroused resentment and, at times, rebellion and permanent schism. They were not substantial doctrinal differences, as was the case in the Reform break with traditional Jewish Orthodoxy. Still, while minor by comparison, such distinctions were taken very seriously by those to whom religion was of fundamental significance. Within the Spanish and Portuguese congregation, there were also differences between the older community – many of them Canadian-born – and the newcomers, most of whom had immigrated from England, Germany, and Poland. Of the latter, some had remained in the congregation and were in one way or another "rather troublesome," according to the young Clarence de Sola, who was probably reporting his father's impressions of the congregation's annual meeting in his diary in April 1872. In some of his letters to Isaac Leeser, himself of German origin, Abraham de Sola revealed his disrespect for these newcomers who belonged to the other synagogue, which was sometimes referred to as the "German school" or *"dem Paleischer Minyan."*[72] It was usually with ill-disguised disdain, if not contempt, that such references were made to those with strange accents and manners, who lacked a proper sense of deference to the bearers and defenders, like the de Solas – Abraham and his sons, Meldola, Gershom, and Clarence – of the proud tradition of the Sephardim.

For the latter, the mid-Victorian era was a period of remarkable integration into the social and economic life of Montreal. While the de Solas were at the very apogee of the city's Jewish social pyramid – rabbinical learning, especially when recognized by McGill University, carried great prestige – they were not by any means alone. Some, like Samuel Benjamin, who was elected alderman for Centre Ward in 1849, enjoyed public office,[73] while Dr. Aaron Hart David was appointed secretary to the Central Board of Health.[74] Members of the Joseph, Ascher, Davis, and Moss families were believed to be well-to-do and attained recognition for their business success.

The social life of the sons and daughters of Montreal's affluent Jews included some serious philanthropic endeavours, as well as the *bonhomie* of sports and the frivolities and flirtations at picnics and parties. Not only did most of the young men become members of the Young Men's Hebrew Benevolent Society and the women of the Ladies' Hebrew Benevolent Society, but they also took keen interest in developing a formal structure of Jewish organizations in Montreal. Drawn from both synagogues, these young people seem to have been inspired largely by British rather than American models.

De Sola's son Clarence was probably typical of his generation. He attended the balls and dances and had considerable social contact with members of the Anglo-Saxon elite. His diaries carry no references to antisemitism in any aspect of his early life, whether at school, in sports, or in his active social life. In attending Montreal High School, in playing lacrosse and football, and in genteel social groups, he enjoyed good relationships with teachers, sportsmen, and friends. In school he was known as "Historicus" because of his strong interest in history. If his diary is to be believed, while in his early teens he undertook a remarkable reading program in the classics: Grote's *History of Greece*, Milman's *History of the Jews*, Macaulay's *History of England*, and many other works. He was not especially close to the Protestant establishment but, judging from his diary, he was apparently at ease in their company, and shared much of their outlook, culture, and prejudices. His closest friends, however, were Jewish, and were drawn almost entirely from the small group of old, established, and well-off families associated with the Spanish and Portuguese synagogue. Picnics, outings, extended holidays, and literary and social evenings were almost invariably confined to this intimate group of the younger Jacobses, Davises, Aschers, Mosses, Harts, Josephs, Kellerts, and Samuelses, the sons and daughters of comfortable merchants, manufacturers, and real estate developers who made up the Montreal equivalent of New York's Sephardic "Grandees" and German-Jewish "Our Crowd."[75]

Clarence de Sola's principal preoccupation after finishing high school in 1875 was business. After an apprenticeship with Foulds and Taylor, a non-Jewish firm (which allowed him to be absent on the Sabbath and all Jewish holidays), he entered a number of early ventures and became the agent of various Belgian business interests in Canada. He became a ship-building contractor and an entrepreneur in an assortment of large-scale bridge, railway, and harbour-building enterprises across Canada. Enjoying important connections among Quebec federal Liberals, de Sola expanded his business activity in a very prosperous manner during the Laurier government's tenure in office. His diaries reveal that, between 1900 and 1911, he took frequent trips to Ottawa and had long discussions with Cabinet ministers, and even with the prime minister himself. Through his business connections in Belgium, he became that country's consul in Montreal, an honour which brought him into frequent social contact with Ottawa and Quebec politicians, the Montreal Anglophone plutocracy, governors-general, and a wide variety of English and European nobility.

Despite his considerable personal wealth, the distinction of a learned father, and, most important, the intensely proud lineage of the Spanish and Portuguese Jews – a pride that might have kept him aloof from other Jews – de Sola began to take an interest in the welfare of the Montreal Jewish community, which, in the 1880s and 1890s, was undergoing rapid and far-reaching transformation. During the 1880s Montreal's Jewish population rose by over 170 per cent, several new synagogues were established, and numerous organizations were formed, while the city experienced the cultural diversity carried by these new arrivals.[76] As a younger man he was only perfunctorily involved in philanthropic causes, but in 1882 the plight of hundreds of refugees arriving in Montreal from Eastern Europe following the pogroms of that year moved him profoundly.[77] He was again shaken in 1903, in 1905, and by the events of the First World War. Thus, despite his youthful indifference (which was shared by many other members of the small Spanish and Portuguese group, as well as by Montreal's British-born Jews), de Sola was drawn sympathetically to his people in their hours of adversity.

He was also fastidiously faithful to the Jewish religion. Throughout his entire life he always kept the Sabbath, ate only kosher food, attended synagogue each week, read the Tanach (Bible) regularly, studied Hebrew, taught Sunday school at the Spanish and Portuguese synagogue, and took great pride in helping to build and decorate its *succah* (booth) for the festival of Succoth. He carefully observed the holidays in the traditional Orthodox manner according to the Spanish and Portuguese *minhag*. His Sephardic pride was coupled with a sense of responsibility to uphold the Orthodox traditions, to combat the forces of internal disunity within North American Jewry, and to foster defence mechanisms against the persecution of Jews abroad.[78]

In March of 1881, with substantial community support, a small group including Clarence de Sola set up a Montreal branch of the Anglo-Jewish Association. Their purpose was to act in concert with the London-based association, which had been established ten years earlier to protect Jewish rights in countries where Jews were threatened.[79] This organization helped to mobilize Montreal's Jews to receive the wave of pogrom refugees who reached the city during the next few years. Its formation indicated that a major segment of the community saw itself as parallel to that segment of British Jewry headed by the Montefiores and Rothschilds, which took an active interest in the fate of their persecuted co-religionists in Eastern Europe and the Middle East.[80] The organization was not only paternalistic and philanthropic, it also – like its English model – reflected ethnic pride, sense of duty, and social conscience. And as the counterpart of ethnic organizations like the St. Patrick and St. Andrew's societies, perhaps the two most prominent in Anglophone Montreal at that time, the Anglo-Jewish and the Young Men's Hebrew Benevolent associations were part of the quest for respectability – acceptance, even – in the best circles.

Similar to American Jewry in structure and concerns, Canadian Jewry was by 1860 nevertheless significantly different. Many of the most pressing issues confronting American Jewry, such as the immediate and urgent question of realigning Jewish life to a modern liberal environment, were not the leading items on the Canadian Jewish agenda.[81] No evidence is yet available to indicate that Reform surfaced in Canadian Jewry at this time, and vigorous debates between its growing number of supporters and the traditionalists were absent north of the forty-ninth parallel. Even though de Sola threw himself into the American fight alongside Leeser and Isaacs, he was only a soldier in the ranks of Orthodoxy's army, never an officer. Not until much later in the century did Reform make any inroads into Canada, and then only when its followers removed themselves from existing congregations to establish their own congregations.[82] When de Sola attempted to join the drive led by Leeser to form a Board of Delegates of Hebrew Congregations in the 1850s, he was told that, because he lived in British North America, he was not welcome to participate – an indication that leading American Jews thought Canadian Jewry did not share their problems.

Of course, the distinctions between the two Jewries were not just qualitative. In 1850 the American Jewish population numbered some 50,000 souls and fifty congregations, fifteen in New York city alone, whereas in all of British North America there were a mere 451 Jews in 1851.[83] As a result of the immigration of the 1850s, though Canada's Jewish population more than doubled to 1,186, the number of Jews in the U.S. increased by about 100,000, to a total of 150,000 by 1860. The number of congregations in Canada had increased from the two in Montreal to a total of five, the additional three being in Toronto, Hamilton, and Victoria, but meanwhile another 135 congregations had emerged in the United States. Thus Canadian Jewry simply did not have the numbers to make religious dissent organizationally sustainable, except in Montreal – where the second synagogue was apparently every bit as traditional as the first. From 1861 to 1871 Canada's Jewish population increased by a minuscule number to 1,333 persons, while that of Montreal actually decreased.

The Jews who migrated to Canada in that early Victorian era were probably not significantly different in their social origins and financial wherewithal from those who went to the United States. The recent synthesis of American Jewish history by Arthur Hertzberg emphasizes the findings of historians that, contrary to myth, German Jewish immigrants of the 1850s were not political refugees from the failed revolutions of 1848.[84] They were mostly in flight from poverty and were "the poorest and the least educated."[85] As many as half of them were from Bavaria, mostly the children of petty tradesmen and cattle dealers from country towns where economic opportunities were limited. Many others came from Posen, the eastern-most province of Prussia, and Bohemia and Moravia. The migrations of Jews to Canada included many from these regions, but others were British-born, or long-time British residents. Their British origins or sojourns may have affected their political and social outlook.

The crucial difference between the Canadian and American Jewish communities lay in the social and political contexts in which they then existed. In contrast to the United States, where, since 1850, a single – albeit increasingly divided – nation had existed from sea to sea, governed from Washington under a constitution "conceived in liberty," British North America consisted of separate and widely scattered colonies until Confederation in 1867; indeed, the territorial union was completed only in the 1870s, when the Northwest Territories, Manitoba, British Columbia, and Prince Edward Island were brought into the Dominion. Even then, Canadian national identity was still unformed and relied largely upon British co-ordinates, while Canadians grappled with the over-riding reality of the two ways of life and thought in the English and French sections of the country.

In Montreal this fundamental French fact was made strikingly obvious by the magnificent religious edifices, like the new Roman Catholic cathedral arising in the 1850s on Dorchester Street, by the sounds of the French language among about half of the city's population, by the outpouring of journals in the 1840s, by the emergence of powerful personalities like Bishop Ignace Bourget and George-Etienne Cartier, and by the continuing importance of the Sulpician Order in the economic life of the city.[86] The question of how Jews should adapt themselves and their faith to the new nation, which defined itself ambiguously as a "dominion," never arose because – unlike the United States, which was based on a statement about philosophically derived first principles – Canada was founded, in the words of the British North America Act, "under the Crown of the United Kingdom . . . with a constitution similar in principle to that of the United Kingdom."[87]

Except to a tiny minority of intellectuals, the meaning of Canadian nationality was not an issue, and late-nineteenth-century nationalist thought expressed an essentially British view of Canada's history, national character, and mission.[88] Implied here were broad extra territorial co-ordinates of Canadian national identity which, unlike the ideas expressed in the Constitution of the United States, laid down no first principles and promised no secular redemption. Instead, Canadians received the more sober, less inspiring, and less demanding pledge contained in the British North America Act that the Dominion government was empowered "to make laws for the peace, order and good government of Canada." Thus, in the era of Abraham de Sola, the political and social contexts of Canada's largest Jewish community reflected a set of continuing differences from those affecting Jews in the United States.

Montreal's population, of course, was defined variously by ethnic, linguistic, and religious allegiances, while it was divided economically into several levels, from common labourer to business tycoon, and occupationally into about five major divisions (agricultural, commercial, domestic, industrial, and professional). Although measurements of wealth are not available, the fact that benevolent societies were required indicates the existence of an increasingly serious problem of Jewish indigency. On the other hand, the Jewish well-to-do were able to afford large homes, servants, expensive lifestyles, and generous holidays. There existed plutocrats, too – like Jesse Joseph, who possessed substantial real estate and corporate interests. But occupationally the Jews of Montreal in the 1850s and 1860s were heavily concentrated in commercial pursuits.[89] In 1861 fully 55 per cent of Montreal's gainfully employed Jews were in commercial pursuits, almost two and a half times the rate among the city's population as a whole. This was accentuated during the 1860s. The 1871 census returns reveal that nearly 63 per cent of the Jews gainfully employed were in commerce, nearly three times the rate of the entire city's population. There were no Jews in agriculture, and only two in domestic service in 1861, four in 1871. The number of Jewish profes- sionals actually declined from fourteen to eleven during these two decades, as did the number and percentage of Jews in industrial occupations. Thus, the middle-class and commercial character of the community was heavily pro- nounced in this period.

The concentration of Jews in commercial activity did not mean, however, that even a majority of them were well off. One study of Jewish residential pat- terns in 1861 and 1871 demonstrates that, while some upper-middle-class Jews could afford to move during the 1860s from their homes on Viger Square to the fashionable "new town" neighbourhood that was opening up south of McGill College, a new and much poorer Jewish enclave was emerging in the St. Lawrence Street area. Here lived most of the Jewish pedlars, pawnbrokers, commercial travellers, hatters, tailors, rag-shop owners, silverplaters, and glaziers.[90] Most were Polish-born and were, apparently, recent immigrants. Thus, at least a decade before the beginning of mass migration of poor Jews from Russia in the 1880s, fairly sharp economic divisions existed alongside the ethnic and religious differences within the Montreal Jewish community.

CHAPTER

4

Profit and Loss on the
Urban Frontier

Mark Samuel, who ran a men's hat shop on Montreal's Notre Dame Street in the early 1850s, probably did not know what was being written about him in the R.G. Dun and Company credit report of 1852.[1] The entry under his name read "said to be a very honest Jew," signalling to potential creditors the message "here is one you can trust."[2] Not all Jewish businessmen in Montreal were accorded such praise. Most received far worse, and might be described as "close fisted Jew," "trying to get the best of a bargain," or simply "Jew, cannot trust." These descriptions were more derogatory than the kinds of characterizations that were attached to local businessmen of other national or ethnic origins, like Irishmen, Scots, Americans, and French-Canadians, and no doubt reflected an antisemitism that was widely current at the time. Jews had a reputation for shrewdness, toughness, and dishonesty that went far beyond the reputed canniness of the Scot, or the sharpness of the Yankee trader. The prevailing assumption seems to have been that one *really* had to be on guard when dealing with a Jew, and those who reported confidentially to Dun's agency clearly made it their business to find out who was a Jew, to try to scrutinize that person's dealings more closely than they would otherwise, and to make a specific point of that in their reports. A comparison of Jewish merchants identified by Dun with those listed in the 1861 and 1871 Montreal manuscript census returns indicates that the Dun reporters had an accurate knowledge of who was a Jew.[3]

One obvious question is "Did antisemitism matter?" If it had not existed, would Jews have fared better in the business environment of mid-nineteenth-century Central Canada? As noted earlier, the commercial community that controlled the economic life of Montreal had included a small number of Jews since the Conquest – as well as a few Germans and Italians – amid the Anglo-Celtic majority of Scots, Americans, English, and Irish, and the minority of French Canadians. By about 1850 a few members of the Jewish community were listed among the local merchants who dominated the increasingly diverse business affairs in the city. Jews owned shares in the chartered banks; David David even sat on the boards of the Bank of Montreal and the Lachine Canal Company.[4] Moses Judah Hayes, the police chief, was the owner of the Montreal waterworks until he sold the company to the city in 1845.[5] He was one of the few wealthy Jews who, besides owning shares in all of these ventures and in ships, both sail and steam, held substantial quantities of real estate.[6] Some were so successful that, although they were still denied membership in the most elitist organizations of the rich Anglo-Celts, they enjoyed considerable status and influence. Because of his great learning, Abraham de Sola held an appointment at McGill. Meanwhile, Jesse Joseph, the president of the Montreal Gas Company and by far the richest Jew in Montreal, was amassing a vast amount of first-class urban real estate.[7]

In what ways was the Jewish experience in the Canadian business world unique, or at least noticeably different from that of the Scots, Americans, English, and French Canadians? Did they constitute a separate business enclave, to a significant degree working apart from the rest in a kind of Jewish business ghetto? If so, did they separate themselves, or were they excluded by reason of antisemitism from certain sectors of business? In business, did antisemitism really matter? And, if it did, in what ways did it restrict Jews from progressing or from entering certain fields?

Some studies of Jewish life in the United States during the nineteenth century – Steven Hertzberg's book on Atlanta, Elliott Ashkenazi's on Louisiana, and William Toll's on Portland, Oregon – reflect the influence of the new social history in American Jewish studies.[8] All three works are based upon analysis of the manuscript census data, Dun and Company credit reports, and records of fraternal orders and synagogues, as well as diaries and correspondence, and they evaluate the processes at work in the creation of Jewish business groups, predominantly mercantile, in those places. Toll stresses the importance of family-based commercial networks in which Jewish single males from south German and Bavarian small towns moved to Portland in the 1850s to pioneer in petty commerce, often as pedlars. When moderately successful, they brought out wives and members of their immediate and extended families from Germany. Relying on savings, commercial experience, and credit generated by family or fraternal institutions, some of them became wealthy through commercial and industrial enterprise. Toll emphasizes that Portland's Jewish business class evolved independently of the non-Jewish environment and notes that, while business contacts developed between Jews and Gentiles, antisemitic attitudes such as those reflected in Dun's credit reports forced Jews to rely essentially on themselves. Both Hertzberg and Ashkenazi make much the same argument.

David Gerber's scholarly study on the Jews of Buffalo argues that the Dun reports reflect the persistence in America of the image of Shylock – the parasite, the predator, the fraud, the arsonist, the seller of trinkets – in short, the stereotypical Jew.[9] He argues that discrimination against these "Shylocks" forced the Jews to adopt alternative economic strategies, such as borrowing from within immediate family networks, and creating partnerships and other means to circumvent a "credit squeeze" forced upon them by the prevalence of this negative image. Ashkenazi goes further and claims that in New Orleans "some Jewish wholesalers of dry goods and clothing concentrated on supplying hundreds of small Jewish country retailers throughout Louisiana and neighbouring states" and that "a singularly Jewish trade developed, with its own mechanisms and its own peculiar methods of payment."[10]

How well do these patterns apply to the Canadian context? Some of these features – migration, family connections, intercity networks and patterns of ethnic business association – were well-established throughout Canadian business in the mid-nineteenth century. Studies of the Hamilton and Montreal business communities illustrate that these same patterns prevailed among Scots and Americans in Canada's commercial world at that time.[11] Borrowing from family and friends and forming business partnerships with them were widespread practices, despite the growth of incorporated companies for capital-intensive developments like banks, canals, and railways. If Canadian Jews employed extended family networks for finance, they were conforming to the existing customs among all businessmen, of whatever background or affiliation, during this period of rapid economic growth, diversification, and modernization.

In the 1840s, 1850s, and 1860s, Montreal was the premier city of the United Province of Canada, which embraced Canada East and Canada West – the new official names for the old provinces of Lower and Upper Canada, which became Quebec and Ontario at Confederation in 1867. The booming exports and imports that fuelled the city's growth in these decades sparked enormous expansion in all sectors of its economic life. Old banks expanded while new ones were founded; insurance enterprises began to flourish. Always the hub of St. Lawrence River traffic, Montreal emerged in the 1850s as Canada's pre-eminent railway centre as well, and the steamboats and sailing craft that crowded the waterfront competed for the lucrative passenger and premium freight traffic. Manufacturing enterprises abounded, both in the processing of primary products and in the production of manufactured goods for the Montreal and regional market. This colonial metropolis experienced continuing growth and sophistication as its commerce and population grew, while its expanded railways – like the Grand Trunk, with its magnificent Victoria Bridge – strengthened the city's influence throughout Canada.

Jews constituted no more than half a per cent of Montreal's population between 1840 and 1880,[12] and most of them were in businesses of various kinds – largely jewellery, tobacco, dry goods and textiles, and clothing manufacturing. In all of these sectors family connections were overwhelmingly important in the formation and continuation of partnerships, capital formation, and marketing.

While there were relatively few Jewish businessmen dealing with jewellery, or in "fancy goods" (which included trinkets and decorations), the Dun reports reveal some fascinating information about their capital, connections, and style of business. Moses Ollendorf, a forty-four-year-old German Jew, arrived with some capital in 1848 and started by repairing jewellery and engaging in small-scale retailing.[13] After failing in 1852, he recommenced business on a modest scale as an importer and wholesaler dealing mainly with Jewish pedlars. By 1862, following a second failure in which he paid off his creditors, he was reported to be worth some $15,000 and described as "a shrewd cunning Jew [who] lives in great style." He assisted a brother, a local soap-maker, and helped put his son-in-law, Lewis Anthony, a small-scale clothing manufacturer, into business in Toronto.[14] A member of the English, German, and Polish congregation, Ollendorf contributed handsomely to the campaign to build its first synagogue in the 1850s – so much so that he was elected its first president in 1860.[15]

Abraham Hoffnung, another German Jew, arrived in 1855 at the age of twenty-five, with inventory worth about $8,000, to start selling watches; he had been in St. Louis, Missouri, for several years, probably working with relatives or friends.[16] Like Ollendorf, Hoffnung was an importer and wholesaler, dealing mainly with English suppliers. He prospered and was estimated to have made a profit of $5,000 to $6,000 within two years. He benefited from the excellent credit he enjoyed in London and, probably, from his marriage to the daughter of John Levy, a well-to-do local tobacco merchant. Hoffnung's business was well regarded, though the Dun reporter complained in October 1858 that he "belongs to a class regarding whom it is next to impossible to learn anything certain." This meant that Jews were secretive about their business dealings – a very frequent complaint, and perhaps one of the reasons why Dun's reports were filled with pointed references to "people of that class." By March of 1860, Hoffnung was estimated to be worth $10,000 and his annual turnover was judged to be $25,000, on a stock of about equal value. In August of 1860 he was joined by a young English Jew, George Wolfe, one of two brothers who had been partners in a small jewellery business since arriving in 1858 with an $8,000 inventory that had been supplied by a sister-in-law.[17]

Gottschalk Ascher was another German-Jewish merchant in Montreal.[18] He had arrived from Glasgow in 1841, at age fifty. He sold watches and jewellery and by 1857, the date of the earliest Dun reports on him, was thought to be doing well, though the reporter complained that it was difficult to get information about his obligations. By that time Ascher had already established a branch store in Toronto run by his sons, Jacob and Albert. Ascher bought merchandise in both New York and Glasgow and, despite severe setbacks in 1857 (possibly because of the sons' takeover of the Montreal store), he was soon back in business, though on a much reduced scale. By that time his son Albert – who had married Rachel Joseph, the daughter of a very wealthy, old Montreal Sephardic family – was the firm's travelling salesman. The marriage into wealth did not help the business, however, and by 1861 it was sputtering.

The short-lived partnership of Dinklespiel and Bumsel, organized in 1859, was made up of Michael Dinklespiel, another German, and Michael Bumsel, a Swiss, both of whom had immigrated in the mid-1850s.[19] This was a wholesale house, and Bumsel – a jewellery pedlar until he teamed up with Dinklespiel – seems to have been its salesman. The leading partner was Dinklespiel, who was supported by a brother in New York who became the effective owner of the business by 1861. After starting well, the firm closed down in October of 1862, following an auction of its stock and a settling of its accounts. Dinklespiel went to California, probably as his brother's agent, while Bumsel returned briefly to Europe, possibly to peddle jewellery in the Swiss countryside, and then journeyed back to Canada to take up business, also briefly, in Toronto, where he cut a sad figure.

Henry Davis and Julius Lander, both Germans, began to import jewellery and fancy goods through Lander's connections in Germany in 1861.[20] They sold mainly at wholesale, to pedlars like Samuel Silverman, whose wife kept a millinery shop in the city, and to Herman Danciger, a German who had migrated to Montreal from New York, where he had run a clothing store for several years. They supplied Simon Hart, who, with his wife and son, Philip, also had an interest in a pawnshop[21] with William Silverstone, another German. Silverstone left that partnership in February of 1863 and set up his own pawnshop with Louis Albert, a former pedlar.

And finally, David Ansell, though not a jeweller, might be included here, because he imported various kinds of glassware and toys.[22] An agent for several German firms, he arrived in 1862 from Queensland, Australia, where he had served an apprenticeship in this line. He had excellent connections in Frankfurt, where his father was an important glass manufacturer with outlets in London, Paris, and Hamburg. By 1869 Ansell was reported to be worth from $8,000 to $10,000 and enjoyed a good reputation. "He evidently knows how to make money," commented Dun's investigator after noting that Ansell claimed to have made $10,000 in 1868 alone, "a result few would expect from the quiet business he does." Besides knowing how to turn a handsome agent's profit in his various lines, Ansell speculated in property. In 1871, for example, he financed the building of a row of stone houses worth about $20,000 (and mortgaged for only $7,000). That year he employed six travelling salesmen, including one working exclusively in the United States. By 1874 he was reported still to be doing well, though following a "peculiar style of doing business," while estimates of his personal wealth ran as high as $50,000. He suffered serious reverses a year later, perhaps because of the depression, and in November of 1875 he was forced to make an assignment (a form of bankruptcy) with his liabilities totalling $130,000 against assets of $40,000. Although Dun's registers lose sight of him at this point, Ansell went into other business ventures, apparently with great success. He was one of the most important figures in Montreal's Jewish community for nearly another forty years, taking a very active role in charitable work among the city's Jewish immigrants, in the colonization of Jews on the western Prairies, and in Quebec political issues that affected Montreal Jewry.[23]

Nearly all of these Montreal Jewish jewellers were German. Most clearly arrived with considerable capital or inventory, and benefited from business and family connections in Germany, Britain, or the United States, which supplied them with vitally important agencies for specific lines of merchandise, credits, and information. Several acted as wholesalers to local pedlars, or upcountry traders, many of whom, apparently, were also Jews. But not all of them prospered; about half enjoyed only transitory business lives.

The Jewish presence in Montreal's tobacco trade, by contrast, included practically no Germans. Most Jewish tobacconists had small-scale enterprises which apparently enjoyed very few family or other credit connections abroad. There was one giant tobacco firm, that of the Joseph family, headed by Jacob Henry Joseph. They were Sephardic Jews who had originally settled in Berthier in about 1800, then in Quebec City in 1814, and finally in Montreal in 1830.[24] Their business was so large, well capitalized, and sound that in October 1858 a credit report rated them "As good as the Bank. You may trust them [for] all they will buy," and in February 1859 "Jews and 'Rich as Jews'."[25] The firm occupied huge premises where the various tobacco products were manufactured and prepared for distribution across the province. By October of 1857 the Josephs also held other assets, possibly real estate, worth over $200,000. A year later Jacob Henry was reported to be building a house for $40,000, and was believed to have a net worth of at least $100,000. He became an officer of the Montreal Board of Trade and the harbour authorities, and a supporter of a number of charities.[26] In 1866 he took in Alexander Hart as a junior partner, as he was too busy with other lucrative interests in real estate and extensive share holdings in local telegraph, railway, banking, and elevator companies.[27] He and his brother, Jesse, also a rich and diversified investor, were Montreal's only Jewish tycoons of that era.

By comparison, most of the other Jews in the tobacco business were much smaller fry. Of these, John Levy (whose daughter married the jeweller Abraham Hoffnung) was apparently one of the most successful, at least for a brief period during the 1850s. An immigrant from Manchester, Levy began business in 1843 on a small scale. Ten years later, using credits from New York City firms, he was prospering and, according to the Dun reporter, "making money . . . owns [real estate] and is said to be rich + good."[28] Thought to be worth from $18,000 to $22,000, he was doing between $60,000 and $65,000 worth of business annually. A Dun reporter noted that Levy put on "a princely entertainment" for his daughter's wedding in March of 1858. But Levy died the following August, leaving his widow and ten children – and his creditors – with a rat's nest of tangled finances. His wife, Gertrude, settled with the creditors, most of them in New York, for fifty cents on the dollar, and continued the business, though on a much reduced scale and solely in retail. She opened a shop in Quebec City and gave it to one of her sons to manage, but it closed a few years later and Mrs. Levy was forced to take in boarders to help meet expenses, while eking out a meagre living in her own small shop in Montreal.

Samuel Davis arrived in Montreal from New York with substantial means about 1864. A cigar-maker by trade, he began manufacturing "medicated" cigars and selling part of his output at two stores he opened in Montreal.[29] If some of his accounts turned sour, he would sell them off at a discount to recoup whatever he could, thus staying as liquid as possible. Though in good standing in Montreal, Davis did not use his credit there, somewhat to the mystification of Dun's reporter, preferring instead to draw on his New York contacts. In August 1868 he brought Lyon Silverman – who invested $4,000 – into the firm as a partner. Eighteen months later, however, despite their preference for "good accounts," the firm was forced into bankruptcy as a result of a failure of one of its major creditors. The firm had liabilities totalling $17,700 against assets of only $8,500.

Two years after settling his debts at 40 per cent, Davis was back in business, with the help of his New York creditors and a new partner, Jacob L. Moss, a former local pawnbroker who invested $20,000. By October of 1874 their firm was thriving and they employed seventy-five workers, who produced cigars which sold at their store in St. Lawrence Hall, and at wholesale in Quebec and Ontario. Less than a year later, Davis and Moss claimed to be doing $300,000 business a year, while being supported by substantial lines of credit at both the City Bank and Molson's Bank. The firm had thus shifted from sole reliance on New York to at least partial dependency on the Montreal banks. Samuel Davis' son, Mortimer, was investing his enormous energy in the business, which expanded widely in the 1880s and 1890s; Mortimer became known as Canada's "tobacco king," and was a multimillionaire.[30]

Most of Montreal's Jewish tobacconists, however, were petty retailers or simple pedlars. Essentially transient, they usually struggled for a few years and finally disappeared. Henry Jacobs and Michael Michaels, formerly of Guelph, opened a small retail and wholesale shop in Montreal in 1860.[31] They eked out a living with a modest stock-in-trade and limited credit. Abraham Levey and Humphry Michaels attempted to do the same in their shop, which opened in 1858,[32] but circumstances forced them to become pedlars within a year. Rebecca Warner operated a retail store in the 1850s for her husband, an undischarged bankrupt, with the backing, according to Dun's somewhat suggestive report, "of parties who take a *peculiar interest in her.*" In November of 1858, with heavy debts outstanding, Rebecca and her husband suddenly left town for parts unknown, never to be seen again in Montreal. Then there were Zacharias and Delapratz, German Jewish cigar-makers from Connecticut who blew into Montreal in August of 1866, ran up substantial debts, and hightailed it out of town two years later, leaving their creditors high and dry.[33] Samuel Brahadi, an English Jew and a cigar-maker, set up a small shop in 1861 and did a reasonable trade until he was forced out of business in 1869 as a result of debts accumulated by his brother, Abraham (of whom more later), for whom he stood guarantor.[34]

Thus, in the tobacco business, aside from the Joseph family's large firm and John Levy's smaller company, there existed a group of very small-scale Jewish retailers and cigar-makers who were characterized by financial weakness and transiency. In the clothing business, however – a traditional Jewish area of enterprise in its various branches: retailing, wholesaling, manufacturing, and importing – the pattern of Jewish participation was much different.

Most of the Jews operating in this sector manufactured caps and hats and furs. Some, like Mark Samuel, the "very honest Jew" referred to earlier, simply made hats and caps and sold them at retail, in shops which were often left to the wife or an older child to manage, while the father peddled merchandise door to door in town or out in the countryside. Some furriers sold at retail and wholesale in stores in Montreal, like Bernard Levin and Moses Davis, Germans described as "decent men of their class" who operated a substantial store on Notre Dame Street where, after 1859, they also sold clothing.[35] Some bought up furs for export. Abraham Brahadi, an Englishman – formerly a professional singer who, allegedly, had abandoned his wife and son in London – arrived in Montreal in the late 1840s and gradually developed a business which became so fashionable that it attracted "the better kind of French Retail Custom" trade.[36]

The most prominent clothier from the mid-1830s until the early 1860s was a native of Manchester, William Benjamin, who, with his brothers Samuel and Henry, owned three distinct but interconnected businesses – clothing, dry goods, and carpets – each operated by one of the brothers.[37] By the end of the 1840s, their aggregate worth was estimated to be about $200,000 and their thriving dry goods and clothing outlets were rated as the best retail stores in town. Consequently, they enjoyed a high rating with creditors in New York and England, especially with a family firm in Manchester. However, by 1860 they were in trouble. Their trade had declined seriously over the previous year or so, according to one report in November 1860, "on account of the prejudice felt toward them as Jews," though another report stated – perhaps more accurately – that "the retail business in which they are engaged is not successful owing to competition." In 1861 they closed out all their operations, except for a wholesale dry goods outlet in Quebec which they left with William, and moved back to Manchester, where Samuel and Henry set up a dry goods export house.

Only a handful of Montreal Jews were involved in the manufacture of ready-made apparel at this stage. In the mid-1840s, the Moss brothers, David and Edward – who had operated an import clothing business – were manufacturing men's work clothes on an enormous scale[38] in a factory next to the Lachine Canal, where they employed eight hundred workers. By 1856 they were exporting $200,000 worth of clothing annually to Melbourne, Australia, where their two brothers had wholesale and retail outlets.[39] They were known to be rich, not only from their lucrative clothing business, but also because of their highly profitable sideline of private banking, in which they lent out money and "shaved notes," as the Dun reporter disparagingly described it, by discounting commercial paper.[40] This sideline was so rewarding that, in March of 1858, the Mosses began cutting back on manufacturing in order to concentrate on banking. They retired to England in March of 1864, giving the clothing business to their sons, Samuel and Jacob (Edward's), and Jacob and Hyam (David's). The two pairs of brothers, with occasional guidance from their fathers in London, proceeded to enlarge operations. By January of 1873 they had about $250,000 invested in fixed and working capital and had expanded so much that they were selling merchandise on doubtful credit, to "a weak class of customers," as Dun's investigator put it. But they were willing to take these risks because handsome profits on good accounts more than compensated for losses on a few bad ones. By 1878, Samuel Moss had become the principal partner in the firm.

Finally, there was Moses Gutman, an American who, though trained as an engraver, gave up that trade a few years after he emigrated to Canada in 1857, to work for the Mosses as an invoice clerk.[41] After some nine months, Gutman joined the Benjamins in their Quebec outlet as a bookkeeper, meanwhile studying the clothing business. In 1863 he formed a partnership with Mona Lesser, a salesman for a major New York hoop-skirt manufacturer who had moved to Montreal in 1860 to try his luck. Gutman started off with twenty-eight women workers in 1863 to manufacture low-priced lines, while Lesser served as the firm's salesman, travelling mainly in the countryside, where cheaper goods were more marketable. Gutman soon emerged as the principal partner and, even though he was an undischarged bankrupt, he commanded substantial credit in New York, where the firm bought almost all of its supplies. Dun's reporters remained cautious about this firm, even though its owners were deemed to be hard-working and steady men who apparently did not seek credit in Montreal. By May of 1869, Gutman and Lesser were "selling goods at cutting prices and pushing trade too hard for their limited means," a practice which the reporter deemed to be "a little too sharp." Gutman left the firm in 1871, while Lesser carried on. By September of 1874, however, he was in serious financial trouble. "This state of things," it was reported, "has been occasioned by the many rapid changes of fashion entailing losses to his customers and ultimately on him by which his capital was used up." After the partnership ended, Gutman teamed up with two others, Edward Morris and Alexander Saunders, to manufacture gloves, and they opened an outlet in Toronto.

In the clothing business, therefore, there were few sparkling performances. The exceptions, the Mosses and the Benjamins, were either well supported by continuous credits from family abroad, or based upon substantial cash and merchandise in hand. Even in clothing manufacturing, where Jews were so successful, some of them were just beginning at mid-century. Apparel production in Montreal was booming by the early 1870s.[42] But all the major Montreal manufacturers, aside from Moss's, were owned and operated by Anglophones like Hollis Shorey, Edward O'Brien, Edward Small, and the Peck brothers.[43]

Toronto was undergoing the same processes of economic change in this period, as its western frontier in Upper Canada (later Canada West, then Ontario) filled up with settlers who created farms in the interior. From Toronto's docks, steamboats and schooners plied Lake Ontario to ports on both the Canadian and American sides, making possible important linkages with the United States and thus lending the city's economy a certain independence from Montreal. Some of the railways across Canada West, like the Northern and the Great Western — both built during the 1850s — reinforced this facility. Meanwhile, local banks serviced the expanding regional economy, and industries oriented to the expanding local and hinterland markets began to thrive in the decades following the union of the Canadas in 1841.[44] In nearby Hamilton, still a lesser commercial centre, the Great Western Railway's completion in 1857 and the location of its repair shops there began the processes of transforming the city into a centre of heavy industry.[45]

In Toronto, economic activity among Jews was focused heavily in jewellery and fancy goods, apparently a field offering them an easy entrée into business. The brothers F. and E. Gunther started up a small jewellery business in 1856 or 1857, "without much capital," according to Dun's reporter.[46] The Aschers of Montreal operated a successful Toronto branch.[47] Michael Bumsel, having failed in Montreal, retreated to Switzerland and then moved to England, where he failed again. He turned up in Toronto in 1857 and was quickly spotted by the reporter as "a hard case"; Bumsel's credit, he reported, was "very doubtful at best . . . he does not inspire any confidence here."[48] Soldiering on, Bumsel nevertheless proceeded to carve out a vast peddling hinterland between Quebec and London, "selling jewellery and watch materials to small dealers and retailers." A few months later, Dun's reporter still regarded Bumsel as a "hard case" with no property and "no settled abode," and advised potential creditors to exercise "the greatest caution" in extending credit to this man of "irregular habits and general char[acter] . . . [with] nothing to bind him here and having no apparent wealth . . . a travelling Jew." His reputation for failure having followed him, Bumsel drifted away, presumably peddling jewellery somewhere out on the Canadian frontier until the end of his days.

M. Feintuch, another jewellery pedlar, showed up in Toronto in the spring of 1863. "A Jew of the regular type," Dun's reporter snorted; Feintuch was "not in good repute and is not sold to here by the trade."[49] Although he was thought to have "made some money [by] peddling . . . [he] is a risky customer and only pays when he can't help it." "He should be avoided," the entry continued, because he "could pack up and leave at any moment." Feintuch, however, was thought to be "doing well," despite Dun's discouraging report. But he too disappeared from view a few months later, also presumably drifting away to improve his fortunes elsewhere.

I. Guttstam, a German Jew, reached Toronto in the early 1860s and opened a business dealing in fancy and dry goods. Believed to have "some money," Guttstam was not too successful in Toronto and, according to Dun's reporter, was "sharp and attempted to smuggle," presumably a reference to a business manoeuvre which led to a seizure of some of his assets.[50] Guttstam's fortunes apparently improved when he moved to the Bradford area north of Toronto, where he bought a farm, built a new house, and was reputed to have five or six pedlars working for him through the countryside.

Judah George Joseph, the first Jewish settler in Toronto "prepared to strike roots" in the city, was an optician and stockbroker.[51] When his name first appeared in Dun's reports in August of 1848, he was noted as "very respectable, A Jew, s[ai]d to have a gr[ea]t deal of money," although "it is not easy to find an est[imat]e of his real w[orth] or position."[52] He had gone bankrupt in Cincinnati, where he was a lawyer, and "in various kinds of merc[antile] business," but in Toronto – where he had been in business since about 1843, according to a Dun's reporter writing in 1854 – Joseph was doing well and enjoyed a good reputation. "For a Jew his eng[age]m[en]ts are all O.K., I sh[oul]d say Good. . . . I have a doubt ab[ou]t Jews generally, but consid[er] him an exception." Until his death in 1857, Joseph's business prospered and his reputation remained intact.

Two other Toronto Jewish families, the Samuels and the Rossin brothers, were also well-to-do. Marcus and Samuel Rossin reached Toronto in 1842, and set up a jewellery and fancy goods business. Wheelers and dealers, the Rossins were "open to any speculation they think they can make money out of," the Dun reporter sniffed; they "will buy anything from Bacon to Silk gloves if they are only sure of a profit."[53] Anticipating an economic boom in the 1850s as a result of Toronto's extensive new railway linkages to south-western Ontario, in 1856–57 they built the Rossin House, Toronto's biggest hotel, an opulent establishment on King Street, just in time for the commercial depression that struck the city that year. They were apparently having serious financial difficulties with it by early 1861. Dun's reporter noted that "the Rossins had to take or keep [it] to prevent its being closed." This commitment, along with other speculations in downtown Toronto real estate, put the brothers in financial jeopardy "to the extent of all they had ever made," although they limited their losses by "getting back into [the] hands of original owners a large amount of RE."[54] Speculating meanwhile in calf-skins and cigars, the brothers were described as "sure to make money if they enter trade again as they contemplate doing." The hotel burned down in November of 1862 and within the year the brothers were reported to be manufacturing tobacco products, while contracting for the construction of a railroad in Kansas! Much of their real estate had been seized by various creditors, the rest was heavily mortgaged, and the insurance on the hotel had been paid to other creditors, but the Rossins managed to salvage some of their fortune by selling the property on which the Rossin House had stood. "If they are successful they will pr[oba]bly be all right," wrote Dun's reporter, no doubt amazed at the remarkable financial dexterity of the brothers Rossin. They were soon to disappear from Toronto forever, Samuel to the United States in 1863 and Marcus, the following year, back to Germany.[55]

Another entrepreneur with U.S. connections was Jacob Englehart; he and a group of other New York Jews associated with a firm described, somewhat mysteriously, as "whisky-rectifiers" Sonneborn Dryfoos and Company financed the development of the early oil industry in Western Ontario in the 1860s.[56]

Notwithstanding the mercurial financial prominence of the Rossins, Toronto's premier Jewish family by the mid-1850s – and easily the wealthiest – was that of Lewis Samuel, an Englishman who arrived there in 1855. It was he who took the initiative in mobilizing eighteen Jews to establish Toronto's first

Jewish congregation, in September of 1856.[57] This was only a year or so after he had arrived in the city to start a hardware business, after a business apprenticeship of seven years in New York, Syracuse, and Montreal.[58]

When they first attracted notice from Dun's reporters, in August of 1858, the Samuels – Lewis was joined by his brother, Mark – were "not cons[idere]d to be of much consequence," partly because "there is so little known of them."[59] Consequently, one reporter complained a few months later that "there is a good deal of contradiction in the reports respecting their standing." One thing was clear very early: they sold "at very low rates," thus undercutting competitors and "creat[ing], a bad feeling [against] them amongst the trade." The firm was able to sell cheaply partly because the brothers kept only a small inventory and "are exceedingly close, live over their store . . . and are very attentive and pushing. They sell at almost anything to get money." An additional and probably more important advantage was the fact that they generally paid cash – a practice also employed by their contemporary Timothy Eaton – to buy merchandise at discounts, sometimes even for bargain prices.[60] Thus they could usually undercut the prices of competitors. Another advantage was the connections the Samuels had in Quebec, Montreal, and New York "who purchased bargains in job lots, remnants, etc." Perhaps the most important factor in their success, however, lay in their access to a ready source of capital in a Liverpool Jewish family, the Hoffnungs, who helped to finance them in their first few years. "The Hoffnungs opened their hearts to us," Lewis' son, Sigmund, later recalled; "over the years they were to lend my Father and Uncle the sum of fifty thousand pounds, without security and at very low interest." With this kind of backing and the Samuels' "exceedingly close . . . very shrewd . . . and persevering character in a g[oo]d many things," as Dun's reporter put it in September of 1860, they had a good start in Toronto's commercial world.

By 1861 their business was doing very well and the firm enjoyed a fine reputation. Dun's reporter described them as "('Jews') of excellent character and business ability." Their trade was large and profitable, "making money." Although their full worth was not known, they were prompt and regular in meeting their obligations. Mark moved to Liverpool, where he did much of the firm's purchasing, serving in the classic role filled by so many British partners in Canadian firms based on transatlantic partnerships.[61] Dun's reporter was well informed of this feature: "one of the bro[ther]s now resides in England," he wrote in November of 1863, "where he picks up job lots." They were considered to be good for their "engagements," but the complaint that "very little is known of their means" suggests that the Samuels kept their affairs strictly to themselves. But their credit in Toronto was obviously very good despite their secretiveness. In 1869 they were thought to be worth about $75,000 and doing $300,000 a year in business. Therefore, when they bought out the stock of a local metals importer in 1871 for $18,000 – spread out over twenty-four months – the normally cautious Dun reporter did not flinch, even though the deal meant that the Samuels were increasing their risk by moving heavily into a new line of trade.

In 1871 the Samuels did $350,000 business, but uninsured losses incurred in Chicago – due to the fire that destroyed the city that year – set them back somewhat. Dun's reporter often commented favourably on the family's frugal lifestyle, a virtue admired by the Victorians. Despite the onset of a serious depression in 1874, the Samuels were nevertheless able to survive. In December of that year, the Dun report stated that their annual turnover was about $500,000 and their losses so small that they would still make a profit. In fact, the annual statement showed that profits amounted to $23,300 and the firm's net assets came to $78,000.[62] The depression and ensuing credit squeeze had apparently not hurt them seriously; in 1875 they were still "thought to be doing well" and were worth between $75,000 and $100,000.

While they focused on hardware and metals, the Samuels' early business necessarily took them into other fields. Because of a lack of ready cash, "business often was on a semi-barter basis," Sigmund Samuel recorded in his memoirs.[63] His father was frequently compelled to accept commodities like hides, tallow, or beeswax in partial payment for goods, and on one occasion took beaver pelts in exchange for tin plates. Such were the necessities of trading in an under-developed, cash-starved frontier economy such as Upper Canada's largely still was in the 1850s and 1860s. Therefore the Samuels were alive to the possibilities for profit in the commodities export trade, which developed into an important part of their business. When Sigmund became a partner in 1869, the firm was shipping large quantities of wood products abroad.

The Samuels imported pig iron and lead, and many goods and commodities as well. Quantities of copper, tin, zinc, brass, pipes, wire, stove plate, Russia iron, and chemicals arrived by ship and rail. Casks of bristles were brought from Poland to be made into brushes, glass came from Belgium, marble from Italy, and linseed oil, tin foil, and horsehair from other countries.[64] Assisted by the burgeoning railway network spreading from the hub of Toronto, the Samuels sold at both wholesale and retail to customers throughout south-western Ontario – in Brampton, Brantford, Paris, Stratford, St. Mary's, and London. They did business in Chicago and, after 1881, in Winnipeg, during its brief economic boom at the start of the Canadian Pacific Railway's construction.

In nearby Hamilton, virtually all mid-century Jewish businessmen were German immigrants and, like their metropolitan co-religionists, concentrated largely in selling jewellery and fancy goods. The brothers Leander and Leopold Rosenband (the latter in partnership with three Dray brothers) sold fancy goods and cigars.[65] Though they owned no real estate, according to Dun's reporters they did "a very fair business," were good businessmen, and enjoyed a sound credit rating, even though Dun complained that "it is impossible for us to know really what [their] standing [capital] is." By 1859 the Rosenbands and Drays were apparently doing a large business at a small store in the city, and in peddling and "getting up raffles" for their merchandise through the surrounding countryside. By October of 1859 the partners, "shrewd keen Jews [with] no visible means," were doing "a large trade" and were "thought to have money." The partnership was dissolved in 1860, however, the Drays departing the city and Leopold Rosenband continuing the business alone. A Dun report of April 1861 rated him as a man of "very exalted bus[iness] ability good char[acter] + habits. Has always a good bal[ance] to his credit at B[an]k." With an estimated $12,000 capital, Leopold was able to pick up "bargains for Cash," enabling him to sell merchandise at low prices. In Hamilton there was "nothing against him, except that he is a German Jew, which in some quarters prejudices his credit." He was certainly a German Jew "of the better sort," the report went on, but though "supp[ose]d good . . . no one can tell." By November of 1862, Rosenband had got out of the fancy goods trade and into a tobacco manufacturing concern with Frederick Schwartz, a former brewer who, if also a Jew, was not noted as such by the investigator working for Dun's that year. Rosenband gave up the Hamilton business scene altogether after the early 1860s, presumably to look for opportunities elsewhere in fancy goods, tobacco, or other ventures.

Two Polish Jews, Prince and Levy, started a jewellery business in Hamilton in the mid-1850s, but by 1857 they were in serious financial trouble and they failed in rather bad odour with creditors.[66] Several brothers named Hofeller opened a clothing store in the early 1860s, but they lasted only long enough to attract notice as "German Jews, not deserving of cr[edit] . . . sh[oul]d be avoided." The same was written of the clothing dealers I. and L. Desbecker, two "of the numerous German Jews we have here . . . no one knows anything about them." Such was also the case of L. Loeb and Co. – Loeb sold dry goods but "nothing favourabl[e] [was] known of him" – while L. Levi dealt in fancy goods for a few years in the mid-1860s before drifting off to the United States.

Isaac Stine, another German immigrant, set up as a clothier in the early 1860s, was thought possibly to be worth as much as $10,000 but "possibly he absconds tomorrow . . . German Jew, don't trust him"; in March of 1862 he was described as "worthless."[67] J. Hirschfield sold hoop skirts in the early 1870s, but disappeared.

Off in the hinterland, there were a few Jewish pedlars and storekeepers who operated, mostly transitorily, in towns and villages that served as local market centres. Early nineteenth-century frontier Upper Canada was served by numerous pedlars who helped to provide "agencies of retail and wholesale commerce."[68] While Toronto, Hamilton, and many other towns were emerging as significant commercial centres by 1850, there was enough entrepreneurial space in rural areas for these itinerant traders to conduct petty commerce from wagons, horseback, or, at its most primitive level, simple backpack. In Paris, for example, Thomas Coleman, who was described as "an English Jew," ran a general store in the 1840s, but by about 1850 he had abandoned business and was living handsomely on the proceeds of his father's estate and some valuable real-estate holdings in Paris itself. A few years later, Coleman departed for St. Paul, Minnesota.[69] In nearby Brantford, a rising place in the 1860s, two German Jews named Strauss (possibly father and son) sold clothing; they were thought to have a stock worth $300, to be "steady and always on hand when any bus[iness] is to be done," and worthy of "credit for a sm[all] sum."[70]

In London, J.W. Ezekiel, a Polish Jew who had lived in London, England, for some years, started a millinery and ready-made clothing business in the early 1850s but came to be known as "not safe: not a man of principle, a Jew of a 3rd rate stamp . . . a rascally Israelite and not to be trusted on any acc[oun]t." Ezekiel left town in 1856 after closing up business, and moved on to Detroit, where he was arrested for debt.[71] B. Morritz operated a clothing store in London from May of 1856, did pretty well by all accounts, and was judged to be "of g[oo]d character and hab[it]s and tho[ugh]t s[a]f[e] for purchases," but by July of 1858 he was out of business and had moved away.[72] Samuel Kohn set up a tobacco shop in the city in 1859 but disappeared within two years.[73]

Jewish traders were also to be found in Brockville, Stratford, Victoriaville, and St. Andrews by the 1850s and 1860s, though often for only a year or two before drifting away to look for a better business frontier.[74] George Benjamin, who had lived in Belleville since 1834 and prospered as owner-editor of the *Belleville Intelligencer* and *Hastings General Advertiser*, served as member of the legislature of the Province of Canada for North Hastings from 1857 to 1863. He was the first Jewish MP in Canada.[75] In nearby Kingston, the brothers Abraham and Samuel Nordheimer gave music lessons and operated a music store between 1840 and 1844.[76] In 1857 German-born Simon Oberndorfer, a cigarmaker by trade, established a successful cigar factory; he became one of the founders of the Jewish community there by the end of the century.[77] There is evidence that numbers of other Jews came, stayed a few years, and drifted away. Men on the move they were, ending up who knows where, moving their stock by wagon or buggy, or occasionally even hot-footing it out of town.

Though little is known about the small Jewish enclaves in most Ontario towns and villages in the late nineteenth and early twentieth centuries, there is some information about a fascinating group located in and around the village of Lancaster, in rural Glengarry County, a few miles north-east of Cornwall. This tiny Jewish community was founded by Noah Friedman shortly after he immigrated to Canada from Poland in 1857.[78] He was followed by Harris Kellert, his brother-in-law, ten years later.[79] They and their families presumably constituted the majority of the Jewish population of ten persons in Glengarry County in 1861, but they were followed by many others, including Abraham Jacobs and his large family.[80] By 1871 the community numbered thirty-nine, while nearby villages in Stormont County had nineteen Jews and the town of Cornwall had twenty-six. This Glengarry–Stormont–Cornwall group continued to exist for the next twenty years, although its numbers declined slowly. The Jews in Glengarry were essentially pedlars and general store owners, or both. However, many of the original settlers moved to Montreal, where family connections, Jewish educational and religious facilities, and more opportunities for business – notably in that city's burgeoning wholesale clothing business – were available. Kellert and Friedman formed a fancy goods wholesale business before becoming clothing manufacturers.[81] The Glengarry experience foreshadowed the fate of many small Jewish communities: initial settlement, followed by growth over a decade or two, and then decline as the younger generation moved to cities to follow other business or professional careers.

Overall, Jews were essentially marginal men in the Canadian business world in the mid-Victorian era, when all sectors were experiencing such massive growth. With some notable exceptions, they were merely petty and transitory retailers or pedlars of jewellery, fancy goods, tobacco, and cheap clothing. Many of them were driven from their shops by the ill winds of the business cycle, bad luck, mismanagement, incompetence, or under-capitalization. Yet they were not all merchants and pedlars. Butchers, bankers, agents, restaurateurs, and auctioneers were included among the peripatetic penny capitalists who drifted into Canada's cities and towns for a few years and then, blown over by a bad season or two, moved on to try their luck elsewhere – though never far from the scrutiny of R.G. Dun and Company's assiduous investigators.

Were Jews adversely affected by the antisemitism that was clearly manifest in the business world? In very few cases is there evidence that it mattered enough to force a business failure. The evidence indicates that, in the competitive (if not cut-throat) world of business in the mid-nineteenth century, a Jew was as welcome a creditor or client as anyone else – provided, of course, that he was good for his commitments. Non-Jews did business with Jews despite the existence – possibly even the prevalence – of attitudes that held Jews in contempt, fear, or mistrust. They were, after all, an alien cultural element, most of them relatively new to the scene. At the time "political and commercial realities . . . were multidimensional. Men formed loyalties and took positions on the basis of race . . . , religion . . . , region . . . , national loyalty . . . , personal ambition . . . , as well as calculated economic interest."[82] Canada was still characterized by a considerable degree of the ethnic segmentation which had existed since the late eighteenth century, and suspicion was not limited to Jews. Irish and American businessmen in Montreal deeply resented the dominance by the Scottish "old boy" network of practically all major sectors of the local economy, while French Canadian businessmen seem to have operated largely in their own sphere. These business networks continued to exist, and immigrant Jews – or other outsiders – would not likely be invited into the potentially profitable railway stock flotations and other lucrative ventures that were promoted by Montreal's and Toronto's established, rich, and politically well connected businessmen.[83] Everyone, Jews included, understood that that was the way business was done. Who, except those under duress, would share such deals with perfect strangers – and with Jews, to boot? Jewish businessmen could not have been unacquainted with antisemitism before they immigrated, and were likely not surprised to encounter it in Canada.

It appears, furthermore, that most immigrant Jews preferred doing business with fellow Jews. Time and again, Dun's reporters complained of the difficulty of getting information about Jewish businessmen and said that, when possible, Jews seemed to prefer using their credit with their British and New York connections – often eschewing opportunities for credit in Montreal. To Dun's sharp-eyed investigators it seemed that some Jews were living better than their assumed volume of business would allow, a sign that their real financial standing was unknown. Despite continued investigation, Dun's reporters found it extremely difficult to fully penetrate the veil that hid the business affairs of some Jews, who may have operated on the assumption that credit supplied by family or friends was more reliable than bank loans, which could be recalled without notice, and that relatives and partners were more trustworthy than strangers. Yet, if such exclusionary attitudes were not confined to Jews, the Jews did carry a unique history of persecution. In Germany and Poland they had long suffered from various disabilities inflicted on them by the authorities, one of these being the periodic confiscation of accumulated wealth through impositions and special "Jew taxes."[84] Secretiveness, therefore, was a special hallmark of this subculture, in which authorities and institutions were seen as real or potential oppressors. It was perfectly natural that such attitudes should continue to prevail among Jewish immigrants.

For the most part, then, the history of the Jews shaped their business attitudes and behaviour. They were largely marginal to the major economic transformations under way between the mid-1840s and the 1870s. Aside from the Josephs in the Montreal tobacco business and the Mosses in the apparel manufacturing trade, they were absent from the dynamic sectors of urban industrialization — like shipbuilding, flour milling, sugar refining, and the flourishing iron-fabrication shops located in Montreal's industrial quarters along the river and the Lachine Canal; nor were they participants in Toronto's and Hamilton's spectacular industrial growth of the 1860s and 1870s. Neither were they much involved in those cities' flourishing banks and insurance companies, and railway and steamboat ventures. As well, with a few exceptions, Jews were absent from businesses importing iron goods, wines, liquors, and textiles, and from those exporting flour, grain, timber, and other commodities. But this was not because of antisemitism; it was principally due to lack of experience and connections in such enterprises. It is evident, therefore, that at this stage in the development of Canadian capitalism, Jews as a group had no important role.

Virtually all the adult male Jews were petty merchants in the fairly specific business sectors that have been discussed above. With only a few exceptions, notably the Joseph brothers, none was involved in Montreal's great financial, transportation, and manufacturing sectors — and the numerous powerful incorporated companies — for which the city became famous, and through which it came to dominate the national economy that emerged towards the end of this period. And in Toronto and Hamilton there appears to have been no Jew of financial prowess like the Josephs'. Jews began as marginal men, in the sense that they engaged mostly in the petty commerce of jewellery and fancy goods, tobacco, dry goods, and cheap clothing, much of it sold to storekeepers (some of them Jews) living in upcountry towns and villages, or peddled through the rural areas of Upper and Lower Canada. Nevertheless, unlike their co-religionists in Altanta, Buffalo, and

New Orleans – where Jewish businessmen from importers to pedlars developed "a singularly Jewish trade"[85] in which Jews operated largely within a Jewish business world – their Canadian counterparts do not appear to have been nearly so restrictive. The sale of clothing, both wholesale and retail, provided a major springboard for Jewish entry into what was by 1871 already one of the leading industries in major Canadian cities – the manufacture of men's and boys' apparel, while tobacco merchandising gave them another major manufacturing opportunity in Canada. But the full efflorescence of the Jewish presence in these sectors lay some twenty years in the future.

CHAPTER

5

Beginnings in the East
and the West

Even before Jews settled in the Province of Quebec, there was some Jewish contact with the British colonies in Newfoundland and Nova Scotia, and with the French fortress of Louisbourg on Ile Royale, or Cape Breton. The New York merchant Jacob Franks dealt in tea, shipping some to Newfoundland and some through Cape Breton in the early 1740s.[1] In 1748 the executive of London's Spanish and Portuguese synagogue, then searching for a refuge for the city's Jewish poor, considered founding a Jewish colony in Nova Scotia.[2] Four years later the project was still alive. In October of 1752 the *Halifax Gazette* reported that:

> The congregation of the [London] Jews in general, that is to say the three synagogues, have chartered three ships of 500 tons each and are going to send 100 poor families over with provisions for a year after their arrival and £10 in goods on three years credit to set them up. They are to sail in three weeks time.[3]

Although the Maritime region was still experiencing naval conflict between Britain and France, the scheme was mooted for a few years more, though nothing ever came of it.

Considerable numbers of Jewish traders arrived in Halifax shortly after it was founded in 1749, as a British naval and military counterpoise to the massive French bastion of Louisbourg. A number of Jews moved there from Newport, Rhode Island in 1751, including Israel Abrahams, Isaac Levy, Nathan Nathans, and the four brothers Abraham, Isaac, Naphthali, and Samuel Hart, "all of whom were sons of German Jews, who had settled in England."[4] By the 1750s there were many Jews among the army and navy purveyors and the merchants who supplied the civilian population, which numbered 4,000.[5] Israel Abrahams and Nathan Nathans were New Yorkers who moved to Halifax in 1752.[6] A cemetery was acquired and some sort of community was established. The Jewish presence continued in the Nova Scotia capital into the 1760s,[7] but the community gradually died out as trade with New England dwindled following the Non-Importation Agreement of 1765. The outbreak of the American Revolution temporarily ended the trade between Halifax and the American colonies;[8] the cemetery land was appropriated for a provincial workhouse.[9]

Samuel Jacobs, who later settled at St-Denis in Quebec, was present early in 1758 at Fort Cumberland, "where he apparently engaged in the liquor trade." Jacobs was also a partner in a brewery at Louisbourg between 1759 and 1761.[10] In the early 1750s Israel Abrahams manufactured potash and petitioned the Board of Trade to employ him to restrict others in this business.[11] Jacobs and Abrahams were joined by several others, including Naphthali Hart, Jr., who formed a partnership with Abrahams; they became "large scale merchants and packers of mackerel."[12] They may have done business with the Newport shipowner Aaron Lopez, whose ships traded with merchants in Newfoundland and the Gaspé.[13] Lopez owned numerous vessels plying the eastern seaboard of North America. His crews engaged in whaling off the Newfoundland coast, and traded mustard, rum, cordials, and onions to merchants in Halifax and Quebec City.[14] With other Newport merchants, Lopez had interests in the Gulf of St. Lawrence cod fishery, as he "followed his advantage wherever it beckoned, to nearly every important harbour between Quebec and Florida."[15] A man named Nathans ran the Halifax mackerel fishery from nearby Russell's Island (now Horseshoe Island), and, at his home situated on the Northwest Arm, lavished generous hospitality on his friends and associates.[16]

There were at least two Jews among the Loyalists who sailed from New York to Nova Scotia in 1783, Jacob Louzada from Bound Brook, New Jersey, and Abram Florentine, a Tory businessman from New Jersey and New York; however, there is no evidence of precisely where they settled, or how long they stayed.[17] A few others may have lived in Saint John shortly after it was founded in the 1780s.[18] There was also Isaac DaCosta, an English Jew of Dutch origin and of Spanish-Portuguese lineage, who claimed to have lived in Nova Scotia in 1765–66. Before the Commission of Enquiry examining Loyalists' losses, he claimed ownership of over 20,000 acres in the province, and said he had settled six families there at his own expense.[19]

Two Jews whose surnames were Abraham and Phepard acquired land in the 1780s in the border region between Nova Scotia and New Brunswick, and assimilated into the local population. A Dutch Jewish immigrant, Nathan Levy, became a Lutheran in 1752 and settled in Lunenberg, where his descendants still reside.

Samuel Hart, formerly a merchant in Philadelphia, moved to Halifax in 1785, perhaps because of his reputed Tory sympathies during the American Revolution. He set up in business as a general merchant and ship's chandler, traded extensively with the West Indies, and engaged in shipping, notably with Shelburne County. Some seventeen years before his namesake, Ezekiel Hart, was elected to the Lower Canadian Assembly in 1808, Samuel Hart was elected from Liverpool to the Nova Scotia legislature in 1791 and took the oath of office "on the true faith as a Christian," even though he was at that point still a Jew. However, he was soon baptized an Anglican and became a pewholder in St. George's Church. He seems to have been content with a minor role in the legislature but remained there until 1797. In good standing with the governor, Hart secured several large land grants in Nova Scotia and prospered so much from all his various businesses that by 1801 he owned more than £4,000 worth of real estate.[20] He maintained a large country estate near Halifax where he entertained lavishly, perhaps too lavishly, because his social ambitions eventually outran his purse. He died in 1810 and was buried in St. Paul's churchyard in Halifax. Three Jewish merchants, Alexander and Isaac Levi and Aaron Moses, were doing business in Halifax between 1813 and 1817, but there appear to have been no other Jewish businessmen operating in the city at that time.[21] Out in Windsor (not far from Halifax), in the early 1850s, lived B. Louis, who was believed by one investigator for Dun and Company to be of "Jewish descent," a feature that possibly explained why there was "a g[rea]t deal of 'Wash'[junk]" on his shelves.[22]

Saint John was the base of some Jewish pedlars in the eighteenth century and even of "an unusually large number of Jewish farmers . . . most of [whom] married into the Christian majority."[23] At Chatham, the booming timber post at the mouth of the Miramichi River, a merchant named Joseph Samuel ran a general store for some thirty years before he retired in 1856.[24] As well as selling imported English goods, Samuel bought up furs, and though regarded as "a respectable Jew" he was also thought to be "cautious like most of his nation." In 1855 he set up another store in partnership with a nephew, Morden Levy, at Miramichi. Here they engaged in the salmon fishery. Samuel transferred his business interests to his son, Solomon, in 1857 and retired to England. The cousins continued the business, opened a branch at Richibucto, stood well in the community as far as their credit went, and prospered. A contemporary report by an investigator for Dun's observed that Levy "puts up fish, and does [a] rather extensive bus[iness] at Richibucto and does a quieter bus[iness] at Chatham." The store at Chatham was sold in March of 1863. Levy died the following year and, though Solomon Samuel carried on for a while, he slips from view in 1865, beset by his growing dispute with the heirs of Levy over the business and other jointly held assets.

Both Prince Edward Island and Newfoundland experienced only sporadic Jewish settlement in the nineteenth century, though Solomon Solomons, Newfoundland's first postmaster, appointed in 1805, may have been a Jew. "There is more than ample reason to believe that throughout the nineteenth century there was . . . a continuous Jewish settlement on [Newfoundland]," in coastal trading and the seal fur business. English Jews named Ezicial settled on the island in the early 1800s, and others like Lacque and Levi were involved in the seal trade in 1834.[25]

By 1871, Saint John's Jewish community was sizeable – the Dominion census of that year reported forty-eight Jews living in New Brunswick, all but a few of them in the port city. Saint John was Canada's third-largest city, after Montreal and Toronto. A major port and regional banking and commercial city, it was also a promising industrial centre. Most Jews were in some form of business. Solomon Hart, a tobacco merchant who had settled in the city in 1858, was joined in 1862 by Nathan Green, his brother-in-law. Born in Amsterdam, Green apprenticed as a cigar-maker (he claimed to have learned this craft from Moses Gompers, father of Samuel Gompers, the famous American trade union leader), moved to New York in 1850, and finally settled in Saint John. Here he developed a large business in manufacturing and selling tobacco products all over the Maritimes.[26]

The Hart–Green clan of Saint John expanded rapidly and numbered fifteen by the late 1860s, serving as the nucleus of what was to become the first significant Jewish community of the Maritime region. The Harts and Greens were joined in 1878 by Abraham and Israel Isaacs, who ran a successful cigar factory on Princess Street. Other families followed in the 1880s, and by 1896, when the community numbered some thirty families, a congregation named Ahavath Achim – Brotherly Love – was formed to conduct services and employ a rabbi.[27] Close ties were maintained with Boston for both religious officials and supplies of kosher foods. In fact, the first religious services were made possible in the autumn of 1879 through the support of Boston's Jewry, who supplied a cantor, a

Torah scroll, and the vital tenth man to make the necessary quorum.[28] When the campaign to build a synagogue was begun in the late 1890s, substantial assistance came from Boston and New York.[29] The synagogue was completed in 1898.

Halifax's Jewish community re-established itself in the last third of the nineteenth century after disappearing in the 1820s, when the last of the eighteenth-century founders' families died out, assimilated, or departed.[30] By the 1890s a new community was in gestation, fuelled by a wave of immigrants arriving from Europe. While only 18 Jews lived in the city in 1891, there were 102 a decade later.[31] The Baron de Hirsch Benevolent Society was formed in 1891 and a synagogue was built on Starr Street four years after,[32] to mark the start of what was to become a thriving community.

Jewish communal beginnings on Canada's west coast were more auspicious than the fragmentary and scattered settlements on the Atlantic. This was in part because a synagogue, with all that its development implied, was built in Victoria in 1863, within five years of the arrival of the city's first Jew. Another major factor was the relative size of the Jewish immigration in 1858. "As I write these lines there is an extraordinary excitement in California. New gold mines have been discovered in the British possessions north of the Washington Territories on the banks of the Fraser and Thompson rivers," Daniel Levy announced enthusiastically in June of 1858, in his report from San Francisco for the Paris newspaper *Archives Israélites*.[33] "There are few Jews among the pioneers who are almost entirely miners with pick and shovels, and a few speculators well provided with capital. . . . However a few left on the last two steamers." He recognized that if the Hudson's Bay Company's trading monopoly was extended, keeping out others, "it will be a real disaster for our co-religionists in commerce here, who would thus see a large part of their trade leave California and would be unable to follow it themselves." But "if they are admitted to trade freely there, you will soon hear of new Jewish communities at Victoria . . . and other places, which to-day are only small trading posts, but may become within a few years great centres of population and flourishing ports in which the commerce of the world will meet." No wonder, then, that even before Governor Douglas finally announced in 1860 that Victoria was a free port, "the flow of ships brought golden inundation by waves of eager miners" followed by "entrepreneurs with capital, store and hotel keepers, commission merchants and real estate buyers, who were ready to invest in the business which they envisaged would accrue to Victoria from its service to the gold fields."[34] Among them were a number of Jews who got passage on the crowded ships that made the four-day trip from San Francisco to the bustling town of Victoria.

Frank Sylvester was among about fifty Jews – most of them moving directly from San Francisco – to reach Victoria on July 17, 1858. He arrived with some cash and high hopes of doing business in the city, which was booming from the traditional trade in furs and fishing, as well as from the lucrative traffic in supplies to the goldfields on the Fraser and Thompson rivers, where burgeoning communities of miners were panning for gold.[35] Sylvester was followed by others, including the five Oppenheimer brothers, who were also attracted to the Fraser River rush. The German-born Oppenheimers – Meyer, Godfrey, Isaac, Charles, and David – after business ventures in Ohio, Texas, and Louisiana, set up stores at Yale, Fort Hope, Lytton, and Barkerville, in the heart of the goldfields, as well as a store and warehouse in Victoria which became the base of their operations after goldmining died out in the Cariboo district.[36] Other early Jewish settlers included the brothers Selim and Lumley Franklin, English Jews who arrived via San Francisco in 1858 to become auctioneers and real-estate agents,[37] while numerous others who settled, at least briefly, in the Cariboo towns of Yale and Barkerville passed through Victoria.[38] The Sutro brothers, Adolph, Gustav, and Emil, arrived in 1858 to establish a branch of their San Francisco–based tobacco business.[39]

While some came from Britain, Australia, or New Zealand, most Jews came from California, where, even though of German or other origins, "they had already become accultured to Anglo Saxon society prior to arrival in Victoria."[40] While a few of these Jews were actually miners, most were pedlars and merchants.

The German Jewish traveller I.J. Benjamin noted in 1862, in his *Three Years in America*, that "about a hundred Jews live here," continuing:

> Only a few are married. The beginnings of the city of Victoria are really due to the Jews. For, no matter how many persons streamed to the island at the outbreak of the gold fever, they scattered again . . . to all corners of the world when their disillusion followed only too quickly. . . . More and more Jews settled here, and the German element was increasingly represented by them.[41]

By 1863 there were 242 Jews in Victoria, making it the second-largest Jewish community in British North America.[42] Not all of them, to be sure, remained in Victoria, at least all the time. Many, like the Oppenheimers, conducted business in the interior, mainly at Barkerville and Yale; some later moved on to the Cariboo district, while others moved up-island to Nanaimo.[43] But the Jewish population of Victoria was a modestly significant percentage of the city's total population, fluctuating between 4 and 4.8 per cent.[44]

Many of the Jews were general merchants, and acted as agents of family businesses in San Francisco, which were the source of most of the non-perishable goods and provisions required by miners in the interior.[45] Others lived briefly in the interior as agents of Victoria-based houses. Some served as express agents and others operated pack trains to and from the goldfields.[46] A few were itinerant traders. By 1863 there was a total of twenty-two Jewish-owned clothing and drygoods stores in Victoria, fourteen selling groceries and provisions, thirteen selling tobacco and fruit, and ten selling various other items, obviously a major commercial presence in this small town.[47]

And it was in this capital city that the first British Columbian congregation was formed. It began in 1858 with the formation of a *minyan* for prayer, and the establishment of a benevolent society for tending the sick and burying the dead, known as Chevra Bikkur Cholim V'Kedusha.[48] In May of the following year, plans were made to buy land for a cemetery, and this was accomplished in 1860.[49] In late August of 1862 the congregation was established on a formal basis with a constitution whose preamble stated that:

> Whereas, according to the holy ordinances of the House of Israel, it is highly necessary to adhere to the religion thereof, and to attend to the dying and burying of the dead; and Whereas the Israelites of Victoria, B.C., are desirous to fulfill the ordinances of our venerated and holy religion, which has been continuously handed down to us by our forefathers. Therefore, we hereby unite to form ourselves into a Congregation this fifth day in the month of Ellul and the year 5622, corresponding to the 31st day of August 1862.[50]

Two weeks later the congregation, which then had forty-nine members, resolved to build a synagogue.[51] Abraham Hoffman, the congregation's first secretary, reporting to the congregation on November 22, invoked the aid of Providence

> so that the congregation though slumbering yet in its infancy may one day attain the magnitude of a mighty institution, a shrine for the destitute, a school for our youth and the blessing for those that seek the House of G-d in prayer. Though fate has brought us far from home, may we not in the turmoil, troubles and anxieties sometimes cast a lingering look upon the religion that our forefathers upheld so faithfully – the religion that was planted in our hearts by a loving father and a doting mother when first we knew how to lisp the name of G-d.[52]

Hoffman urged the membership "to build a synagogue as speedily as possible . . . our numbers are certainly large enough and there remains but the will to accomplish our end . . . the balance for a commodious place of worship can easily be raised by subscription." "We can safely count upon 35 members," he reported, adding that "the pecuniary affairs of the congregation are very flourishing." Construction was already well advanced when Hoffman reported to Dr. N. Adler, the Chief Rabbi of the British Empire, who had enquired about the welfare of Victoria's Jews, that "we have resolved with the will of G-d to erect a temple which will be an honour to Him and a credit to us." The congregation had now increased to nearly sixty-eight members, fifty of them heads of families. In all, Hoffman calculated the number of Jews in Victoria as "upwards of 30, the most of whom with proper examples will . . . no doubt soon join our congregation."[53] But financing the new building, he informed the rabbi, required assistance: "Our brethren on [this] side have assisted as far as their means would permit, and I trust that [those] in the Old Country will not refuse to lend their aid which will be the means to accomplish our religious task."

The document listing subscriptions to the synagogue reveals that the project was assisted by many non-Jews, who donated a substantial sum of money.[54] Support came also from Baron Rothschild and Sir Moses Montefiore in London.[55] The building, whose total cost was $9196.60, was completed on November 3, 1863 and opened with considerable celebration and fanfare – including the St. Andrew's Society, the French Benevolent Society and the Germania Singing Club, Masonic officials, local politicians, and a huge crowd led by the band of HMS *Topaz* from the Royal Navy dockyard at nearby Esquimalt.

Even though it was endowed with an impressive new synagogue, the organized Jewish community of Victoria grew only slowly. With the decline of gold-rush fever in Victoria, it began to drift away. People left not just for economic reasons, apparently. Many were young men who had come up in 1858 or 1859 as representatives of San Francisco businesses, probably with no intention of staying on after an initial foray lasting a year or two.[56] The percentage of single persons in Victoria's Jewish population declined from a high of thirty-eight in 1858 to twenty-two in 1863, while the number of families grew from thirteen to sixty-five in the same period.[57]

A building was one thing; religious observance was quite another. M.R. Cohen, the congregation's first "minister" (a title used by rabbis in England), complained to its president in early November of 1863 that "our synagogue arrangements at present are anything but satisfactory or likely to draw religious light upon us as a Congregation of Israel."[58] There was, he complained, no proper schedule for services on the Sabbath or on holidays, "which keeps the people from attending this Synagogue instead of finding a pleasure in visiting it . . . and our rising generation . . . must suffer by it, to whom the Synagogue service if properly conducted forms the principal fountain of their religious life." The children, Reverend Cohen observed, must be taught to "know the difference between the *kernel* and the *shell* and thereby appreciate the time they spent [in synagogue]." "The present age," he continued, "demands of us some improvement in our religious affairs and unless some steps are taken in the matter I fear that all your labour . . . in erecting so noble an edifice . . . will prove 'Labour in Vain'." He called for a public meeting "of all Israelites of Victoria" to consider this "and other matters for the welfare of our holy faith."

From twenty families in 1863–64, the membership increased to thirty-eight by 1899.[59] But the community failed to grow to any greater degree because Victoria's development stalled after the 1880s, when Vancouver began to emerge as Canada's major west-coast commercial and transportation centre and when gold-rush fever declined. Because the community was so small, it had great difficulty in employing a rabbi and in meeting the other expenses of the synagogue.

Many of the community's founders were anglicized Jews who mixed easily in the city's social, cultural, and political milieu, as is evident from the public careers of Selim Franklin and Henry Nathan in Victoria, and the Oppenheimers in Vancouver. Franklin was elected to the Vancouver Island legislative assembly in 1860 and, after a challenge on the grounds that he had not taken the oath "on the true faith of a Christian," was allowed to take his seat.[60] Henry Nathan, who arrived in Victoria in 1862 from England, was elected to the legislature of British Columbia in November of 1870 as member for Victoria. Nathan actively promoted B.C.'s entry into Confederation in 1871 and became one of the province's first members – and the Dominion's first Jew – to sit in the House of Commons.[61]

Vancouver's Jewish community began in the early 1880s and grew slowly through the next two decades. In a city that was initially created by the Canadian Pacific Railway as its western terminus and headquarters, the orientation was largely landward. The city's railway yards, wharfs, warehouses, and shops were built to service the railway, commercial, and industrial activity that grew in the decade and a half between the completion of the CPR in 1886 and the beginnings of large-scale settlement on the Canadian Prairies in the late 1890s.[62] But although the Vancouver story properly belongs in later chapters that will cover the mass migration and communal development of that era, it is important to note the early connection between Victoria's and Vancouver's Jewish experience.

By the early 1880s, David and Isaac Oppenheimer foresaw the future economic importance of the western mainland terminus of the CPR.[63] The Oppenheimers were among the leading promoters of Vancouver's growth; David had been buying prime land in the area since 1878 and, with subsequent purchases through their Vancouver Improvement Company, controlled large tracts in the Coal Harbour and English Bay districts. Patricia Roy writes: "Along with other private landowners, he lobbied the British Columbia government to assist the C.P.R. to extend its line westward from Port Moody and encouraged other private owners to join him in selling 175 acres to the railway." After opening a wholesale grocery house in 1887, David Oppenheimer concentrated on the urban development of the city and took a keen interest in politics. He was acclaimed Vancouver's first mayor in December of 1887 and helped to organize the Board of Trade; he vigorously established basic urban services, and actively encouraged industrial development. Indeed, as Vancouver's premier booster, he apparently even travelled to Europe to seek investors for several ambitious industrial projects. He personally invested in electrical and tramway utilities which served areas in which he held substantial landholdings. There were charges of "boodling," a contemporary word for corruption. Nevertheless, in his own time Oppenheimer continued to enjoy a reputation as the "best friend Vancouver ever had."

Vancouver's Jewish community grew very slowly during the 1880s, although a tiny Reform congregation was formed in 1884 under the guidance of Solomon Philo, a religious leader of German origin.[64] Orthodox services were organized around the same time by Zebulon Franks, an immigrant from Russia. But only in 1910 was the first synagogue built in the city.

There were few similarities between the two cities' communities. Their origins were entirely different. Whereas the Victoria community was established by essentially middle-class and moderately well-off Jews of German origin from San Francisco in the 1850s and 1860s, Vancouver's Jews were mainly poor, working-class, or lower-middle-class immigrants from Russia and Poland from the 1880s onward. And while the fortunes of Victoria slowly waned after 1890, those of Vancouver grew. From the beginning, Victoria's Jewry included a significant percentage of single men; Vancouver's evolved from the migration of family groups who left Eastern Europe to settle where they could earn a living.[65]

In any event, what is evident from these earliest east- and west-coast Jewish communities in the nineteenth century is that their origins were similar to those of Montreal's communities in the eighteenth century. Most of their initial settlers came from nearby areas of the United States; the majority of Montreal's earliest Jews had moved north from New York, Newport, and Philadelphia, while Nova Scotia's moved up from New York and Boston, and Victoria's arrived from San Francisco. Those American cities had not usually been long-term homes to the migrants; they had often been no more than sojourning places for immigrants from Bavaria, Alsace, Posen, Amsterdam, or London, who might have lived in several other locations before that. Most of the migrants then were young men, often unmarried, who moved in response to both their perception of opportunity elsewhere, and their limitations or failure where they lived. As is clear from scholarly studies of mobility in Hamilton in the 1860s, those who moved on were very often the ones who could not "make it" – the marginal people who had not yet achieved economic well-being.[66] The phenomenon of "men on the move" affected Jews in the same way as it propelled other people in North America from place to place in search of the fortune that often proved elusive or fleeting.

What is equally significant about these Jewish migrations into British North America – and often out of it, either back to points of origin, or to new commercial frontiers – is that the earliest east and west coast transients and settlers were essentially no different from their Christian contemporaries who moved in from American or British metropolitan centres. Both Maritime and Pacific British North America were frontiers on the outer fringes of metropolitan societies. Resources and personnel migrated from the south, though both often originated in Britain or Europe, while the vital structure of government was decidedly British. And whatever early Jewish presence there was in Nova Scotia or British Columbia evolved under the British flag, administration, and imperial policies. Thus, though both regions were frontiers, they were British imperial frontiers. British Columbia was a "counter frontier . . . projected from London and Victoria in response to influences and pressures from other frontiers," particularly from the U.S.[67] Yet, while the governmental context was British, California – mainly San Francisco – was a "major source of economic influence in British Columbia from Confederation to the 1890's."[68] Nova Scotia and New Brunswick, on the other hand, were fully integrated into a North Atlantic commercial world centred on Britain.

Just as Lower Canadian Jews returned to New York, Philadelphia, Newport, or London to find wives, borrow funds, or recruit kinfolk to join them in business, or seek religious assistance for their communities, so the Nova Scotia, New Brunswick, and British Columbia Jews returned to their own jumping-off points for the same reasons. The key lines of communication, family ties, and economic relations thus ran in two directions – north and south, and east and west across the Atlantic. But until the late 1890s there was no unified Canadian Jewish community; the various communities began in isolation from each other, as had those in the United States, where, until the mid-nineteenth century, there existed no organizational structure to provide a semblance of national Jewish cohesion.

Another salient feature of British North American Jewry was the national background of its members. Most were of English and German origin until the 1880s – with the exception of Montreal, where there were some Polish Jews by the 1850s. And yet the early importance of the German element did not result in the emergence of the Reform movement. The Germans in British North America were not as numerous as they were in the United States. The decidedly British nature of British North America was more important, and religious leadership continued to come from the British metropolis, London.

PART III

THE EMERGENCE

OF A NATIONAL

COMMUNITY

1882–1900

6

"Where There Is No Bread, There Is No Torah"

Towards the end of the nineteenth century, Eastern Europe became Canada's greatest source of Jewish immigration. Over two million Jews left the Russian and Austro-Hungarian empires and Romania between 1880 and 1914, chiefly for the United States, South America, and the British dominions.[1] Over 75 per cent came from the Russian Empire, which then included a huge area of central and eastern Poland and Lithuania. Here, a combination of changing social, political, and economic factors had made the lives of Jews difficult since the mid-1800s, and the pogroms that broke out in May of 1881 violently underscored the precarious position of the Jewish community in czarist lands.

For a century Russia had governed the large Jewish population that inhabited the western territories she had acquired with the partitions of Poland by Prussia, Austria, and Russia in the late eighteenth century. In keeping with czarist policies of confining virtually all subjects to their places of residence, and in recognition of problems arising from the presence of a huge new Jewish population, the Jews were restricted to the area known as the Pale of Settlement, which had been created by the czarist government in 1791.[2] The Pale included the Polish and Lithuanian *gubernii*, or provinces, the southern Black Sea territories recently conquered from the Ottoman Empire, and a few other provinces that were later opened to Jewish settlement. The Russian Jewish population would be confined to these areas – twenty-five provinces in all – under a variety of laws and restrictions until the fall of the czarists in 1917: "these decrees were intended to serve the national and economic interests of the state by preventing competition of the Jewish with Russian merchants and encouraging settlement in the desolate steppes of southern Russia. . . ."[3]

The question of what to do with these Jews had been a serious concern of government officials since then. Non-Christian, non-agricultural, and non-Russian, they were seen by contemporaries as a problem to be solved by the implementation of policies of Russification and Christianization. No other minorities in the expanded empire were viewed as targets for such assimilation-ist efforts. Jews, therefore, were unique in experiencing this kind of persecution under Nicholas I and Alexander II: Ukrainians, White Russians, Lithuanians, Poles, and Germans were not then subjected, in varying degrees, to policies intended to assimilate them to Russian culture. Jews were considered a great danger to Russian Orthodoxy.

Various approaches were attempted to Russify the Jews. In 1827, Czar Nicholas I implemented a policy known as "cantonment," by which Jewish boys were compelled to serve six years of special instruction, from age twelve to eighteen, before beginning a regular period of twenty-five years' service in the Russian army; this was intended to achieve conversion of these children — some of them in fact taken at age eight — to Christianity and to Russian culture. This policy was deemed to be unsuccessful and was abandoned in 1856, but not before thousands of boys were forcibly converted or done to death in special military barracks. The horror of their fate was revealed by the Russian radical Alexander Herzen, who encountered a convoy of cantonists in Siberia in 1835:

Boys of twelve or thirteen might somehow have survived it . . . but little fellows of eight and ten . . . Not even a brush full of black paint could put such horror on canvas. Pale, exhausted, with frightened faces, they stood in thick, clumsy, soldiers' overcoats, with stand-up collars, fixing helpless, pitiful eyes on the garrison soldiers who were roughly getting them into ranks. The white lips, and blue rings under their eyes, bore witness to fever or chill. And these sick children, without care or kindness, exposed to the icy wind that blows unobstructed from the Arctic ocean were going to their graves.[4]

The implementation of this policy within the Pale was put in the hands of Jewish authorities, who were made personally responsible for filling regional quotas for cantonists. These communal leaders often took children from the poorest homes, from parents with the least influence, by using *khapers*, kidnap-pers, who seized children, incarcerated them, and handed them over to the army. Thus the policy engendered deep and lasting class-conscious bitterness within the Jewish community, as well as towards the czarist regime. Associated policies such as the ukase of 1851 required all Jews to secure documents attesting to which of the five social categories they belonged to; this put a much more severe conscription burden on the poorest sector of the community, officially deemed "useless."[5] Policies such as these left Russia's Jews with an abiding fear and detestation of military service, and also supplied an important stimulant to their desire to emigrate.[6]

In 1840 the government began establishing schools to teach Jews secular subjects, in the Russian language, so that they would be emancipated from their backward culture and fully integrated into the Russian people. Though the schools were opposed by Jewish religious leaders, they attracted growing numbers of young Jews, and by 1857 had enrolled 5,711 pupils – a small percentage of the school-age Jewish population, to be sure, but a significant group which "laid the foundations for the subsequent large-scale entry of Jewish youth into . . . Western pursuits."[7]

By the late 1850s the new czar, Alexander II (r. 1855–81), had begun to introduce legislation to Russify Jews by "toning down these conversionist policies."[8] During the first ten years of his reign, cantonment for army conscription was abandoned, Jewish rights of settlement were liberalized, and universities were opened to all, while the new local advisory assemblies (*zemstvos*) allowed Jewish participation. Jury trials were introduced, military service was reduced from twenty-five to six years, and the serfs were freed. For many Jews these and other reforms seemed like the dawn of a bright new era. Many Jewish intellectuals attended Russian schools and universities, entered the professions, and adopted the Russian culture and language; a small number even converted to Christianity. But the "broad masses" of Jews "had responded very little to the 'reforms' of Alexander's early years. The few gratuities offered them thus far had been insufficient to fill them with a burning desire to 'fuse' with the Russian people."[9]

Alexander II, though of a gentler nature than his father, was no more liberal in spirit; his attitude to the Jews of his empire was tainted by continuing fear and suspicion. As a result, "the high hopes of the Jews that they would obtain civic equality in [his] reign . . . did not materialize."[10] The movement for Jewish emancipation received a serious setback with the outbreak of the Polish uprising of 1863, which sparked a rise in Russian patriotism, and Russian fear of disaffection among minorities like the Jews. Antisemitism was further rekindled and strengthened by the "revelations" of the Jewish apostate Jacob Brafman, and a spirit of reaction effectively reversed the early Alexandrine reforms of anti-Jewish policies. The Russification of Jews through education and civic equality was, to all practical purposes, a dead issue by the end of the 1870s. In 1876 military service laws for Jews were toughened, and the following year severe limitations were placed on the eligibility of Jews for service on juries.[11] The antisemitic press began new campaigns to discredit Jews and even elements of the liberal press published anti-Jewish articles. A three-day anti-Jewish riot erupted in Odessa in 1871, and ritual murder charges were brought against several Jews in the Caucasus in 1879. Was there a future for Jews in the empire of the czar?

The outbreak of pogroms in several Ukrainian provinces in April and May of 1881 were believed to mark the beginning of a new czarist policy towards the Jews. They were not unused to pogroms, the violent outbreaks that periodically brought down on them murder, rape, arson, looting, and destruction of property. In the 1871 Odessa riot, when synagogues, homes, and shops had been looted and destroyed, the authorities had not only refused to intervene, but had even blamed the Jews for the outbreaks.[12] Worse still, at least for the city's Russified Jewish intellectuals, was the fact that many of their non-Jewish colleagues justified the pogroms on the grounds that Jews created the economic conditions that made these outbreaks inevitable.[13]

The 1881 pogroms erupted spontaneously shortly after the assassination of Czar Alexander – one of the assassins was a Jewish woman – and there was probably little direct relationship between the two events.[14] The policies encouraging the assimilation of Jews into Russian society since the 1840s had clearly not worked, and a new official attitude towards Russian Jewry was emerging. As Pobedonotsev, a highly influential czarist official, is reputed to have expressed it, "One third will die, one third will leave the country and the last third will be completely assimilated within the Russian people."[15] Thus, when the pogroms began in May of 1881, they were exploited to fit in with a new strategy aimed at eliminating the "Jewish problem" and of drawing off the energy of the revolutionary movement.

The promulgation of the May Laws of 1881, while pogroms were still in progress, provided further clarification of the government's revised position on the Jews. Though for many years official restrictions on their movement beyond the Pale had been ignored, and substantial Jewish communities had developed in St. Petersburg, Moscow, and rural areas of Ukraine and Crimea, Jews were now prohibited from living outside the Pale and even from moving to rural areas or villages within its confines. Their residence in villages had come under severe restrictions since the 1860s, when new regulations had the effect of severely limiting the number of Jewish innkeepers.[16] Travel outside the boundaries of the Pale was prohibited to Jews except by special permission, which was given only to certain categories of merchants, for limited periods. Jews living outside the Pale – even ex-soldiers, to whom some latitude had been allowed – were required to leave their homes and move to towns within its borders. A contemporary French observer of these events, Anatole Leroy-Beaulieu, wrote in his study of Russia in the 1880s:

> In some localities, the Jews, after having been allowed to settle on this strip of borderland, were abruptly removed in obedience to some sudden ordinance. This very thing happened in Volhynia, in 1881. The expulsion ruined thousands of families. But it was only partial; the poor were ruthlessly expelled; the rich bought themselves off.[17]

Meanwhile, new restrictions were being implemented on Jewish entry into gymnasia (senior high schools) and universities. Inside the Pale, Jews were limited to a maximum of 10 per cent of the student body. Moreover, they were officially barred from the civil service, the army, and the judiciary, unless they were willing to be baptized into the Russian Orthodox Church. Changing economic conditions imposed increasingly severe hardships on them, and they also experienced a change in the country's intellectual atmosphere. Consequently, many Jews who had embraced liberal and reformist movements and had favoured Russification now turned to a solution through socialism or Jewish nationalism instead. The year 1881 marked the start of substantial Jewish emigration from the Russian Empire, some of it to the United States. Other minorities, such as Poles, Lithuanians, and Finns, also showed a strong tendency towards emigration to the U.S., and between 1900 and 1914 their emigration "accelerated as rapidly as that of the Jewish immigrants."[18] Nevertheless, a far higher proportion of Jews emigrated than of these minorities.[19] Many Jews seeking higher education began to move elsewhere, chiefly to Germany, Switzerland, and Austria; by the 1880s and 1890s, there were substantial communities of Russian Jewish students and intellectuals in university centres like Berlin, Vienna, and Geneva.

While avenues to university education affected mostly middle-class Jews, the Jewish masses suffered the more basic hardships of unemployment and severe poverty, as well as poor housing and health conditions. Leroy-Beaulieu observed the miserable living condition of Jews in Russia and commented:

> The competition between them is homicidal. . . . The majority work at nominal prices. There are few countries where labour is cheaper.

Accordingly, nine tenths of these Russian Jews are a prey to all the horrors of the sweating system. Crowded into close and fetid lodgings, unventilated, inaccessible to light, several families in one room – the families almost always numerous – these miserably lean Jews, married before they are twenty, wrestle with all the ills and diseases entailed by destitution. Nothing saves their bodies and souls from the deleterious effects of extreme poverty, but temperance, endurance, and religion.[20]

A major cause of their deteriorating economic situation was the new legislation restricting migration, which prevented Jewish traders and artisans from doing business in country districts. Jewish tavernkeepers and storekeepers were ejected, while the growth of co-operative marketing among farmers severely reduced the trade of Jewish grain, cattle, and produce dealers; many were forced out of these areas.[21] Equally serious was the fact that crafts like tailoring, shoemaking, carpentry, tinsmithing, blacksmithing, and cabinetmaking, which working-class Jews had traditionally entered, were experiencing a crisis. Trends towards the industrialization of these trades forced many Jewish artisans into factory employment. Because of restrictions on movement which limited their market potential, moreover, these and other Jewish craftsmen experienced overcrowding that tended to severely depress wages and living standards. Traders and pedlars forced out by the same limitations drifted towards petty, almost nebulous commerce that barely disguised the poverty and aimlessness of their economic existence. Living only on air, as it seemed, they were known as *luftmenschen*. Meanwhile Jewish cabbies, porters, draymen, and wagon drivers had been adversely affected by railroad and, later, tramway developments in southern Russia, where new rail lines had disrupted trade at the port of Odessa in the 1870s.[22]

In Poland, many Jews who were being dislodged from their traditional economic existence gravitated into the new textile factories that had opened up in Lodz and Bialystok. This caused an enormous expansion of the Jewish population in these cities. In Lodz their numbers rose from 2,886 in 1856 to 98,676 by 1897, and the Jewish percentage of the city's total population increased from 11.7 to 31.8.[23] In Bialystok their numbers rose from 9,547 to 47,783 and from 69 to 76 per cent between 1856 and 1895.[24]

Because of restrictions on movement outside the Pale, competition among Jewish pedlars and petty traders increased to such an extent that many turned to industrial occupations. A noticeable trend towards the proletarianization of the Jewish population was under way by the 1880s, especially in the north-western provinces of Lithuania and White Russia. Data collected in the official government census demonstrated that "in these Provinces there is a rapid shifting from the commercial pursuits to industrial work,"[25] notably in the tobacco, food, and clothing industries. Thus, one observer of this trend concluded, "economic conditions, such as opportunities and local demand, have a much more decisive influence [on them] than mere national preelection."[26]

Some Jews were even taking up farming in colonies and on independent farms. By 1897 nearly 200,000 Jews derived their living from agriculture. Jews were crowding into the handicraft trades; Leroy-Beaulieu noted that "numbers [of Jews] are tailors, shoemakers, locksmiths, joiners, saddlers, coachmen, butchers, tilers, painters, dyers. Although they prefer trades requiring more deftness than strength, many are carpenters, smiths, masons, road builders. Most stone houses in western cities have been built by Jewish hands."[27] However, there were also growing numbers of unskilled labourers as well: agricultural workers, cabmen, diggers and stonebreakers, lumbermen, craftsmen, ragpickers, teamsters, and water carriers.[28] Observing the condition of Jewish longshoremen and carriers on the Odessa and Nikolayev waterfronts, A. P. Subotin wrote:

> From their external appearance it is difficult to guess at their nationality, so strong, rough, and muscular do they look. Their wages, besides being very low, rarely more than 50 copecks [about 25 cents] for a whole day's work, are seldom regular, their employment almost accidental, and the large numbers of these laborers anxiously waiting for an opportunity to earn a few copecks, and crowding the so-called market (or the open public ground) is one of the most distressing pictures of each and every Jewish town.[29]

"The initial stages of the development of capitalistic industry . . . required a perceptible decline in the economic condition of the Jewish artisan, in the early eighties, to force him into the ranks of the industrial army," historian I.M. Rubinow noted.[30] By 1907 there were from 100,000 to 150,000 Jewish factory workers in the Pale, mainly in textiles and clothing – a number limited only by the laws restricting Jewish settlement beyond the Pale and by the antisemitism that prevailed in German-owned textile factories in Lodz and Bialystok.[31] By 1898, in the north-western provinces, Jews constituted over 50 per cent of all workers in the glove, brush, match, tobacco, soap, button, tanning, candle, wool spinning, flour milling, and beer brewing industries.[32] By the end of the century, the Jewish working class in Russia embraced some half a million artisans, apprentices, and factory operatives.

Much of the urban increase could be attributed to the natural growth of Russia's Jewish population, which rose from about one million to about four million during the nineteenth century, largely due to a rapid decline in the Jewish death rate, which fell off more precipitously than that of the general population.[33] The difference can be explained by "the greater stability of the family, the smaller number of illegitimate children, the infrequency of venereal disease, the higher status of women within the family, the care lavished on babies and small children, abstinence from alcohol . . . and the lengthy tradition of charitable deeds."[34] The validity of such assumptions still needs to be tested. In any case, the fact that the Jewish urban concentration rose more than the overall Jewish population clearly indicates that demographic shifts were under way and that the Jews were rapidly becoming urbanized, with major concentrations emerging in the large cities of the Pale. But because of limitations on economic improvement among their Jewish masses, and higher than average rates of population increase, this process of urbanization brought little relief: "To survive in the teeming provincial towns [of the Jewish Pale], which had limited opportunities for earning a living and intense competition, required industry, marketable skills and quick wits."[35]

In the cities, Jewish poverty abounded, and it was worse in Lithuania and Poland than anywhere else in the empire. In Vilnius, a contemporary observer stated, "fully 80 percent of the Jewish population . . . do not know in the evening where they will obtain food the next morning."[36] Communal authorities in Warsaw, Minsk, and Vilnius established houses to shelter poor vagrants, while in the provinces of Kaunas, Vilnius, Grodno, Piotrków, Kielce, Radom, and Lublin fully 22 per cent of all Jews were on communal poor relief. The situation was only slightly better in Ukraine, where 20 per cent of all Jews were on relief, and where major sheltering homes had to be built in Berdichev, Elizavetgrad, Kremenchug, and Odessa to accommodate the totally destitute. And in all of the major centres throughout the Pale, such as Kherson, Nikolayev, Ekaterinoslav, Zhitomir, and Daugavpils, one in every four Jews was forced to turn to local Jewish charities for winter fuel. Economic pressures inside the Pale were tightening severely by the 1880s and 1890s. Beggars abounded and Jewish criminality, prostitution, and juvenile delinquency were emerging as disturbing new social problems.[37]

Although Jews in Galicia and Bukovina had a far better political environment, under the Austro-Hungarian crown, than their Russian co-religionists, the prevailing economic conditions were apparently as bad, or worse. In Cracow, Tarnów, Przemyśl, Brody, Lvov, Ternopol, Kolomyya, and Chernovtsy there was massive economic suffering, and throughout the two provinces over 5,000 Jews starved to death each year.[38] In Romania, meanwhile, the economic situation of the Jews was aggravated by severe semi-official persecutions – an especially savage pogrom occurred in Galati in October 1868 – and by humiliating regulations which continued even after the 1878 Congress of Berlin had made the granting of civil rights to Jews a condition of Romanian independence; the Romanian government found elaborate legalistic ways to circumvent those stipulations. Indeed the situation worsened, as Jews were forbidden to enter most professions, or to sell commodities like tobacco, salt, and alcohol, which were declared a government monopoly.[39]

Jewish reaction to these deteriorating political and social circumstances, along with the pogroms of the eighties, was characterized by the emergence of new intellectual currents within the Pale. Enthusiasm for the Haskalah, Jewish Enlightenment, waned among intellectuals who had been enamoured of its ideals and the promise of a better life in a liberalized and reformed Russia. By the end of the 1870s many Jewish narodniki (intellectual communalists) felt betrayed by the new antisemitic manifestations evident in the irregular underground publication Narodnaia Volya (Peoples' Will), while other liberal and progressive Jewish thinkers were becoming disillusioned by signs of antisemitism among their non-Jewish colleagues, where they least expected it. The violence, persistence, and spread of the pogroms disturbed them deeply. That there was a multi-faceted "Jewish problem" in the Russian Empire was self-evident. An answer to the question of how to solve it was not.

For a growing number of Jews, adherence to tradition and the Torah was no longer the answer. The authority of the rabbis was declining, except in the remote towns removed from the intoxicating ideas and material influences of the cities. Not that the religious life was disappearing, by any means. The great Talmudic academies continued and new ones emerged in Lithuania and Poland. Under the powerful influence of charismatic rabbis, Chassidism thrived – especially the Belzer and Lubavitcher sects, in remote areas of Poland and Ukraine, as well as in Galicia and Hungary. Meanwhile the moral influence, even among some secularized Jews, of renowned rabbis like Israel Meir Ha-Kohen, known as Chafetz Chaim, was of consequence on a wide range of issues.[40]

What was to be done? There were a variety of answers to this question, as Russian Jewry went through a period of "inner upheavals" and "revolutionary results in . . . the structure of Jewish society."[41] The Maskilim, Russifiers and assimilators who continued to argue for civil emancipation and reforms within Jewish religious canons, had long been influenced by Enlightenment ideas imported from Western and Central Europe, and by the Russian liberal press, such as the popular St. Petersburg journal *Voskhod*. Russian Maskilim, indeed, established a number of schools in cities like Warsaw, Riga, Kishinev, and Odessa to propagate their ideals of integration, social reform, and occupational diversification, including projects for Jewish agricultural settlement.

But support for these aspirations was limited among the Russian Empire's Jews. Unlike the communities in Western Europe, "in Eastern Europe there was no influential social stratum . . . that aspired to closer contact with the non-Jewish world and culture. . . ."[42] The Russian Jews were intellectually, materially, and socially removed from the contexts in which the Enlightenment thrived, like that of mid-nineteenth-century Germany. There, Jews influenced by the Haskalah aspired to what they considered to be a higher culture. Russian Jews, on the other hand, did not believe that the cultural milieu surrounding them was in any way superior to their own.

By the 1860s, the Russian Haskalah had consequently begun to assume a somewhat different form from the one it took in Central and Western Europe. Hebrew, not German, became the literary language of the Russian Maskilim, and a new secular Hebrew literature began to emerge; it flourished as poets, essayists, and journalists like Isaac Levinsohn, Abraham Mapu, and Judah Gordon began to adapt the ancient language of prayer and religious literature to the world of secular ideas, to political debate, and literary expression. While this movement was under way, a concurrent efflorescence of Yiddish, the lingua franca of East European Jews, was also taking shape. Hebrew could reach the educated youth – the important cadre of *yeshiva* (Talmudic academy) students, for example – but Yiddish literature was accessible to the masses. Like Hebrew literature, Yiddish was intended to disseminate the Haskalah to enlighten the people and open their minds to reform, modernization, and other cultures. Through the pens of Sholem Aleichem and Isaac Loeb Peretz, among others, Yiddish literature evoked the complexity of the East European Jewish historical experience, and its travails in the transformations of late-nineteenth-century Russian economic and social life.

But the Haskalah in Russia was different from that of the West not only in its positive affirmation of aspects of Jewish culture but also in its complete failure to undermine – or even significantly weaken – traditional Jewish religion. With the exception of Odessa and Warsaw, two cities open to certain Western influences, the Jewry of Russia were not receptive to the reformist religious impulses emanating from Germany, where emulation of Christian religious modes was growing popular by the mid-nineteenth century. For the overwhelming mass of Russia's Jews who observed the laws and traditions of their faith, therefore, Orthodoxy prevailed. Unblemished, as it were, by Western "modernization," traditional Judaism remained steeped in the study of the Torah and in rigid adherence to its precepts. Yet even within this world of pious and generally unquestioning adherence to the faith, faint but significant reverberations of a transforming intellectual milieu were felt.

Not even the most fervent adherents could completely escape the effects of those external changes. As the struggle between Chassidism and its opponents abated in the early nineteenth century, fresh religious currents emerged, notably in Lithuania, where new and autonomous *yeshivot* were established and where the *musar* (ethics) movement developed. Reflecting both the fervour of Chassidism and, more, the Enlightenment impulse for reform, *musar* stressed the importance of study for both men and women, while "its exponents . . . tended to engage in self-examination and to express contempt for 'the vanities of this world'."[43]

But now there were other voices, like that of Moses Hess. Hess, like Marx, Engels, and Lassalle, was one of the major founders of German social democracy, and in 1862 published *Rome and Jerusalem.* Hess was a German Jew and a universalist left Hegelian to whom "the solution . . . to the Jewish problem at [an earlier] period in his life was assimilation and integration into the revolutionary Universal socialist movement," now, in his pathbreaking book, he called for "the establishment of a Jewish socialist commonwealth in Palestine."[44] Hess believed that the "Jewish problem" had both national and socioeconomic dimensions, and would only be resolved through a Jewish state. He thus, foreshadowed by two decades the emerging national consciousness among Jewish intellectuals in Russia itself. Perez Smolenskin, editor of *Ha-Shahar* – "Morning Star" – turned from the Haskalah to nationalism and emigration as a pragmatic solution to the problems of Jewish existence in Russia. Only in Palestine, he argued, could a practical resolution of these problems be found, because only there could Jews "be dispersed across the whole socioeconomic spectrum."[45]

Other Odessa Maskilim, such as Moshe Leib Lilienblum and Leon Pinsker, came to essentially the same conclusions. In September of 1882, Pinsker, an intellectual and communal worker once favouring assimilation, published his pamphlet "Autoemancipation: An Appeal to his brethren by a Russian Jew." Summoning Jews to a program of national revival that would breathe life into the "ghost" they had become, both in their physical enslavement in Eastern Europe and in their spiritual captivity in the enlightened West, Pinsker too advocated a territorial solution. Whether in America or in Palestine, he argued, Jews could achieve the full realization of their true national personality only in a territory of their own. This auto-emancipation would be achieved, he averred, if Jews took "the first step towards national restoration."[46] This concept of Jewish nationalism was now put forward in the Hebrew journals Ha-Melitz, "The Advocate," published since 1860 in Odessa, and Ha-Shahar, which began in Vienna in 1868.[47] Meanwhile, a revolution in Jewish life was demanded with renewed vigour by the former Maskil and assimilator Leib Osipovich Levanda, and by a lively group of new writers enamoured of Jewish nationalism: writers, poets, and novelists like Odessa's Ahad Ha'Am (born Asher Ginsberg) and Hayim Nahman Bialik.

These were the Zionists, the members and supporters of the Chovevei Zion, "Lovers of Zion," a nationalist movement spreading widely among Jewish youth throughout Russia and Romania. Shortly after the first pogroms, they advocated that national renewal could be achieved only in the land of Israel, the ancient homeland of the Jewish people. In Kharkov hundreds of students and other young Jews formed themselves into the Bilu (from Isaiah 2:5, "House of Jacob, Come Ye and let us go"), with the purpose of emigrating to Palestine in order to create "a political centre for the Jewish people."[48] Although only fifty-three of these idealists ever reached Palestine, they formed the vanguard of the waves of Russian pioneers who would dedicate their lives to building a new Jewish society and culture, while at the same time laying the foundations for a reconstituted polity in Palestine.

But the Zionists were in a minority; the vast majority of Jews were motivated by more practical concerns, such as putting bread on the table, and the anguish of their life in Russia stimulated other messianic hopes, among them various forms of socialism. Economic transformations, especially the rise of a proletariat – some of it working for Jewish employers – sharpened the differences between the classes within the community and gave rise to tension and conflict. Jewish workers were organizing co-operatives, work stoppages, and unions from the 1870s in Lithuania and Belorussia, as industrialization began to break down traditional craft associations in the textile, tobacco, and brush trades.[49] As early as the 1850s, Jewish apprentices in the clothing trades had been organizing themselves into hevrot (clubs), forerunners of modern trade unions, to demand better conditions.[50] Socialism appealed to many young intellectuals whose revolutionary ideas and frustration with the disabilities of life in Russia made them ardent supporters of this movement for revolution, and for Jewish autonomy within a reformed Russian state.

Others had notions of rebuilding their lives by moving to America and living as simple farmers in communities organized on collectivist principles. Calling themselves the Am Olam (Eternal People), they formed chapters in a number of Russian cities. In 1881 a group of seventy artisans and students left Elizavetgrad for America, and the following year another contingent of about seven hundred followed, from Kiev, Kremenchug, and Odessa.[51] Four Jewish farming colonies were formed in various parts of the United States from these groups, the most long-lasting being "New Odessa," near Portland, Oregon. While only short-lived, Am Olam did supply a small cadre of committed idealists to the early American Jewish socialist movement. It also provided a cautionary example for later idealists who experimented in Jewish agricultural settlement in the United States and in Canada, where they hoped to find a new Garden of Eden.

The Jewish experience in Eastern Europe was clearly undergoing a crisis during the late nineteenth century. The murder of Jews in Ukraine and the destruction of property made it all too clear that Jewish political and social emancipation was unattainable in the Russian Empire. But the tide of emigration did not reach large proportions until the 1890s, and grew larger still in the years immediately before the First World War. So the emigration was not caused by pogroms alone, and it is doubtful if they were even of major importance; indeed, emigration rates declined later in the 1880s. Shmuel Ettinger's conclusion that "this migration was the consequence of demographic, economic and political developments" seems a more accurate summation than his statement that "this emigration movement was largely a 'flight to emancipation'." The average Russian Jew did not aspire to emancipation, even if he could understand what that word meant. He and his brothers and sisters were too poor, too uneducated, and too religious to be influenced by such ideas. Generally speaking, the Haskalah never penetrated below the ranks of the Jewish intelligentsia and the middle class, except perhaps in Odessa. Most of the masses were suffering more from poverty than from a lack of political and social emancipation, and even religion was of little solace—as the Talmud says, "Where there is no bread, there is no Torah."

CHAPTER

7

Beginnings of Western Colonization

While these transformations in Jewish social and intellectual life reflected the changing context of Russian Jewry, they also stimulated rising Jewish emigration. Rates of departures fluctuated, indicating a sensitivity to changes in economic conditions and to business cycles in both the country of origin and the countries of destination. In fact, Russian Jewish emigration increased only slowly in the early 1880s, accelerated in the early 1890s, then declined slightly until 1905, when it rose substantially and maintained a high, though uneven, level until 1914.[1] Pogroms and political upheavals – such as the failed revolution of 1905 – were still not the major factors; poverty and perceptions of better economic opportunities in America remained the forces that propelled Jews from the Old World to the New.

Canada received about 10,000 Jewish immigrants between 1880 and 1900.[2] It is not clear, however, what percentage of them were transients who migrated to the United States soon after arrival. It would be safe to assume that the rate of re-migration of Jews back to their countries of origin – despite recent revisionist views – was extremely low, as it was in the United States, where, in contrast to general net immigration (i.e. immigration minus remigration) rates of about 65 per cent, Jewish net immigration for the period 1908–14 stood at about 93 per cent.[3] On the basis of these estimates, Canada can be assumed to have netted about 9,300 of the 10,000 immigrants.

Between 1881 and 1901, Canada's Jewish population grew from 2,443 to 16,401. Decennial censuses distinguished between "Jews by race" and "Jews by religion," the former exceeding the latter by less than one per cent before 1931.[4] This study uses the figures of "Jews by religion" on the assumption that, while those accepting the designation obviously were not all religious in the strictest sense, they did acknowledge themselves to be part of the Jewish collectivity. Other calculations show that the decennial growth rate of Canada's Jewish population was 164.88 per cent during the 1880s and 157.06 per cent during the 1890s, compared to total population-growth rates of 11.76 and 11.13 per cent. In other words, the Jewish population of Canada grew at about fourteen times the rate of the population as a whole, and enjoyed one of the highest increases of any ethnic community in the country during those decades, except for Poles, Ukrainians, and Scandinavians.[5]

If the Canadian Jewish community experienced a net growth of about 700 per cent in two decades – an overall increase of about 14,000 people, of whom perhaps 9,300 were immigrants – the rate of natural increase would seem to account for a significant percentage of this growth. If the fertility and death rates of Jews in Eastern Europe were the same as those of immigrants from the same areas, and if those of the existing Jewish community of 1881 were the same as those in the general Canadian population, then natural increase would account for about half the non-immigrant Jewish population growth.

It is clear from 1891 census returns for Jews living in Canada's major cities that a significant percentage of this growth can be accounted for by immigrants who resided for a time in the United States, Britain, or Germany. Whether they moved on directly from American ports of entry like New York or Boston, or came north after residing in the United States for some time, has not yet been established, although birthplaces of children suggest that the latter was true in many cases. But it seems evident that a significant proportion of the increased population may be accounted for in this way. Clearly, the complex process of immigration was an important part of what has been described as the mingling of the Canadian and American peoples.[6] A historian of Hungarian migration to Canada before 1914 has noted that "one of the basic facts of Hungarian immigration to Canada is that most of the first and many of the later Hungarian newcomers came via United States."[7]

While official government attitudes towards immigration in the late nineteenth century were not as sharply defined, as restrictionist, or as rigidly enforced as they became after the First World War, and notably after 1925, there was a distinct preference throughout the century for farmer-settlers to populate the country. Long before Confederation, governments in Canada promoted settlement for military defence or for economic purposes in various ways, and it became an article of faith that agricultural settlement was best. Numerous immigration schemes brought Irish, Scots, English, and German farmers to settle backwoods areas of Ontario. After 1867, provincial as well as federal governments pursued immigration policies that were intended to settle these isolated regions with immigrant farmers.[8] In the 1870s, Icelanders and German Mennonites were brought to Manitoba on the assumption that, as sturdy farmers (though Icelanders were mainly fishermen) cultivating unoccupied regions, they would add to the nation's wealth. The Dominion government, which controlled the public lands in the Northwest Territories, was directly involved in immigration and settlement, and promoted farming settlement on the Prairies. Dominion lands policy became an integral part of Canada's national policy of development. And so, when immigration of Russian Jews began on a small scale in the spring of 1882, it seemed natural that questions would be raised concerning their suitability for farming in the vast Northwest Territories – which stretched from the western border of Manitoba to British Columbia.

In January of that year, reports began reaching Canada of persecutions of Jews in Russia.[9] In Montreal a group calling itself the Citizen's Committee Jewish Relief Fund, a city-wide organization with considerable support in the Christian community, was formed in response to news of the atrocities. Editorials condemning the excesses in Montreal newspapers expressed sympathy for Russia's Jews and pressed for public support to assist any of them who might arrive as refugees in Canada. In February, the Montreal *Gazette* urged Dominion officials "to make proper provision for the hospitable reception of such of them as may land on our shores." "The people of their own race and faith, of whom many living amongst us occupy positions of respectability and influence," the *Gazette* continued, "will of course do all that is in their power for the succor of their unfortunate brethren, but it is no less incumbent on Christians of all denominations to give a helping hand, which shall atone, to some extent at least, the brutal usage by those who profess to serve the same master."[10] The Anglican Bishop of Montreal, William Bennett Bond, who headed the Citizen's Committee, solicited subscriptions and raised over $4,600 by mid-September. The *Gazette* regularly kept its readers informed of the latest donations.[11]

By this time, all important Jewish charity groups in the city – the Young Men's Hebrew Benevolent Society, the Ladies' Hebrew Benevolent Society, and the Anglo-Jewish Association of Montreal – had joined together to form the Jewish Emigration Aid Society (JEAS) in order to co-ordinate their efforts to help the expected refugees.[12] Probably modelled on the similarly named society established in New York the preceding year, this committee took on the immense task of providing food, clothing, housing, furniture, medical aid, jobs, and, often, transportation to other parts of Canada and the United States.[13]

The new organization barely had time to prepare before the first group of 260 Russian refugees – who, according to the *Gazette*, "were not particularly distinguished for cleanliness," – arrived on May 15 at Bonaventure station.[14] Within days a large building in Montreal's waterfront area was converted to a dormitory, relief, and medical centre for them. Those who could not be accommodated there were boarded with local Jewish families.[15] The Mansion House Committee of London, England, organized by that city's major Jewish societies to assist Russian Jews immigrating to Britain, sent some money to assist the Montrealers. By June 21, 180 refugees had been housed there and employment had been found for most of them, while many others were given help as they passed through Montreal to destinations in the United States, Ontario, and Manitoba.[16]

Once the refugees of 1882 had moved on or settled in, the Citizen's Committee and JEAS were disbanded. Though short-lived, these organizations marked the beginning of a general understanding of the need for co-ordinated action by all of Montreal's Jewish philanthropic societies to meet an emergency.[17] Organizations similar to Montreal's JEAS were set up in Toronto and Winnipeg, where both Jews and sympathetic Christians contributed to the relief work. Toronto's emergency committee leased an old hotel and even used a synagogue to provide refugees with temporary housing.[18] In all three cities, moreover, Christian concern manifested itself forthrightly in the form of substantial and sustained financial and moral support.

The migration of Jews to Canada during the 1880s and 1890s was to some extent based on the belief that, as well as providing a refuge from persecution and poverty, Canada offered the possibility of widespread Jewish agricultural settlement, and might become a new Eden for a distressed people. While Canada's west was widely viewed at this time, by both Canadian and imperial planners, as a land of opportunity for agricultural development, it was also thought of as a place where Europe's displaced Jews might be settled as farmers.[19] Some interest had been shown in Montreal in 1874 in a Jewish colonization society but nothing had come of the idea.[20] Proposals for Jewish colonization were gaining considerable support among American Jewish charity organizations, which were generally opposed to massive Jewish immigration, especially of poor Eastern European Jews who crowded into the cities and presented these organizations with enormous financial burdens.

Equally distressing was the fact that American Jews were faced with the embarrassing presence of "uncivilized" Jews, whose outlandish dress, odd manners, petty commercial occupations, Yiddish language, and fervent religiosity detracted from the carefully cultivated image the American Jews attempted to present to Christian society. Many of Montreal's Jews were now moving from the downtown up into the fashionable West End, and were soon to erect expensive synagogual edifices there.[21] At a meeting of Jewish organizations in Paris, France, in 1878, an American delegate voiced strong opposition to the migration of "surplus poor" Jews to America, saying that only "strong and active" immigrants were welcome.[22] Acting on both selfish and philanthropic impulses, western Jewish organizations promoted a number of colonization schemes in the United States during the 1880s, most of them failures. Begun by immigrants who were enthusiasts of the Russian Am Olam movement, they quickly succumbed to the problems of inexperience, shortage of capital, poor choice of land, and weak or misguided follow-up.

It was therefore entirely understandable that such proposals should be raised in Canada, or elsewhere, for this country which had opened the newly acquired Northwest Territories to settlement through the Dominion Lands Act of 1872. The act was "the landmark legislation that introduced the principle of the free homestead in Canada."[23]

The Canadian High Commissioner in London, Alexander Galt, who was greatly interested in promoting immigration to Canada's Prairies, wrote to Baron Rothschild in January of 1882, strongly proposing the migration of "the agricultural Jews to our North West."[24] A few weeks later, Galt confided to Prime Minister John A. Macdonald that "[A] large proportion [of Russian Jews] will still be found with sufficient means to establish themselves in Canada. . . . I found the American Jews were actively promoting emigration to the United States, and I thought what was good for them, could not be bad for us."[25] This proposal was essentially intended to prevent a large-scale influx of "Old Clo" — a contemptuous reference by Macdonald to the cry of London's Jewish used-clothing pedlars, by which he meant poor Russian Jews. "[T]hose unhappy Jews take up more time than bargained for," Galt wrote to Macdonald in early February of 1882. "But it is very necessary, or we might have a lot of them thrown upon our shores unprovided for. By being on the committee I can prevent this."[26]

What Galt and Macdonald were really seeking was not significant Jewish settlement on Canada's Prairies, or a few Jewish "Cheap Jacks" and "Chapmen," who would have been useful to the Conservative Party in the West.[27] A Jewish colony might provide, as Macdonald put it confidentially to Galt, "a link, a missing link . . . between Canada and Sidonia [Jewish financiers]." In the same letter he told Galt, "After years of ill-concealed hostility of the Rothschilds against Canada, you have made a great strike by taking up the old clo' cry, and going in for a Jew immigration into the Northwest. . . ."[28] For what was vastly more important to Macdonald than Jewish voters or Conservative Party drummers was the hope of attracting some Rothschild money for the Canadian Pacific Railway – then under construction by a company desperately short of funds – or for other development projects. And if acquiescence to some Jewish immigration was the price of an entrée to the Rothschilds and other London Jewish financiers, it was well worth it. Such cynicism "was pervasive in [Canada's] official circles." Reflecting the politicians' outlook, the governor-general's secretary, Colonel I. De Winton, wrote to Macdonald in mid-February, "if the English Jew will subscribe liberally and settle his Russian brother why shouldn't the Canadian [government] get the benefit of the transaction[?]"[29] Galt had put the matter in clear perspective in a letter to Macdonald in late January 1882: "The Jewish persecution in Russia has induced me to write Rothschild suggesting that I would like to discuss with him the feasibility of removing the agricultural Jews to Canada – I have only sent my note to-day. It seemed not a bad opportunity of interesting the Hebrews in our NorthWest."[30]

In contrast to the cynicism and opportunism among the country's political leaders, at least one official – John Taylor, the Dominion government's Icelandic agent at St. Andrew's, Manitoba – appealed to the Marquis of Lorne, the governor-general, for a suitable block of land in the north-west for Jewish settlement, on humanitarian grounds. "Providing new homes far removed from the cruelties and atrocities so shamefully perpetrated on this people in the name of religion," he stated, "would be a lasting credit to this country. . . ."[31] In May the Lord Mayor of London, J. Whittaker Ellis, wrote to Louis Davis, president of the Anglo-Jewish Association of Montreal, that "at the suggestion of Sir Alexander Galt, the Mansion House Committee are sending a considerable number of the Russo-Jewish refugees to Canada, the more able bodied to Winnipeg." He added that "Sir A. Galt had given my committee so glowing an account of the charity and benevolence of the Canadian Jews that I feel sure that this suggestion will meet with your ready acceptance."[32]

Encouraged, or maybe intimidated, by such impressive support, early in 1882 John and Hyam Moss, Louis and Samuel Davis, and Moise Schwob, all of them prominent members of Montreal's YMHBS and the JEAS, formed a settlement and land company, the International Colonization Association, with a projected capital of one million dollars, to establish communities of Russian and

Polish Jews in the north-west. Given the financial limitations of even the tiny well-off sector of the Montreal Jewish community, they were probably hoping for support from London or other European Jewish plutocrats. They proposed to start by moving one hundred families out west the following spring.[33] Supported by other Montreal Jews and the local press, they sent Lazarus Cohen, a local notable, to Ottawa to confer with the Minister of Agriculture, John Henry Pope, who gave assurances of his interest and desire to assist.[34]

While projects for Jewish colonization were being discussed, several contingents of Jews had reached Winnipeg in the spring of 1882: 23 arrived on May 26, 247 on June 1 and 70 on June 10 – in all, 340 people to a community of only a handful of families. Even the best efforts of the community to house and feed the new arrivals and to find them employment were only partially successful. One of the newcomers, S.F. Rodin, poured out his disappointment in a lengthy letter to *Ha-Melitz*, the Odessa Hebrew daily, which reported regularly on the new agricultural settlements in North America.[35] Informing his readers that he wrote from "Winnipeg (in the country of Canada, North America) Sunday, week of Parashat *hukat* (June 18/6), 1882 (5652)", Rodin wrote as follows:

> On the Friday of Parashat, *selah* the 22nd of Sivan . . . we were the first contingent sent under the auspices and financial responsibility of the London [Mansion House] Committee, arrived in the city of Winnipeg (which is situated on the Winnipeg River to the south and which is about a thousand Persian miles from the Atlantic Ocean). . . . I don't know where to dip my pen as I write these words – shall it be in the inkwell before me or in the abhorrent tears which stream from the cheeks of the people who came here with me. Like an outcast, I sit looking towards the sky, and I hear voices of their weeping, lamenting the days of their youth which have passed away quickly with poverty and grief in an arid and sunken land. Their words and groans tear my heart and pierce my inner parts to the very depths. . . .[36]

By September, however, Rodin was much more optimistic about Winnipeg, and wrote somewhat apologetically to *Ha-Melitz* readers that "perhaps I have somewhat exaggerated."[37] He reported that the immigrants had successfully worked on railway-building and sewer-construction crews, earning between $2.50 and $3.00 per day. He was perhaps inspired by the promise of urban greatness brought on by the railway construction and land speculation Winnipeg was then experiencing, during the economic boom of the early 1880s. Comparing the Winnipeg immigrants with those refugees who had reached New York and still languished in sheltering homes, Rodin continued:

> The farmers, willing to work, endeavour with their own hands to earn
> their livelihood without relying upon the generosity of strangers. . . .
> Here in [their] new country, even the cultured and well-bred among us
> have soon discarded their starched shirts and lacquered shoes, and have
> set themselves to work.

But while there was some satisfaction with employment prospects, Rodin
reported the immigrants' great disappointment with the lack of opportunities
for providing their children with a Jewish education. "One is grieved," he
wrote, "with things educational and spiritual, which are growing worse daily.
Our children wander recklessly about the streets and humiliate us in the eyes
of our neighbours."[38]

Jewish agricultural settlement in western Canada could have had no better
a Canadian agent than Alexander Tilloch Galt, an entrepreneur who had cut
his business teeth in the British American Land Company, a weak and faltering
Lower Canadian enterprise which, under his guidance between 1844 and
1855, experienced a spectacular turnaround.[39] A successful railway financier,
member of the legislative assembly of the United Province of Canada through
the 1850s and 1860s, and twice Minister of Finance, Galt was a key architect
of Confederation. Briefly serving as Minister of Finance in Macdonald's first
government, he resigned in 1868 and fulfilled a number of major diplomatic
responsibilities, including the post of High Commissioner in London in the
early 1880s. He invested in development projects in western Canada, especially the southern Alberta coalfields. Together with other investors, he
became one of the major promoters of mining, lumbering, steamboating, and
townsite development out in the prairie hinterland.[40] The prospect of more settlers migrating to the west, and the possibility of enticing London Jewish
financial backing for some of these projects, fitted nicely into his new financial
interests. With his excellent political and business connections, Galt was in an
ideal position to help Jewish settlement projects.

After returning to Canada in May of 1883, Galt continued his efforts on
behalf of Jewish colonization, serving as Canadian agent for the Mansion
House Committee, which collected and distributed large sums of money for
the welfare of the Jewish refugees of 1882.[41] In early April of 1884, he wrote
to an official in the Department of the Interior concerning the prospects for
settling the forty to fifty Jewish families then waiting in Winnipeg for
arrangements to be completed. "I now have the money to help them from the

Mansion House Fund," he wrote, asking "as an exceeding important favour" that four homesteads – instead of two, as provided in the Dominion Lands Act of 1872 – be allowed to occupy each 640-acre section in the region.[42] Thus each family would have 160 acres of land. Intensive settlement "will be of the greatest Service," he advised. This would allow him to house all four families in one dwelling and supply them in common. Still unsure of where to settle his charges, Galt insisted that "good, easy worked land [with] wood, water and proximity to the Railway are the requisites" and inquired, "where can you find some ten or twelve sections that combine these qualifications."[43] The matter was urgent, as it was already April 1: "Time is of so great importance that I have intended to go west the moment I have the answer."

Galt's plan, with some modifications to satisfy the legislation, was approved,[44] and Winnipeg officials of the Dominion Lands Commission consulted with Louis Wertheim, a Winnipeg businessman, in selecting a homestead location. Although western officers of the Dominion Lands Commission were not prepared to give the project urgent consideration, Galt reported to the Department of the Interior in early May that a site had been found for thirty families in townships 11, 12, and 13, range 2 west of the second meridian. He requested that even though only a small part of these lands would be taken up immediately, "the government may be pleased to reserve the remaining vacant homesteads and pre-emptions in the Townships . . . until the result of the present experiment is known," or about six months.[45]

These efforts resulted in the establishment of twenty-eight families in a colony near Moosomin in 1884.[46] The Mansion House Committee provided each family with a loan of up to $600 to buy cattle, implements, and food.[47] Land was selected in the District of Assiniboia, south-west of Moosomin, and in the spring of 1884, twenty-seven settlers took up homesteads there. Occupying 8,968 acres – an area which included pre-empted land (additional quarter-sections) as well as homesteads of quarter sections – the farmers were faced with almost insuperable barriers. Financial support from London was inadequate, and during the first year the settlers called on the Winnipeg Jewish community for assistance. Crops failed that first year, and were struck down by hail in 1885. Morale seemed to be falling precipitously, and when the colony's rabbi was stricken with disaster in 1886, the Moosomin settlers lost heart and many began to leave.[48] Their unsuitability for farming was so obvious that "petitions were sent to London to send no more of them":[49] "There was not a farmer amongst them nor were they trained mechanics, and they made very poor laborers." The Dominion immigration agent at Brandon reported in 1887 that, though occupying good farmland, they had not done well "and were never adapted for agricultural pursuits."[50]

Broken financially and spiritually, the Moosomin settlers refused to repay the loans they had received from the Mansion House Fund in 1884, and a long legal and political squabble ensued over these debts, as well as over the rights of Moosomin settlers who had registered their lands. Until his death in September of 1893, Galt was pestered by the messy financial aftermath of the Moosomin project. In May 1886 he had warned that a failure to settle the claims "will close the door upon all further effort on the part of the friends of the Jews in Europe."[51] Some of the original settlers returned in 1887, bringing others with them in the hope of rejuvenating the project, which they renamed "New Jerusalem."[52] The Dominion lands agent in Whitewood would report later, in 1892, that they had "built several houses, with the ruins of those houses left by their predecessors." They too failed after putting in one crop, "which, unfortunately was so badly frozen that they were discouraged, and this band also deserted . . . leaving a few houses and stables. . . ." A fire ravaged the colony in September of 1889, putting an end to its existence.

Meanwhile, five Jewish families had settled near Wapella, in the District of Assiniboia, in 1886, with the assistance of Herman Landau, a London Jewish financier connected with the CPR.[53] Led by its founders, John Heppner and Abraham Klenman, the tiny colony grew slowly over the years.[54] Between 1886 and 1907 the Wapella district attracted about fifty Jewish families to local homesteads. Others settled in the towns along the new CPR branch line from Brandon to Estevan, and in 1891 a group of farmers led by Ascher Pierce and his family settled at Oxbow in the Northwest Territories.

Although all homesteaders on the Canadian Prairies faced long and severely cold winters, short growing seasons, and the isolation and privations of farm life, Jewish homesteaders suffered "additional handicaps."[55] Unlike most other homesteaders, Jews came with "virtually no previous farming experience" and had little capital to buy implements, animals, and basic household amenities. Conditions at Wapella during the early years, therefore, were especially harsh and primitive. Homesteading in a wooded area of heavy black soil, where poplar trees provided building materials and fuel, the early colonists, who were drawn mostly from southern Russia and Bessarabia, scratched out a living by hauling wagonloads of wood to nearby towns to sell for a dollar a load, or by working for neighbours. Meanwhile, they cleared their land – a few acres each year – for growing wheat, oats, and barley. The first houses were often just dugouts covered with sod roofs; these were followed by more substantial dwellings built of logs and clay, whitewashed for appearance. Household furniture was scarce. "Who needed furniture?" Fanny (Pelenovsky) Brotman remembered many years later. "We were looking for something to eat. You can't eat furniture. . . . We put hay on the mud floor and we all slept on the floor."[56] Most of the scant "furniture" they had was of the crude, homemade variety.

Religious services, she recalled, were held regularly on the Sabbath and on the holy days, when Jewish farmers came to the settlement from miles around. "They would stay over two days on Rosh Hashanah, and they'd come the day before Yom Kippur. We didn't have enough beds, so they slept on the floor. And we would have to cook for everyone."[57] One of the colonists was specially trained in *shechita*, so it was possible to have local kosher chicken and meat. But they had a hard life and many drifted away.

Ekiel Bronfman was one of the early Wapella settlers. He arrived there with his wife Mindel and three children in the summer of 1891 and experienced the harsh conditions the colonists faced in those years of long dry summers and early frosts.[58] These disasters made a lasting impression on four-year-old Harry Bronfman, who later recalled that the family's wheat froze and that his father spent the winter of 1891–92 "going into the bush, cutting logs, loading them onto a sleigh and drawing them twenty miles" to sell for "money to buy a sack of flour, a few evaporated apples, dried prunes and probably some tea and sugar to bring back to his family. . . ."[59]

No other new settlements materialized during the 1880s, even though Galt publicly professed to take an interest in such projects, which for some years, according to his official biographer, "kept him in close touch with the Montagus, Rothschilds, and other leaders of the Jewish community in London."[60] Privately, Galt was deeply disappointed by the failure at Moosomin. "I regret to say my Jewish colony at Moosomin is a failure. The [settlers] have sold their cows – the cattle I gave them – and turned to their natural (!) avocation of peddling," he wrote in early 1888 to an official in Ottawa. Referring to the failed settlers as "vagabonds," he continued, with utter disregard for the facts, "The only comfort I have is that from the start I protested against the experiment as I never thought they would make farmers."[61]

When a more ambitious western settlement project was begun in 1892 by the Baron de Hirsch Institute – as the YMHBS had been renamed in 1891 – for a number of families who had petitioned for support, it met with greater success. Baron Maurice de Hirsch gave huge sums of money to various Jewish charities[62] to try to help solve by radical means some of the main problems facing the Jews of Eastern Europe. He believed that they must not only be removed from the

congestion, poverty, and hatreds of their environment, but must also be reha-
bilitated in such a way that these miserable conditions could never again
develop. One of the prime reasons, in his opinion, for the violent anti-Jewish
outbreaks in Eastern Europe was the fact that Jews were considered different
from others. They must, he thought, be made more like their neighbours, and
settled in large numbers as sons of the soil in new lands like Argentina and
Canada. Thus Jewish life must be reconstituted in a revolutionary manner.
While Theodor Herzl, the founder of the modern Zionist movement, insisted
upon a political solution to the "Jewish problem," the baron emphasized that
the social and economic structure of Jewish life in Eastern Europe had to be reformed from the bottom up. In this way his outlook was similar to that of the
Jewish radical socialists who insisted that a national home was not enough, but
that the very fabric of Jewish society had to be reconstructed in order to nor-
malize the Jewish people. This paradox of the multimillionaire entrepreneur as
radical was lost on the baron's generation, who saw his work as essentially philanthropy, though perhaps of a rather advanced kind.

The baron made use of YMHBS and, after 1891, the Baron de Hirsch Institute, to further his plan of settling Jews in the uninhabited lands of the Canadian north-west.[63] Yet the immediate impetus behind this very important
aspect of the society's work came from neither the baron, through the Jewish
Colonization Association (his agency for implementing his schemes to settle
Jews in the New World), nor the YMHBS, but from the colonists themselves.
The story of their initiative is instructive for its insights into the enthusiasm
shown by members of this small group for the radical reconstruction of their
lives. At a meeting of the society's advisory board, called the Baron Hirsch Fund
Committee,[64] in late March of 1891, "a letter was read, signed by fifty-one
Jewish families residing in Montreal who stated that they have been residing in
this city from one to five years and have been engaged in various occupations."
They asserted "that they have been unsuccessful in these occupations and
asked for assistance in order to go to the North West where they would be able
to farm."[65] While the YMHBS wrote to the Minister of Agriculture, John
Carling, a delegation was sent to Ottawa to interview him about the possibilities of another Jewish settlement in the west; meanwhile, interest was shown by
the New York committee of the Baron de Hirsch Fund.[66] The YMHBS wrote
to the baron "acquainting him of our circumstances and the negotiations in
progress for colonising our unfortunate coreligionists in the Canadian North
West."[67] In September 1891, the society established a separate Colonization
Committee whose chairman, Montreal merchant David Ansell, continued

contact with the Dominion government.[68] In Ottawa, Dominion Lands Branch officials – perhaps mindful of the Moosomin failure – reacted cautiously to these overtures.[69]

Although it was clear that nothing could be accomplished before spring, the YMHBS board was trying to prepare the ground. In November of 1891, community activists Harris Vineberg and David Friedman[70] were added to the Colonization Committee. They interviewed the prime minister on the subject of suitable lands, and came up with a proposal that the abandoned Moosomin colony land still held in trust for the Mansion House Committee by Galt be turned over to the YMHBS for this project.[71] Meanwhile the Montreal colonists informed the board that they intended to approach the Jewish Colonization Association (JCA) in Paris to request direct assistance from Baron de Hirsch,[72] and asked the board for "general support in their undertaking." Obviously annoyed with such independence, Ansell, Vineberg, and Friedman "strongly advised them to abandon this ill-advised scheme. It was fallacy to imagine that their attendance would have any weight and it was only wasting money to proceed on their journey."

But the colonists' delegates went to Paris anyway. In February 1892, Dr. Sonnenfeldt, director of the JCA, sent the institute (as it now was) a list of the settlers, asking whether it was prepared to establish and supervise the project if the JCA gave it financial support.[73] After some debate, the board agreed, provided they retained the right to select the colonists, since "they certainly could not accept the list as it stood," and the JCA agreed to the hiring of an expert to supervise and assist the settlers. An experienced and reliable person, a Mr. C. McDiarmid – formerly a farmer in Huntingdon County, Quebec – was sent to the north-west to survey a number of suggested sites.[74]

In March, news came from Paris that a grant of 100,000 francs[75] would be provided by the JCA and the Alliance Israélite Universelle.[76] A committee was appointed to select "not more than 40 men . . . to be ready at a moment's notice to proceed to land, the females and the children to be left behind till the weather was more favourable." McDiarmid accepted the appointment as resident supervisor of the colony and immediately began purchasing supplies. However, agreement on the best site had not yet been reached. Surveyors had examined a number of alternatives to the Moosomin tract, including a site close to Regina.[77] Ascher Pierce[78] advised a location near Oxbow, and McDiarmid was sent west to investigate; he agreed on Oxbow. By now it was April and the food supplies, horses, tools, and implements were being assembled.[79] The last snags in the remittance of the necessary money from

Paris were being cleared up, and the final selection of twenty-six families was made.[80] This group was to be joined by ten more families from Winnipeg and three from Regina. McDiarmid was dispatched west again on April 16 to prepare as much as possible for the colonists. A *shochet* was employed and a *sefer torah* was borrowed from the Sha'ar Hashomayim synagogue.[81] And all was in readiness for the tedious rail journey to Oxbow. On April 19, the settlers appeared before the board to sign the agreements, which were, the institute's minutes recorded, "translated into Hebrew and German [Yiddish] so that everyone should thoroughly understand its contents. . . . They were then addressed collectively and informed of the duties they would be expected to perform and exhorted to be industrious in their new station in life and to live peaceably with their neighbours and respect the rules and laws of the country which they had now adopted as their own."[82]

An eleventh-hour delay developed when McDiarmid telegraphed on Sunday, April 24, that he was investigating another parcel of land "a few miles beyond [west of] Oxbow."[83] This gave the board further opportunity to plan the colony and they determined that the colonists should "work first as a community and proceed as rapidly as possible with ploughing and seeding" and that no division of property should be made for several weeks after they arrived. Until then four work parties were to be formed, each under a local farmer selected and supervised by McDiarmid.

On Wednesday, McDiarmid wired that he had selected lands from the new tract he had been investigating in township 3, range 5 west of the second meridian in the District of Assiniboia, and that the colonists could now be sent. The board determined that the group should leave the following day.[84] The possibility of another delay arose when several colonists vehemently protested against having to leave on Thursday, which would mean having to travel on the Sabbath. However, "they had since consulted their Rabbi and were informed that in cases of necessity it was perfectly allowable." On Thursday, then, the men, some with their families, left by CPR from Windsor station. Some of their friends and the loved ones who would follow came to see them off, as did most of the board members of the institute.

Although they attempted to establish some independence,[85] the colonists of the new settlement – named Hirsch, aptly enough – required considerable material assistance and technical advice from the institute for several years. The brief comments in the minute books reflect the weariness of their back-breaking labour, their disappointment with poor crop yields in the early years, and their loneliness, without even the railway locomotive's whistle to break the silence of the prairie night. But these records also show that the institute shared the tangible problems and expended much of its strength and ingenuity to solve them. The Colonization Committee maintained regular correspondence with McDiarmid, who wrote often about the needs of the colonists, the stock in the general store,[86] the cost for necessary supplies, and the colonists themselves.[87]

The institute soon proposed establishing a school in the colony and approved the hiring of a midwife.[88] As early as August they were worrying about ensuring an adequate supply of coal, and in February about matzos for Passover.[89] (It was eventually decided that the matzos would be baked at Hirsch itself.)[90] So optimistic were its members that they even speculated on the possibility of establishing more settlements if the JCA was favourable.[91] They sent voluminous reports to the baron, often enclosing letters from the farmers themselves to impress him with the need for more funds.[92] In mid-July David Friedman and Moses Vineberg visited the colony to supervise the allocation of a quarter-section of land to each settler.[93] On their return they reported at length on the state of the settlement and on some of the significant problems beginning to surface there. A second group of colonists was getting organized during the summer of 1892,[94] but the society viewed many of them as "not proper people to be sent away as they were already earning a living in the City,"[95] reflecting an outlook that colonization was a form of philanthropy.

The Montreal group then sent a delegate named Lerner to Paris in August, to appeal directly to the JCA and the Alliance against the decision to refuse them support. It worked; two months later twenty-two families were sent out to join the colony,[96] only a few days after the JCA telegraphed its intention of sending another $16,500 to "complete the purchase of cattle, implements and food for the [new] colonists."[97] And in November the Alliance advised the board to send Lerner to the colony to join his colleagues. Though the board grumbled "that Lerner was a great agitator and . . . would be a disturbing element in the Colony," they complied. Some members believed that the Alliance and the JCA should take charge of the colony[98] and relieve them of its problems.

And problems abounded at Hirsch. McDiarmid was recalled to Montreal in late November of 1892 to answer numerous complaints from colonists. For failing to keep harmony in the colony, he was fired.[99] Realizing that the colony would require continued assistance at least until the next year's crop could be harvested, the board appealed to the baron, who replied that the JCA would send a further $12,000 to pay outstanding accounts and buy the necessary supplies, "but that under no circumstances would any further sum be given."[100]

Despite this warning and the profusion of problems, the board sustained its interest in the management of Hirsch. New managers were appointed and sent out west in February,[101] while William Baker, an employee of the institute, was also dispatched "to complete the Land Certificates, the Mortgage deeds in accordance with the terms of the Dominion Land Act, to adjust the accounts, to form the School Districts and perform such other duties as are immediately required for the welfare of the Colony and the Colonists."[102] Upon his return I. Roth, who had been sent to inspect the colony, informed the board of how it stood in general, of the needs and eccentricities of the farmers,[103] and of the administration of his predecessor, McDiarmid.

By the beginning of May 1893, the institute's executive considered that most of their work would soon be drawing to a close, and that the colony should, within the foreseeable future, be able to manage itself.[104] Each settler now had his own homestead of 160 acres, some draught animals, at least one cow, and a supply of tools. The colony provided some of the larger and costlier implements for common use. Most encouraging of all, the first harvest had been substantial, if not abundant.[105] The settlers had begun to develop their own community life and would soon enjoy a school and a synagogue of their own.[106] A post office was to be opened, and the CPR contemplated extending a branch line from Oxbow to Hirsch.

Even with these promising omens, Hirsch colonists needed further assistance, largely because of subsequent crop failures. Also, the JCA found it impossible to superintend the establishment of Jewish farmers in Canada from its offices in Paris and refused to provide for a paid official in Canada; consequently the institute's board members, though reluctant to continue this work, felt that, as the beneficiary of much of the baron's philanthropy, the board was morally bound to continue.

In mid-October of 1893, a robbery at the colony's store and a disturbing report from Ascher Pierce that "the Colonists were trying to sell their cattle and farming implements"[107] made it clear that the colony's future was uncertain. The institute was compelled to vest Pierce (perhaps the most valuable adviser to its colonization work) with the power to protect its property, especially the cattle and the store. The board knew that "the condition of the Colonists was very distressing"[108] and that, unless something was done, the whole project was in danger of disintegrating. It appealed to the baron for help. Meanwhile, on November 20, Lazarus Cohen set out to view the situation at Hirsch.[109] On his return in January, Cohen reported on what he had discovered concerning the deterioration of the colony. He had fired the manager and attempted to clear up the mystery of the store robbery, and had left Hirsch in the hands of the most reliable colonists he could find.[110] Cohen estimated that more than $15,000 was required to keep Hirsch going until spring. Another appeal for assistance was sent off to the baron, whose stolid silence to the last request, in October, was somewhat unnerving. While the board awaited his answer, further trouble in the colony was reported in February.[111] With still no answer from the baron by March, the board was desperate. Seed had to be bought soon. The colony still had no manager, and the board asked the local Hudson's Bay Company agent to recommend a suitable replacement.[112] Isaac Mendels was employed as temporary manager and set out for Hirsch, where he settled outstanding business accounts and attempted to reassure the distraught colonists. On his return to Montreal in September 1894, he set out a plan of temporary assistance for the colonists.[113]

These measures made little difference to the success of Hirsch. References at the institute's board meetings during 1894 and 1895 indicate that there was a good deal amiss in the colony: lands were being abandoned, crops were poor, and the settlers were experiencing considerable privation. The drama and challenge of establishing a colony in the west had disappeared, and the tedious and arduous task of keeping the project going remained. Nonetheless, the future of the colony still seemed promising, and the gradual recruitment of new colonists eager to try their luck as farmers brightened everyone's hopes. When several Jewish families farming near Red Deer[114] pleaded for help from the society, Mendels visited them and supervised their removal to Hirsch, where they took up some of the abandoned farms. The colony struggled on through the late 1890s, though it relied on continuing handouts from the JCA.

The Baron de Hirsch institute was never again called upon to establish settlements, although it did provide assistance and guidance to at least one other Jewish colony which sprang up, apparently spontaneously, near Wapella.[115] In 1900 the JCA's colonization work was taken out of the institute's hands and Isaac Mendels, now the paid manager of Hirsch, was given direct charge over all JCA settlement work in the Canadian west. Thereafter, the only connection of the institute with Hirsch was through its supervision of the school, and in 1903, even this last vestige was removed. The JCA set up its own Canadian committee in 1908, and three of its six members were from the institute. But this was a tenuous connection with colonization, and merely a shadow of the years when the institute had interested itself in some of the most minute details of life at Hirsch — as when the board had decided, in 1893, that "no new

Passover dishes be purchased but that lye be procured and the Colonists directed to clean their dishes therewith."[116]

Like other such projects, Jewish colonization in Canada was complicated, hazardous, and expensive. The Jewish experience was not much different from that of others who tried to make a living by farming on the Prairies, or anywhere else in Canada. As far back as the settlements of United Empire Loyalists in Upper Canada in the 1780s, and of Scottish crofters, British ex-soldiers, and Irish peasants in the nineteenth century, group settlement had proved to be initially costly and only moderately successful. On the Prairies, experiments in settling other ethnic groups – Hungarians, for example – in the 1880s and 1890s had met with mixed results, including significant rates of departure by original members.[117] In fact, "the record of the first Hungarians in the West closely resembles that of the pioneer Jewish homesteaders." Even the colonies of Icelanders, who were deemed to be excellent settlers, experienced high rates of failure.[118] Overall, statistics of homestead abandonment indicate that failure rates among western Canadian farmers were extremely high.[119] Jews were no more successful than others, and probably less so than Mennonites, Doukhobors, and Mormons, who brought substantial communal unity and farming experience with them.[120] From this perspective Hirsch has to be judged at least a limited success.

There were more Jewish farm colony experiments on the Prairies in subsequent years, some of them moderately successful and others of only fleeting duration. The lure of the open plains as a place for the rehabilitation of East European *luftmenschen* continued to interest many. But the JCA's Paris officials were less sanguine about Canada than about Argentina, where enormous sums of money were invested in the settlement of tens of thousands of Jews in colonies on the pampas.[121]

Canada's Jewish farm colonies were similar in some ways to those begun in the United States during the 1880s and 1890s, in that they were small and poorly organized. But there were differences between the American and Canadian experiments. The colonies in Oregon, Colorado, the Dakotas, Michigan, Louisiana, Arkansas, Virginia, and New Jersey were established as agricultural utopias by leaders who were "sublimely indifferent to the need for careful planning," and that they to some degree fit into the American tradition of such experiments, as well as representing a kind of forerunner to the Israeli kibbutz model that began to emerge after 1900.[122]

In the Canadian colonies, on the other hand, such utopian ideals appear to have been less prominent, and there were no charismatic individuals associated with their founding. The colonies were initiated by people who felt the call to farming to improve their material lives, and who appealed to philanthropies in Montreal and Paris for support. After the JCA became more involved in Canada in the early twentieth century, the differences between the major Canadian and American Jewish agricultural experiments became much sharper. Whereas, in the United States, virtually all efforts at Jewish colonization were abandoned (except in places like Woodbine, New Jersey, which was close to New York), in Canada the major farm colonies in the west were strengthened, and new ones were established. While utopianism in the United States had collapsed, pragmatism in Canada continued and steadily expanded until the 1930s – even into the 1950s. Thus, while colonization constitutes an interesting but brief paragraph in American Jewish history, it is a significant chapter in the history of Jewry in Canada. What is more, the Canadian Jewish farming experience was unique in the Anglo-Saxon countries. In South Africa, New Zealand, and Australia, no such organized experiments were undertaken, even though those three dominions possessed large tracts of unsettled land. Canada's history of Jewish colonization was similar to Argentina's, where, by the early 1900s, efforts were in full flower, while the most dynamic experiments in the regeneration of the Jewish people through agriculture were under way in Palestine.[123]

At the end of the 1890s, however, Jewish colonization attempts in Canada's west were, at best, a qualified success. It was becoming clear that Jewish immigration must be based on the expectation that Jews would migrate to urban centres, and that their prospects for success were therefore limited by the absorptive capacity of the Canadian economy. In a survey of economic conditions in 1907, a year of serious recession, the JCA's agricultural expert, Dr. Sonnenfeldt, concluded that Paris should "not plan on sending [to Canada], in the coming years, more than 10,000 people a year, until industry develops and provides work for more hands."[124]

So, for major Jewish organizations at least, Canada was not the new Eden where major colonization efforts would take root and a new agricultural Jew would be created. Such a destiny was reserved for Argentina, Palestine, and, later, Birobidzhan, in the Soviet Union. Large-scale colonization on the Prairies was impossible without massive support from the JCA, and even had this organization favoured Canada, it seems unlikely that Dominion officials could have been persuaded to change the extremely unfavourable opinion they had formed of Jewish farmers. What Dominion Lands officials interpreted as a failure at Hirsch "played a significant role in the evolution of Dominion

Lands Policy and its administration."[125] Officials blamed Jews for their own administrative bungling "and the complexities inherent in the legislation regarding colonization companies tended to be forgotten in the shuffling of papers related to the troublesome 'Jewish business' as it came to be known."[126]

That such a substantial part of Canadian Jewish assistance to co-religionist immigrants took the form of western colonization efforts underscores the fact that Canada (or Montreal, at least) believed it could not cope with the influx in any other way. Nevertheless, Canada was a place of opportunity and refuge for these immigrants – though a poor second to the United States, which took in over 80 per cent of those leaving Russia and similar proportions from Austro-Hungary and Romania. Canada's political economy was at a less advanced stage than the American one during these decades. The west still beckoned, as it had in the United States a generation earlier, and the unofficial national agenda was to conquer that territory. And if the move to populate the Prairies with Jewish families was less than successful, it resulted in substantial growth of the Jewish communities in the major cities. Montreal, Toronto, and Winnipeg registered remarkable changes as a result of the influx, not just in numbers but in the very character of their communal life. The East Europeans had arrived.

CHAPTER

8

Travails of Urbanization

Whatever pressures Canadian Jews had felt previously to assist destitute or sick immigrants paled to insignificance beside the urgency they experienced during the influx of the 1880s and 1890s. Like their sister communities in New York and Philadelphia, those of Montreal and Toronto were forced to appeal to West European and British Jewish organizations to stop sending more immigrants and help support those who had already arrived. While financial assistance came from agencies like the Mansion House Committee and the Jewish Colonization Association, it was never enough to meet local needs.

The new arrivals had other problems besides poverty. Until the 1880s, most Jewish immigrants to Canada came from Britain or Germany; they possessed, or quickly acquired, the necessary language and commercial skills for making a living and adapting to their new home. But the vast majority of Russian, Austro-Hungarian, and Romanian Jews who arrived in the 1880s and 1890s brought no such experience or facility. Their culture, and that of successive waves of migrants from those countries until the First World War, was partly formed by the political and social context of Eastern Europe and by the Yiddish language they employed in their everyday lives. Their political consciousness was shaped less by the pogroms of the early 1880s than by the intense intellectual fermentation that was forced throughout the Pale by those disasters.

We have seen from contemporary surveys of late-nineteenth-century social structure in the Pale that Jews, like other immigrants to North America, migrated mainly for economic reasons. Yet this is not to suggest that most

Jewish immigrants were necessarily impoverished. We have no way of knowing whether they were less well endowed economically on arrival than those who had preceded them. While some of the immigrants of the 1880s made heavy demands on the philanthropic societies in the major cities, it is unlikely that they were a majority. The records of the Young Men's Hebrew Benevolent Society (the Baron de Hirsch Institute after 1891) suggest that only a minority received help. Many others may have needed it but, given its limited resources, the "Baron de Hirsch" could not do much for them. Aside from informal networks of mutual assistance, Jews – like everyone else in Victorian Canada – were essentially on their own.

The sheer numbers of immigrants during the 1880s and 1890s overwhelmed Canadian Jewry. Although an older, larger, and institutionally better endowed community than Toronto's, Montreal Jewry was nevertheless severely strained by its staggering rate of growth during these years. While Montreal's total metropolitan population grew by some 55 per cent in the 1880s and by 25 per cent in the 1890s, during the 1880s the city's Jewish population rose from 811 to 2,473, and in the 1890s to a total of 6,941 – an average of nearly 300 per cent in each decade.[1]

The growth was accompanied by demographic change, as reflected in school enrolments, urban demographic patterns, and the location of synagogues. In the 1880s and 1890s immigrants were concentrated in an area between lower St. Lawrence Boulevard (and along nearby cross streets) and St. Catherine Street, while the older community had already begun to move west and north into the newer suburbs at the foot of Mount Royal. In 1882 the English, German, and Polish congregation moved from its building on St. Constant Street to a large new synagogue on McGill College Avenue, in the upper west end. Ten years later, Shearith Israel, located since 1839 on Chenneville Street, moved to an impressive edifice on Stanley Street. Meanwhile the Reform congregation, which had originated in 1882, also settled into a new structure on Stanley Street.

As the older community migrated, the newcomers filled – and overfilled – the spaces they had left. A new congregation of Russians, called B'nai Jacob (Sons of Jacob), occupied the vacated St. Constant Street synagogue, while newly arrived Romanians, who had organized themselves as the Beth David (House of David) congregation in 1886, acquired the synagogue on Chenneville. Other newcomers formed still more congregations, most of which worshipped in modest places like rented halls or lofts for years before they could acquire their own premises. There was Beth Yehuda (House of Judah), another group of Russians, organized in the 1890s; Chevra Kadisha, which was formed in 1893 and worshipped in a factory on lower St. Lawrence Boulevard; and Chevra T'hilim (Brotherhood of Psalms), a group of Russians and Lithuanians which started about 1903 in a rented flat on St. Charles Place.[2] Meanwhile, a small synagogue was erected in 1900 by the Jews living out in the industrial suburb of Lachine. Besides these, there were other *minyanim* which met for prayer in rented rooms or apartments, where they engaged in the eternal labour of separating the sacred from the profane.[3]

But it must not be assumed that the new arrivals were all, or even mostly, religious Jews who found their principal means of Jewish affiliation in a synagogue or house of prayer. Many other associations, some only transitory, were formed to encourage affiliation with friends and former neighbours from the old land, and to help lessen the hazards of sickness and death in their new surroundings. One such type of organization, known as a *landsmanshaft* (organization of fellow townsmen), arose to provide sick benefits, prepaid burials, temporary help to widows and orphans, and interest-free loans.[4]

Some of the immigrants took to peddling various goods around the city or out in the countryside – the same kind of penny capitalism that was pursued by many Jews who had arrived a generation earlier. In Montreal the Baron de Hirsch Institute provided small loans for some of these pedlars in the early 1880s but, for unexplained reasons, decided to discontinue the practice a few years later. Whether or not they were able to get municipal licences, however, pedlars proliferated. By 1905 Jewish pedlars were so numerous in Montreal that the *Canadian Grocer* complained that they had "established themselves seemingly irrevocably."[5] Other forms of small-scale commerce abounded: clothing, confectionery, fish and grocery stores, kosher bakeries and butcher shops. A few people were employed as religious slaughterers, teachers, or rabbis. These and other service workers, many of them self-employed, may have constituted as much as 30 per cent of the Jewish gainfully employed, the same level that obtained in Russia in the 1890s.[6]

The production of ready-made clothing was booming in the 1880s and 1890s. Protected by high tariffs since 1879, and stimulated by rising demand within the province of Quebec, and in the more distant hinterlands, the industry saw its output double in value in the 1870s and rise again in the 1880s. By 1900, clothing production was the province's second-largest industry.[7]

Many Jews gravitated towards employment or enterprise in the clothing industry. It was comparatively easy to do. Apparel of all kinds was produced in Montreal, the major centre of the industry in Canada since the 1850s,[8] and the demand for labour was constant. Jews became clothing workers in factories, where all of the production was carried out on the premises, or in home work-shops, where only parts of a suit or other garment were sewn up. By the 1880s a new class of clothing manufacturers had emerged in Montreal – including Harris Vineberg, Mark Workman, Harris Kellert, David Friedman, Solomon Levinson, and Lyon Cohen – all of whom needed labour for their factories. These men were breaking new ground in an industry that was already well established in the city, and was dominated by large and powerful non-Jewish firms.[9]

Noah Friedman and his son David started in the clothing manufacturing business in a small way in 1881, after spending some years running a store in Lancaster, Ontario. They were joined two years later by Noah's brother-in-law, Harris Kellert, also newly arrived from Lancaster.[10] The Friedman Company grew into an immense business which manufactured men's ready-to-wear that was sold across the Dominion. Harris Vineberg, once a pedlar in the Ottawa Valley, started manufacturing men's and boys' suits in 1882 as the "Progress Brand" company.[11] Abraham Jacobs, Solomon Levinson, and Jacob Cohen, after serving their business apprenticeships as pedlars and petty retailers around Lancaster, moved to Montreal during the 1870s and set up successfully as menswear manufacturers. Levinson established a retail clothing business in Montreal in 1874, and the small-scale production of clothing, made up by home labour in the countryside, to supply his own business.[12] Able to produce more goods than he could sell in his own store, Levinson established a whole-sale outlet in 1880. In 1894 he was joined by his son, and in 1900 by his brother, to form a clothing manufacturing firm which became one of the largest in Canada.[13] What attracted all these men to this particular industry was the fact that, as former traders and, in some cases, retailers, they had a good under-standing of what types of goods would sell, and of the outlets for selling them. Also, the industry required relatively little fixed capital. Sewing machines had been manufactured in Montreal, Toronto, and Guelph since the later 1850s, and were readily available at relatively low prices. The plentiful supply of female labour in the towns and villages around Montreal kept costs low.

The St. Lawrence valley, the Ottawa River lumber camps, the Eastern Town-ships, and the Maritime provinces served as a vast marketing frontier for Mon-treal clothing producers. Served by several railway systems that reached into these regions, and, after 1876, by the Intercolonial into the Maritime provinces, Montreal was also soon to become the terminus of the Canadian Pacific Railway, which would extend the city's market potential all the way to Vancouver, through the promising wheatlands of Manitoba and the Northwest Territories. Thus Montreal's Jewish clothing manufacturers were entering an industry that held great promise, in a city that spawned several new industries (cotton textiles, tobacco, railway rolling stock, and metal products) based on the prevailing expectations of great future growth. Many Jews were willing to work in this industry, at least temporarily, and to endure the low wage rates, seasonal unemployment, and sweatshop conditions which earned notoriety and public outrage during the Dominion royal commission investigations into labouring conditions in 1889, 1896, and 1898. Also, because Jewish communities included a large number of tailors, many Jews had worked in this industry in Eastern Europe. The lesson of how most of their Jewish employers had become manufacturers or contractors was not lost on the immigrants, and that role model was emulated time and again in subsequent years. Besides having the example of the Mosses and the Benjamins of an earlier generation, the immigrants were witnesses to outstanding Jewish success in this business.

There are few surviving records of the Jewish clothiers and workers in Montreal during the 1880s and 1890s. Decennial censuses provide indicators of aggregate growth, while the three royal commissions give some evidence of the increasing presence of Jews; they note that in Montreal and Toronto Jews were operating as contractors, and that conditions among them were especially poor. Testifying before the Royal Commission on the Relations of Labour and Capital in 1886, Montreal wholesale clothier James O'Brien stated that he gave out work to several Jewish contractors, some of whom employed up to thirty workers. A number of these Jewish contractors also testified, and indicated that many, if not all, of their employees in their home workshops were members of their own families.[14] While official reports indicate that children constituted only about 6 per cent of the workforce in Canadian clothing factories, their proportion of the labourers in contractors' shops was undoubtedly much higher.[15] Jewish activity in the clothing industry increased. By 1895, all but a few of two dozen major clothing contractors in the menswear sector were Jews who operated small shops employing up to twenty workers in the Lagauchetière–Lower St. Lawrence street area, then the heart of the city's Jewish quarter.[16]

The report of Alexander W. Wright, who led the Commission on the Sweating System in Canada in 1896, produced evidence that Jews acting as contractors for large clothiers were employing their own families, including many underage children who were often forced to work until late at night.[17] Two years later, Mackenzie King's report on the production of post-office uniforms revealed the same pattern of small-scale Jewish contractors operating family workshops in homes or lofts, with inadequate sanitation or ventilation. So pointed were the references to Jewish sweatshops in King's report and in a feature article he wrote for the Montreal *Herald* that the *Jewish Times* published a strong editorial attack on these conditions in Montreal.[18] Meanwhile, evidence presented by Quebec's inspectors of industrial establishments confirmed the existence of a serious problem.

Throughout the immigrant districts of Toronto and Montreal, King's investigation revealed a widespread system of oppressive working conditions which was as exploitative as it was unhealthy. Clothing shops were found to be unsanitary, crowded, poorly ventilated, and dangerous – and their workers very poorly paid. The shops operated on a piecework basis which encouraged long hours. While shops usually ran to a sixty-hour week, King found that one Toronto contractor worked his operatives thirteen hours a day, seven days a week.[19]

Wages varied considerably, depending on the specific job performed and the worker's skill. Wages of operators, basters, and pressers averaged between $9 and $12 per week, although in one shop King found an especially efficient presser earning $18 to $20 per week. However, young women in their early teens, who were essentially apprentices, earned only $3 to $5. In many shops, these girls were paid nothing while they learned the trade, and were often fired after they began demanding wages.[20] Piecework and subdivision of labour created conditions akin to an assembly line. In the production of a coat or jacket, for example, fifteen separate production processes were involved; these called for the work of a trimmer, pocket-maker, seamer, stitcher, lining-maker, joiner, sleeve-maker, under-baster, finisher, sleeve-lining feller, basting feller, button-seamer, hand presser, edge-presser, and seam-presser. King recognized that "all this division of labour tends to make men mere cog in wheel – if he had whole section [garment] he could exercize brain – if [only] one cog – can't do anything else, nerve wracking." He identified a serious problem, not only in the needle industry but in the modern industrial process – the separation of the worker from the end product of his or her labour.[21]

While King did not comment on the industry's seasonality, which resulted in layoffs for most workers during a considerable part of the year while manufacturers awaited the orders transmitted through commercial travellers from country retailers, this too was a major problem. Although some manufacturers kept small numbers of workers employed during the slack season, producing stock for inventory, many hundreds of pressers and operators were out of work during the winter months, when orders tended to be slow. Needleworkers and their families thus experienced serious privation. Conditions in the industry never really improved, and contributed, a generation later, to the poverty and misery that were rampant throughout the city's Jewish quarter during the winter of 1913, when a serious depression hit the city.[22]

All three royal commissions pointed out that only the merchant tailors, milliners, and dressmakers manufactured entirely on their own premises – though even some of them sometimes contracted out part of their output. The vast majority of those manufacturing large production runs of clothing – mainly cheaper grades of menswear – utilized outworkers through the medium of contractors. The clothier or manufacturer, who acted as a wholesaler, undertook to produce specific garments; he sold, either at his own factory or through travelling salesmen or at retail in his own store. The pieces of these garments were cut at his factory from whole cloth, with tailor's shears, bench-mounted knives, or the recently invented steam-powered machines that could slice through twenty thicknesses at once. He sought out contractors and, once an agreement on price and delivery date had been reached, the pieces were marked, matched, and bundled. Contractors took them to their workers, who operated either at their homes or in the contractor's shop, which was usually located in his home or in a loft somewhere in the city.

Because contractors had little or no capital requirement – not even rent for a shop or investment in sewing machines, if they could get their operators to work at home on their own machines – there were few barriers to entry into this business. Many Jews who had some knowledge of clothing production or marketing even became subcontractors, taking on part of the contractor's work. Manufacturers would therefore put the work out at low prices, realizing the likelihood that some contractor, hungry for employment, would have to accept his terms. The contractor, in turn, would offer his workers low piece rates determined by competition for work in the trade. Workers could accept or reject, but could improve the terms only with difficulty.

In this Hobbesian crushing system of undeclared economic war of "all against all," the wages were kept low and working conditions were at minimum levels.[23] Should workers complain, contractors, some of them known as "sweaters," could find other willing hands, in the city itself or in the surrounding countryside. Low wages and poor working conditions were "all the fault of the 'sweaters'," one contemporary observed, "as they are constantly undercutting the prices in order to get the work and the wholesalers are continually playing one lot against the other."[24] Married women workers – most of them employed at home, where they were confined by social custom and domestic responsibilities – were in such a weak bargaining position that they were open to severe exploitation by the contractors.[25] To the manufacturer and the contractor it did not matter who did the work, as long as it was done properly, on time, and at the lowest possible price. The system of contracting had worked more or less this way since the 1860s, some twenty years before significant numbers of Jews started to appear in the industry. Thus, Jews did not create a new system; they moved into an existing one that provided a door of economic opportunity.

Reports by provincial inspectors of factories on the existence of sweatshops in the Montreal clothing industry received full exposure in the *Jewish Times*. In February 1898, the *Times* revealed that

> in the tailors' workshops kept by Jews in private houses, the space is small, badly aired, and unprovided with special conveniences for women. . . . The workshops . . . are most defective. Located in old buildings, private houses, lanes, and back-yards, sometimes in basements, but oftener in garrets, they lack equally in air, light and cleanliness. Besides the hygienic question, the other abuses are excessive working hours and low wages. . . . Piece-work is responsible for many evils.[26]

The paper called upon the "Baron de Hirsch" to start a program of training Jewish immigrants in a variety of trades. "But a surer remedy," it continued,

> lies with the wholesale merchants themselves; for if, instead of becoming philanthropists for one day at the annual meeting of the Benevolent Society [the "Baron de Hirsch"], they would examine the condition of their work people and determine that the misery which these wretched people undergo should not be laid at their door, a different state of affairs would exist.

A year later, when the inspector issued another report condemning Jewish sweatshops, the *Times* again did not mince words:

> The conditions under which Jews are thus publicly reported as being in the habit of conducting their industries requires plain speaking. They should not be tolerated. Not only in physical matters, but morality, the character and reputation of the Jews of Montreal are at stake. Those who are in touch with the parties indicated should spare no effort in the endeavour to bring about a better state of affairs.[27]

Yet, despite these exposures and exhortations for reform, the evil continued unchecked.

While they were willing hands, and even included some skilled tailors earning relatively high wages in the manufacturers' own premises, or "inside shops," Jewish workers in Montreal and Toronto soon joined fellow clothing operatives to fight for better conditions. The first union among Jewish garment workers in Montreal, a branch of the United Garment Workers of America, was organized in 1892. There is no evidence of how long it survived, how many members it had, or who its leaders were. Like a sister organization established in Toronto around the same time, this union marks the beginning of Jewish participation in the struggle against employers, Jewish and non-Jewish alike. The unions attempted to exploit the fact that clothing was a seasonal item that had to be delivered on time. Retailers were reluctant to accept late deliveries, except perhaps at very large discounts, so work stoppages or strikes at the beginning of a season could seriously damage or completely ruin a manufacturer's sale, and weaken his credibility with retailers.

Unions provided an additional vehicle for economic and political self-expression among the immigrants, like the synagogues and *landsmanshaften*. They are also evidence of the growing divisiveness within the Jewish community of Montreal. Considering the origins, dates of arrival, and outlooks of these old and new groups, this was natural enough. Jews had never been politically, economically, socially, or culturally homogeneous, and many in the older and more established community had little in common with the immigrants. By the 1890s, charities such as the Baron de Hirsch Institute and the Ladies' Hebrew Benevolent Society were dominated by those who had arrived between the 1840s and the 1870s. The more established members of the Spanish and Portuguese community tended to participate less in running these and other charitable organizations, whose executive bodies now consisted mostly of members of the English, German, and Polish congregation. However, members of both congregations came together in many contexts, not the least important being the marriage canopy under which, for example, a Vineberg would marry a Hart. They also shared the Montefiore Club, a business and social association of well-to-do Jews who could not join the St. James, the Mount Royal, and other clubs to which Montreal's Anglophone elite belonged. They formed Montreal branches of the Anglo-Jewish Association, the Jewish Colonization Association, and, in 1899, the Federation of Zionist Societies of Canada, under the leadership of Clarence de Sola.[28]

Because of the scale of the relief and educational work carried out by the Baron de Hirsch Institute in Montreal, it was the city's most important Jewish charity organization. Part of the baron's $20,000 grant in 1890 was used to purchase a small building which became the real focus of much of the institute's activities. It provided temporary accommodations for immigrants. Some of them were newly arrived wives and children of men who had come to Canada a few years earlier. While attempts were made to reunite the families, the wives and children remained in the "home," the children attending school in the same building. Frequently a husband had died or disappeared completely, and the widowed or deserted woman was sent back to Europe or to friends elsewhere in Canada or the United States.

The "Baron de Hirsch," as the building and the organization were now known, was located near the Champs de Mars, in the heart of the district then inhabited largely by Jews. Various social and cultural organizations, including the Ladies' Hebrew Benevolent Society, the Hebrew Citizenship Association, the Palestine Colonization Society, the Ladies' Aid Society, the Sons of Benjamin, the Young Ladies' Work Society, and the Hebrew Benevolent Loan Society, began using the building regularly,[29] and it became a community centre. But its most valuable use was as a school. Established almost as soon as the building was acquired, the school had two significant features: provision of free education for the children of that rapidly growing segment of the community which could not afford even the nominal fees at the Protestant schools, and preparation of the many children who could not speak or understand English enough for entry into the Protestant schools. The school had both a charitable and educational function in the local Jewish constituency. It was staffed by W.H. Baker, who served as principal, and several teachers, one of whom taught Hebrew.

Despite the obvious need for such a school, which from the very beginning enrolled more than two hundred pupils, it suffered from weak financial support. What remained of the baron's grant was rapidly being used for immigrant relief and colonization. Fairly regular but meagre assistance came from the Alliance Israélite Universelle; money came from the baron or the JCA less frequently, and of course there was some from supporters in Montreal itself. Altogether, however, this was not enough to keep things going, and other sources of revenue were soon explored. Officers of the "Baron de Hirsch" soon came to demand a portion of the school taxes paid on property owned by Jews in the city of Montreal. This brought the society into direct conflict with the Spanish and Portuguese synagogue, in a contest which brought into focus the complex question of the legal position of Jews in the educational structure of the province of Quebec.

The Spanish and Portuguese had operated a day school for their own children under the direction of their minister, Reverend Meldola de Sola, son of Abraham de Sola. To finance it, the members of the congregation in 1886 exercised their right under the law to allocate their school taxes (levied on their real property) to the Roman Catholic board of school commissioners. This body, which educated only a very small number of Jewish pupils – Montreal's Jews overwhelmingly attended Protestant schools – agreed to turn back 80 per cent of these monies to the Spanish and Portuguese congregation, retaining 20 per cent simply for acting as broker. This arrangement considerably damaged the position of Jews in the Protestant school system, where the number of Jewish pupils was rapidly increasing. The Protestant board did not get much financial support from the immigrant parents, most of whom were by definition poor and most unlikely to own any real estate; it was the Spanish and Portuguese who possessed property. In the spring of 1889 the Protestant board attempted to have the legislature pass a bill which would interfere with this arrangement, but the congregation engaged prominent Montreal lawyer Frederic D. Monk, who succeeded in getting an exclusion clause for Jews inserted into the bill.[30] Out of a total of $2,800 paid in school taxes by Jews in the city in 1892, $2,200 was paid by members of that congregation.

The indignant "Baron de Hirsch" officers believed that, as the educator of many more pupils than attended the Spanish and Portuguese synagogue school, their institute should receive a portion of this Jewish tax money. Several meetings with the officers of the synagogue ended in failure. After one meeting in March of 1891, Maxwell Goldstein concluded that "the Jewish public of Montreal should be informed of the impasse at a mass meeting of the community."[31] Other members of the "Baron de Hirsch" advised moderation. Lewis A. Hart, who was also a member of the Spanish and Portuguese, believed that "the members of the Congregation were not a unit in regard to the School-tax question" and presumably tried to lobby fellow-congregants to relent, but to no avail.[32]

On May 19, the "Baron de Hirsch" appealed directly to the provincial government to intervene,[33] asserting that the reason why the Spanish and Portuguese had set up their own school was because they were unable "to have their minister [Meldola de Sola] appointed under salary as the Hebrew teacher in the Protestant Schools."[34] The Spanish and Portuguese argument that "nobody else has a right to complain" about their private deal with the Roman Catholic board was "against the whole tenor and spirit of the School Acts, which were framed for the education of the masses, and not for the benefit of any particular individual or Congregation." And while the Spanish and Portuguese school was supposedly open to all Jewish children in the city, regardless of ability to pay, it was in fact inaccessible to most because of its location. It was for this reason that David Ansell, head of the "Baron de Hirsch" school committee, rejected the offer from Gershom de Sola (brother of Meldola) to take 100 to 135 of their pupils into the congregation's school.[35] Ansell argued that "as a solution of the difficulty . . . the School Tax derived from the Jewish Real Estate proprietors of Montreal . . . should be distributed among all properly established schools in the city, in proportion to the number of Jewish children bona fide attending and taught at the said schools . . . ." He also reminded the government that the 250 Jewish pupils who attended Protestant schools were backed by only $600 in Jewish tax money. They warned that the Protestant schools "have threatened to close their doors to Jewish children, if the present state of affairs continues."[36]

The acting government leader, Louis-Olivier Taillon, and his Cabinet also heard from a deputation from the Spanish and Portuguese congregation several days later, but the matter remained unresolved. The provincial secretary, Louis Pelletier, wrote to Meldola de Sola warning that since "we feel that the distribution of the Jewish school taxes are [sic] not as equitable and fair as they should be . . . it will suffice to call the attention of the interested parties to those facts."[37] If the question was not fairly settled within a few months, Pelletier continued, "the Government will decide as to what course ought to be adopted."

Gershom de Sola, as president of the congregation's school committee, offered to pay the "Baron de Hirsch" school $500 annually "so long as present conditions exist [i.e. the arrangements with the Catholic board]."[38] Ansell rejected this offer as being "totally inadequate and disproportionate"[39] since, if the total amount of $1,750 received by the synagogue were divided between them on a per capita pupil basis, the "Baron de Hirsch" would be entitled to most of the sum. Ansell asked for $1,200 for the academic year 1892–93 and reminded de Sola that this was only an interim solution: "The principle of the equitable distribution of the School Tax remains still to be decided," he continued; "in this, others than the Baron de Hirsch Institute are interested, and my Committee cannot and would not do anything which would jeopardize the right of Jewish children to freely attend the Public Schools of this City. . . ."

Ansell then appealed directly to the provincial secretary, who wrote to Meldola de Sola, suggesting a settlement. De Sola's evasive answer was not satisfactory, and the congregation was warned that:

> In the event that an amicable arrangement is not reached soon, it will be necessary to study the question to determine whether the Protestant and Catholic school commissioners have the right to make the decision to

give part of the moneys they receive to schools which are neither Catholic nor Protestant.[40]

A few days later, de Sola offered $800 to settle an issue now so notorious that it was being freely discussed in local newspapers.[41] The institute's school committee again refused, offering instead to accept $1,000.[42] The congregation demurred and the impasse continued.

The "Baron de Hirsch" had the support of the overwhelming majority of Montreal's Jews. A petition which circulated asking for an amendment to the education legislation had the backing of every synagogue (with one obvious exception), fraternal society, and charitable organization in the community. This fact, as well as the intrinsic merits of the institute's case, had unquestionably impressed the Quebec government, which was now thoroughly annoyed with the intransigence of the Spanish and Portuguese congregation. By using its political influence through John Smyth Hall – MLA from Montreal's St-Antoine riding, and provincial treasurer – the Spanish and Portuguese were, however, able to alleviate much of the government's unfavourable attitude towards them. At the end of November, the office of the Provincial Secretary demanded that the congregation give the "Baron de Hirsch" school $800 for the current scholastic year[43] "for a fair and equitable distribution of the Tax."[44]

The congregation, attempted to attach a proviso to the "grant," that it was to constitute "a complete and final settlement" of the "Baron de Hirsch" claims,[45] and that this sum would be paid only as long as the agreement between them and the Catholic board was in force. But Meldola de Sola was cautioned on December 15, 1892 that "the Government cannot accept the conditions mentioned in the [congregation's] resolution."[46] The $800 was to be paid "for this year, reserving the settlement of the question, in a definite way, hereafter, for years to come." Ansell, certainly cognisant of the strong official tide running in favour of the "Baron de Hirsch" claims, wrote the congregation to the same effect.[47] Though the congregation protested that the government's action was arbitrary,[48] Pelletier replied that unless the Spanish and Portuguese accepted the decision "forewith [*sic*] and voluntarily . . . I regret to have to state to you that we will take energetic measures to force a settlement."

The congregation tried everything possible to stave off government legislation that would compel them statutorily to share on a per capita pupil basis. When Taillon visited Montreal in December of 1892, Meldola de Sola tried to convince him "that the matter should be looked into anew when he returned to Quebec."[49] A bill that was introduced in the Legislative Assembly in early

February to settle the issue once and for all was stalled, and the whole issue was in limbo during the spring and summer of 1893.

In September, the controversy began anew with the "Baron de Hirsch" school committee reiterating their complaints to the provincial treasurer.[50] The Protestant board's secretary, hoping to avert a repetition of the previous year's bitter wrangle, wrote to Meldola de Sola that he hoped "we are agreed that we will not have all the trouble over this matter that we had last year." The rabbi replied that, as far as "trouble" was concerned, "there will be none from any initiative of ours," and that he hoped "the arrangement may continue as last year."[51] Hall then suggested that, since the Spanish and Portuguese school committee had received $2,605.05 from the Catholic school commission in 1892, he presumed "that the amount [$800] will be increased this year on account of the increased valuation of the property."[52] Hall pleaded with him "to do differently with these people than was done last year." He pointed out that the "Baron de Hirsch" was "educating a much larger number of people than you are in your school," and suggested that the Spanish and Portuguese pay them $1,300, or about half of the receipts. The "Baron de Hirsch," he warned, "are quite determined, and they have quite a number of members supporting them, to bring in legislation, if necessary, to put the matter right." But Gershom de Sola refused "to contribute more [than $800]. . . . [This] could not be done without seriously injuring and crippling our school."[53] Hall was despondent.[54]

The "Baron de Hirsch" was clearly winning public opinion to its cause,[55] including *La Minerve*, a leading Montreal daily, which in December 1893 published a lengthy editorial in support of the "Baron de Hirsch":

> The . . . [institute] say to the former "Come and help us in the education of our children, in your own interest, if you wish your property to be respected later." "By what right," the former reply, "do you make such a demand? You do not frequent our synagogue; our congregation has a legal existence; according to the laws of this province we have a right to keep our money for the education of our children. What is it of yours that we have more money than you? We use it to pay our masters better. We make our pupils more comfortable, and build more luxurious schools. The law protects us; you have no right to say anything or to claim anything from us! This reasoning is in perfect accordance with the law but it sins against justice.[56]

Anxious to escape this quarrel, the Catholic school commission announced in April 1894 that it would stop payments to the Spanish and Portuguese until the matter was resolved,[57] and gave notice that, as of July 1, school taxes on property owned by Jews and paid to the Catholic school commission would be distributed "for the instruction of Jewish children in the manner the Board may think proper." The Spanish and Portuguese, now seeking a way out of the impasse, raised their offer to the "Baron de Hirsch" to $900. It was accepted,[58] and de Sola wrote the Catholic board worriedly in the hope that "as the Baron de Hirsch school's acceptance of our proposal disposes of the school dispute, we presume that the resolution to which you refer will now be withdrawn, and that matters will run on as they did before the late dispute arose."[59] The Catholic board replied that "your request cannot be granted."[60]

The Catholic board now pushed vigorously for a final resolution of this nagging problem. Early in September of 1894 they asked the Council of Education of Quebec whether it would be legal to appoint a joint commission of the Protestant and Catholic school commissions to administer the Jewish taxes in Montreal.[61] Since the "Baron de Hirsch" knew that the Catholic board favoured dividing the money on the per capita basis originally suggested by them, they were quick to endorse the proposal.

Faced with the resolve of both the government and the Catholic board, the Spanish and Portuguese congregation surrendered. In late 1894 they reassigned Jewish school taxes to the Protestant board of school commissioners, on the understanding that Meldola de Sola would be appointed as Hebrew teacher to these schools.[62] While the Protestants were placated, the claims of the "Baron de Hirsch" were still not settled. But the Protestant board recognized that the school was a very valuable support for their own system, and decided to subsidize it with an annual grant of $1,500, a sum which rendered the school independent of assistance from the baron or the Alliance by putting it on a more assured financial basis.

The dispute was now resolved but, despite the fact that "Baron de Hirsch" had won out in the interests of the Jewish community as a whole, there was a downside. The Protestant board were now more conscious of what they came to view as a growing "injustice" – having to educate a rapidly growing number of Jewish children without adequate compensation from school taxes on Jewish-owned property. Even though they received all Jewish school tax monies after the imposed settlement, these amounts were not enough to cover the costs of educating Jewish children. By 1899, when Jewish enrolment in the Protestant schools stood at 749 – having increased from 269 in 1890 – and when Jews constituted over 8 per cent of the total student body in Protestant schools, the board was deeply worried about the costs of accommodating them.[63] In an ominous public statement issued in mid-February of 1898, one board member indicated that the Protestants were near the end of their patience:

> It is all very well for people to talk about children of different creeds sitting together on the same bench, a very nice phrase, and I would like it if all could be educated together, but I suppose the [Jews] on the bench have no legal rights there, and they are pushing off those who have and who pay for the bench.[64]

Two years later, in an effort to force the issue to public attention – especially that of the Quebec government and the whole Montreal Jewish community – the board changed its regulations, to restrict entry into their schools to children of Jews who paid their school taxes to the Protestant board. Henceforth children of other Jews, who were not taxpayers, would be admitted only as a matter of grace.

Outraged and alarmed, the Jewish leaders prepared to fight what would turn out to be a long, bitter, internally divisive, and, ultimately, losing battle. It would arouse strong feelings in Francophone Montreal as well, particularly in the Roman Catholic hierarchy. At least one newspaper, the militantly ultramontane *La Croix de Montréal*, used this issue as a springboard for a "great outpouring of antisemitic writing," from late 1894 until the paper's demise in the spring of 1895.[65]

The work of the "Baron de Hirsch" school continued despite these clashes over finances. Not much is known of its curriculum. Strong attempts were made to ensure that the children learned English quickly, although this did not interfere with the teaching of what other children learned in the city's schools. Mr. Gordon and one assistant taught Hebrew subjects, although apparently not as intensively as some people in the community would have liked. Some parents preferred to send their children to special Jewish schools – attached to the new synagogues and the smaller congregations springing up in the Jewish district – or to private teachers. The "Baron de Hirsch" school attempted to inculcate a sense of pride in Canada as well as in Jewish traditions. In 1898 a cadet corps known as the Hirsch Cadets, affiliated with the Jewish Lads Brigade of England, was formed for the boys. They were equipped with uniforms and, with their wooden rifles shouldered, they were drilled up and down the nearby Champs de Mars by the redoubtable Mr. Baker, now transfigured as "Colonel" Baker.

The rising tide of Jewish immigrants during the late 1890s conditioned much of the "Baron de Hirsch" activity throughout this period. The number of people in the "home"; the cost of feeding, clothing, and housing them; their transference to other places; the amount, kinds, and costs of medical treatment in both outpatient clinics and hospitals; and even the number of burials in the newly acquired[66] cemetery all absorbed the energies of the society. By far the largest proportion of the immigrants during the 1880s and 1890s were from the Russian Empire, although precise figures are not known as no official statistics of immigrants' ethnic origin were kept before 1900.[67] Nor can it be accurately known how many immigrants petitioned the "Baron de Hirsch" for assistance in any one year, as only sporadic attempts were made to keep records.[68] Yet there are constant references in the minute books to immigrants arriving, to their being met at the ships, to lost baggage and searches for lost family members. Many needed at least temporary lodging, beside meals and clothing; some wanted to be sent to New York, Winnipeg, Toronto, Chicago, Cincinnati, Omaha – or back to Europe. Confusion and mistrust led to many unusual petitions: at least one individual wanted information on changing roubles into dollars.

Towards the end of the decade, Romanian Jews began to outnumber the Russians. In 1900 alone, 2,202 Romanians arrived in Montreal, most of them needing assistance.[69] They posed tremendous problems. Through July and August nearly 300 arrived each week. The society moved many of them to other places and enlisted the aid of committees in Toronto, Winnipeg, Hamilton, and London. Of these Romanians, 783 settled in and around Montreal, 599 were sent to the United States, and the rest were distributed to Winnipeg, Toronto, Sydney, London, and Hamilton.[70]

Most of the money to achieve all this came from abroad. The baron's original gift of $20,000 was supplemented many times by special grants for immigrant care, especially during 1900. The Alliance Israélite Universelle supported the school generously. The Baroness de Hirsch donated in excess of $20,000 for a new school building, and left the institute almost $89,000 when she died in 1899. By contrast, funds raised in Montreal were abysmally low. In 1900, when the JCA sent $12,000 to help support some 2,880 immigrants, $1,500 to help maintain the "home," and $10,000 towards the construction of a new building (and the Protestant school board donated $2,000 towards the school), the institute raised only about $1,100 from its members and supporters, along with a few special donations for matzos and coal.[71] The reasons for this startling discrepancy between local and outside contributions are not easily explained. Members of the executive, of course, and many others from the general membership, spent numerous hours each week attending meetings of the board of

directors and of the relief, colonization, burial, collection, or school committees. The institute physician attended the sick two days each week, and visited
indigent patients in their homes or in hospitals – and all he got was honour. Both
the notary and the solicitor spent much time on the growing amount of complicated and expensive legal work. Board members would often make trips at
their own expense, to Quebec City to discuss the school question with ministers, or to Ottawa to deal with problems pertaining to Hirsch and other settlements. When immigrants arrived, members of the executive were often there to
meet them; they laboured hard to find them lodging and jobs, offered them
advice, and sent them to their destinations elsewhere.

Nonetheless, the very fact that a rapidly increasing proportion of its funds
came from outside Montreal meant that the institute served essentially as an
agency of the baron and the of JCA. Even more important was the fact that the
contributions of the baron, for colonization, the handling of immigrants, and
the school, drew the institute into the role of administrating these funds. Direc-
tives from Paris accompanied most of the baron's grants, and those of the JCA,
and the institute was required to send them detailed financial reports. The colonization experiments at Hirsch and elsewhere on the Prairies highlight this
new "agency" status. The purposes of the institute were changing in order to
encompass new roles that suited the designs of the JCA. The Montrealers did
not reject the baron's and JCA's surveillance because this would probably have
resulted in the curtailment of the support. Montreal was at or near the end of a
migration chain that began far off in Russia and Romania. Jewish committees
in the border cities of Germany and Austria found it impossible to turn immigrants back; if they and the agents of the powerful JCA could not stem the tide,
the Montreal organization had even less of a voice in determining how many
refugees should come to Canada – and when.

The "Baron de Hirsch" had accomplished a great deal in the ten years from
1890 to 1900; a western colony had been painfully but successfully established, a school thrived, and the homeless and bewildered could find rest in
the "home." In addition to these tangible possessions, the institute now had
an unchallengeable prestige, thanks to its victory over the oldest and probably most prominent institution in the community, the Spanish and Portuguese synagogue, in the school tax question. The "Baron de Hirsch" served
as the self-appointed spokesman for the majority of the city's Jews, and after
the school tax issue was settled, and with the allegiance of dedicated and
aggressive leaders, it emerged as the physical and political fulcrum of the
community. In the last few years of the decade, the "Baron de Hirsch"

entered its "golden age," which saw the flowering of many of the services initiated in the 1890s.

In 1893 their Christian middle-class sisters in eastern cities and towns had established the National Council of Women of Canada – which had distinctly Christian overtones – to advance a number of important women's causes, and Jewish women followed suit in 1897. The National Council of Jewish Women was organized in Toronto and later spread to Montreal and other major cities, where members conducted a variety of programs dedicated to helping new immigrants with visitations and English classes. The council also ran summer camps for children and recreational activities for girls, and provided help for problem children.[72]

Public reaction to the increasing number of Jews in Montreal during the 1880s and 1890s seems to have been, with some exceptions, fairly benign. The major newspapers manifested no alarm or animosity. But Jules-Paul Tardivel's newspaper, *La Vérité*, began publishing antisemitic articles in the early 1880s, most of them drawn from militant ultramontane publications in France.[73] In 1886, Tardivel made favourable references to Edouard Drumont's diatribe *La France Juive*, as well as to other French antisemitic publications. In the early 1890s Tardivel wrote more antisemitic material himself "and ceased to rely exclusively on material reprinted from French newspapers to address the Jewish question."[74] In October of 1890 he urged his readers "to be on guard against the Jews, to prevent them from establishing themselves here. . . . The Jews are a curse, a curse from G-d."[75] *La Vérité* also provided a platform for other French Canadian antisemites, such as Zacharie Lacasse and Raoul Renault,[76] while Tardivel's antisemitism was echoed by Amédée Denault, who, in his newspaper *La Croix de Montréal*, published much material in this vein between 1893 and 1895, either borrowed from French antisemites or locally produced. Many of these antisemitic articles were published between November 1894 and March 1895, in the first stage of the infamous Dreyfus affair.[77]

The Dreyfus affair, which was the occasion for antisemites in France to mount a crescendo of virulent abuse against Jews,[78] generally found only faint echo in Quebec. The Montreal daily *La Patrie* approved the decision of the court martial that condemned Dreyfus for treason in 1894, and reported some of the antisemitic material from the French press during the related libel trial of Emile Zola in 1898, and a few independent French Canadian newspapers were pronouncedly anti-Dreyfusard and antisemitic throughout.[79]

In a lead editorial during the second Dreyfus trial in 1899, *La Presse* – the French daily with the largest circulation – on the other hand, proclaimed that "we are neither Dreyfusist, nor anti-Dreyfusist," and urged upon its readers " As we in this country follow English law in criminal matters, we do not accept, especially during a trial, that the accused should be considered guilty."[80] *La Presse* was headed by Jules Helbronner, an Alsatian Jew, who was one of Quebec's leading journalists, a staunch liberal and a champion of workers' rights. Widely known as a Jew, Helbronner — who never denied that fact — nevertheless enjoyed a lengthy career in the French press and wide respect among French Canadian liberal thinkers.[81]

The most avowedly antisemitic of the major Montreal newspapers in the late 1890s was not a French Canadian publication at all, but the daily serving the city's English-speaking Catholics, the *True Witness and Daily Chronicle*, which carried strongly partisan material during both trials. The lead editorial of December 11, 1897, proclaimed:

> Of course it is possible that Captain Dreyfus may have been condemned [for] a crime of which he is innocent. But it should be borne in mind that the highest authorities in the French Army, and all the members of the court martial by which he was tried, have declared their belief that he did commit the crime of selling important military secrets to the German War Office. The Chamber of Deputies has also by a very large majority affirmed its conviction that the charge was fully proved.[82]

This was, on the evidence to date, not an unreasonable position. But the *True Witness* then proceeded to wax eloquent on "the rise of antisemitic feeling on account of the undue prominence attained by Jews in the financial, political and journalistic world." From this point onwards, the paper was unabashedly in the camp of the French anti-Dreyfusards. In reply to a complaint in the *Jewish Times* against this antisemitic line, the *True Witness* replied that "nothing could have been further from our minds than to attempt 'to poison the minds of our readers' against the Jews. . . . Because a man is a Jew, it does not follow that he is incapable of committing a crime. . . ."[83] Following Zola's libel conviction in February of 1898, after he published a letter alleging conspiracy in the Dreyfus case, the *True Witness* editorialized that "No one who has read the letter . . . can have the least doubt as to his guilt. . . . Fancy France's honour being personified by the filthy novelist Zola."[84] Referring to other recent cases of treason in the French army and navy, the *True Witness* continued: "None of these cases excited more than passing interest, but . . . had these men been Jews, it *would* have been otherwise." To the credit of the newspaper's editors, they did backtrack considerably after dramatic developments indicated that Dreyfus might have been innocent all along. In late September of 1898 the newspaper referred to Dreyfus as "this unfortunate man" and to his public degradation and humiliation before the garrison of Paris followed by his "banishment to a lone and barren isle. . . ."[85]

The *Montreal Star*, on the other hand, strongly proclaimed Dreyfus' innocence throughout the second trial in September of 1899.[86] As for *La Minerve*, it demonstrated a somewhat patronizing, amused, and sometimes genuinely curious attitude towards the culture of these new arrivals. If it was occasionally mildly prejudiced, it printed little that could be described as outright antisemitism in its pages.[87]

It is difficult, therefore, to see much difference between the attitudes of the mainstream Anglophone and Francophone Montreal press towards the Jewish community in the 1880s and 1890s. A certain ethnic stereotyping was characteristic of the time – Italians seemed to be on the receiving end of much of it – but, in Montreal at least, it was seldom vicious; nor was it in any way comparable to the virulent anti-Asiatic campaigns that were then under way in British Columbia.[88] This is not to say that nasty, even rabid, printed antisemitism did not exist, as witness the fringe newspapers *La Vérité* and *La Libre Parole* (*Illustrée*), which propagated some poisonous anti-Jewish libels. Some of the most vile forms of Jew-hatred would surface in certain French Canadian clerical circles during hearings of the Plamondon case in Quebec City in 1912. The few anti-Jewish fulminations of the enigmatic nationalist Henri Bourassa in 1906 were also in the future, though his attitudes may have reflected what he had been taught in his youth. While overt antisemitism was present in Montreal, it was at this point no more a feature of the Francophone community than of the Anglophone one.

Still the Dreyfus case and its impact on public opinion had had a marked effect on segments of Montreal Jewry. Increasingly concerned about the growing antisemitism in Europe, a number of Jews, headed by Lyon Cohen and Sam Jacobs, a prominent lawyer and influential figure in the Liberal Party, had decided it was necessary to found a weekly newspaper, the *Jewish Times*, for "the advocacy as well as the defence of Jewish rights as free citizens of a free country." In an editorial in its first issue, in December 1897, the *Times* declared that the conviction of Dreyfus was a "dark constitutional crime . . . an antisemitic plot which showed the weakness of the French judicial system and the inability of the French government to protect its citizens"[89]:

> The Dreyfus trial should not cause our people to lose courage or give up the fight against our modern inquisition. The darkest hour is before the

dawn and who can say that the end will not be a repetition of the story of Haman and Mordechai, and that France, the modern Persia, which has hitherto tolerated our people in its midst, may come to see that the Jew can combine within himself the qualities of attachment to his ideals with devotion to the land that sustains him.

Well into the following year, the *Jewish Times* was publishing numerous reports on the case, stressing Dreyfus' innocence and opposing the antisemitism that the case had aroused in Canada. Lyon Cohen, Sam Jacobs, and the other owners were deeply concerned about the image of Jews in Christian eyes.

Throughout its seventeen-year existence and changing ownership, the *Jewish Times* remained the newspaper of the Montreal Anglo-Jewish community, which was centred mainly in the upper-middle-class, West End suburbs. The paper also circulated extensively in Ontario, in the Maritimes, and, to a lesser extent, on the Prairies. Editorials tended to emphasize the need for Jews to show that their religion was equal to that of their Christian neighbours, and the fact that Jews were unquestionably true and loyal citizens, devoted to Canada and the British Empire. Non-Jews must not generalize from Dreyfus' alleged disloyalty to France – as did Maurice Barrès, a founder of the Paris-based magazine *l'Action Française*, who formulated the memorable antisemitic phrase "That Dreyfus is capable of treason, I deduce from his race."[90]

After the outbreak of the Boer War in 1899, Jews were urged to support the Empire, while the exploits of Jewish volunteers such as Captain Hyman Lightstone in the Canadian Contingent, and Dr. J. Alton Harris, who joined the British Army, received considerable coverage – as did the award of the Victoria Cross to an English Jew.[91] Jewish military achievements past and present were glorified; Jewish participation in the American naval and military forces during the Spanish-American War was also highlighted. (Revenge, at last, for the Inquisition!) The *Times* told its readers, for example, that eleven Jewish sailors had been killed when the *Maine* blew up in Havana harbour. In an era when military achievements were generally glorified, the *Times* wanted everyone – especially Christians – to know that Jewish boys could also fight and die for their country. Such valiant warrior Jews, the paper opined, were a great boost to Jewish history and pride.[92]

In August of 1900 the paper reported that, on a visit to Winnipeg, Rabbi Ashinsky of Sha'ar Hashomayim – Cohen and Jacobs' own synagogue – had delivered a rousing speech at the Rosh Pina synagogue extolling British supremacy. Because British institutions were based on justice and equality, he predicted that Anglo-Saxons would eventually rule the world. Jews, the rabbi urged, should pray for the Queen twice a week, because "it would be through the British that the Jews would ultimately be returned in full possession of their Holy Land."[93]

Cohen and Jacobs' purpose in establishing the *Jewish Times*, then, was not just to report but also to guide and educate non-Jew and Jew alike in what they regarded as the realities of Jewish life in Canada. And this included instruction to Jews about correct behaviour (conveyed in the regular column "As Others See Us"), the lack of which, they warned, helped to explain why Jews were not readily admitted to polite society.[94] Jews who sought admission to fancy resort hotels, they cautioned, were trying to barge into that society without learning the proper manners: "These are the sort of people who have brought discredit on Jews as a whole and, until they learn better manners, we will all have to suffer for their sins."[95] Other editorials showed concern about the effect on the Jews' image of the development of a specific Jewish quarter: "those of our community who have the good of our people at heart should do all in their power to prevent the formation of a Ghetto in this city" by inducing Jews to spread out.[96]

This emphasis on what the owners hoped would become the acceptability and equality of Jews, and coverage of the social activities of those living in the West End, left the *Times* little room for report or comment on what was taking place down in Montreal's inner-city quarter, where the majority of the city's Jews lived and worked. The political, cultural, religious, and benevolent life of downtown Jewry was therefore seldom seriously discussed. Instead, the "Baron de Hirsch," the Ladies' Hebrew Benevolent Society, the Young Ladies' Sewing Circle, and other West End charities received major coverage. The occasional mention of the concerns of the downtown Jews was almost always couched in condescending terms which emphasized their poverty and the need for better-off Jews to be more generous in rendering them assistance.[97]

What was also absent from the columns of the *Jewish Times* was any significant attempt to inform, analyse, or comment on the social and economic changes then underway in the Province of Quebec, which was being transformed by massive industrialization and urbanization. Nor were the far-reaching changes being experienced by many of Quebec's leading young intellectuals who were creating a dynamic and powerful ideology of French Canadian nationalism objectively evaluated, although its antisemitic aspects were sometimes featured. Apparently, neither the *Times* owners, nor its editor until 1909, Carol Ryan, thought that these matters were of much importance to their readers. On the other hand, the major French and English newspapers of Montreal published numerous well-grounded, objective, and detailed accounts of many major events taking place in the Jewish community of Montreal.

The *Jewish Times* openly supported Zionism as a solution to the "Jewish problem," and in particular the territorial Zionism of Theodor Herzl. A homeland for the Jews, not necessarily in the Land of Israel, must be created in order to relieve the oppressive conditions of the Jews in Eastern Europe. With the outbreak of new pogroms in Kishinev in 1902, Herzl began favouring a proposal to establish a temporary refuge in British Uganda. When this idea came before the Sixth Zionist Congress in August 1903, the Russian Jews rejected it by a dramatic refusal to attend the Congress sessions.[98] *Jewish Times* editorials supported the Uganda proposal and the subsequent formation of the Territorialist Organization, which favoured establishing a Jewish homeland anywhere, not necessarily in Palestine, and continued quixotically to support the Uganda project even after it was finally rejected. Such attitudes were perhaps not surprising; the problems created by the flood of Jewish immigration might be obviated altogether if Jews could readily find refuge elsewhere. Zionism, which served both broadly philanthropic and more immediate communal purposes, attracted substantial support from the Montreal Jewish elite.

By 1900, Montreal's Jewish community had not only grown but also changed considerably in character. With its sizeable numbers of Romanians and Russians, it was certainly more diverse, and there was a more decidedly East European flavour present. There existed a distinct class structure as well, tending to sharpen differences among the city's Jews; workers in contract or tailoring shops and clothing factories, machinists in the CPR or Grand Trunk yards, tradesmen, pedlars, and small storekeepers had different economic agendas than the owners of substantial real estate, clothing manufacturers and contractors, and owners of large businesses. They employed different strategies for achieving economic security.

Measures of achievement are elusive; growth in numbers, wealth, associations, and synagogues are only a few kinds of achievement. But in comparison with the city's Irish Roman Catholics, by 1890 a more numerous community, Montreal's Jews registered but modest accomplishments. Besides some five churches and parishes, the Irish Roman Catholics supported an orphanage and a college, and boasted several building societies, several newspapers, and strong influence in a local savings bank. Many of the city's Irishmen had achieved success not only in commerce and industry but also in journalism, the judiciary, and public service. They had ensured their countrymen a share of jobs in the police force and fire department, and regularly sent representatives to the House of Commons, the provincial legislature, and the Montreal city council. As the new century opened, the Irish had "arrived," to the extent that they were no longer "Irish Canadian."[99] They had developed their own separate institutions within the Montreal context of French Catholics and English Protestants by successfully establishing a communal uniqueness of being both English-speaking and Catholic.

In contrast, Montreal's Jews had minor achievements to register. While some were successful in business, and the older sub-communities had built impressive synagogues, most communal institutions, particularly those devoted to education, were weak and underfunded. Jewish charity had to draw enormous financial support from Paris and London to keep from collapsing altogether, there being so little forthcoming from the city's Jews themselves.

Toronto and Hamilton were much newer communities. Off in the west, Victoria's had already peaked in size. And although the London, Saint John, and Halifax communities were by the 1880s numerous enough to establish *minyanim*, the synagogues would come later.[100] These centres experienced slower rates of growth than Montreal's 280 per cent increase during the 1890s. Toronto's Jewish population, for example, grew by slightly more than 100 per cent during the same decade, Hamilton's by 50 per cent, and Winnipeg's by about 90 per cent. Ottawa's Jewish population, on the other hand, rose by 800 per cent during the nineties, both Windsor's and Saint John's by over 900 per cent, and Quebec City's by 600 per cent.[101] Perhaps even more significant is the fact that by 1900 all of these communities had reached sufficient size to establish various institutions. All of them, as well as Halifax, London, and Vancouver, now possessed synagogues – most of them rather modest structures, but nevertheless major bridgeheads to communal strength, and symbols of collective commitment to the values and traditions of the Jewish faith.

Off in Winnipeg, the tiny Jewish community, numbering only a few families in 1881, had grown to 645 persons by 1891 and to 1,156 a decade later. The Shaarey Zedek (Gates of Righteousness) congregation was formed in 1880 and the Rosh Pina (Head of the Corner) followed in 1890.[102] Many Jews took to peddling in order to make a living, and because this challenged the interests of the city's established merchants, pedlars' licence fees were suddenly raised in March 1891, to reduce the competition. This imposition was accompanied by a rise of antisemitism in local newspapers. Winnipeg Jews entered municipal politics by putting forward Lewis Wertheim as candidate for alderman "largely as a defense mechanism to ward off [the] aggression and hostility" that had arisen in the city, "and to achieve acceptance and equality."[103]

Although the Toronto Jewish community began much later than Montreal's and had only half its population in 1900, the social and economic patterns were very similar. Instead of two older synagogues, Toronto possessed only one, Holy Blossom, which had begun in the 1850s and had been housed since 1875 in a modest new building on Richmond Street. But the immigrants of the 1880s and 1890s, like those who came to Montreal, were not grafted into the existing community. Here, too, considerable differences between the forerunners and the later arrivals were in evidence. Indeed, in Toronto they were in some ways even greater, because by 1898, when Holy Blossom's magnificent new edifice on Bond Street was opened, the congregation had adopted elements of Reform, including services largely in English, mixed seating, organ music, a choir, and more permissive rabbis.[104] In Montreal, on the other hand, both major synagogues were decidedly Orthodox, and the Reform group was very small.[105] Yet these significant distinctions in liturgy and ritual observance were of less importance in dividing Toronto's older and newer sub-communities than the social and cultural barriers between them. Sigmund Samuel, the son of a well-to-do hardware merchant who had been the "moving spirit" in building the Richmond Street synagogue, records that, while he received his secular education at Upper Canada College and the Toronto Model School, his formal Jewish education was limited to after-school tutoring for his bar mitzvah.[106] Although he experienced some anti-Jewish discrimination, Samuel became very wealthy and circulated among Toronto's best circles. Other Toronto Jews – the Nordheimers are a case in point – were so assimilated that they were regarded as Gentiles.[107]

The increasing numbers of Canada's Jewish population, which rose from 2,443 to 16,401 between 1881 and 1901,[108] greatly affected the community in several ways. Jews carried with them important intellectual baggage that reflected changes in both the world Jewish context, of which Canada was then a minor part, and the North American environment, in which Jews were only one of the newly transplanted groups of immigrants. Russian Jewry was experiencing the tensions between two post-liberal ideologies that had emerged from the failure of the Haskalah to solve the "Jewish problem." Jewish socialism was one major ideological frame of reference embracing many variations that stressed a form of Jewish national self-realization within the socialist philosophy.[109] The Jewish *Bund*, the most popular expression of this outlook in Russia and Poland, strove for the realization of Jewish national autonomy within a socialist state. Zionism, on the other hand, was a nationalistic movement stressing a Jewish political and cultural revival in the land of Israel, a strategy of exodus that was based upon rejection of Europe. The success of Zionism in Canada, and the Federation of Zionist Societies in Canada, suggests that there were many who were eager to support the Zionist cause. Indeed, some Montreal Jews took Zionism seriously enough to attempt to settle in Palestine in the early 1890s – a degree of commitment rare among Canadian Jews, most of whom were content to lend their support from a distance. The rise of socialist thought among the broad mass of Canadian Jews of this era is evidenced by the formation of cloakworkers' and other unions in the garment trades after 1900. Among the settlers on the Prairies there were likely some adherents of the Am Olam and other utopianist movements – early forerunners, perhaps, of both these radical and collectivist ideologies.[110]

These were Jewish solutions to the "Jewish problem" in Russia. But of what relevance was either of them – autonomism or nationalism – to the situation of Jews in Canada, where the prevailing political culture was essentially British? Clearly there was no "Jewish problem" in Canada as there was in Russia, where there was an increasingly severe crisis in practically all levels of Jewish life. But there were problems affecting Jews in Canada, some of them unique to Jews, just as there were problems affecting other immigrant groups – or, in some respects, the population in general – having to do with the transplantation of people from one social, economic, and political context to another.

Canada's Jews were beginning to be confronted by many features of this country's special and subtle national personality – its French–English duality, and the "sense of mission" among many of its Anglophone intellectuals – an outlook matched by the emergence in French Canada of a national ideology combining ultramontanism, messianism, and anti-statism.[111] At the same time, many Canadian Jews understood that, while part of "Amerika," Canada was in many important ways a different society. This was not as secular, as democratic, as nationalistic, as liberal a nation – at least theoretically – as the real "Amerika," the United States, even though Canada held out to them the same promise of freedom from persecution, and of a better material life for them and their children. It must have seemed a paradox to the Jews settling in Canada that they had arrived in a country where a major province like Quebec, should be reminiscent of Eastern Europe – with its masses of poor peasants, its extensive system of Roman Catholic religious institutions, and a ubiquitous state-recognized clergy. Was there a shock of recognition, however transitory?

PART IV
THE EAST
EUROPEAN ERA
1900–1920

CHAPTER

9

Transformations in the Era of Laurier and Borden

Jewish immigration rose during the first two decades of the twentieth century to levels which have never since been equalled, while total immigration to Canada increased dramatically during the same years. Between 1901 and 1911, net Jewish immigration amounted to 56,055, while another 42,029 Jews arrived in the following decade.[1] These figures are based on annual arrivals via Canadian ocean ports and American entry points, minus emigration, principally to the United States. There was clearly a substantial movement of Jewish population to and from the United States. However, Canada gained more Jewish population than it lost from these cross-border transfers. From 1901 to 1911, 22,266 Jews entered Canada from the United States, while only 12,121 left for the United States. During the next decade the figures were 43,758 and 31,931, a much closer ratio, due mainly to substantially larger migration from Canada to the United States between 1915 and 1917, possibly because of the war. It is worth noting that the years of the greatest Jewish immigration to Canada – 1904 to 1908 and 1912 to 1914 – coincided fairly closely with the peaks in aggregate immigration.[2]

Most of the Jewish immigrants concentrated in the metropolitan centres. Between 1901 and 1911 Montreal's Jewish population grew by more than 400 per cent, while Toronto's increased by nearly 600 per cent,[3] although the growth rates between 1911 and 1921 were a much more modest 60 and 70 per cent respectively. The secondary Jewish centres of Ottawa and Hamilton also grew dramatically during these decades, by about 400 per cent from 1901 to

1911 and 70 and 50 per cent respectively during the next decade.

The most noteworthy growth between 1901 and 1911 occurred in the west. Winnipeg's Jewish community experienced a staggering 800 per cent increase and Vancouver's grew by nearly 500 per cent. Calgary's Jewish population rose from one to 604, while Edmonton's, Regina's, and Saskatoon's rose from zero to 171, 130, and 77 respectively. Fort William increased from 13 to 267, Port Arthur from 3 to 76, and Brandon from 73 to 271.[4] As well, tiny communities emerged in many smaller western towns which had previously had no Jewish inhabitants: Selkirk, Portage la Prairie, Dauphin, and Winkler in Manitoba; Melville, Yorkton, Moose Jaw, Canora, Lipton, and Estevan in Saskatchewan; and Lethbridge in Alberta. During the 1910s tiny Jewish populations emerged in dozens of other prairie towns and villages. By about 1921 the numbers in most of these places had stabilized, while many declined sharply during the 1920s.[5]

This growth in the Canadian Jewish population outside metropolitan centres and secondary cities was also occurring in central Canada, especially in south-western and northern Ontario. London's Jewry grew from 206 to 571 to 703 from 1901 to 1911 to 1921, Kitchener's from 10 to 226 to 298, and St. Catharines from 30 to 109 to 225, while figures for St. Thomas, Owen Sound, Peterborough, Brantford, Guelph, Chatham, and Sarnia rose markedly. In "New Ontario," Sudbury and Sault Ste. Marie grew, while Cobalt, Cochrane, Englehart, Timmins, and North Bay developed sizeable Jewish populations.

Jewish concentrations in the Maritime provinces also increased. Saint John and Halifax more than doubled their Jewish populations from 1901 to 1911, while new communities sprang up in Glace Bay, Yarmouth, Moncton, Fredericton, and, over the next decade, in New Waterford.[6]

These statistics reveal that the Jewish population of Canada was spreading out to smaller urban places in response to expanding economic opportunity. This was reflected in changing regional distribution: By 1911 roughly 21 per cent of the Canadian Jewish population lived west of the Ontario–Manitoba border, an increase of 4 per cent over the previous decade.[7] On the other hand, in 1901 some 5 per cent of the country's Jews lived in the Maritimes; this decreased to a little over 3 per cent in 1911 and to 2.7 per cent in 1921. Ontario's percentage of the Canadian Jewish population rose from 32 in 1901 to 35 in 1911, and increased again to nearly 38 per cent by 1921, while Quebec's percentages dropped steadily from 45 to about 35 between 1901 and 1921. These trends reflected the national population distribution, as the prairie economy expanded enormously during these decades, while that of the Maritime provinces experienced general stagnation and decline relative to the national economy.

The importance of this distribution into smaller places across Canada lies not so much in the numbers involved. They were, after all, not of sufficient magnitude to constitute a significant demographic shift away from communities in metropolitan centres, which, as noted above, continued to grow at very high rates. The point about Jewish communities in Glace Bay, Brantford, and Moose Jaw, to take regional examples, is that they represent another dimension of the Canadian Jewish experience. Jewish life in these places differed in important ways from life in Montreal, Toronto, and Winnipeg, where Jews constituted a critical mass – a substantial minority in neighbourhoods, schools, and workplaces. Small-town Jews had little such compactness. There were too few of them to form a distinctive neighbourhood, and because they were almost entirely small-scale businessmen like storekeepers, pedlars, or junk collectors, they had to deal daily with non-Jews. They lived among non-Jews, and their children were often the only non-Christians in the public schools they attended. It might be said, therefore, that they lived on a kind of cultural frontier between the Jewish and non-Jewish worlds; they were more directly exposed, on the one hand, to those influences which drew them away from their identity as Jews, and on the other, to the need to understand, assert, explain, and defend that identity on almost a daily basis.

The small-town Jew – for the most part – did not enjoy the luxuries of *landsmanshaften*, political clubs, and various forms of cultural expression that were readily available in large Jewish centres. His major forms of Jewish association were decided for him: the local synagogue, the B'nai B'rith lodge, and, for the women, Hadassah and the synagogue Ladies' Auxiliary. For the youth, after 1917, there was usually a branch of Young Judaea. There were, of course, minor variations, but this was the essential organizational structure of small-town Jewish life by the early 1920s. Most Jewish cultural life came filtered through the organizations within that structure, as well as in Yiddish newspapers and magazines from New York, Toronto, and Montreal, or from an occasional speaker, frequently a Zionist fund-raiser. Small-town Jews huddled close to each other for mutual support: here, nothing could be taken for granted.

The first communal obligation, usually undertaken by those Jews intending to settle permanently in the town, was to purchase land for a cemetery, like Abraham after arriving in Hebron. The biggest task in each of these communities, however, was the establishment of a synagogue, and this usually took years to accomplish. Initially meeting for prayers in someone's home, the community would later meet in a room above a downtown store, then move to a converted house, and, much later, to a commodious, modern structure designed by an architect (whose plans might be amended several times after heated disputation among local "experts"). For the most part, these immigrants were people of modest means, who had little to spare and knew that the Lord's worship required no grand edifices. Plain and simple structures, stark by modern standards, these little *shuls* in Glace Bay, Brantford, Yorkton, and Edenbridge were adorned only by stars of David in a few windows and an embroidered curtain in front of the Ark containing Torah scrolls. Occasionally, biblical symbols of lions, menorahs, and eagles would be painted, and one wall of Windsor's Tifereth Israel was graced by a passage from *Pirke Avoth* (Sayings of the Fathers): "Be bold as a leopard, light as an eagle, fleet as a hart, and strong as a lion, to do the will of thy Father who is in heaven."[8]

For the Jews of Glace Bay, Brantford, and Medicine Hat – and the many towns and cities in between – the synagogue became the centre of their Jewish lives. They drew up constitutions for their governance. "All men of Jewish faith can become a member of this Corperation [*sic*] by making application and paying three dollar fees," the 1902 constitution of Kingston's Independent Hebrew Congregation solemnly declared, but continued: "any person marrying contrary to the law of Judaism shall be excluded from the rights and privileges of this Corperation."[9] Here English, Galician, Lithuanian, Polish, Ukrainian, and Russian Jews – and perhaps, later, a few Germans and a sprinkling of Czechs and Hungarians – came together uneasily, but of necessity, to assemble and pray in awkward unison.

All of the town's Jews, religious and non-religious, *yeshiva* graduates and those with lesser learning, Zionists and Bundists – even the town Communist – gathered on the High Holy Days, and faced east towards Jerusalem to sing the Lord's praises and utter ancient pleas for redemption. With their mixture of national origins, cultural backgrounds, economic levels, and political affiliations, small-town communities emerged as special places where their tiny numbers forced Jews into a unity, sometimes discordant, and an unnatural cohesion which made the establishment of national organizations like the Federation of Zionist Societies of Canada easier than it might have been otherwise. For many years the Federation (later the Zionist Organization of Canada) along with the Hadassah and Young Judaea organizations, provided these little communities, which had few institutional supports, with vital linkages to the metropolitan centres and programmes for Jewish identification.

The economic structure of small-town Jewry, unlike that existing in metropolitan centres, was from the beginning overwhelmingly commercial. Here there was no Jewish working class like that beginning to emerge in the cities;

the majority engaged in storekeeping, usually in men's or women's clothing, furniture, or shoes. Others might operate a grocery wholesale, a theatre, a flour mill, a candy store, or a dry cleaning shop.[10] Many of these people began as pedlars selling merchandise from small carts or buggies from farm to farm in rural areas, or along the streets in towns and villages, securing the merchandise on credit from a Toronto, Montreal, or Winnipeg wholesaler. In a few years he might have done well enough to open a small store. Instead of cash, some pedlars would take livestock or produce as payment, while still others accepted any scrap metal, hides, or furs that farmers had for barter. Thus, small-town Jewish commerce typically began on a partially rural basis, with the pedlar providing an exchange function, not simply selling merchandise in return for cash. Those seeking scrap metals, for example, often offered new kitchen utensils to farmers in exchange for cast-off implements. Such metals would be hauled back to the pedlar's yard, knocked apart with sledge hammers, thrown into piles, and sold off to brokers who bought up scrap for shipment to the steel mills in Hamilton, Sydney, and Sault Ste. Marie. Others collected rags, cleaned and shredded them, and sold off the product as "shoddy" to mills. Some dealt in hides and furs which they assembled, cleaned, sorted, and sold to brokers from the city.

Max Vanger, an immigrant who arrived in Saint John in 1910 at age sixteen, toured parts of Nova Scotia and New Brunswick buying up old rubber goods (boots and raingear, mainly), tea, lead, hides, and scrap metal, though he also at times worked as a shoemaker, a cutter in a pants factory, and a lumberjack.[11] It was an odd combination of jobs, but was probably typical of occupational and class mobility for many Jews and other immigrants in this era. David Stemeroff, a tailor by training, learned bricklaying, carpentry, and rudimentary farming before becoming a pedlar in scrap metals in the Mitchell area of western Ontario.

These dealers served as commercial intermediaries between the nearby farms and the metropolitan centres. Pedlars and storekeepers offered much the same kind of link between the rural community and the growing populations in their towns, while, as purchasers from Montreal, Toronto, and Winnipeg wholesalers, they also linked the towns to the metropolises.

Although in these settings Jews accepted work in a variety of occupations, they gravitated to commercial pursuits. According to Edmund Bradwin, a teacher for Frontier College and a well-informed observer of life and labour in northern railway-construction camps from 1903 to 1914:

> The Jews, while not numerous, are always in evidence during any period of railway activity when large numbers of men are employed in camps.

Few Jews engage in manual work. There are exceptions, however, and persistent able workers they are even in the most strenuous tasks. But they usually prefer to do their own planning. As tailors, peddlers, jewelers, and small traders of various kinds they follow the steel, locating temporarily in the small towns which spring up in its wake. It is only occasionally, or by special permit from the head-contractor, that peddlers are allowed in the camps ahead of the steel, so these small dealers, ensconced in their tar-papered shops at the small construction hamlet, wait to do business with the man going in or coming off the line. Quite frequently, too, the Jew is ubiquitous at a frontier town as the proprietor of an employment office for shipping men to camps and works.[12]

One of the major purposes of the formal organization of the community was to provide for religious needs, such as kosher meat and fowl, instruction of children, and prayers. Teachers who doubled as ritual slaughterers were employed, among them saintly men who served all their lives in one or more of these communities for whatever could be afforded in wages. Some were ordained rabbis, graduates of great Polish or Lithuanian talmudic academies, cast ashore, as it were, in Halifax or Brantford, brimming with learning and zeal for the Torah, but usually required to spend most of their lives providing rudimentary religious services in these isolated communities. Missionaries they were, to their bewildered people scattered across half a continent.

Of all the metropolitan Jewish communities, Winnipeg's grew fastest over the years 1900 to 1920. It increased from 1,156 to 9,023 between 1901 and 1911 and reached 14,837 a decade later.[13] As the city expanded so remarkably during these years of western Canadian economic growth, and emerged as a capital for many European ethnic groups, so it became as well the Jewish metropolis of the Prairies. In fact, its Jewish community constituted a larger percentage of the total civic population in 1911 and 1921 than in any other Canadian city.

Jews flocked to Winnipeg in such numbers for much the same reasons that so many other elements did during the period. The city's total population increased by more than 300 per cent between 1901 and 1911.[14] Touted by its ambitious business community as "the Chicago of the north," Winnipeg was the most important transportation and commercial hub of the Canadian Prairies, with the potential of also becoming an industrial and financial centre.[15] Immigrants heading for farmsteads in Saskatchewan and Alberta jostled with railway contractors and labourers, salesmen, agents, and local construction workers who flooded into this crossroads city; they crowded the Dominion government's immigrant sheds, the hotels and rooming houses, and its major thoroughfares. Into this collecting station came also a backwash of people who had tried prairie farm life and given up. They swelled Winnipeg's North End district, constituting a growing social problem that attracted the attention of social reformers like the Reverend James S. Woodsworth, who became the superintendent of All Peoples' Mission there in 1907.[16]

During the early 1900s, Winnipeg's fast-expanding Jewish community established a wide range of educational, cultural, and welfare institutions. Living at such a great distance from the rest of the Jewish world not only forced Winnipeg Jews to do virtually everything for themselves, but also infused them with an energy that made their efforts strikingly successful. By 1920 this community had established a parochial school system embracing separate institutions for children of supporters of religious or various left-wing views. Groups for theatrical and choral performances, for reading, discussion, and debate, and for numerous Zionist, mutual aid, and philanthropic purposes sprang to life. A newspaper, *Dos Yiddishe Vort*, was founded in 1911 by Harry Wilder, and a few years later the *Jewish Western Bulletin*, an English-language weekly, began publication.[17] Both circulated among Jews throughout the Prairies.

Location was another factor contributing to this dynamism. Winnipeg was situated in a region where substantial numbers of non-Anglophone immigrants, all of them often lumped together as "foreigners," were a political and social fact. Jews were included among Ukrainians — sometimes known as Galicians or Austrians — Poles, and Germans (Icelanders, having lived in Manitoba since the 1870s, were obviously not foreigners), in an ethnic agglomeration that constituted nearly half the city's population by 1913. In one North End school in 1911, Jewish pupils constituted the largest single group by nationality, but they were a minority among children of Christian immigrants from the British Isles, the United States, Scandinavian countries, Germany, Austria-Hungary, and the Russian Empire.[18] In such a variegated population, the Jews, like the members of other ethnic groups, perhaps felt the need to assert their group identity the more strongly.[19]

The area of first settlement for most Winnipeg Jews was the North End, located north of the CPR yards and its main line east and west. This included Ward 3, where between 1901 and the 1930s upwards of 88 per cent of the Jewish population lived.[20] This whole district north of the underpass on Main Street was a populous region that also housed large proportions of the city's other immigrant communities. In the early 1900s Jews tended to concentrate in a fairly narrow belt between Main and the Red River.[21] By 1921 the centre of Jewish population was located at Selkirk Avenue.[22] While they constituted a majority in certain parts of these districts, Jews lived close to the other immigrant communities, especially the Ukrainians, Poles, and Germans, in large measure peacefully – if not with perfect mutual understanding. The need to make a living and to create separate cultural institutions diverted attention away from the renewal of old acrimonies, while the diversity and newness of the city's social setting temporarily overrode those old feelings.

But such harmony was not to last.[23] The old animosities reemerged: Ukrainians, to many Jews, were murderous, drunken barbarians, while Jews, to many Ukrainians, were Christ-killers, unmanly weaklings, and ruthless exploiters. Residents of the same North End areas, Jews and Ukrainians began to compete with each other for a place in municipal politics as a vehicle for gaining acceptance, recognition, and clout in the larger society of Winnipeg, which was dominated by Anglo-Saxons.[24] Efforts to elect aldermen and school trustees who had the support of both communities broke down after 1911, and "the unfriendliness of the Jewish–Ukrainian political competition . . . brought to the surface hatred and fear" in the 1914 municipal elections.[25] While the tensions did not end and "political rivalry between Jews and Ukrainians . . . continued . . . in Winnipeg until well into the post–World War II period," left-wing Jews and Ukrainians eagerly supported Communist candidates in the interwar period.[26]

The Jewish influx to Winnipeg in the early 1900s included a substantial number of Zionists and radicals. Their top priority was the education of their children in paths of ideological correctness, and they quickly discovered that the existing Jewish schools were inappropriate for such aims.[27] In 1906 the Zionists started their own school, attached to the new B'nai Zion synagogue in the North End. Within a year the school, now called the Winnipeg Hebrew School–Talmud Torah, and directed by Rabbi Kahanovitch, had an enrolment of 150 pupils. Six years later it moved to larger quarters and became for some years what Harvey Herstein calls "the heart of the Winnipeg Jewish community."[28]

The radicals began their foray into education not long after the Zionists. Their literary and cultural club, the Yiddisher Yugend Farein (Jewish Youth Organization), launched the National Radical School in 1914, following lengthy disputations that continued for many years over the content and orientation of the curriculum, the language of instruction (whether Yiddish or Hebrew), and the precise ideological pitch of socialist teachings.[29] The last question was an especially contentious issue and led to a split in 1914, the radicals leaving to form their own school. Called the Arbeiter Ring (Workmen's

Circle) school, it got under way, shakily, in 1917, and more effectively four years later, with a program that included Yiddish language and literature as well as Jewish and working-class history.[30] Meanwhile the Shaarey Zedek congregation had operated its own religious school since 1915. Besides these institutions, many a *melamed* (private teacher) also served the area. With such broad educational facilities, Winnipeg may have been one of the best endowed Jewish communities in North America. These schools served not only as vehicles for the transference of Jewish culture – in its several manifestations – but as "prime socialization agents" for the immigrant children, providing them with the knowledge and culture necessary for entry into Canadian society.[31]

Winnipeg's Jews made their living in a variety of ways. The vast majority were drawn into the city's burgeoning commercial and manufacturing sectors. Data on Jewish occupational distribution in the 1931 Dominion census reveals that the vast majority of gainfully employed Jews, both male and female, were concentrated in the retail and wholesale trade and in manufacturing, chiefly in clothing, textiles, furs, and metal products. There were also significant and growing percentages of clerical workers, as well as professionals. A number engaged in building and construction.[32] Thus, while they made up only 6.5 per cent of Winnipeg's population by 1931, Jews constituted 68.4 per cent of all furriers, 72.4 per cent of hawkers and pedlars, 35.4 per cent of tailors, 32.8 per cent of retail merchants, 13.1 per cent of sheet metal workers, and 18.5 per cent of teachers. They made up a sizeable percentage of the city's salesmen, commercial travellers, lawyers, and physicians.[33] A substantial number had blue-collar jobs, chiefly in trades associated with clothing, furs, metal products, and transportation.

Winnipeg's Jewish proletariat before 1914 had included fifteen workers, mainly typographers, employed by the *Dos Yiddishe Vort*, numerous tailors who produced women's coats and suits at Jacob & Crawley, sheet metal workers at various factories producing ovens and other appliances, and packing-house workers at Swift's and other plants.[34] Women, it should be noted, constituted a larger number in the Jewish workforce of the clothing industry than men in 1931 (385 versus 298), and in clerical and personal service occupations, and were a sizeable proportion of the total Jewish component in the professions and in occupations associated with fur, leather, wood, and paper products.

Small Jewish communities in Calgary, Regina, Edmonton, and Saskatoon also grew with remarkable speed over these two decades. Jews had figured among fur traders at Rocky Mountain House as early as 1869, as storekeepers at Qu'Appelle in 1877, in CPR construction gangs in 1882, and among the founders of Calgary and Edmonton.[35] In 1906, Calgary Jews purchased land for a cemetery, rented space for religious services, and hired a *shochet*. In Edmonton a congregation was organized that year for the same purposes, and in 1907 a Hebrew school was opened. The Jewish community of Saskatoon was founded around 1905 by William Landa, a carriage-maker.[36] Regina's community was begun the same year and grew quickly, to 130 people in 1911, 495 in 1916, and 860 in 1921, by which time a synagogue, a rabbi, a cemetery, and a school had been acquired.[37] The communities in Prince Albert, Moose Jaw, and Medicine Hat, flourished too, along with those in a number of other towns and villages that sprang up during the western wheat-boom years between 1900 and 1913.

Even more remarkable was the impressive growth in the number of farm colonies in Saskatchewan. Now under the direct management of the Jewish Colonization Association, the settlement projects there were professionally managed and well financed, as the JCA also stepped up its efforts in Argentina and Palestine.

While the history of Jewish farming settlements on the Canadian Prairies has received much scholarly attention from writers who stress the "achievements" represented by Hirsch and later colonies, Anthony Rasporich is less romantic on this subject. The bald facts as he sees them are that, by 1931, of all Jews (for whom records were available) who had farmed on the Prairies, over 60 per cent were no longer living on farms.[38] In 1921 only one in four Jews living in rural areas was directly engaged, as a primary producer, in agriculture, forestry, or mining.[39] There were 700 Jewish farm families in all of Canada in 1921, the peak year of the colonization movement, most of them in Western Canada. But that farm population dropped significantly over the next decade, and by 1931 the whole Jewish agrarian involvement was in serious trouble. Ten years later, the Depression had all but wiped out the colonies, even though some families still held on for another generation.

Although "Jewish sons persisted in farming longer than the average universal rate of rural persistence in the second generation,"[40] the farming movement had clearly failed to realize the goal of generating a significant Jewish rural life in Canada. Like the very much larger settlement schemes fostered by the JCA in Argentina, the Canadian Jewish colonies suffered from confusing changes in management and the social conflicts that arose in the early years, perhaps because of an overdependence on the JCA. Limitations on immigration introduced in the mid-1920s severely curtailed recruitment of new settlers in Europe, so that many settlement populations never reached viable size.[41] While all of these factors were, no doubt, important in the ultimate failure of the colonies, it is clear that – in contrast to colonies established by Mennonites and Hutterites – the Jewish settlements lacked the internal coherence of commanding communal religious beliefs and values. Nor were these settlements based on the kinds of strong social ideals that underpinned the kibbutz movement then emerging in Palestine, where, despite enormous difficulties – not the least of which was almost complete initial ignorance of local conditions – Jewish agricultural efforts succeeded.

To point out their failure, however, is not to denigrate the enormous effort and idealism that lay behind these settlement schemes. Following the establishment of Hirsch in 1892, the colony experienced serious tensions which resulted "in a frequent movement of settlers out of the colony with new ones recruited in their place."[42] Nevertheless, the JCA continued to attempt new projects. In 1901 some 365 Romanian Jews were established in the Lipton–Cupar area of the Qu'Appelle Valley, even though government officials were skeptical of the scheme, given the fact that few of these settlers had any knowledge or experience in farming.[43] The Paris-based JCA, which up until then had operated through a committee of the "Baron de Hirsch" in Montreal, responded to complaints of inefficient management by shifting control of its Canadian operations to an affiliated New York organization, the Jewish Agricultural and Industrial Aid Society. But this too proved unsatisfactory, and in 1907 the JCA changed direction again and established its own Canadian organization, with an office in Montreal.

In assessing its accomplishments up to that point, the JCA discovered that Hirsch had only twenty-four farmers, with 2,529 acres under cultivation, while the Lipton–Cupar settlement had fifty-six farmers who had put only 500 acres under plough.[44] Despite these modest results, the JCA nevertheless supported other such projects. Some began spontaneously, like Bender Hamlet in 1903, at Narcisse, north of Winnipeg, and Edenbridge, in 1906, near Melfort, Saskatchewan. Another, Sonnenfeld, was established in 1905.[45] Other Jewish homesteaders started farming in many other parts of the Canadian Prairies before the First World War, some of them with the support of the JCA but others independently. It is not clear, however, whether or not JCA support made any significant difference to the probability of success of a particular settlement or individual farmer.

What has been less than adequately examined is the life of the Jewish men, women, and children in these settlements. Their daily lives, their ambitions for themselves and their families, their attitudes towards Jewish and other neighbours or to the land itself, as well as the transformations they were inevitably experiencing are usefully touched upon in the published memoirs of a few early settlers. *Land of Hope*, by Clara Hoffer, and *Uncle Mike's Edenbridge*, by Michael Usiskin, were written by settlers reflecting in their later years upon their pioneering experiences, their survival strategies in balancing their lives as homesteaders and as Jews, their shifting mentalities as they moved from Europe to Saskatchewan, and their adjustment to the Canadian prairie environment in the ongoing tension between culture and material context. Something of these transformations can be derived from Clara Hoffer's recollections, taken from a diary in Yiddish about the experiences she shared with her husband, Israel Hoffer, and his father, Reb Moshe, who had come to Saskatchewan from Galicia in 1906:

> As a pious Jew, he was probably berating himself . . . for having given in to his headstrong son and for having allowed himself to be led into the wilderness, like a lamb being led to slaughter. It was true God was everywhere. But to go to the wild sprawling prairie countries where there were no Synagogues, no scroll, and not enough Jewish men for a minyan, was the height of madness . . . what was he doing here. . . . In the Old Country he had been revered as a learned, as a respectable man. Pah on his son's obstinacy.[46]

The distance from familiar sights, sounds, and smells, from family and friends, from the synagogue, from other Jews in a ferociously cold, flat land, were – at least in retrospect – deeply depressing to a man of Reb Moshe's age, fifty-seven. "This is the place my son wants to call home," he said bitterly to a visitor, "this wilderness with no trees and no water except what is in the slough."[47]

In the rough atmosphere of the Canadian frontier, the ignorance of Jewish customs that prevailed among other farmers could lead to some perilous situations, as one incident at Hirsch demonstrates:

> The new shocket [sic] had moved into the rooms built for him at the back of the Synagogue, and the dedication of the building was planned for a night in November, 1912. It was the first day of Chanukah and they had decided to light the first candle in the Synagogue. . . . It was peaceful and comradely until the outside door opened and 20 men entered the building, unshaven, dirty, grimy, wearing greasy overalls, old sweaters and torn jackets covered with chaff. They were a threshing crew who had finished up some late work and decided to take in what they thought to be a dance in the lighted Synagogue. . . . Each intruder reached out for the

nearest girl or woman and began pushing clumsily around in circles. . . .
"Let's throw them out," the young men said to one another.

. . ."Wait" Israel [Hoffer] cautioned them. "They didn't come to make
a commotion, just to dance." . . . "I have something to say to you. . . . This
is our Synagogue, not a dance hall. We are here to dedicate the building
and celebrate a religious ceremony, the beginning of a Holiday.
However, our ladies have provided food for the evening and they tell
me there will be enough for you. We bid you welcome to our food. Boys
let's put up the tables."[48]

After thirty-three years of working on his farm at Edenbridge, Mike Usiskin
recalled the appeal directed at London Jews in 1906 by the "rabbi" of the colony:

Flee, my friends, from the London fogs and the chaos that eats away at your
hearts. Flee from the confusion of busy streets . . . flee from the tenements
and the bosses that live off your blood, sweat and tears; flee from that
two-faced society where politicians don't say what they think, and don't
think what they say. Come to Edenbridge. Come where the air is fresh.
Everything is so peaceful. . . . The forest here is so vast that personal
expansion has no bounds. You can live here by your own resources. . . .
Come help us tame this wild land . . . we need you. Come please come!
You will not regret it.[49]

Usiskin succumbed to the call, travelled to Canada, and when he got to
Edenbridge

encountered Jews who came from all over the world . . . [South] Africans,
Europeans, Americans, and a new breed called Canadians. Each had his
own distinguishing feature: the African wore a light shirt; the Lithuanian,
tall boots; the American wore a leather jacket; and the Canadian, a fur
cap with flaps pulled down over his ears, and Edenbridge-style overalls –
a checker-board of patches.[50]

The settlers' most important preoccupations, judging from these memoirs,
were not so much the practical problems of wresting their living from the soil
amid the often hostile environment of the Prairies, as emotional and social
issues. Hoffer worried about relationships with Christian neighbours and tensions emerging within the Jewish community itself, while Usiskin's overriding
concern was the realization of his youthful ideals of enjoying the liberating
effects of physical labour on the land, of seeking the brotherhood of man, and

of building in rural Saskatchewan a new arcadian Jewish life far from urban travails. The women of these colonies appear to have left almost no memoirs, and, until further research is done among letters or other documents that may survive, we can only imagine their perspectives on lives of domestic toil in harsh surroundings, with husbands ground down by incessant labour and uncertain rewards, while their children were growing up as strangers to them in this new land. Doctors were often far away, most close family and friends were still living in the old country, and the ways of the new country were so unfamiliar. These women look out from old photographs with puzzled sadness or wry hopefulness, and almost palpable weariness.

What the colonization of Jews in western Canada accomplished was both actual and mythical. Though small in number and tiny in size, the colonies existed for some seven decades as tangible evidence of Jewish ability to cope successfully with an agricultural life in which, though many failed or gave up, some survived. The soil did indeed beckon to and nurture a small number who would never trade the broad prairie sky for the narrow horizons of a Canadian city, or the feel of their own wheat between their fingers for the dubious touch of a clothing contractors' garment pieces.

Some of the major reasons for the decline of these Jewish colonies – in comparison with those established in Western Canada by the Mormons – were of a social, religious, and institutional nature.[51] The Mormons' efforts succeeded while the Jews' failed because Mormons built compact colonies of contiguous settlement, were committed to building "a new Zion in the wilderness" as a refuge from persecution, and enjoyed the benefits of very substantial continuing material and moral support from their mother church in Utah. The Jews, on the other hand, did not establish such close-knit settlements, with the consequence that vital needs of social contact and religious requirements (a *mikveh* – ritual bath, kosher meat, and a synagogue) were very difficult to meet. Furthermore, the Jewish agricultural experience in the Canadian west was not based on anything like the religious idealism of the Mormons; Jews settled essentially for economic reasons, hoping – like so many others – to make a living from the soil. And finally, support from the JCA was not as generous or as sustained as that which came from Utah for the Mormons. Consequently, Jewish efforts were unsuccessful. Lack of sufficient farming experience was likely another weakness of the Jewish enterprise. Most other immigrant groups settling the West, including the Mormons, had an agricultural tradition. By contemporary standards, many of the early Ukrainian settlers also arrived with substantial capital resources (being "peasants of means"), and this too facilitated their adjustment to the demands of prairie farming.[52]

Even with the spread of Jews into small cities, towns, and villages, and the increasing activity in the farming colonies, the most dramatic growth – as we have seen – occurred in the metropolises of Montreal, Toronto, and Winnipeg. As they expanded, these communities also experienced the problems associated with the transference of so many people to a new environment. The immigration process showed up many of the social problems affecting Jewish communities on both sides of the Atlantic, including poverty, mental illness, crime, juvenile delinquency, desertion, and child abuse. There were also many divisions within the community. Some of these problems, no doubt, were brought from Europe, where the contemporary migration from towns to cities brought about significant changes in communal life.

Poverty, sickness, and burial were the most serious problems presented to all of the metropolitan centres. In Montreal, the "Baron de Hirsch" and its associated charities, notably the Ladies' Hebrew Benevolent Society, were extremely busy after 1900 attempting to meet pressing responsibilities in all of these areas. There were so many burials of Jewish indigents (including 139 children) in 1908, for example, that available spaces in local Jewish cemeteries were all used up.[53] Because the institute's doctors' caseloads jumped from 787 to 2,162 between 1907 and 1913, the Herzl Health Clinic was established to cope with the sick, many of them afflicted with tuberculosis. For these cases a sanatorium, the Mount Sinai, was established in the Laurentian highlands near Ste.-Agathe, while for the growing numbers of children needing care an orphanage was built in the city's western suburbs.

In the late nineteenth and early twentieth century, Toronto's Jewish neighbourhood was the "Ward," or "St. John's Shtetl."[54] In this narrow downtown area bordered by Yonge, University, Queen, and College streets, there lived about half of all the city's Jews, who formed a majority of the ward's total population. A slum by early-twentieth-century standards, it attracted notoriety for its crowded conditions, filth, squalor, poverty, and lack of adequate sanitation. But it did serve as a reception area for the vast majority of the Jews who migrated to the city in the Laurier years, and it became so overwhelmingly Jewish that, by 1912, 87 per cent of the pupils in the district's two elementary schools were Jews.[55] Here they created, "a miniature Jewish civilization in the heart of Anglo-Saxon Toronto," with all of "the amenities and security of the shtetl" they had left behind them in Eastern Europe. Convenient to Toronto's burgeoning clothing industry, like the enormous factories erected nearby in

1910 by the T. Eaton Company, the Ward also offered cheap housing, especially in the crowded and filthy rear tenements filled with tiny, dark rooms. As Jewish children crowded the classrooms of Ward's Hester How public school, as "foreigners," school officials worried about how to "Canadianize" them.[56]

In this small area of poor immigrants the light of the Torah shone forth. Synagogues abounded. The magnificent Goel Tzedec (the Lithuanian *shul*), modelled on London's Roman Catholic cathedral of Westminster, was opened on University Avenue in 1907; the Machzikei Ha Das (the Galicianer *shul*), a less impressive edifice, was built the year before, on Terauley Street.[57] Numerous others arose: the Shomrei Shabbos (Sabbath Observers) on Chestnut Street, four major congregations on Centre Avenue, and several *shtiblach* elsewhere in the Ward. Stores selling Jewish foods, kosher restaurants, delicatessens, candy stores, offices of steamship agents, clothing stores, sweatshops, and Jewish bookstores added to the *shtetl*-like ambience of this district, whose Jewish population was already declining. The move westward had begun and the centre of Toronto Jewish life reemerged in the next decade in the Spadina area.

A number of mutual benefit societies appeared in Toronto in the early 1900s, helping in their way to lessen the pain "of alienation, loneliness and rootlessness in a strange new country," as well as the economic problems of adjustment.[58] Membership consisted mostly of Jews who could not afford synagogue membership or were secularists. Three types of mutual benefit societies existed in the Toronto Jewish community – the non-partisan and ethnically mixed, the left-wing, and the *landsmanshaften*, whose members were all from the same area. Altogether, there were thirty such organizations in the city by 1925: ten *landsmanshaften*, eight ethnically mixed societies, and twelve branches of the left-wing *Arbeiter Ring* (Workmen's Circle)[59] with memberships from as few as 80 to as many as 500.

There was a decided working-class orientation to these associations, even those that were not Workmen's Circle lodges: the Pride of Israel and the Judaean Benevolent and Friendly Society "often gave assistance to striking workers."[60] Benefits usually included payments during illness (excluding those caused by immoral actions) for the member and his family, doctors' visits, and free burial in the society's own cemetery. Many also provided small loans at low interest rates. The price of this protection was probably significant, costing each member as much as two weeks' wages annually.

Just as important were the social and psychic benefits provided by the *landsmanshaften* through associations with fellow townsfolk who could share a reminiscence about now-rosier old times in, say, Czestochova, Miedzyrecz,

Ostrow, or other Polish towns and cities, where bearded rabbis, town fools, pious women, village peasants, and *cheder* (Jewish school) children crowded the square on market days, collecting in front of memory's camera and calling out in Yiddish: *"Long leben zolstu"* ("Long life to you"); "Don't forget us"; "Come back for a visit, rich Canadian!" The Workmen's Circle lodges provided the cohesion of an ideology that stressed left-wing politics and Jewish cultural autonomism, a comfort both to working men in an exploitative economic climate and to Yiddish speakers who supported the rich efflorescence of that language in the early twentieth century.

To those without the protection of such associations, cash, coal, food, bedding, and cooking utensils were dispensed by the Toronto Hebrew Ladies Aid, from 1899 on; similar organizations sprang up for specific congregations, along with charities offering maternity care and child care and other social assistance needs.[61] And in 1909 the Jewish dispensary was established to supply the poor with medicines and medical advice. An orphanage was established in 1910 and an old-age home in 1913.

In Winnipeg, in 1909, the Hebrew Benevolent Society, which since 1884 had provided relief for the needy, jobs for the unemployed, railway tickets for those intending to resettle elsewhere, help for the farm colonies, and assistance for other communal efforts, was reorganized as the United Hebrew Charities.[62] Differences of opinion over priorities between the poorer and more numerous Jews of the North End and those of the prosperous south side were resolved by an amalgamated organization called the United Relief of Winnipeg in 1914.[63] Two orphanages were established by 1917, and in 1919 the Jewish Old Folks Home of Western Canada was founded.

Orphanages housed not only those children who were bereft of both parents, but also those abandoned, or left with only a single parent – usually a woman – who had too many children to look after adequately. Besides these unfortunates, there were children who were so badly abused or improperly cared for by parents either criminal, mentally ill, or incompetent that they had to be taken into communal care.

Such breakdowns of family life were not unknown in Europe. Nor, of course, was Jewish criminality. Organized gangs of Jewish criminals were a well-known phenomenon in Odessa and Warsaw in the early twentieth century.[64] While illicit activity of all kinds was attributed to Jewish criminals in these and other cities, "Jews in the Diaspora have generally been less involved in crime than the populations among which they lived" because of communal restraints, close family ties, high educational standards, low alcohol consumption, and other social controls.[65] Nevertheless, prostitution and the international traffic in women for immoral purposes attracted considerable Jewish criminal activity. One account of Jewish participation in the "white slave" trade emphasizes that this nefarious business that spread to North and South America had its origins and source of supply in Eastern Europe.[66] As late as 1920, Lillian Freiman of Ottawa voiced deep concern in an address to Hadassah members overs the fate of orphaned Jewish girls in Eastern Europe who were being lured to South America "into a future worse than death [by] these human vultures."[67] However, contrary to legends about enticement and entrapment of young Jewish girls from poor families – often after hasty marriages to men posing as rich American Jews looking for brides[68] – most of the women being trafficked were willing participants in this trade. Between 1880 and 1920, some 20,000 to 30,000 women were moved through illicit channels to all parts of the world, though mainly to Argentina.

While only a small part of this traffic appears to have extended into Canada, the "Baron de Hirsch" took notice of the danger and co-operated with international organizations and the National Council of Jewish Women in attempting to arrest its spread. From time to time Montreal was alleged to be the scene of some of this activity, and Vancouver a way-station on the Pacific.[69] In September of 1908, the Toronto newspapers reported the arrest and deportation to the United States of two local Jews, well known to the Chicago police as brothel-keepers, who were wanted on charges of white slavery.[70] But the 1915 Toronto Social Survey Commission noted that a few Jewish pimps were doing business in the Ward, probably servicing mainly a Jewish clientele, and there were allegations that most of the city's bootleggers were Jews and Italians.[71] The fact that some prominent Montreal Jews – like Samuel Schwartz and Rabbi Nathan Gordon – took part in various campaigns to suppress corruption and vice, including rampant prostitution, was a reflection of their progressive and reformist impulses rather than of any sense of guilt over Jewish participation in such crimes.[72] In sharp contrast to Buenos Aires, New York, and other American cities where Jewish criminality became notorious, no serious charges were made against the Jewish communities in Canada, although occasional allegations were voiced.[73] Perhaps this reflected the fact that Jewish criminality was never a significant public issue in this "peaceable kingdom." There were no Canadian counterparts to such New York Jewish toughs and mobsters as Kid Twist, Yuski Nigger, Big Jack Zelig, Dopey Benny, Kid Dropper, and Gyp the Blood.[74]

In larger centres like Montreal, juvenile delinquency attracted the attention of the "Baron de Hirsch" and affiliated organizations. The orphanages were sometimes used as repositories of children whom parents could not deal with. In Montreal there appears to have been a problem of Jewish boys being arrested for illegally selling newspapers without municipal licences; others were in court on criminal charges. So serious was the problem perceived to be that a magistrate publicly noted the fact that so many Jewish youths were being brought up before him. There were enough of these youths, convicted on a variety of charges and sent to a provincial correctional farm for boys at Shawbridge, Quebec, to attract special rehabilitative efforts from the institute. In Toronto, meanwhile, a Jewish branch of the Big Brother movement was organized in 1914 to respond to juvenile delinquency, which was rising "in undue proportion to the population." "The situation was becoming more serious daily," one contemporary later reflected.[75]

The lives of Jewish immigrants were dominated by the search for economic survival in this new land where, in the era of prime ministers Laurier (1896–1911) and Borden (1911–20), the wheat boom, war, and recovery created enormous growth and rapid modernization. Immigrants pursued different strategies to seek a livelihood; their family biographies tell of the struggle, confusion, and anguish that were common to most. Allan Grossman, born in Toronto's "Ward" in 1910, was the seventh child of Moses and Yetta Grossman, whose migration from Poland to Canada stretched over two years, from 1907 – when Moses came with his son Levis – until 1909, when Yetta arrived with the rest of the family.[76] While waiting for his family to arrive, Moses did a succession of labouring jobs, including laying railway ties. In 1912 he became a pedlar and, like so many others, collected rags and bones for recycling by paper and glue manufacturers. Pushing their little carts along city streets crying out, "Rags, bones and bottles. Any rags today, lady?"[77] these pedlars became a fixture of the Jewish urban scene.

Moishe Lazarovitch migrated from Romania to Montreal in 1911 and was followed two years later by his wife and children.[78] A deeply religious Jew who was unable to find work in his occupation of bookkeeping, Lazarovitch spent his days in study and prayer at home and in a local synagogue, seeking redemption in the slums of Montreal, "a dark, brooding, silent man" with "a strong sense of the unimportance of this world,"[79] while his family struggled to make ends meet. In 1912 Louis Zuken, a pottery worker from Gorodnize, Ukraine, unemployed after leading an unsuccessful strike, arrived in Winnipeg, where he found work in a meat packing house; two years later he brought over his wife, Shifra, and their children to live in the city's North End.[80] In December of 1921, Joshua Gershman left Warsaw to join his father, who farmed near

Winnipeg, only to find that his father was dead. He had left the family behind in Poland in 1913, hoping to save enough to bring over his wife and children.[81]

Kalman and Yetta Klein reached Montreal in the summer of 1910 with three children, their five other offspring having preceded them to North America.[82] Formerly a pedlar in pottery items, Kalman found work as a presser in a clothing factory and laboured over hot irons for the rest of his working life in the garment-manufacturing sweatshops along St. Lawrence Boulevard. Eleven years later, Morris Lewis, a leather worker, left Svisloch in Belorussia for Montreal; in a few months he brought over his wife, Rose, and their three children.[83] He got work in the clothing industry and joined the Amalgamated Clothing Workers of America,[84] striving towards recognition of labour's dignity and the brotherhood of workers, Jew and Gentile, male and female.

The transition from Old to New World exposed – and perhaps in many instances created – certain social problems. Among the most serious was the breakup of families during the migration process. While East European Jews had a very high rate of migration in family units – compared, for example, with pre-1914 Italian immigrants, who were mostly young single men seeking enough money to buy land back home – many Jewish male breadwinners did immigrate ahead of wives and children. Others left their families at ports of debarkation like New York and Montreal while they sought employment elsewhere. In the process, contact was sometimes lost, through accident or neglect, or even by design, as some husbands sought to escape their responsibilities. Such desertion became so grave a problem that American Jewish charities organized the National Desertion Bureau in 1911 to track down husbands "on the lam," many of whom had skipped over the Canadian border.[85]

Early in 1913, New York's Industrial Removal Office (IRO) relayed to Winnipeg a message received from their St. Petersburg correspondent, who was trying to locate a man who, six years before, had emigrated to Fargo, North Dakota, "leaving his old parents in Russia. As there are now 2 years that he sends neither letters to his parents, who besides are sick and without means, we request you . . . to get information . . . regarding the reason for his silence and urge him to care for his old parents."[86]

Other correspondence between Canada and the IRO illustrates the range of obstacles and frustrations experienced by immigrants. One man claimed he could not help his brother and sister come to Winnipeg because he had been unemployed for some time.[87] A husband and father who worked on a dairy farm pleaded for help in bringing his family from New York to Winnipeg, where "he would be in a position to support them on their arrival."[88] Another asked for help on similar grounds, claiming that while with earnings of nine dollars a week "he could nicely support his wife . . . if they were together . . . [he] is unable to contribute anything towards transportation as he has to prepare a house and some furniture for the arrival of his family."[89] A Montreal junk pedlar, who was a distant relative of two recent arrivals, offered to furnish them with handwagons so that they could start peddling.[90] A Montreal Jewish official offered to bring the sick husband of a distraught woman to the city from New York only if he agreed to have a physical examination "as you know that unless the man can stand the severe Canadian climate he will only become a burden to this community."[91] An official writing to the IRO from Toronto in August 1913 stated that the children of a tailor who still resided in Europe "are not well disposed to their father and do not wish him to come" to Toronto, where they now lived.[92]

The stories of working children are especially heart-rending. A home visitor for the "Baron de Hirsch" reported in December 1907 on thirty-four hard-luck cases among immigrants in Montreal.[93] Ten-year-old Mary Vangorofsky worked as a tailor for $1.50 a week to help her widowed father support two other children. Golde Steinberg, age thirteen, assisted her mother, who worked as a washerwoman to help support four other children. Fannie Hofobovitz, age thirteen, earned $2.00 a week working as a tailor, while two sisters aged eighteen and fifteen earned another $14.00 to help a widowed mother and another sister. Fannie Ganofsky and a seventeen-year-old sister together earned $7.00 a week making cigarettes to support a widowed father and three other children. Max Kaufman, a teenaged orphan, was paid $3.00 a week as a messenger at Morgans department store. Fannie Taitelbaum, age twelve, worked in a clothing factory earning $2.50 a week to help her widowed shoemaker father support five other children. Myer Klagman earned $4.00 a week as a clothing-factory worker to support an unemployed father and four other children. Pasa Bookman, who made paper boxes for $2.00 a week, was the sole support of her family of four, including an unemployed father. The same was true of Peritz Chedlac, age twelve, who earned $2.00 as a tailor. Most of the child operators, pressers, tailors, and workers were employed in Jewish-owned clothing firms like Hart's, Vineberg's, and Kellert's. Most of these children apparently did not go to school.

What is clear, then, is that Jewish immigration to Canada during the early twentieth century was not an organized and regulated flow. It was fraught with much chaos and confusion. Organizations on both sides of the Atlantic – not to mention helpful individuals, often local rabbis – were hard put to deal with even the most desperate cases among the huge numbers of arrivals.

The immigrants came from a culture in which men and women – as sons and daughters, as husbands and wives – traditionally had sharply defined roles in their families as well as in their economic and religious activity, throughout their lives. But the New World social context effected some changes. Because the evidence is fragmentary and anecdotal, generalizations are risky, but, even before emigrating to Canada, some Jewish women had determined to pierce holes in the barriers preventing them from following paths to educational and economic improvement. In pre-revolutionary Russia, a girl from a traditional family, Rae Stillman, insisted on being allowed to learn to read and write Russian "like the other [Christian] girls and be good at it."[94] Against her parents' wishes, she learned Russian and found a job in a factory; at age seventeen she married her boyfriend and left her family for Canada.[95] Fanny Sky recalled that her mother, the daughter of a well-off family, had a good education and wrote letters for people in her town, while Rose Wohlgelertner attended a business academy in her native Lvov.[96] Bella Isaac graduated from the gymnasium in Marburg, Germany, and Elizabeth Kestler from a junior high school in Žilina, Slovakia.[97] There was apparently a significant number of exceptions to the general rule that girls were taught crocheting, sewing, knitting, and mending to prepare them for life as "a good wife, able to raise her children, and also [to] help her husband whenever she could. Nobody had a special occupation. They were just housewives."[98] Or, as Betty Mazerkoff succinctly remembered: "Housewives were different, they didn't expect much out of life."[99] Whether in Eastern Europe or in Canada, such was indeed the pattern for most women: endless drudgery in the home, numerous pregnancies, and subordination to males in the home, synagogue, and society.

But this "world of our mothers" began to change in Canada. Here "the relative wealth and high degree of acculturation of Jews from western Europe allowed for rapid adjustment to New World feminine ambitions, just as it reinforced their fear of any threat to their integration into Canadian life."[100] The first generation of Jewish women immigrants who arrived in the mid-nineteenth century from Central Europe were influenced, by social reform ideas then current among their non-Jewish contemporaries, to try to "deliver Jewish women from their second bondage of ignorance and misery," while "their eastern European sisters organized their own groups."[101] Eastern European women who had arrived in Canada during the 1880s and 1890s formed the Hadassah organization in 1917 for the welfare of women and children in Palestine. But the Jewish women of the third wave of immigration, during the Laurier boom after 1900, were often workers in factories, and because of their lack of familiarity with the English language they "shied away from joining English-speaking groups like Hadassah." Their class culture inclined them to socialist organizations, like the Labour Zionists, the Social Democratic Party, and the Bundist Workmen's Circle. Despite barriers put up against them by the Jewish unions and their Jewish co-workers, "Jewish women played an important part within the Jewish labour movement . . . [with] militancy and class consciousness. . . ."[102] North American social and economic conditions were inducing different segments of Jewish society to conform to new norms, which were changing the role of women within the community.

The enlargement of the Canadian Jewish community during the years between 1900 and 1920 brought into play both realities transferred from Eastern Europe and particular social imperatives in the contemporary Dominion of Canada. A culture of ancient lineage that had long been subjected to the social and political forces of the Pale of Settlement came into a nation whose promise was as yet unfulfilled. The adjustment of these immigrants, and the routes by which they sought accommodation to their new environment – their survival strategies – demonstrate the resulting interaction between their imported cultural context and the raw realities of a nation whose economic destiny was still publicly defined in terms of staple production, and whose identity was obscured by unreconciled national dualities. In the clothing industry, traditional Jewish occupations like tailoring provided an entrée and a springboard for Jewish-led trade unions – a kind of immigrant success story, in which – to a great extent – Europe imposed itself on Canada. The modest success of Jewish farm settlements demonstrates, conversely, that, in the short run at least, this fragment of the European context could not easily be transplanted to the new environment.

What were the processes by which the Jewish immigrants of Eastern Europe became Canadianized, and what happened to their culture on the way? For an understanding of those transformations we must examine the intellectual and social changes taking place within the community as it attempted to reach an understanding of what it meant to be a Jew in a young nation undergoing its own metamorphosis.

10

"If I Forget Thee, O Jerusalem"

Since the very beginnings of their presence in the Dominion of Canada, Jews had adopted various routes to accommodate themselves to their environment. Accommodation involved survival and adjustment – preservation and defence, as well as change and reassessment. The survival of Jewish culture and its traditions, literature, language, and social values in Canadian civil society required numerous changes. Such accommodations had two major and not easily compatible purposes, the preservation of a culture and the realization of good citizenship. That there could be limited identities within the would-be Canadian national identity – notably Quebec's – was not lost on the Jewish community. But French Canadian nationalism carried a most distressing baggage train of antisemitism, as we shall see.

Some Jews of the older community had already been drawn to service in the militia, to civic positions as justices of the peace, mayors, and councillors, while a few others had made their way on the athletic, musical, or university scene. In the nineteenth century, such individual accommodation strategies were often rewarded with considerable success, probably because of the small size of the Jewish community and the absence, among most of its members, of the ideologies that had historically defined Jewish identity in religious terms. This traditional outlook changed dramatically at the end of the nineteenth century with the advent of ideas promising political solutions to the Jewish problem in Eastern Europe. Socialism and Jewish nationalism, which were the vehicles of a complex revolution in the self-understanding of vast numbers of these Jews, were brought to Canada in the 1880s and 1890s to become an integral part of the debate on the Jewish future. What is particularly interesting about the intellectual dimensions of Canadian Jewish history in the late nineteenth and early twentieth centuries is not the adaptation by many individuals to their environment – important as that is – but the ideas and institutions in which definitions of Jewishness and Canadianness came together. Would the belief in the existence of Jewish nationhood current in Eastern Europe before the First World War be compatible with the diverging nationalistic aspirations of English and French Canada?

The experience of the Canadian Zionist movement is an important example of the modifications that the local environment imposed on the idea of nationalism associated with the establishment of a Jewish national home in Palestine. At the first Zionist Congress, held in 1897 at Basle, Switzerland, Theodor Herzl's formulation of political Zionism was a declaration of intent. His call to his sympathizers a year later to organize local Jewish support for the movement was never intended to challenge their identity as good citizens of the countries in which they lived.

The ideas associated with Jewish national revival in the ancient land of Israel had taken root in Canada even before the rise of the Zionist movement. As early as 1887, a branch of the Chovevei Zion (Lovers of Zion) organization was formed in Montreal by a local Hebrew teacher, Alexander Harkavy, who subsequently moved to New York, where he achieved great eminence as a Yiddish lexicographer.[1] Another Montreal Zionist group, formed five years later, was known as Shavei Zion (Return to Zion); in 1894 some of its members – under the sponsorship of the Paris Rothschilds – actually attempted to start an agricultural colony at Hauran, in the north-eastern corner of what is now the Hashemite Kingdom of Jordan.[2] After a harrowing year of unremitting toil in the colony, problems with local officials, and repeated plundering by Druse neighbours, the Montrealers returned to Canada, much sadder and considerably poorer than when they had left.

But the new political Zionism movement which Theodor Herzl set in motion by the publication of his *Der Judenstaat* (*The Jewish State*) in 1895 and the convening of the first Zionist congresses in 1897 and 1898 revived hopes for a national revival in the land of Israel. In 1898, Zionist groups sprang up in Montreal, Toronto, Winnipeg, Kingston, Hamilton, Ottawa, and Quebec.[3] In November of 1899, a national organization of these groups – the Federation of Canadian Zionist Societies – was established, and over 500 memberships (known as shekels, for the ancient Hebrew coin) in the world Zionist organization – and nearly twice as many shares of the Jewish Colonial Trust (which was intended to be the financial instrument of the Zionist movement) – were sold to hundreds of Jews across Canada. A few months later, Clarence de Sola of Montreal, the president of the federation, triumphantly cabled to Herzl, "Canada Takes 1,000 Shares of the Jewish Colonial Trust." Not content with these successes, de Sola, who enjoyed the support of a devoted and growing group of followers, set about spreading the Zionist message to as many Jews as could be reached from the Atlantic to the Pacific – even in the isolated farm colonies on the Prairies.

In examining the early history of Zionism in Britain, Stuart Cohen concluded that "individual communities developed distinctive patterns of political association which, despite their overall adherence to a recognizably Jewish political tradition, were framed as specific responses to the peculiarities of their different situations." In Cohen's view, "Jewish history is necessarily heterogeneous,"[4] and is largely determined by Jews within local contexts. British Zionism, he discovered, was a sickly flower from the beginning, because the local Jewish elite saw the movement as a threat to their image as loyal British citizens, while many of the new immigrants were equally wary. Gideon Shimoni points out that, in South Africa, binational context was conducive to the community's becoming a bastion of intensely loyal Herzlian Zionism.[5] In South Africa Jewish identity, therefore, was essentially Zionist. In the United States, on the other hand, such a clear-cut normative identification was not possible because of both demographic factors and pre-existing and competing political ideologies and structures.[6]

Canadian Zionism was stronger than the American variety, and Zionism followed "divergent paths" in the two countries because of several factors. These mainly were: British chauvinism among Canada's Jews; the country's binational character and the absence of a countervailing pan-Canadian nationalism; the religious conservatism of Canadian Jews and their wide geographical dispersion; the organizational genius of Clarence de Sola himself; and the general "conservatism" of Canadian society.[7] At any rate, the early movement was indeed moulded by de Sola, who for twenty years headed the Federation of Zionist Societies of Canada, and was its titular leader, chief spokesman, and major ideologue.[8] Through the prism of his Zionist career, we may see how the movement evolved in a period of significant numerical growth and geographical spread, as well as one of far-reaching social and economic changes in the Canadian Jewish community.

Clarence de Sola was the third son of Rabbi Abraham de Sola and Esther

Joseph, and grew up in a milieu of social prominence and financial comfort.[9] The de Solas not only effectively led Montreal's Jewish community but were also relatively well integrated into the Anglophone society, thanks in part to Mrs. de Sola's substantial private income. Clarence attended the High School of Montreal and lived with his family in a large West End home close to his Jewish and non-Jewish friends. Although not as scholarly as his distinguished father, Clarence – according to his diary – maintained a rigorous and ambitious program of reading, mostly history. He closely followed domestic and foreign political affairs, especially British, and, like most late Victorians, was fascinated by the great European and imperial conflicts.[10]

Religious beliefs, growing concern for the welfare of Jews everywhere, a family tradition of communal leadership, and strong pride in his Sephardic heritage, together fuelled de Sola's intellectual and emotional predisposition to Zionism, and the activist role he was there to assume. In the early 1880s he came under the influence of Dr. Moses Gaster, leader of the Sephardic congregations in England; in the 1890s Gaster would be one of the few prominent rabbis in Britain to espouse Herzl's Zionism openly. De Sola reported regularly to him on the progress of Zionism in Canada, and received in return news of the movement in Britain and Europe, as well as encouragement and advice.[11]

Having launched their campaign in 1899 with the founding of the Federation of Canadian Zionist Societies, de Sola and his associates in Montreal and across the country were tireless in spreading the message. Montreal rabbis Meldola de Sola and Abraham Kaplan delivered pro-Zionist messages from their pulpits, and Rabbi Aaron Ashinsky could be relied upon to address the immigrant Jews in Yiddish. From Toronto, Dr. John Shayne, Moses Gelber, and, later, Sam Kronick carried the cause to English- and Yiddish-speaking audiences across southern Ontario, and in Ottawa Archie Freiman soon became deeply involved.[12] Youth and women's organizations flourished. In Toronto, Zionist clubs were so numerous and active that in 1910 they united to purchase a house for their meetings. These local groups affiliated with the federation.[13]

From Winnipeg, M.J. Finklestein, Harry Weidman, and H.E. Wilder served in various capacities on the federation's national executive. All were highly influential men in the west; Finklestein was an important local lawyer, and at the time one of the few Manitoba Jews in that profession, while Wilder was one of the proprietors of *Dos Yiddishe Vort*, the Yiddish weekly which circulated to Jewish communities across the Prairies.[14] In these vibrant western communities, especially in Winnipeg, Zionism put down deep roots in several ideological directions besides the centrist stem of the federation. And in smaller places both in the west and in the Maritimes, a cadre of devoted workers developed, men and women who for years ran local campaigns and attended national and regional conventions, selling the fifty-cent "shekels" which denoted official membership, emptying Jewish National Fund boxes, and trying to collect on pledges. Thus, while Montreal and Toronto were easily the largest centres of Zionism, the movement was highly active in many of the smaller Jewish centres. As it grew across the Dominion its affairs became increasingly complex, and, as de Sola preferred to deal with policy matters, he delegated some responsibilities to an executive committee called the Administrative Bureau, headed by Leon Goldman.[15] Although de Sola still served actively as leader, spokesman, and representative of the movement, Goldman handled more and more of the federation's business, in conjunction with the bureau, each of whose five members took responsibility for a separate fund-raising department – including the JNF, the Jewish Colonial Trust, and the Herzl Forest of new trees in Palestine. At Montreal headquarters, Goldman, a retired businessman, watched over the organization's daily affairs, while de Sola, now happily relieved of these matters, dealt with "the big picture," visited branches, and corresponded grandly with fellow "world leaders."

In Montreal, key intellectuals like Dr. Wortsman and, later, Reuben Brainin, successive editors of the *Keneder Adler*, and Hirsch Wolofsky, the publisher, supported Zionism, although they were not always pleased with de Sola's autocratic manner and lack of cultural depth. Several major businessmen also joined the movement: Joseph S. Leo, a leading optical company executive and insurance director, was active in Montreal Zionist circles and served for twenty years as secretary of the federation, while Abraham A. Levin, a wealthy manufacturer of braids and trimmings, was the federation's treasurer for seventeen years.[16] Women also played a major role in early Canadian Zionism; they formed their own associations and national connections, while early on they adopted their own special projects in Palestine and laid the basis for the Hadassah organization, which emerged in 1917. Children and youth were organized into clubs called Young Judaea, and in 1917 a separate national association of that name was formed by McGill law student Bernard Joseph.[17]

By 1910 the federation was attracting growing numbers of Jews to its constituent organizations throughout Canada. Its total national membership rose from a few hundred in 1899 to 1,000 in 1903, over 2,000 in 1906, and nearly 6,600 in 1920, when the total Canadian Jewish community numbered a little over 125,000 people.[18] Although this was only one in every nine or ten adults – a modest segment of the nation's Jews – it is important to note that the movement attracted a significant proportion of the members of small communities located in lesser towns and cities, beyond the metropolitan centres of Montreal, Toronto, and Winnipeg. Of nearly 6,600 members in 1920, for example, the non-metropolitan communities, which had only 23 per cent of the Jewish population, supplied nearly half.[19] In many of these centres, almost all adult Jews were members. The shopkeepers, pedlars, and tradesmen, who were overwhelmingly newly arrived immigrants, formed local societies which affiliated with the federation. Many leading members of these new communities, like Isaac Cohen of Kingston and Bernard Myers of Saint John, were East European immigrants of the 1890s or early 1900s. While no doubt many of these individuals brought their Zionism from Europe, as new arrivals they were susceptible to appeals from leading Jews like de Sola, whose direction of the Zionist cause provided, in their eyes, a Canadian as well as a Jewish legitimacy to the movement. The federation, moreover, offered the only sustained organizational link between the various Jewish communities of Canada, not only binding them together for a common purpose but also supplying a forum in which their representatives could meet. Thus, aside from the widespread intrinsic appeal that Zionism had as a cause in its own right, the federation offered a nationwide vehicle for Jewish expression in Canada, as a forum for voicing domestic concerns and a significant training-ground for leadership in the national community.

While directing this expansion, Clarence de Sola and his Montreal associates had a very keen sense of independence – which sometimes came across as hubris – from the American Zionists, who were beset by what de Sola considered to be far too much internal dissension and unnecessary duplication of organizations. In December 1901, de Sola advised Theodor Herzl to nip this problem in the bud, while pointing out that, because of weakness and confusion among Zionists in the United States, Zionist associations in Des Moines, Detroit, and Syracuse had recently asked to join the Canadian federation instead.[20] In a letter to Max Nordau, Herzl's successor as president of the Zionist World Council, in February 1910, de Sola underscored the success of Zionism in Canada as opposed to the experience in Britain and the United States. According to de Sola, the "larger contribution per capita of our population than in any other country" had been due "to the fact that we have insisted all along on the strictest discipline in our ranks, with the result that our organization is strong and united, and schismatics have always found themselves in an utterly hopeless minority."[21] Not long afterwards, de Sola dispatched a somewhat acerbic letter to the Central Zionist Bureau in Cologne, sharply disagreeing with proposed constitutional changes which would allow more than one central authority in a country. De Sola wrote, "the greatest fault of the Jewish people to-day is their unwillingness to submit to discipline." "In Canada," he boasted, "we have had a rigid almost military discipline in our Federation."[22]

Although this letter reflected considerable arrogance, de Sola's belief that the Canadians were better organized was not his alone. As early as 1903, Herzl's adviser, Jacob de Haas – who, after visiting Canada and the United States, had a good basis of comparison – wrote to Herzl that "the movement here [in Canada] appears to be stronger and more solid than in the United States and altogether considerably different." Implying a comparison with unnamed American Zionist figures, he continued, "de Sola works very hard and is popular."[23]

It is clear that, right from the beginning, de Sola was determined to run his own show. In March of 1899, in reply to a letter from Professor Richard Gottheil, the president of the Federation of American Zionists, requesting that the Canadians co-operate with their fellow Zionists in the United States, de Sola had stated that the Canadians felt strongly

> that the autonomy and individuality of [their] Federation should not be sunk or lost sight of. . . . As you must be aware, the Canadian Jews have always maintained a very independent course in their communal affairs. . . . This feeling . . . is not dictated from any lack of good feeling towards our neighbours, but is simply the natural feeling of people living in a separate country, in which, to a certain degree, the sentiments and traditions are different from those of the neighbouring country.[24]

Different political and social contexts, in his view, made for separate forms of Zionist expression.

This independent attitude carried over to some of de Sola's associates. In 1919 Leon Goldman, who had a somewhat peppery personality, expressed his indignation to Shmarya Levin that the American Zionists had taken credit for Canadian contributions to the post-war Palestine Restoration Fund, and shekel purchases, by failing to inform Copenhagen otherwise: "You can easily imagine the hindrance which is caused to our efforts when we appeal for funds without being able to produce public recognition of funds already remitted." He warned that contradictory and unclear correspondence created an unfavourable impression in Canada, making it difficult to get "wholehearted support."[25] But while the centrist federation and its successor, the Zionist Organization of Canada, maintained a jealous independence from counterpart organizations in the United States, the various left-wing Zionist organizations in Canada developed fairly close ties with sister societies south of the border. These ties were especially strong in several of the youth movements, which were essentially branches of the American organizations.

Goldman was at pains to let world Zionist leaders know how far they might presume on the goodwill of Canadians. In February 1920 he wrote to London asking to be informed about discussions at a recent session of the actions committee "so as to enable us to be in a position to discuss intelligently the workings of our Organization, when we are dealing with our branches and affiliations in this Country. . . ."[26] A few years later he firmly asserted Canadian independence within the world Zionist communion when, in response to several dunning letters, he replied that fund-raising would be conducted by Canadians with due regard to local conditions, which were apparently beyond the capacity of the German officials to understand: "while we appreciate the extreme importance and dire necessity of raising as much money as possible for the work of the Restoration Fund, we cannot lose sight of the limitations of the Jewish community of this country," which numbered barely 120,000 souls whose "material wealth . . . cannot be compared in any degree with that of our brethren in the United States of America."[27] After the First World War, he said, Canadian Jews had been subjected to "campaigns after campaigns" for Palestine, for Ukrainian pogrom relief, and for local purposes. The community's limitations had to be understood. Moreover, he protested against the kind of propaganda Zionist officials were employing to extract money out of Canadian Jewry:

> It is not necessary to bring to our notice the report of the conditions in Eastern Europe in order to induce our organization to do their duty, for [we] are fully aware of those conditions and very much alive to the necessity of obtaining vast amounts of money for the work of reconstruction. [But] we do need propagandists of the higher type. . . .

De Sola's philosophy of Zionism, as expressed in his addresses at Canadian Zionist conventions, never seems to have altered very much from the program set at the First Zionist Congress, in Basle, in 1897: the establishment of a Jewish national home in Palestine and the strategies adopted by the leaders of the world movement for its implementation. In a general sense, he was a loyal supporter of Herzl, perhaps partly because he was mesmerized by Herzl's personality and speeches, as well as by the respect and honours accorded to de Sola in London at the Fourth Congress in the summer of 1900, and by the private visit he had paid to Herzl in Vienna in the preceding June. His insistence on autonomy stopped at the Canadian borders. His failure to attend any other congresses, even though Herzl, Nordau, and others encouraged him to do so, is evidence of his complete willingness to accept decisions about strategies and tactics from those who, he believed, understood these matters better than he. At later Zionist congresses, the Canadian federation was, more often than not, represented by English or American delegates, or by any Canadian Jews who happened to be travelling to Europe. An examination of the congress proceedings reveals that, after presenting perfunctory reports, Canadian delegates were never active in the debates.

This subservient attitude was not unique to de Sola or to the Canadian Zionists. Jews living elsewhere within the empire – in South Africa, for example, far from the dynamic centres of world Zionism – were also willing to accept direction from headquarters, and to concentrate on establishing efficient organizations within their own countries. To Clarence de Sola, the businessman who regularly negotiated contracts with Cabinet ministers and senior civil servants, the discussions between Herzl and the Turkish sultan, the kaiser of Germany, Emperor Franz Joseph of Austria, and other European potentates were an entirely understandable and acceptable way of securing recognition of Palestine as the Jewish national home. He delighted in news of Herzl's high-level diplomacy, and frequently embellished his letters and speeches to Canadians with information on the progress of these negotiations.

All the same, de Sola kept himself well informed of events, through his correspondence not only with Rabbi Gaster but also with Zionist figures elsewhere – including, of course, those at the movement's headquarters in Vienna, Cologne, and Berlin. He read the English Zionist press, the Vienna-based organ *Die Welt*, and, initially, the *Maccabean*, the American Zionist monthly, which he circulated to Canadians in order to keep them informed of developments abroad. Once the Montreal-based *Jewish Times* became more favourable to Zionism in 1900, de Sola saw this publication as a better vehicle for influencing Canadian Jews, and he subsequently lost interest in the *Maccabean*.

In response to the early anti-Zionism of the *Times*, which in 1898 considered the movement's "goals to be politically unattainable and economically unfeasible,"[28] de Sola and other Zionist spokesmen denied that there was any conflict between Zionism and patriotism. The issue of dual loyalty, loyalty both to Canada and to Jewish national revival, never seems to have bothered him.[29] In a letter to one supporter, he stated:

We regard the idea that the reestablishment of the Jewish state would throw suspicion upon the loyalty of Jews residing in other lands as too absurd to call for serious reply. To our minds, the Zionist movement aims at securing a home for Jews living in countries where they are suffering oppression. Those, who like ourselves, enjoy the same privileges as the other citizens of the countries we live in declare most emphatically our loyalty to the countries we live in notwithstanding that we are a nation.[30]

Despite the early concerns expressed in the *Jewish Times*, the loyalty question did not at this time become a major issue in Canada, as it did in the United States.

As already noted, de Sola strongly favoured discipline and order, two elements which he found to be sadly lacking in Jewish public life. He believed that, with firm direction, Zionism could bring order out of a chaos and disunity which had held Jews everywhere back for many years. In a letter to de Haas early in 1903, shortly after several hundred delegates and observers from Halifax to Vancouver had attended the federation's third convention, in Montreal, de Sola exulted over "how wonderfully our movement is uniting the scattered parts of our race."[31] He wrote in a similar vein to Jews in cities all across Canada. Encouraging Joseph Enzer of Fort William to form a local Zionist society, he wrote, "remember that one of the great aims of Zionism is to organize our entire race and solidify it under one governing body; hence there is a principle at stake in gaining the adherence of the inhabitants of even the smallest village." In this and many other letters, de Sola carefully explained that the purpose of this unity was to achieve the goals of the Basle program, which included obtaining a legally secured home for the Jewish people in Palestine, the physical and economic development of that homeland, and the awakening of Jewish national and spiritual consciousness through the development of Hebrew literature and everything that would raise the cultural level of the Jewish people.

Although cognizant of the importance of political Zionism as the beginning of an all-embracing Jewish revival – and while he seems to have understood the far-reaching nationalistic implications of the movement – de Sola also conceived of Zionism in more practical terms. To a Jew in New Brunswick, he explained that the aim of the Zionists was not to "restore the whole of the Hebrew race to Palestine. The object . . . is simply to restore to that country that portion of our race who are at present suffering from persecution, and who, as a consequence, are emigrating and seeking new homes."[32] He argued that "for an organized mass of people to flood these western countries under no direction, "and with no proper training for agriculture, or other means of living, will be disastrous, and must naturally only produce misery." The only feasible and businesslike solution was to settle these people in Palestine, where they could be self-supporting in agricultural or other pursuits. Thus, de Sola saw Zionism as a practical solution to a problem facing the Jews of Canada, on whom the burden of European immigration would otherwise continue to fall.

Although de Sola often publicly stated, especially at annual conventions, that there were two tasks for Zionism in Canada – education and fund-raising – it is clear from his correspondence that fund-raising was by far the more important goal. Indeed, from the very beginning, the federation set this as its first priority. In addition to the shekel, the basic membership fee for Zionists everywhere, and the sale of Jewish Colonial Trust shares, the Jewish National Fund to purchase land in Palestine was adopted early on as a special Canadian cause. Raising money was, in de Sola's mind, exactly the kind of work best suited to Zionists. "Mere ebullitions of sentiment would prove inadequate unless supported by concrete achievements," he told the delegates to the national convention in January 1911.[33] "When we gather in Convention annually, the first thing that interests us is to see how much practical work our Federation has accomplished during the year, . . . above all, how much we Zionists have contributed in hard cash to the funds of the Movement." For most members of the federation's constituent associations, de Sola's prescriptions for action seemed acceptable. There were some internal tensions within the federation as to whether the mere gathering of money deserved as much attention as education or, as one dissenter, Abraham Fallick of Toronto, put it, "the proper understanding of Zionist principles and institutions."[34] But most members agreed that "Our Movement aims at an ideal but we are practical enough to recognize that it can only be attained through that which is material."[35] He would brook no opposition from Fallick, "a man of no influence in the community, a comparatively recently arrived emigrant" who had dared to attack "the leading Jews in Canada, and the power and authority that they represent." Such leading Jews, he observed, contributed "about four-fifths of the . . . funds of the Movement every year in Canada [which] has been the cause of the success of Zionism in this country. . . ."[36] De Sola thus made it abundantly clear not only that large donors were the ones who kept the federation alive, but also that fund-raising was virtually the only activity of note going on within the federation. Dissenters like Fallick and a few others, who wanted to enrich its cultural program, had to knuckle under or get out of the organization.

As time went on, fund-raising became the even more firmly fixed *raison d'être* of the federation and the measure of its success. What world Jewry demanded of their Canadian brethren was financial help, and while it was given in generous measure, through gargantuan undertakings like the million-dollar Emek Hepher scheme – an enormously ambitious and expensive land purchase in Palestine in 1927 – the habit of giving became a substitute for a deeper, more positive experience that might have laid the basis for a Jewish cultural renaissance in Canada. Canadian Zionism developed few cultural dimensions, except in relatively small ideological offshoots like Farband or Poale Zion (Labour Zionism) or Mizrachi (Religious Zionism), or in the youth movements. It is perhaps arguable that the Russian and Polish Jews who, by 1910, made up the largest proportion of Canadian Jewry needed little of this cultural stimulation: they may have brought all they needed for a lifetime from Europe. But if they had, it remained, for most, a matter of conviction only; discussion, debate, and exposition of Jewish culture within the Zionist movement did not attract many participants. By the end of the First World War, Canadian Zionism had produced no more than a handful of intellectuals with the ability to energize the movement or even challenge the federation's leadership.

Given his priority of fund-raising, de Sola was never prouder of the Canadian Zionists than in 1910, when at his suggestion they launched the Jewish National Fund. The purpose of the fund was to purchase land in Palestine for reclamation and settlement. This was exactly the kind of practical work he wanted Canadians to undertake, and he took special interest in raising the necessary first $10,000; once that amount was subscribed and collected, he had the federation take up further land purchase commitments the following year.[37] He also gave approval – however guarded – to the plans of a Winnipeg branch of the Ahuza, a movement, dedicated to settlement in Palestine, to buy a 3,500-dunam tract of land (3.5 square kilometres) at Sheikh Munis, north of Tel Aviv, where the Winnipeggers planned to settle and farm.[38] Negotiations for this purchase were well advanced when they were interrupted by the war. The scheme eventually lapsed.

In fund-raising for various projects, in the size of its membership, and in the adherence of women and youth, the federation was in a generally healthy condition by 1914. But the economic and political crisis of East European Jewry during the war raised serious problems and, for a time, significantly altered its hitherto unchallenged power, influence, and legitimacy as a Canadian Jewish communal institution, and as the official spokesman of Jewry in the Dominion. Also, the war highlighted many major transformations wrought by immigrants

in the social and intellectual life of Canadian Jewry, which challenged the legitimacy of Zionism as the sole vehicle for Jewish national aspirations. As well,
the war gave rise to discontent among young intellectuals within the Zionist
movement, who dissented from the philosophy espoused or represented by de
Sola and his association, because of the emergence of rival Zionist agendas.
The effects of the war on Canadian Jewry, therefore, were profound.

By 1914, the majority of Canadian Jews were East European immigrants
who had arrived during the great migrations after 1900. Whether these immigrants were located in Glace Bay, Montreal, Brantford, Regina, or Vancouver,
their hearts lay in the East, in the Russian, Ukrainian, Galician, Polish,
Romanian, and Lithuanian towns and villages where their close relations now
found themselves in war zones. From 1914 to 1921 the Yiddish press, which
by 1914 included three Canadian papers that readers often supplemented
with Yiddish dailies from New York, carried news of starvation, forced migration, and pogroms.

Among the most important and interesting manifestations of Zionist activity in Canada during the war was the recruiting campaign undertaken for the
Jewish Legion, a 5,000-man force – the first Jewish military formation in
modern times – organized to fight under Britain's General Allenby for the liberation of Palestine from Turkish rule. Following the 1917 decision of the
British government to recruit British and American Jews to this special force,
the agreement of the Canadian government was sought. Hundreds of Jews
already in the Canadian Expeditionary Force – both volunteers and conscripts
– indicated a desire to transfer to the Legion.[39] The Borden administration,
which had introduced military conscription in June of 1917, agreed to allow
the British to recruit Canadian Jews who were "not subject to conscription in
Canada,"[40] and an officer from the British army arrived late in 1917 to begin a
recruiting drive across the country.

Yitchak Ben-Zvi and David Ben-Gurion, respectively future president and
future prime minister of Israel, had been travelling throughout North America
in 1915 and 1916 to recruit young Jewish men for a pioneer army called
Hechalutz (the Pioneer), to serve in Palestine once the war ended. The two-
man mission was greeted with considerable enthusiasm by Jews in Toronto,
although Ben-Gurion was disappointed with the actual recruitment. In August
1915, only seven men signed up in Toronto, where Ben-Gurion had hoped to
enlist 15.[41] In Hamilton he found only one qualified man, a professional jockey
who wanted to join the *shomrim*, a force of mounted watchmen; the rest he
rejected as "not suitable material. . . . Most of them are forty or fifty years old

and burdened with families."[42] An invitation for him to address a meeting in Montreal was withdrawn for lack of interest, and a gathering in Winnipeg, according to one observer, produced "a serious failure [because] . . . Ben-Gurion is a very weak speaker and is no great agitator."[43] In 1918 both Ben-Gurion and Ben-Zvi joined the Legion, and assisted in recruiting in the United States. American and Canadian recruits – at least 300 of the latter – were sent to Windsor, Nova Scotia, for three weeks of basic training before being shipped overseas to British army training depots. Later that year they were sent to Egypt as the 39th Battalion of the Royal Fusiliers.

Writing to his wife days before embarkation, from temporary quarters at the Citadel in Halifax, Ben-Zvi described the view. To a Russian Jew who had laboured as a pioneer in the harsh conditions of early-twentieth-century Palestine, it was an idyllic scene:

> The fort stands on top of a high hill at the foot of which an inlet of the Atlantic invades the dry land. And the area is covered with grass and oak trees – all around, everything is green. Only here and there does one see occasional huts and houses – these are the houses of local farmers, each widely separated from its neighbours, or the huts of the fishermen, who get their living from the ocean's rich harvest. The hills and the bay, the forests and the multitude of boats remind me very much of the shores of the Bosphorus, near Constantinople. . . . This is exactly the same landscape: a multitude of ships go back and forth, and they can all be seen from the top of the hill where the fort stands. Whenever I see the ships my heart expands within me. I gaze towards the East, across the ocean, and in my mind's eye I see my homeland, half of it redeemed and half of it enslaved.[44]

Bernard Joseph, the McGill law student who had formed Young Judaea, participated in the Legion recruiting campaign and joined up himself. For him, as for a number of others, the experience served to reinforce an already deeply embedded Zionism. After completing his law degree at McGill in 1921, Joseph would return to Palestine with his wife to practise law. Later, having adopted the Hebrew name of "Dov" to replace "Bernard," he would pursue an active political career in Jerusalem. But although a small colony of Canadian soldiers settled at Avichayil, a village north of Tel Aviv, most of them eventually returned to Canada. Persistent harassment of the Jewish soldiers by British military police in Palestine in 1918 and 1919, and the complete ban on visitations to Jerusalem, contributed to their frustration and anger. Several who loudly and physically objected to this discrimination – including four privates from Toronto – were court-martialed for disobedience and mutiny and served terms in military prison before being given amnesty.[45]

Recruitment to the Legion was a good index of Canadian Jews' enthusiasm in 1917 and 1918 for a national home in Palestine under British sponsorship. The Balfour Declaration of August 1917 elicited widespread emotional outpourings, and not just from Zionists; Canadian Jews marched through the Jewish sections of major cities, attended numerous emotional rallies, and listened to countless messianic speeches from rostrums and pulpits across the land. Long-standing Anglophiles like de Sola waxed eloquent at this revolutionary new turn in Jewish history. At last there was to be a home for the Jews in their sacred ancient land, the setting of the first and second Jewish commonwealths millennia before. But would they regard Palestine as the national home for all Jews, themselves included, or continue to see it as a refuge for the persecuted?

For the overwhelming majority, the latter was true, and the idea that the national home would be under British sponsorship was taken to mean that the refuge would be larger, stronger, and much more secure. And, like the rest of the Jewish world, Canadian Zionists believed that, because their cause had received the imprimatur of one of the world's great powers, the dream would be fulfilled soon. Thus, while the character of Zionism in Canada changed little from its essentially philanthropic orientation, its intensity grew, largely because of the legitimacy provided by the Balfour Declaration and, later, by the mandate the League of Nations gave Great Britain to proceed.

From its earliest years the Federation of Canadian Zionist Societies had received regular goodwill messages from prime ministers, provincial premiers, and other levels of government. Some of this may have been self-serving. Liberal politicians, having more of a political debt to the Jewish community, may have felt particularly compelled to be favourable to their supporters' concerns. But all of this public attention was very necessary to the Zionists, because they were part of a movement which emphasized the acquisition of world approval for their cause. In the Western democracies such approval was relatively easily acquired. In Canada, where a certain marginal identification with British imperial aspirations and grandeur remained, support for the mandate was considerable. Favourable editorial comment in the newspapers indicated that the idea of a Jewish national home in Palestine, under British control, had at least some public acceptance.[46]

The dislocation and destruction of the First World War had disrupted much of the early Zionist reconstruction in Palestine. The Turkish authorities had expelled many Jews and interned others; meanwhile, development had languished and settlements had declined. Worst of all had been the immense human suffering in the Jewish communities there, particularly in Jerusalem, where the population was composed mainly of elderly people largely dependent on charity. While the Turks remained in control, little could be done directly by Canadian Zionists to assist Palestine Jewry. Funds raised in Canada had usually been transferred directly to the international body; its headquarters had been located in Germany until 1914, when the offices were hastily transferred to neutral Copenhagen so that Zionists on both sides could continue to communicate. Before 1917, however, relatively little practical work could be accomplished even from neutral countries because of Turkish suspicions, although by 1917 American Jewish relief organizations were allowed to distribute medicine, food, and other forms of relief.

The wartime experience of Canadian Jewry helped greatly to crystallize a number of developments within the Zionist fold. The leadership of the Canadian Zionist movement had in many ways reflected the demographic nature of the community in the critical year of 1914, when sizeable immigration from Europe had stopped for the duration of the war. By 1914 the overwhelmingly East European makeup of the population had been evident not only from a glance at immigration figures over the previous decade and a half, but from the Yiddish spoken by most Jews, the organizations they founded, and what one might call an outlook on Zionism and Jewish life in general which many of them shared. Labour Zionism and Religious Zionism had arisen, along with many other groups such as Territorialists, Anarchists, and Bundists, as well as scores of mutual aid societies and trade unions. Many immigrants, then, especially those living in the large cities, did not officially support the federation.

Thus, even though the Federation of Canadian Zionist Societies was the only national Jewish body – a Canadian Jewish parliament, so to speak – it was not very broadly based, or representative of all segments of Jewish political opinion or all social classes. The severe crisis in European Jewish life brought on by the war had a catalytic effect on the masses of Canadian Jewry, who were moved to perform prodigies of joint action such as they had never undertaken before. And in the process of developing this co-operation, which was finally achieved only at the end of the war, the right of the federation to speak on behalf of the community was challenged, and defeated, by the new-found collective action of the immigrants.

Besides raising the question of convening some kind of national congress to discuss a broad range of issues affecting Jews in those critical times, the war created serious political difficulties for all Zionists – especially those living in countries like Canada, which were fighting against Germany and its ally Turkey. Sensitive to the problems which might impede the realization of their aims in Palestine (and endanger what had already been achieved) if the Zionist cause was identified with either side, the world Zionist organization's executive had sought to remain neutral. De Sola was instructed to conduct federation affairs with circumspection. What this meant, essentially, was that money could not be sent directly to Palestine, but had to be forwarded through American relief organizations. Still, the war had the effect of seriously reducing fund-raising until about 1917, because of the uncertainty of the fate of the *yishuv* (Jewish settlement) and the emergence of other, more pressing concerns.

At the onset of the war de Sola and the federation had been uncertain as to what they should be doing, and so had appeared to be doing little, if anything, to preserve the movement's strength in Canada. Among those dissatisfied with de Sola's failure to provide more dynamic leadership were young intellectuals and professionals like Abraham Roback, Louis Fitch, and Hyman Edelstein, all of them contributors to Montreal's *Canadian Jewish Chronicle*, the successor to the *Jewish Times*.

The wartime period also accentuated the Montreal Jewish community's vulnerability within French Canada, where the war effort was unpopular, while it highlighted the fact that the federation was beset by bitter internal economic conflict and serious structural problems.[47] This variety of issues combined to affect the lives of a significant and growing number of Canadian Jews to whom, it seemed, Zionism was not directly relevant. To the average Jewish garment worker in Montreal, Toronto, or Winnipeg, for example, the affairs of the Amalgamated Clothing Workers Union were likely to be decidedly more important. And to those working-class Jews who might have been interested enough to join a Zionist group, the middle-class, English-language, fund-raising–oriented Zionist societies, which included clothing manufacturers (whom they considered to be sweatshop exploiters), would have been less than satisfactory.[48] These workers, most of them located in cities, tended to support the more idealistic and intellectually satisfying programs of Labour Zionism and, for the Orthodox, Religious Zionism.

Several women's groups had existed in a number of cities since the first of them, the Daughters of Zion, had been founded in Toronto in 1900.[49] Over the next eighteen years numerous women's Zionist organizations had been formed with the goals of helping Jewish women in Palestine improve health and "home craft" standards in the country (The Jewish Women's League for

Cultural Work in Palestine), assisting in hospital care (the Palestinian Sewing Circle), and other causes. Anna Selick of Toronto had formed the nucleus of Canadian Hadassah in 1916. After a helpful visit from Henrietta Szold, then president of American Hadassah, an organization of women's chapters had been established in Toronto, Hamilton, Brantford, London, and Windsor. Over the next few years most Zionist women's groups in the country came in under the umbrella of Canadian Hadassah, which spread into every city and town in the country. This remarkable organization soon became the most continuously active arm of Zionism in Canada, infusing the movement with a sense of immediate and pressing concern. In large and small centres these women worked fervently for several Palestinian causes – first for the Helping Hand Fund, and later for a Girls' Domestic and Agricultural Science School at Nahalal, a Nurses' Training School in Jerusalem, and a number of other major projects, such as a convalescent home and a tubercular hospital.[50] Innumerable raffles, bazaars, teas, and tag days kept members busy raising money for all of these projects. The leaders of Hadassah, like Lillian Freiman, Rose Dunkleman, and Anna Raginsky, personified the cause in which thousands of Jewish women across Canada worked to help their sisters in Palestine. If Zionism in Canada ever had "shock troops," they were the devoted women of Hadassah and, later, of the Pioneer Women and Mizrachi Women.

The end of hostilities following Allenby's conquest of Palestine opened opportunities for the reconstruction of the Jewish settlements there. Canadians were asked to participate by raising money through the Helping Hand Fund and the Palestine Restoration Fund, both of which were established in 1917. Before the Helping Hand Fund was wound up in 1918, the Canadians raised nearly $160,000, an amount far exceeding the aggregate proceeds of all previous Zionist campaigns since 1899. This success was attributable to several factors, including the full employment, prosperity, and emotions of wartime. In addition, a new and younger leadership had arisen in the communities, especially among women. Lillian Freiman – wife of Archie Freiman, a leading Zionist activist in Ottawa, performed prodigies of campaigning throughout Canada during the war.[51] She employed advertising to spread word of the destitution in Palestine.[52] She then began a systematic coast-to-coast tour (at her own expense) to appeal directly to as many of Canada's Jews as she could reach. Her eloquence opened hearts and purses as never before and the fund collected $160,000 in cash and $40,000 in clothing, medicine, and foodstuffs, including significant contributions from many non-Jewish Canadians. It was the greatest fund-raising drive ever mounted by Canadian Jews and it set a new standard for charitable giving which seemed unattainable a few years before. But the Palestine Restoration Fund, which followed almost immediately on the heels of this drive – and was also led by the Freimans – was even more successful, nearly $275,000 was collected by 1921.[53]

Enthusiasm for Zionism was especially strong among Jewish youth. Many youth clubs had been formed in the early years of the movement, and young people were welcomed at the federation's national conventions.[54] Young Judaea Clubs which had sprung up in Toronto as early as 1913 were absorbed into the new body. Even though Joseph and several other early members of Young Judaea had gone to live in Palestine, the organization did not officially encourage *aliyah* (emigration to Israel) as a goal to which its members should aspire. Rather, it remained essentially what the adult leaders of Canadian Zionism hoped it would be – an educational force

> to advance the cause of Zionism; to promote Jewish culture and ideals in accordance with Jewish tradition . . . to arouse enthusiasm for the study of Jewish history, Hebrew literature and language; to instil in the young a loyalty to the Jewish people and its glorious traditions; to inculcate a devotion to the Jewish homeland in Palestine and an appreciation of the Zionist aim and willingness to serve in the cause for the reestablishment of the Jewish Nation on its own soil.[55]

Within these broad parameters, Young Judaea clubs had soon sprung up in many centres across Canada; a national organization was established in 1919 and a full-time director hired in 1924 to manage its educational program. In promoting the Zionist ideal, Young Judaea achieved considerable success. Although it later faced competition from more idealistic youth organizations which strongly emphasized *aliyah*, the very lack of a clear-cut ideology, beyond a benevolent attitude towards Zionism, meant that it placed no stringent demands on its members. Like its parent organization, therefore, Young Judaea had the kind of broad appeal with which most Jewish youth could identify, and which gave their parents little concern that Zionist enthusiasm would be encouraged to develop beyond a certain point. The educational program was promoted at weekly club meetings, which consisted of lectures and discussions of Jewish history and current events, readings from Jewish literature, the singing of national and traditional melodies, the celebration of Jewish festivals, dramatic presentations, and debates, as well as athletic events.[56] Fostered and largely financed by the federation, later the Zionist Organization of Canada, Young Judaea took on many of its parent organization's characteristics, including the national superstructure, biennial conventions, regional conferences, transnational social contact, and the aura of middle-class benevolence.

The First World War accentuated the fact that certain features of Canadian constitutional and political history had given the Canadian Jewish community a context that differed significantly from that of American Jewry. For example, loyalty to Britain's cause, which waxed positively rhapsodic at times, provided Zionists with opportunities to identify their purposes with Britain's imperial mission. As far back as 1903, when the Uganda proposal (a temporary refuge for Jews in British East Africa) had been under consideration, de Sola had waxed eloquent on the subject of Zion's redemption under the British flag. Fourteen years later, when Allenby's armies were poised in Egypt for an assault against Turkish Palestine, de Sola saw the British liberation of Eretz Yisrael (The Land of Israel) as the dawning of a new messianic age. He even announced at the fourteenth convention of the federation, in 1917, that it was time for the reestablishment of the Sanhedrin – the Jewish judicial body in ancient Palestine – as the supreme court of Jewish law and the governing council of the people of Israel.[57] Canadian Zionists were therefore able to identify their cause within the context of what one historian defines as British Canadian nationalism, and without raising the question of whether adherence to Zionism conflicted with their loyalty to Canada.[58]

When the idea arose of forming the Jewish Legion to fight with the imperial forces in Palestine, de Sola – at first puzzled by the proposal – soon became one of its most ardent supporters. But his work for the Jewish Legion was one of his last acts on behalf of Canadian Zionism. Amid considerable tension and acrimony within the organization, he relinquished the presidency at the 1919 convention, and died a few months later. He was replaced by a provisional committee, which later selected Archie Freiman as his successor. The federation, renamed the Zionist Organization of Canada, went on to undertake even more ambitious fund-raising ventures, continuing the Zionist activity that de Sola had pioneered decades beforehand.

Of course, the progress of Zionism in Canada between the 1890s and the end of the First World War was not determined solely by individuals such as de Sola or his associates. It was the outcome of special circumstances in Canada, which created an environment in which Zionism came to be the most important mode of Canadian Jewish identity in that era. Although non-Zionist groups emerged during the war, Zionism bore the imprimatur of at least part of the elite that de Sola symbolized, and the support of this group – almost an aristocracy, considering de Sola's genealogy, wealth, and position in

Anglo-Montreal society – lent legitimacy to the movement at this stage. It also had the stamp of approval from various federal Cabinet ministers who made brief guest appearances at the federations conventions. And while not all members of the mercantile elite were active Zionists – or, perhaps, even members or contributors – none was an outspoken or active anti-Zionist, or, at this time, did any mainstream or elitist Jewish organization take an anti-Zionist position. In the United States, on the other hand, the American Jewish Committee and leading members of the Reform rabbinate openly opposed Zionist ideas.

Zionism provided Canadian Jewry with an "ideology of survival," as well as an identity. That it was a flawed vision and had problems with leadership is clear. The organization overly stressed fund-raising, to the detriment of education, but this was not entirely de Sola's fault. The message from the European Zionist Federation, and, ultimately, from Jerusalem, was – and unfortunately still remains – "send us more money, and more and still more." World Zionist leaders, with few exceptions, failed to insist that the dream demanded much more than money alone. But it would have been unrealistic to expect de Sola, who was a mere lieutenant in one of the smaller Jewish communities – and a relatively new and unformed one, at that – to do much more than follow orders.

In running the affairs of the federation, de Sola was often self-righteous, pompous, dictatorial, and insensitive. With all that, however, he was a full-hearted Zionist and a proud Jew, devout, serious, and thoughtful, who believed in the inevitability of a Jewish national revival in the land of Israel. He built a large nationwide organization which enjoyed a success that aroused international envy and emulation.

While it was in many ways close to the American Zionist philosophy, Canadian Zionism in de Sola's era had not experienced the same internal power struggles and ideological debate as had occurred in the United States. Zionism in Canada did not have to compete, as it did in both Britain and the United States, with previously established organizations, or with national loyalty. Being a much newer community, Canadian Jewry had had no national coherence or articulated identity before the arrival of Zionism, and it provided both an acceptable structure and an identity. The fact that it remained strong in hinterland communities as well as in the metropolitan centres, indicates its emergence as the normative form of Canadian Jewish identification even as early as 1914.

What was true of the federation was also true of other sectors of the mainstream Zionist movement, like Hadassah and Young Judaea. Canadian Hadassah's achievements in Palestine were remarkable, and the energy, success, and emotional commitment of its members were attributable not only to their Jewish identity; the cause also appealed to "their instincts as women – a love of cleanliness, an abhorrence of disease, [and] a solicitude for the welfare of children."[59] While in some respects Hadassah was at first the women's auxiliary and the constituent party of the male-dominated federation, it soon became separate, as a body devoted to projects that the women themselves selected, sometimes in concert with the Hadassah organization in the United States. Canadian Hadassah charted its own course early on by identifying its own goals, organizing separate fund-raising efforts, and running its own national office. Its early leading spirits were mostly young middle-class women who set out to find an opportunity to serve the movement as women, and to provide a separate voice for women and an emphasis on social welfare in Canada's efforts on behalf of the Jewish national home.

Thus Hadassah was an expression of the earliest impulse among Canadian Jewish women for an independent voice and an emphasis on priorities which they chose to identify and support.[60] In this sense, it was a vehicle for their Canadianization; it provided a medium of accommodation to a number of the cultural and social values that were shared by their non-Jewish sisters. As well, it served as an entrée into society, in both the Jewish and the non-Jewish Canadian world. It raised the profile of Jewish women as Jews, as Canadians, and, above all, as women. Within the Jewish community the moral influence and political power of these women were of great significance. Their leadership's class identity gave the organization a special strength. By 1920, it was the strongest, most coherent, and best-led national organization on the Canadian Jewish scene.

As the mainstream Zionist organization for youth, Young Judaea became in many ways a mirror image of its parent, the federation. In its structure and philosophy it was a vehicle for the Canadianization of large members of Canadian Jewish youth. Its primary purpose was the preparation of the next generation for leadership in the Zionist movement, and so its leaders saw their role as an educational one, to bring members to an understanding of their Jewish roots so that they would "serve in Jewish life on this continent . . . [and] to make a contribution to the perpetuation of the Jewish people, so that the Jew, who has not expended his creative ability, may contribute again to the culture of the world." But there was another goal in Young Judaea, that of saving virtually an entire generation from assimilation. Jewish youth, according to this view, was adrift in North America because traditional East European mechanisms of guidance and control – parents, schools, and synagogues – were no longer able to instil traditional values and culture in the younger generation. "Young people . . . have found it difficult to live as Jews," wrote one commentator in analysing this situation, "and their Jewishness for the most part has not meant enough to them to forgo the comforts and conveniences that could be theirs for the very easy task of forgetting that they are Jews. . . . And so they have sold their birthright for a mess of pottage."[61] Thus the survival of Jewish life was threatened, unless the apathy and ignorance of the younger generation could be arrested by a comprehensive educational program.

Young Judaea was an integral part of the survival strategy implicit in the mainstream Canadian Zionist movement before 1920, and this strategy was largely shaped by the need to create mechanisms for the survival of Jewishness, which was endangered by what was perceived as a breakdown of Jewish culture in North America. The federation and Young Judaea were engaged in establishing definitions of Canadian Jewish identity, and the structure through which it should be expressed. Hadassah helped women define their image, both to themselves and to Canadian society as a whole, in ways that reflected their traditional role as care-givers. Spread nationwide, attracting the energetic leadership of some of the most prominent people in the community, and guided by an accommodationist philosophy, these organizations were among the most important landmarks on the Canadian Jewish scene.

11

"Corner of Pain and Anguish"[1]

As the Canadian clothing industry expanded during the first two decades of the twentieth century, Jewish participation increased enormously. Capital requirements were relatively low, cheap labour was plentiful, and markets abounded in this industry, which was therefore able to escape monopoly control and much government regulation. Clothing manufacturing thus offered an extremely attractive frontier of business enterprise, especially for Jewish immigrants who possessed minimal capital, a capacity for very hard work, and a large measure of willingness to take a chance.

As Jewish contractors proliferated, some of them prospered so much that, as Montreal's *Journal of Commerce* observed in February of 1906,

> wholesale houses are not able to compete due to the low accustomed mode of living [of Jewish immigrants] from South-Eastern Europe and Western Russia (intelligent but ground down) who settle in Montreal. They are driven to make their own garments at home and readily adapt themselves to doing repairs for the second hand shops, and gradually become workers for the wholesale houses. Eventually these people buy their own materials and manufacture for the consumer directly. Many have made a name for themselves in Montreal.[2]

Though this evolution was not complete by 1914 – new firms developed and older ones declined – a number of Jews had emerged as important manufacturers. Competition was rife, and expanding markets placed a premium on flexibility, ruthless price-cutting, mobility, and severe exploitation of workers, particularly women, children, and immigrants.

In an industry with such characteristics it was difficult to organize more than a segment of the employees into trade unions. High turnover rates, the availability of virtually limitless numbers of part-time female workers, the relative mobility of factories (the phenomenon known as the "runaway shop" which was moved out of town to escape unions or use cheap labour), and the tradition of craft unionism, which tried to restrict entry to skilled workers, militated against the organization of the unions that tried to reform poor work and wage conditions. Tailors' unions which had arisen in various Canadian cities since the 1820s proved inadequate for the organization of masses of semi-skilled workers in clothing factories.

The Journeymen Tailors' Union of America had locals in forty-four cities and towns across Canada in the 1890s and early 1900s, but had only a small membership because it was restricted to skilled tailors working in custom shops. Most of these Canadian locals did not survive for long; by 1911 there were only three.[3] Fully aware of market trends towards cheaper custom tailoring and readymade clothing, which were capturing an ever larger share of the men's clothing market, the secretary of the American union warned members in August 1889 that "such work is not being made by our members but by persons who are usually not tailors at all."[4] He admonished members that "we are living under new and ever changing conditions, and we must meet them as they arise or they will overwhelm us" and suggested that members employ helpers to assist them in taking on more work of the cheaper sort, thus expanding employment for union men. But the rapidly rising popularity of readymade clothing undermined the custom tailoring trade. The piecework system used in the production of cheaper grades of clothing was more efficient, as it utilized women and children who were willing to work long hours at home or in sweatshops for low wages; also its extensive division of labour offered more flexibility and higher profits to the manufacturers and contractors.

During the late 1880s, the Knights of Labour included clothing workers in their broad-based industrial unions. In Hamilton and Toronto, several of the Knights' assemblies were composed largely of needleworkers—some exclusively of women—although the effect on wages and working conditions seems to have been transitory at best.[5] Even the growth of a much stronger and more specifically industrial union in the 1880s and 1890s, the United Garment Workers of America (a breakaway organization from the Journeymen Tailors with an industrial rather than strictly craft appeal), had little success in changing conditions.

The UGWA arose in the United States in the 1890s, and quickly organized locals in Toronto, Hamilton, and Montreal.[6] In Montreal the union engaged in a fierce but losing strike at Mark Workman's factory in mid-September of 1900. The union charged that Workman, whose firm specialized in the production of uniforms for the British and Canadian governments, had laid off nine workers to hire illegally imported Romanian Jews allegedly willing to work for one-third the wages. While Workman denied importing these individuals against the immigration laws, he did not deny the firings.[7] The union demanded improvements to wages, which were as low as $5 per week for workers compelled to put in sixteen-hour days.[8] With only 35 out of 300 employees joining the strike, however, Workman continued production with barely a pause.[9]

Unable to prevent employers from bringing in cheap labour, the UGWA could do little to stop the replacement of salaried tailors by women on piecework, or to keep employers from slashing salaries and forcing workers to forgo their Saturday half-holidays without compensation.[10] This latter practice worked a particularly severe hardship on the many Jewish employees who adhered strictly to Orthodox Sabbath observance, although some Jewish employers were willing to allow them to work on Sunday instead. On the other hand, Jewish workers were sometimes militant in defending their religious holidays. During a needle-industry strike in Hamilton in April 1913, they insisted on recognition of Passover, "during which time," a Department of Labour official reported, "none of the Jewish people, and there are many of them among the strikers, would return to work until this particular holiday was over."[11]

Serious confrontations were also erupting in the women's wear sector of the Montreal clothing industry. In March of 1904, workers at Star Mantle Manufacturing Company walked out under the leadership of the newly-organized International Ladies' Garment Workers' Union which won major concessions from the firm's owners.[12] Strikes taking place at other women's clothing companies were often accompanied by violence, arson, lockouts, threats and rapidly rising bitterness on both sides. In February and March of 1910 a lengthy and serious confrontation broke out in the dress and cloak factories owned by Abraham Sommer, a highly prominent activist in the Jewish community.[13]

Piecework, contractors, crowded conditions, dirty garret shops, immigrant labour—the hated "sweating system"—had not improved by the early 1900s, despite the publicity given to it since the late 1880s. Several leaders of the Montreal labour movement pinpointed specific evil conditions. B. A. Larger, president of the Montreal UGWA argued in 1904 that imported female factory-workers, many of them mere children who worked for $2 to $3 per week, were depressing wages generally in the industry.[14] The industry's seasonal nature was another problem; in the periods between the major production runs of July to September for fall deliveries, and January to March for spring deliveries, there were long layoffs for cutters, and only part-time work for operators.[15] Such conditions made it easy for employers to dictate terms of employment with impunity. Even in the face of a powerful open-shop drive in May of 1904, the *Montreal Star* observed, jobs were so scarce in Montreal that a strike would not take place.[16] One firm forced its employees to post a forfeitable $25 deposit each as a personal guarantee that they would not strike. This practice was nothing short of extortion, as some workers pointed out; the employer could foment a strike and pocket the money.[17] Allegedly, some did so.

The UGWA's growing Jewish membership supplied the organization with a socialist[18] tinge. Four major garment strikes were called against a large number of Montreal firms in autumn 1907, to secure union recognition, substitution of wages for piecework, and cleaner factories.[19] Moreover, at S. Levinson, Son and Company, the union demanded that young girls begin work at 7:30 a.m. instead of 7:00, so that they could eat breakfast at home; it also demanded an end of forced "deposits" against strikes.[20] In factories producing women's clothing, a group of Jewish pressers and cloakmakers battling for union recognition had to confront intra-ethnic animosity, as employer A. J. Hart—himself a Jew—demanded that "foreign [Jewish] agitators be deported," claiming that "Not one of our native born employees were affected."[21] In March of 1908, the workers at Freedman Company—owned by community leader Lyon Cohen—struck for a reduction in their work week from sixty-one hours to forty-eight.[22] Other fierce battles ensued all across Canada.[23] In Winnipeg, a bitter and unsuccessful strike by the UGWA in 1908, which included "many Jewish tailors" at the ladies' clothing firm of Jacob & Crawley, lasted more than a year.[24]

But while minor gains were occasionally achieved, employers successfully resisted unionization, as well as attempts to prevent them from employing contractors, whose outside shops were so numerous, so difficult to regulate, and so transitory that they were almost impossible for health inspectors to police effectively, or for unions to penetrate.

The tension caused by increasing competition and rising union militancy brought a rash of strikes in Toronto, Montreal, and Hamilton in 1912. The confrontation began in Montreal in early June when a massive industry-wide strike erupted against the member firms of the Montreal Clothing Manufacturers' Association, which included all the major men's clothing producers. The *dramatis personae* in this protracted and extremely bitter struggle included some of the most prominent members of Montreal's Jewish community, indicating just how closely Jews were identified with the needle trades and what deep class divisions existed among them. At the head of the manufacturers' association stood B. Gardner, owner of one of the city's prestigious menswear firms. Behind him stood a solid phalanx of some of the most prominent Jews in the city, including Solomon Levinson, Harris Kellert, Noah Friedman and his son David, Lyon Cohen, Harris Vineberg, Jacob Elkin, and Samuel Hart – most of whom were connected by marriage or by business ties going back to the 1860s and 1870s, when many of them had been storekeepers and pedlars around Lancaster, Ontario. Well-to-do, established, and powerful men, they had made the slow transition from merchants to manufacturers as contractors on the fringes of the industry, and had emerged as successful industrialists employing hundreds of hands in their large shops, which were located in the city's garment district around lower St. Lawrence Boulevard. Members of the venerable Spanish and Portuguese synagogue, Sha'ar Hashomayim, or the Temple Emanu-el, they lived in fashionable West End suburbs, supported local Jewish charities, and took a keen interest in Jewish public affairs.[25]

The most prominent and active of these worthies was Lyon Cohen; he was born in 1868 in Poland, grew up in Maberly, Ontario, and joined his father, Lazarus, in a Montreal coal and dredging business.[26] He established a brass foundry and in 1906 bought the Freedman Company, which became one of the city's largest and most successful men's clothing firms. As a vehicle for the vigorous defence of Canadian Jews against antisemitism – and as a public service to the Jewish community – in 1897 Cohen founded the *Jewish Times*, the first English-language Jewish newspaper in Canada. He chaired a committee set up to advance Jewish rights in the Montreal Protestant school system and served as president of the "Baron de Hirsch." Well-off, prominent, energetic, and articulate, Lyon Cohen was also charitable, and looked with deep compassion on the sufferings of his people. He went down from his Westmount home to meet immigrants at the docks, and laboured long hours and gave generously to support numerous charitable causes, perhaps remembering that, long years before, he himself had arrived on an immigrant ship in Montreal harbour. Compassion and understanding went just so far, however. Cohen and his colleagues clearly were not willing to sacrifice what they believed to be their vital economic interests by recognizing a trade union in their shops, even though a large percentage of their workers were Jews. Also at issue was their own *amour propre*, which they refused to diminish even for the welfare of their fellow Jews

—especially those who did not share their values. Thus they supported Gardner's denunciation of "professional agitators [who] have created all the trouble," and his refusal to "permit irresponsible demagogues to dictate the terms upon which we will deal with those we employ".[27] Employers may also have resisted unions on political grounds, fearing that these organizations were dominated by radicals or "bolsheviks" who would undermine the social order—and bring shame on the Jewish community.

Who were these "professional agitators" and "demagogues"? Opposing the manufacturers in the summer of 1912 was a joint executive board of forty local UGWA members, headed by A. Gordon, a union official from Baltimore, and Victor Altman, a representative from one of the three striking Montreal locals. They sought union recognition, abolition of piecework, and the end of contracting work to outside shops. The union also demanded the reduction of the work week from an average of fifty-five hours for men and fifty-two for women to a nine-hour day and a five-day week, and wanted an overtime rate of time-and-a-half.

The Montreal manufacturers refused to meet with the union representatives, even though a number of firms had already capitulated;[28] on June 6, union organizer A. Barsky had triumphantly reported to the press that fifteen small manufacturers and two large firms that did not belong to the manufacturers' association had come to terms with the union.[29] The union seemed to be winning, and workers were enthusiastic at prospects of an early victory. They ran a highly successful tag-day throughout the Jewish community to raise money for the strikers' families, indicating substantial public support, and assistance also came from the union's U.S. headquarters.[30] A week or so later, however, violence erupted, and the promise of an early general settlement was shattered. Picketers were beaten up by tough gangs who turned out to be either private detectives or Montreal police plainclothesmen hired by the employers.[31] Non-striking workers were attacked by Union sympathizers and some were seriously injured.[32] Worse still was the adamant refusal of most employers to negotiate. Apparently determined to starve the union out, they closed down their factories on June 18. Workers responded with parades and giant rallies at Coronation Hall and out in Fletchers Fields, where they shouted their determination to continue and were bolstered by speeches from a number of the city's major union leaders.[33] The manufacturers charged that the strike had been called by the parent union in New York to coincide with similar strikes in the U.S., to prevent Canadian workers from emigrating there as scab labour. (Seasonal or permanent migration of workers in both directions across the Canadian–American boundary was a

well-established phenomenon, and there is evidence of this kind of labour transiency among clothing workers, especially among the highly skilled designers
and cutters.[34]) Manufacturers also alleged that the U.S. union leaders wanted to
narrow the price differentials on manufactured clothing in order to keep Canadian goods out of the U.S. market.[35]

The real inspiration behind the 1912 strike was Hananiah Meir Caiserman,
a twenty-six-year-old accountant who had emigrated to Montreal from
Romania only two years earlier. He had worked in a Montreal clothing factory,
and was determined to raise the class consciousness of the city's Jewish workers,
who were now probably 30 per cent of the work force in the clothing industry.[36] Besides organizing the garment workers into separate locals according to
their specific trades (cutters, pressers, cloakmakers), Caiserman also inspired
Jewish bakery workers, by means of highly successful rallies, street demonstrations, and fiery speeches, to force employers to accept the union label.[37] As
well, he organized cultural evenings for these workers and gave courses on
political economy.

Between 1911 and 1913, however, Caiserman's main emphasis was on the
clothing workers' union. Assisted by Louis Zuker, Victor Baranofsky, and Israel
Cheifetz, Caiserman built the separate UGWA locals into a well-organized,
financially sound, loyal, and militant union. The Montreal locals were syn-
onymous in those years with the Poale Zion (Labour Zionists), a left-wing
Jewish workers' movement that had been founded in 1905 in Lithuania, and
had spread rapidly among Jewish manual workers, students, and intellectuals in
Europe, Palestine, and America. Zionist, reformist, and almost messianic in its
emphasis on the reconstruction of the Jewish people, the Poale Zion movement and its intellectual underpinnings had been brought to Canada by the
pre-1914 immigrants from Eastern Europe.[38] This "intellectual baggage" provided Caiserman and his associates with the inspiration for militant strikes for
the UGWA, and, a few years later, for the Amalgamated Clothing Workers of
America. They were battling not just for improved wages and working conditions, but for social justice and recognition of the dignity of labour. When the
June 1912 strike began, Caiserman had behind him all the Montreal Poale Zion
clubs, which taxed each of their members a day's wages. The clubs solicited
funds from Poale Zion groups in other cities to support the $7,000 strike fund
and called a conference of all Montreal labour organizations to build up
support for the strike. Morris Winchevsky, the noted and revered left-wing
Jewish poet, came from New York to give a series of lectures and readings to
provide encouragement to the strikers.[39]

The workers showed spirited defiance all the way through the strike. Two hundred women members donned red sashes and took to the streets at five o'clock one morning to sell copies of *Cotton's Weekly*, a socialist newspaper published in Cowansville, Quebec, containing a long review of the causes of the strike. At the same time they warned the Montreal police that, if they interfered with sales, the paper's editor would be brought to Montreal to sell them.[40] In addition, the strikers gained a valuable ally in Montreal lawyer Peter Bercovitch, who interceded with the police on behalf of the strikers, and in Reuben Brainin, editor of the *Adler*.[41] Bercovitch was a popular figure among the Jewish immigrants. Born in 1879 to recent arrivals from Romania, he was typical of many Jewish men whose upward mobility was based on brilliant scholastic achievement. He graduated from McGill, took a law degree at Université Laval à Montréal, and was called to the bar in 1901; he became a K.C. in 1911, then the youngest lawyer ever to receive the honour in Quebec. By taking on many of the legal problems of Montreal's Jewish immigrants, Bercovitch built a reputation as a champion of the Jewish poor, underprivileged, and workers. An effective speaker, he appeared frequently at Jewish political meetings, and at rallies of fraternal, political, charitable, and social organizations; he often received favourable mention in the city's mildly leftist Yiddish weekly *Keneder Adler*. Its editor in 1912 – Reuben Brainin, Montreal's leading Jewish intellectual[42] – attempted on a number of occasions to arbitrate between the disputing parties in the clothing industry.[43] In the meantime, the *Jewish Times* of 19 July, 1912 – now edited by a progressive-minded young lawyer, Marcus Sperber – recognized that "there is a continual hostility between capital and labour . . . [making] strikes . . . inevitable" but ". . . regretted this strike in question because most of the participants in it are Jews." It called on both sides "to patch up the differences":

> "For shame! You leaders of thousands of men, and you captains of industry should be more considerate, should be more human than to allow the wretchedness and misery consequent upon the strike to continue, because, forsooth, you are proud, and wish the other party to rap at your door."[43]

Montreal garment workers won valuable experience in this strike in meeting tough, organized opponents who used smear campaigns, violence, and "runaway shops." In early July, four major firms announced that they would relocate their factories, Brothers and Hart to Sorel, J.E. Elkin to Joliette, Crown Pants to Cornwall, and Union Clothing to St. John's.[44] But after many weeks of bitterness, the manufacturers and union representatives reached a compromise on July 29. Despite their negotiators' best efforts, the union achieved only a partial victory: a reduction in weekly hours from fifty-five to forty-nine, in stages, and an increase in piece-workers' rates to compensate for this reduction. The union had to drop its demands for wages to replace piecework and for time-and-a-half over-time pay. Worse still was the fact that the manufacturers were able to retain the open shop, thus depriving the union of its most important goal.

The 1912 strike marked the importance of Jews as major participants in the Montreal men's clothing industry, both as manufacturers and as workers. These entrepreneurs were no longer simply small-scale contractors producing cheap garments for wholesale clothiers. Some had graduated from marginal sweatshop operations into modern factories and had become manufacturers and wholesale clothiers distributing to the retail trade under their own labels. Many ran fully integrated operations, or inside shops, which seldom if ever farmed out work to contractors. Furthermore, some of the Jewish manufacturers had by then achieved recognition in the industry for the high quality of their garments.

The lot of the labour force in the Montreal men's needle industry had not changed significantly since the late 1880s and 1890s, when factory inspectors had deplored the pitiable working and living conditions. But industrialization had now furnished the means for achieving a measure of labour solidarity, even class-consciousness, among workers who had previously been segregated from each other in small workshops. Thus industrialization helped to create among Montreal and Toronto Jews what urbanization created among South Italians in American cities: "a community identity and an ethnic consciousness."[45] In the needle industry, identity from the workplace was becoming as important as reli-gious or regional identity. The Poale Zion and Arbeiter Ring, which were organized in 1905 and 1907 respectively, had social, political, and economic goals, and were part of the immigrants' "cultural baggage" rather than products of North American acculturation. But some of their Montreal leaders, like Hananiah Meier Caiserman of the Poale Zion and Herschel Noveck of the Arbeiter Ring, became leaders in the clothing unions,[46] because they recog-nized that solidarity was vital to economic betterment for the workers. The unions – the UGWA in the men's trade and the Cloakmakers (a forerunner of the International Ladies' Garment Workers' Union) in the women's trade – were vehicles for acculturation and the achievement of workers' consciousness, as well as for winning economic goals.

While the Montreal needle industry symbolized a certain kind of transfor-mation and unification in Canadian Jewish urban life, it also provided the

battleground for economic warfare of the kind which the strike of 1912 foreshadowed: bitter and bloody. The fact that Jewish workers were locked in a
struggle with Jewish employers, Jewish strike-breakers, and allegedly even
Jewish gangsters during these confrontations, which continued for another
generation,[47] created deep and long-lasting divisions within communities
where the needle industry was significant. Beneath the surface, Jewish communal solidarity did not exist.

And these divisions reflected not only economic conflicts, but cultural gulfs
as well. Battle-lines in the frequent industry disputes coincided closely with
those divisions which had already begun to develop over the Jewish school
question, and which were to emerge in even sharper focus during the debate
over the formation of a Canadian Jewish congress during the First World War.
Thus, while the emergence of two contending forces at the "Corner of Pain and
Anguish" clearly expressed a classic economic conflict, the associated cultural
and social dimensions were also of far-reaching importance.

In Toronto a 1912 strike, involving 550 workers, lasted a year but failed to
bring satisfactory results for the Journeymen Tailors' Union, which was struggling for a minimum wage scale for a 49-hour week, better piecework rates,
sanitary shops, and equal pay for women and men.[48] In Toronto alone, some
fifty-four contractors' shops producing men's clothing, with an undetermined
number of workers, were identified during the 1912 strike. Rasminsky and
Stein, one of the city's larger contractors, was singled out for unionization by
the UGWA, but the firm refused to yield and the workers returned.[49]

In Toronto, however, Jewish participation in the garment industry was not
nearly as advanced. Although by early 1913 the overwhelming majority of the
city's fifty-four men's clothing contractors' shops were Jewish,[50] few Jews had
become fully-fledged manufacturers. One recent scholarly study of the
Toronto industry reveals that by 1901, while some 15 per cent of clothing firms
were owned by Jews, "Jewish businesses accounted for only two per cent of the
total value of garment factories in Toronto."[51] Though Jewish entrepreneurial
participation increased subsequently, "by 1915, a few men's wear factories and
approximately 50 per cent of all women's wear firms were owned by Jews . . .
they accounted for less than 15 per cent of the production in the industry."[52] In
Toronto, moreover, factory production of clothing was overwhelmingly dominated by the T. Eaton Co. There were therefore few counterparts to the
prominent Jewish clothiers in Montreal.[53] Numbers may have had something
to do with this; the Jewish population of Toronto in 1921 was 34,770, while
Montreal's was 45,802. Contracting was less lucrative than in Montreal because

of slight wage differentials and the greater availability in and around Montreal of part-time workers.[54] Although many Jewish workers were employed by contractors, they were also hired by non-Jewish firms, including Eaton's.[55]

The increasing numbers of Jewish workers secured high visibility in the labour unions. The establishment of mainly Jewish tailoring union locals in Montreal in the 1890s was matched by similar formations in Toronto. By the early years of the century, representatives of these locals were attending UGWA conventions such as the 1906 gathering in Toronto. The general UGWA organizer for Canada, H.D. Rosenbaum, sought to unionize as many workers as possible, and by early 1913 had forced one of Toronto's largest manufacturers, Randall and Johnston, to encourage its contractors to accept union members.[56] Conditions in Toronto remained poor, however. When thirty-three firms granted more than 2,000 workers wage increases of between 10 and 20 per cent, a Department of Labour reporter stated that "Conditions among Gentile girls said to be very good. Among Jewish girls not so good, owing to the fact that a large number of Jewish girls are employed in outside contract shops, also that there is a sub-contracting system."[57] In Hamilton the settlement of an industry-wide strike was delayed until after the Passover holiday because of the large number of Jews among the workers.[58]

In the women's clothing sector, where Jewish manufacturers and contractors were also increasingly evident before 1910, Jews likewise assumed greater visibility. The Independent Cloakmakers' Union of Toronto went on strike in April of 1910 in an attempt to force union recognition. "Many of the strikers," a correspondent of the *Labour Gazette* wrote, "are of the foreign element, Jews and others."[59] In sympathy with the aims of the International Ladies' Garment Workers' Union (ILGWU), many workers came in strongly behind a Toronto organization drive that began two years later. In June of 1912 the eleventh annual convention of the ILGWU was held in Toronto to bolster the efforts of a full-time organizer, M. Koldofski, who had been hired.[60] A strike against the John Northway and Pullan companies early that year resulted in recognition of the union, as well as major improvements in working conditions.[61]

A strike at the Dominion Cloak Company between April and August of 1914 lasted for twenty weeks that were filled with violence in the shop and on the street. A *Toronto Daily Star* reporter, T.W. Banton, wrote to the Department of Labour in early April that it was difficult to obtain particulars because of the conflicting statements; "most of the people concerned are of the foreign element," he wrote, "Jews and others."[62] When the company hired strike-breakers, the violence escalated, and by the end of the month nineteen police court cases – mainly assault charges – were pending, fifteen of them against union members. The firm's plant was sabotaged, and private detectives were hired as increased violence and more arrests ensued. By early August the workers and the union, which had spent considerable sums of money on relief, were exhausted; they called off their strike and admitted defeat. A month later eighty of the workers were still without work.

Relative peace, prosperity, and full employment marked the menswear industry after the bitter 1912 strike and on into the early years of the war. The rapid mobilization of soldiers resulted in full order books for clothing manufacturers, who were generally willing to concede higher wages and better conditions in order to keep production flowing. The number of strikes in the industry fell rapidly. In 1916, however, inadequate wage settlements and a new drive for union recognition caused a major upheaval. Since the development of a huge split in the ranks of the UGWA at its convention in 1914, a new and more radical industrial union had arisen in American men's clothing manufacturing centres. Led by its president, Sydney Hillman, and general secretary, Joe Schlossberg, the Amalgamated Clothing Workers of America (ACWA) was formed. This was an industrial union with a combative style, Jewish leadership, and an emphasis on social justice and collective bargaining which appealed strongly to the Jewish clothing workers concentrated in New York, Baltimore, Philadelphia, Rochester, and Chicago.[63] Tens of thousands of them joined during its early organizing drives after 1914, as Hillman and Schlossberg spoke at dozens of rallies across the United States and Canada. In Montreal and Toronto, support for the Amalgamated spread among the UGWA's Jewish members, who sent Elias Rabkin of Montreal to the new union's first convention in New York. There he reported that "the tailor unions in Canada have been ruined and . . . the conditions of labour have, in the course of the past two years, been reduced to the very lowest state, particularly in the clothing centres of Montreal and Toronto."[64] The Amalgamated New York office sent up an organizer and Canada's first local of the ACWA, No. 277, (the pantsmakers, later led by Joe Shuster), was established in Montreal in 1915.[65]

From their offices at Coronation Hall, near the foot of St. Lawrence Boulevard, UGWA organizers established several locals to cover all of Montreal's twenty major factories, where 5,000 tailors were employed. Joe Shuster, who became a stalwart of Amalgamated, remembered many years later that "conditions were quiet and stable in Montreal under the U.G.W. union" at that time, but that the upheaval in the U.S. headquarters soon affected the Montreal local. A serious factional fight developed between supporters of the Amalgamated and the UGWA.[66] Shuster, Rabkin, and eventually even Caiserman favoured the switchover to the Amalgamated. Meanwhile another branch of the Amalgamated, local 209 (operators and finishers), was formed. In the ensuing months, the union developed a strategy of organizing workers in large plants and forming joint boards to co-ordinate locals in both Montreal and Toronto.[67] Recognition would then be sought as sole bargaining agent in all factories and contractors' shops – creating the union shop. If the giant firms were organized, it was assumed that all others would fall into line.

In July 1916 the union called its first strike, against John W. Peck and Company Ltd., a large, well-established Montreal firm. The results were excellent for the union; it won the company's recognition as bargaining agent for the 400 workers, who were granted a substantial increase in wages.[68] Four months later, another strike, against the huge Fashion Craft Ltd., resulted in another impressive victory. In this strike five locals were involved, including No. 167 (pressers), No. 116 (Cutters), and No. 115 – the French-Canadian local, organized by Adhémar Duquette, who had been recruited to the Amalgamated by Jewish tailors. No. 115 would be the first of several ethnic locals.[69] The firm agreed to stop sending out work to contractors or subcontractors, to recognize the union, to increase salaries by 10 to 15 per cent, and to keep to the nine-hour day and 49-hour week.[70]

Buoyed by these relatively easy victories and a successful organizing drive and strike at the Davis Brothers plant in Hamilton in July,[71] the Amalgamated tried to negotiate similar terms with Montreal's Semi-Ready Ltd. But by now the manufacturers too were organizing. Late in 1916, the Montreal Clothing Manufacturers' Association, a group of menswear producers, was formed to resist unionization and mounting demands for better working conditions. When Semi-Ready's management resisted the Amalgamated, a strike began on December 20, 1916. President A.F. Wood charged that Joe Schlossberg was a German agent whose goal was to undermine the Canadian war effort by interfering with the production of officers' uniforms.[72] The firm immediately began hiring strike-breakers, and J.H. Brownlee, the managing director of Semi-Ready, wrote to Gerald Brown, the Deputy Minister of Labour, boasting that "we have been able to equip our factory without the strikers returning to work."[73] Peter Bercovitch, speaking for the union, labelled the charge against Schlossberg a "baseless appeal to prejudice." Schlossberg pointedly remarked that "in Germany he would have been known as a 'd----d' Jew and it seemed strange to come to Canada to be called a German," while the union's New York attorney declared that, in fact, Schlossberg was a Russian.[74] Bercovitch called on Lyon Cohen, president of the Montreal Clothing Manufacturers' Association and probably Montreal's most prominent Jew, to publicly protest the assertion that Jewish union leaders were Germans. Realizing that these charges were absurd and that they could do serious damage to the image of the community in the heated wartime atmosphere of 1917, Cohen issued a strong denial: "we, the manufacturers, disagree with you leaders and strikers in certain matters, but we agree with your protest against slander." Management never again made these allegations, during this or any subsequent strike, although they did employ other equally rough tactics.

Emotions ran very high a few days later as strike-breakers, under massive police protection, entered the Semi-Ready plant. Several picketers who attempted to stop these "scabs" were arrested on charges of fighting and interfering with the police, while another was arrested for severely beating a strike-breaker.[75] Speaking of the mounting violence on the picket-line, and with the added prestige of having been elected, in 1916, to the Quebec Legislative Assembly, Bercovitch defended the union members at a hearing for their release on bail and asked, "I would like to know under whose orders the police work, those of the city or of the Semi-Ready company," and charged that the company had interfered in the legal process.[76]

By early January of 1917, the strike had spread. All the large clothing companies were now determined to stop the Amalgamated's Montreal organizing drive dead in its tracks, even if this jeopardized their profitable contracts to produce army uniforms. It was significant that Lyon Cohen, the association's president, took the action which precipitated a shutdown in the entire industry. On December 30 he dismissed one of his employees who was a union delegate on the grounds that his union activity had reduced the Freedman Company's production by 30 per cent. After two weeks of unsuccessfully trying to get the worker rehired, the Amalgamated called a strike of the 300 Freedman employees on January 12. Cohen tried then to move his production to other firms, such as Fashion Craft, which had settled with the Amalgamated the previous October and had agreed to secretly manufacture for Cohen. However, Fashion Craft's cutters refused to handle Cohen's goods. They were dismissed, and a general strike erupted in the entire industry. During the next few weeks 3,000 to 4,000 workers from all thirteen firms of the Montreal Clothing Manufacturers' Association walked out in sympathy, and another 1,000 workers were affected when fifty-six independent smaller firms were shut down as the strike spread. By February 12 virtually all men's clothing production in Montreal had stopped.

The real issues were union recognition and collective bargaining. Wage increases and the reduction of hours – and even the use of contractors – though highly important, were not in themselves central and would not likely have shut down the city's entire industry. Indeed, some employers, including Cohen, were willing to increase wages, reduce hours, and even scale down or eliminate the use of contractors. Cohen believed in doing away with subcontracting because, although profitable and often convenient, it encouraged sweatshop conditions which he genuinely deplored. While his own premises were not ideal, they were relatively clean, modern, airy, and, in comparison with most contractors' sweatshops, probably deluxe. Other employers like the Peck company had modern factories.

But recognition of the union cut deeply into the rights these men believed capitalism and private ownership of self-created business had given them. Cohen, their spokesman, identified the crux of the problem when he recounted how the union had forced him to fire a highly productive but unpopular worker; he then explained his perception of the problems caused by shop delegates who came with union recognition:

> Some getting their power as shop delegate, became so arrogant it was impossible to deal with them. . . . This causes a great deal of unrest among the other employees who get so susceptible to fancied insults and every demand on them that they will almost complain if the foreman looks crooked. . . . When a foreman cross[es] the room to show a worker some-thing, the shop delegate gets up to see what he is doing, and then every-body else turns to look. The result is naturally diminished production.[77]

For him, the question was clearly "Who should control the shop floor, the fore-man or the shop delegate?" Other manufacturers argued that the real sticking-point for them was protecting their right to fire incompetent workers.[78] Ultimately the question was one of power. This was the key to understanding "the efforts of labouring people to assert some control over their working lives, and of the equal determination of American business to conserve the prerogatives of management."[79] The concept that anyone but employers should share control of the workplace was completely foreign and totally unacceptable.[80]

To the manufacturers, ownership of the means of production implied absolute control of all aspects of the production process, and the right to change them at will. In this the manufacturers were not unlike other contemporary employers, such as Toronto meatpacker Joseph Flavelle, who believed in the benevolent capitalism which accorded workers year-round employment, a clean working environment, and numerous benefits, but at the same time deplored and battled against unions which demanded recognition as well as all of these improved material conditions.[81] This attitude was not inconsistent with the same men acting in other respects as reasonable employers, as sincerely charitable and dedicated Jewish public servants and public-spirited citizens. Union recognition, which eventually brought the dreaded closed shop in its wake, meant sharing control of the workplace; it also meant possible interference with other aspects of management, and, ultimately, with the pursuit of profits. Because of these implications of the 1917 confrontation, factory owners were prepared to fight a long, bitter, and costly battle, to use vicious, unfair, and seriously damaging tactics against the very class of Jewish poor and underprivileged they were actively helping through the local charities. The union charged that "besides alleging that union leaders were German agents," the Manufacturers' Association, hoping to have Schlossberg deported, had asked the New York Police Department for his record. Some manufacturers who were shareholders in munitions plants, a reference to Mark Workman, president of Dominion Steel Corporation and a large shareholder, blacklisted the striking clothing workers. The union also alleged that, as heads of Montreal Jewish charities like the "Baron de Hirsch," employers denied help to strikers who applied for it. Bitterness spilled over into other sectors of the city's Jewish life. When Lyon Cohen participated in the official opening of a new synagogue, a crowd of clothing workers hooted, jeered, and threatened violence to prevent him from speaking.[82] Economic warfare thus penetrated into the sanctuary of the Lord.

The Amalgamated saw the Montreal struggle as a battle against some of the worst excesses of industrial capitalism. The union and the strike, their newspaper reported, "brought to them a realization of the fact that they were not merely human tools for production of merchandise, rightless, hopeless and aimless, but that they were human beings entitled to the blessings of life, liberty and the pursuit of happiness."[83] This was not self-serving, sentimental propaganda. The Amalgamated was led by men with selfless dedication to social justice and industrial peace, and Hillman, Schlossberg, and Caiserman were undoubtedly sincere. Hillman would tell delegates to the 1918 Baltimore convention of the heartbreaking circumstances he and Schlossberg had observed among Montreal's Jewish, Italian, and French Canadian women clothing workers in 1917:

> But however seasoned and hardened a union representative may be, however much his eyes may have become accustomed to look at faces with misery and sufferings deeply engraved in them, and however much his ears may become adapted to hearing their stories of distress, he can't avoid a severe shock when coming to a shop meeting of his fellow members he finds an audience of little girls, some of them still below their teens, their children's locks hanging over their shoulders and their dresses barely covering their knees. The union's representative, being himself a father, and thinking of his own pink-cheeked little girl, while addressing those child slaves, cannot help renewing his pledge to fight the cannibalistic industrial system, which, not contented with undermining the health of the manhood and womanhood of the nation and send them into early graves, also feeds upon helpless childhood.[84]

But it was not only for humanitarian reasons that the Amalgamated organized the Montreal clothing workers and met the employer's association head on in the 1917 strike; there were practical and strategic reasons as well. Montreal was one of the premier garment-manufacturing centres in Canada, and if the union could secure recognition there, then Toronto and Hamilton clothing workers would probably be more easily brought into the union, thus forcing manufacturers to improve conditions across the country. Strategically, the organization of these centres was important to Hillman because it was probably the only way of establishing stable industry standards of wages and working conditions across North America. This in turn would help to ensure the stability of the industry in general, and prevent the occurrences of wild fluctuations in the labour market that depressed wages and allowed employers to exploit their workers.

Were these efforts an expression of the kind of progressive unionism, of pragmatic, realistic, and businesslike unionism, advocated by Samuel Gompers?[85] Or were they an expression of the more advanced "labour reform ideology" that has been found among segments of Toronto's working class in the late nineteenth century, or of the "persistent practice of workplace control" which is "the critical determinant in many Victorian and Edwardian class struggles?"[86] For a significant number of clothing workers, especially those who were influenced by left-wing reformist ideology, Poale Zion, or the more radical Bundist outlook, these struggles were more than simply bread-and-butter issues, more than Gompers-style progressivism.[87] However, there are indications that for many workers the class struggle, social justice, and Jewish workers' solidarity were less of an issue than they had been only four years before. During the 1912 confrontation, the presence of intellectuals like Hananiah Caiserman and Reuben Brainin, the broad support of Poale Zion clubs, and the editorial backing of an independent though short-lived strikers' newspaper had together created an atmosphere of ideological conflict which was not evident in 1917. This later conflict was clearly an extension of an international organizing drive by the newly formed Amalgamated, whose leaders, Hillman and Schlossberg, were idealistic but pragmatic unionists, not ideologues. And their strategy was one that immediately found acceptance among the vast majority of Canadian clothing workers.

While radicals were clearly an important intellectual and political force in communities like Montreal and Toronto, where there were enough of them to organize clubs, they were not sufficiently influential in the clothing unions at this stage to seriously challenge the moderate labour strategy of Hillman, Schlossberg, and Montreal stalwarts of the Amalgamated like Caiserman and Shuster. What these and the majority of workers seemed to want was better conditions, improved wages, shorter hours, and stability in an industry which they well knew was characterized by unstable—sometimes even chaotic—conditions.

Mediators were not lacking. On January 8, 1917, not long after the conflict began, Sam Jacobs—a leading Montreal lawyer who was a personal friend of Lyon Cohen and other clothing manufacturers—suggested to Schlossberg and Cohen the appointment of the former Minister of Labour, William Lyon Mackenzie King, to arbitrate between the manufacturers and the Amalgamated.[88] Schlossberg agreed to negotiation rather than arbitration, but the employers did not even reply to Jacobs' initiative.

At the same time Montreal's mayor, Médéric Martin, who was increasingly concerned about the economic and social implications of a strike involving nearly 5,000 workers in one of the city's major industries, was also trying to effect a settlement. Urged by the Businessmen's Strike Relief Committee, which invited him and other prominent Montrealers, including Professor Stephen Leacock of McGill, to help, he urged mediation "in order that a basis of settlement, fair and equitable to both parties, shall be arrived at."[89] Though the union expressed interest in Martin's call to discuss mediation, it was rejected by the employers on grounds that they "have already conceded everything, with the exception of the right to control their own affairs which in their

opinion is not a matter which may be arbitrated."[90] They offered instead to
meet separately with their own employees. Martin's suggestion of a three-man
arbitration board was also unacceptable,[91] and by mid-February he concluded

> that the employers while they do not seem to formally refuse to recog-
> nize such Union, seek the means of suppressing it by refusing to confer
> with those who have organized the same and are the principle support-
> ers thereof. . . . The manufacturers refuse to concede anything; they
> decline to discuss with their employees, as Unionists, and object to arbi-
> tration. In view of this stubbornness on their part, I can only repeat to the
> workers what I already said to them, to wit, that they should act with
> calm, but energetically insist on the upholding and recognition of their
> rights. Their cause is just and will ultimately triumph.[92]

It was now a question of endurance. The manufacturers had chosen to fight
at the best time of the year for them, the slack season of January and February.
At the end of this period the workers' bellies would be empty, and with no
alternative employment many would be tempted to break with the new union.
Some producers evaded the strike by employing non-union labour. The firm
Rubin Brothers, for example, boasted that they were overstocked anyway and
could easily carry on reduced production with strike-breakers.[93] The owners of
Atlas Clothing, Messrs Asner and Glickman, and the Modern Boys Clothing
Manufacturing Company reported to the Department of Labour that all their
production was done by contractors; since they used non-union labour, these
firms could continue business undisturbed.

Other small manufacturers, however, were under extreme pressure by the
end of February. Heavily pressed to fill orders to keep up their cash flow and
maintain their government contracts – lest they go out of business entirely –
some settled with the union. On February 26 M. Harris and Sons, whose 175
employees had been on strike for two weeks, accepted the Amalgamated's terms,
and M. Greenblatt, owner of College Brand Clothes, capitulated two days later.
These were only small victories, nevertheless. The bigger firms continued to
defy the union and the pickets kept up their daily vigil at the factories. Financial support for the strikers came from the New York headquarters of the union
and from the Businessmen's Strike Relief Committee.

Meanwhile, numerous incidents of violence on the picket-line ensured continuing bitterness, while the Montreal Police Department's handling of these confrontations did not earn them a reputation for impartiality.[94] In early February,

Israel Solomon and fourteen other strikers were charged with preventing strike-breakers from entering several factories and for mixing it up with police officers.[95] A bomb exploded at the home of one strike-breaker, while another was so severely beaten up by assailants that he lost an eye. Some of this roughhouse was perpetrated by Jewish women; Rachel Black was arrested in mid-February,[96] while Annie Solovitsky, Mary Levine, and Annie Shuta were fined for beating up a strike-breaker. Demonstrations and marches included "un grand nombre de jeunes filles," and *Le Devoir* observed that "A very large part of the demonstrators, especially the women, were by their appearance Israelites."[97] Despite an appeal for moderation from the police commissioner, the violence continued.[98] Tony Calebro was arrested for carrying a revolver which he brandished in the faces of strike-breakers.[99] But all their court appearances did nothing to break the strikers' spirits. They were often attended by friends who crowded into the courtrooms to give them moral support. "The Recorder's Court was jam-packed this morning with Israelites of both sexes," *Le Devoir* reported in early February, "who came to learn the fate of their 32 striking compatriots, who appeared for sentencing."[100]

It was the longest, most bitter, and probably most violent strike in the history of the Canadian needle industry up to the 1930s. Before it was settled in May 1917, more than 4,500 workers were on strike against sixty-nine companies (including fifty-six small independent firms), completely shutting down the production of men's clothing and uniforms.[101] The strike and the issues on which it was fought not only illustrate important aspects of what had become one of Canada's most significant industries; they also highlight major themes in the immigration and settlement of Canada's substantial and rapidly increasing Jewish population.

It is difficult to estimate the effects of the strike on Montreal's Jewish population, which in 1917 could be described as a community only in the broadest sense. It is highly possible that some mediation efforts were started within established community organizations, by major personalities associated with neither side of the dispute – like A. Lesser, who had been instrumental in settling the 1912 confrontation, or some of the city's prominent rabbis. But since many of the major manufacturers and all of the contractors were Jewish, as were virtually all of the union leaders and a majority of the rank and file, the strike can only have sharpened the already deep political, social, and economic divisions. Other frequent, bitter and lengthy labour conflicts involving hundreds of Jewish bakers and butchers during the early 1900s also accentuated those rifts within Montreal Jewry.[102]

Yet other stirring events of 1917 served to impose a kind of unity among Jews, in Europe and in North America as well. Reports of immense suffering among the Jewish masses of Poland and the Ukraine gave rise to separate fund-raising drives which, by 1917, were co-ordinated into one account to support relief to all afflicted Jews in the East European war zones. There was concern over the fate of the Jews in Palestine, where considerable distress and disloca-tion had resulted from the war. These and other issues filled the pages of the *Keneder Adler*, which in those days probably reflected public opinion among the Yiddish-speaking segment of Montreal's population. Rallies, drives, benefits, campaigns, marches, and demonstrations occurred frequently in the Jewish quarter during these dramatic months. The Monument National, the Gésu Hall, and the Gaiety Theatre resounded with Yiddish speeches, songs, poetry readings, and eyewitness accounts of tragic events in Europe and the conquest of Palestine by General Allenby's armies. Synagogues, union halls, clubrooms, cafés, and private homes reverberated with animated discussions of the meaning of these matters. Lines in A.M. Klein's memorable poem "Autobiographical"

> And the two strangers, come
> Fiery from Volhynia's murderous hordes –
> The cards and humming stop.
> And I too swear revenge for that pogrom.[103]

suggest that many individual Jews felt personally involved in the dramatic events of those years. In the midst of the many momentous global concerns that compelled them to unite, stand fast, and dig deeply into their pockets, the local clothing workers' strikes appeared less important. And while it is under-standable that their class conflict was not widely discussed in public, even the events of the strike and the conflicting positions were not examined in great detail in the *Keneder Adler*.

To be sure, the paper carried many reports on these bitter strikes,[104] but the issues and events were not described in nearly as much detail as they were in the Montreal English-language papers, the *Gazette*, *Star*, and *Herald*. More important is that the *Adler*, which, after all, was written for the large Yiddish-speaking segment of Montreal's Jews from whom the clothing-workers were drawn, though generally supportive of the workers, refrained from publishing strong editorials on the dispute until relatively late. Its strike-related editorial-izing was reserved for an antisemitic outburst by a magistrate in Recorders' Court, where a number of strikers were up on assault charges, claiming that

Jewish witnesses were, because of their religion, less believable than Christian policemen.[105] On February 11 the *Adler* announced that it had learned of plans by manufacturers to bring in a large number of strike-breakers from the U.S., and warned the Canadian government to stop them at the border.[106] Four days later it proclaimed that support for the local *schneiders'* (tailors') strike was pouring in from all classes, including Mayor Martin, who was reported as saying that the union's cause was just.[107] Apparently the *Adler's* owner, Hirsch Wolofsky, and the paper's editors did not choose to express opinions on this conflict until public opinion had spoken with one voice.

The *Adler's* cautious and safe approach to a divisive internal conflict, was notably different from the combativeness and daring that had marked New York's Yiddish labour press during the same period.[108] But considering that the *Adler* was the only Jewish daily in Montreal, the restraint is understandable. While New York's Jews could afford the "luxury" of open class warfare, the *Adler's* editor-owner believed that unity in the face of external threats was the only responsible course to advocate, in the small and scattered Jewish communities in Canada.[109]

Though in some respects commendable, this attitude had its price, as frankness was sacrificed for what Wolofsky and his staff decided were the larger and long-range interests of the Jewish people. This high ground, however, was dominated by the men who had time and money to donate to the charities and institutions that had been called into being in order to preserve and defend Jewish interests. The same clothing manufacturers – Lyon Cohen is a case in point – who were battling the Amalgamated tooth and nail during January and February of 1917 were able to attract favourable attention as heads of the fund-raising campaign to assist Jews in Eastern Europe.[110] Thus, through its refusal to take an editorial position on a serious local problem and its failure to meet an issue lest it damage Jewish unity, the *Adler* was party to a serious and lasting injustice. Wealthy Jews were allowed to stand as champions and spokesmen of causes based on the need for Jewish solidarity in the face of worldwide adversity, however real and terrifying those threats became, even as they were fighting Jewish workers. Most Jewish intellectuals remained silent on the irony of this situation. Apparently even Caiserman, who was deeply involved in war relief, chose to remain silent. The irony was not lost on the beleaguered clothing workers. If Wolofsky was not prepared to fully explain the issues – let alone take sides – they would publish their own Yiddish paper. This sheet, which ran for twenty issues during the eight weeks of the strike, seems to have had considerable positive effect on the solidarity of the strikers.

What of the rabbis? If they had anything to say about the strike, none of their comments was ever published in either the *Adler* or the *Canadian Jewish Chronicle*, the Montreal English-language weekly which had succeeded the *Canadian Jewish Times* in 1914. Undoubtedly the most prominent Jewish clergymen in Montreal were rabbis Meldola de Sola of the Spanish and Portuguese synagogue, Herman Abramowitz of the Sha'ar Hashomayim, and Nathan Gordon of the Reform Temple Emanu-el. While his congregation was the smallest of the three, Meldola de Sola was not only Montreal's longest-serving Jewish clergyman, but also one of the most prominent religious figures in the city;[111] he could have wielded immense influence on both parties to the strike. Rabbi Abramowitz, though less prominent, possibly could also have exercised some moral suasion in the traditional role of the East European rabbi as mediator,[112] especially on employers like Lyon Cohen, many of whom were members of his own congregation. He too seems to have had nothing public to say about this strike. Nor is there any evidence that any of these three tried publicly to mediate, or that the strike, or the moral and ethical implications, was even the subject of Sabbath sermons.

What kept these men from speaking out was perhaps fear of their congregants, which could have overcome the interesting similarity in outlook between some of the rabbis and the workers. The rabbis may have recognized that Jewish labour leaders, whether Communists, socialists, or anarchists – all of them "ungodly" – were also pursuing the cause of "social justice" which lies at the heart of Torah teaching.[113] Yet another factor which may have made most rabbis unwilling to take sides was their desire to pursue communal peace (*shalom bayit*), which they might achieve best not by speaking out in public, but by quietly mediating behind the scenes.

Meldola de Sola was both complacent and paternalistic. During the excitement caused throughout the quarter by the deliberate removal of about 1,000 Jews from the voters' lists in Cartier riding in 1904 (preparatory to the federal elections), de Sola had preached a sermon admonishing the Jews to quieten down and be grateful for Canadian citizenship.[114]

In the pulpit of Temple Emanu-el, housed since 1911 in a new Byzantine-style building on Sherbrooke Street West, stood rabbi and lawyer Nathan Gordon, a native of Cincinnati who had served as the congregation's spiritual leader since 1906.[115] His position was made ambivalent by the fact that he was married to Gertrude Workman, the daughter of Mark Workman, and by his membership in the firm of Peter Bercovitch, chief counsel for the Amalgamated. Whatever thoughts he may have had on the issues, the good rabbi was not inclined to make them public. Thus, in Montreal's West End, there were no "troublers in Israel."

There were, of course, other rabbis in Montreal, but they were influential only in the limited context of their own less affluent synagogues, which were attended by working-class Jews, many of them religious, who were among the strongest supporters of the union.[116] An exception was Rabbi Simon Glazer, of the Chevra Kadisha synagogue on St-Urbain Street. He was an immensely popular figure with wide public support – even among the non-observant – who publicly protested Sunday closing by-laws, municipal regulations interfering with the distribution of kosher meat, and other laws affecting the Jewish poor for whom he spoke.[117] An untiring fighter for social justice, he had many a dust-up with the West End rabbis – who tried at least once to publicly discredit him – as, in a Jewish version of the Social Gospel, he carried the prophetic tradition into the streets of Montreal. But he was not likely to influence that section of the city's Jewry to which the manufacturers belonged. And any demands for social justice made from these downtown pulpits were only preachments to the converted; Lyon Cohen would not have been impressed. Perhaps the venerable and saintly Rabbi Hirsch Cohen, a man whose learning, wisdom, good works, and prophetic appearance made him the unofficial chief rabbi of Montreal, might have been able to reduce the conflict, but there is no record that he made the attempt.[118]

In early March of 1917, a memorandum of agreement signed by Michael Hirsch for the Manufacturers' Association and Peter Bercovitch for the union established a committee to inquire into the causes of the dispute and make recommendations for solving it.[119] A board consisting of five members, two appointed by each side and a fifth by the other four, "none of whom are to be connected either directly or indirectly with the clothing industry," was to report within two months while "the employees are to return to work forthwith without reserve of any kind." After lengthy hearings lasting nearly two months, the board's report recommended granting a 46-hour week, a salary increase, time-and-a-half for overtime, and recognition of the union. All these conditions were accepted. The last point had been vital to the Amalgamated; it appears that, despite the already considerable length of the battle, Hillman, Schlossberg, and the Amalgamated members probably would have held fast to win it.

Although the board refrained from recommending a union shop, it did urge that a "conference committee" be elected in each factory by the workers. Union recognition was confirmed by "the fact that the employers signed the agreement with the newly established Joint Board," the central authority of the

Amalgamated.[120] The report was approved by a mass meeting of union members on May 14, and the longest strike until then in the Canadian men's clothing industry came to an end. Settlement of a lengthy strike by the Amalgamated in Toronto had been concluded successfully in March; Hamilton factories were organized at the same time. The popularity of the union increased, membership soared, and – most important of all – a period of industrial peace ensued in that branch of the needle industry for the next four or five years.

Yet, while the strike resulted in a brief respite in the industry's labour wars, it did not bring Montreal's Jewry lasting peace. The strike of 1916–17 was only one vivid, violent outburst of the community's constant tensions. The gulf was an economic one. Enjoying pleasant homes in upper-class, English-speaking neighbourhoods, these Jews tended to absorb the lifestyle and values of the dominant Anglo culture. The sons played sports, attended McGill, and travelled; the daughters performed charity work, took voice lessons, "visited," taught Sunday school – and awaited marriage. The parents formed Jewish social, athletic, and philanthropic societies; they built impressive synagogues in the West End, supported the "Baron de Hirsch" and many other local Jewish charities, and built a downtown Jewish businessmen's club, the Montefiore.

But although they were intent on integrating as much as possible into the Anglophone community, while still retaining their religion and cultural identity, these Jews encountered barriers which prevented them from attaining the complete social acceptance they so much desired. At the same time they were separate from the majority of their fellow Jews down in the quarter.

As significant as the clothing industry was to the overall economic life of Montreal, it was even more vital to Montreal's Jews. Figures for the number of Jews employed in the industry before the 1931 Dominion census are not available; in that year 16.49 per cent of all Jews gainfully employed worked in the industry (compared to 5.69 per cent of all other ethnic origins), while in Toronto, Winnipeg, and Vancouver the figures were 27.42 per cent, 11.88 per cent, and 8.76 per cent respectively. In previous decades, before Jews had achieved a significant degree of occupational mobility, the percentages were probably much higher.[121] Even so, in 1931 Jews still composed 31.2 per cent of all Canadian workers in the manufacture of women's ready made clothing, 40.9 per cent of the workforce in readymade men's clothing, 26.9 per cent in other clothing, and 34.9 per cent in hats and caps.[122] Absorbing such a high percentage of all Jews "gainfully employed," the needle industry, or the "rag trade," as it was sometimes affectionately called, was easily the most outstanding fact of Jewish economic life in Toronto and Montreal during the great migration before 1914, and, in diminishing degrees perhaps, for a generation thereafter. Thus it is central to an understanding of the broad pattern of Montreal's industrial development in the late nineteenth and early twentieth century.

The needle industry was also an important aspect of the Jewish intellectual scene. In the broadest sense, the goals of the labour militants in the UGWA and ACWA represent the universalistic pursuit of social justice. But this pursuit of workers' betterment through unionization, improved wages, and education was a direct importation from Europe, where Jewish workers had been developing an ideology of class action, self-help, and industrial unionism that became widespread during the late nineteenth and early twentieth century.[123] The formation of the ILGWU and the ACWA, and the fervour and militancy of Montreal's and Toronto's Jewish workers during these strikes, are at least partly a reflection of the strength of these movements in their native countries. The fact that these ideas were part of the immigrants' intellectual baggage made them highly susceptible to union militancy when they found themselves in the sweatshops. Certain other European immigrants – Finns, Ukrainians, and Serbs – brought similar and even more militant beliefs; the Jews may well have derived some inspiration from these radicals. Such ideas did not of course float freely on their own; they were supported and modified by similar ideas emanating from North American sources, such as the Knights of Labour in the 1880s and 1890s and the Industrial Workers of the World and One Big Union in the early 1900s.

In the early 1900s, the Toronto local of the Socialist Party of Canada had a large number of Jewish members, including women, while the Social Democratic Party's Toronto Jewish locals, participated in 1911 in efforts to organize a socialist Sunday School.[124] In September 1918 Dominion security officers wanted to outlaw the Jewish Social Democratic Party and monitor the *Israelite* and *Keneder Adler* as part of a general program of censorship and surveillance of ethnic workers and organizations which had been deemed unlawful under an Order-in-Council (PC 2384) and were believed to be "saturated with the Socialist doctrines which have been proclaimed by the Bolsheviki faction of Russia."[125] During Canada's "Red Scare" of 1919, the Royal North-West Mounted Police reported that Jews were believed to be in leading positions of the Russian Workers' Party and "that Jewish radicals were thought to be especially dangerous not only because of their prominence within the Social Bolshevik leadership, but also because they represented a cultural minority which manifested 'the bitterest hostility' towards Anglo Canadians."[126] During anti-alien riots in Winnipeg in January and February of 1919, the business establishment of Sam Blumenberg, a prominent local socialist, was wrecked.[127] A military intelligence report held that Becky and Michael Buhay, members of the Jewish Social Democratic in Montreal were the city's "cleverest and most outspoken" radicals.[128] A few months later, three Jews were included among the five "foreigners" rounded up under Section 41 of the Criminal Code, passed to punish sedition following the 1919 Winnipeg General Strike. Moses Almazov, Sam Blumenberg, and Michael Charitonoff were classified as dangerous enemy aliens, subjected to weeks of surveillance by the RNWMP, and charged with seditious conspiracy. They were threatened with deportation and incarcerated in Stoney Mountain Prison.[129] All were ultimately released, but the threat of deportation hung over them for some months.

In a number of ways, the clothing industry was an "intermediate zone" of Jewish economic, social, and cultural adjustment. "At the corner of Pain and Anguish," Jewish immigrants – as well as many others – received their first Canadian employment, and their first exposure to its industrial system – to urban life with its desperations and opportunities, and to an industry whose conditions aroused class-consciousness and labour unionism. The needle industry was more than just a great Jewish métier; it was a principal focus of Jewish life itself.

Celebrants at a costume ball in Winnipeg in 1909 in honour of the festival of Purim.

Women members of Young Judaea parade proudly through Regina, Saskatchewan, in November 1918, to celebrate the Balfour Declaration favouring the establishment of a Jewish national home in Palestine.

12

"Is It Good for the Jews?"

What kind of place did Jews have in Canadian society by the early years of the twentieth century? What kinds of perceptions were held of them by the Canadians among whom they lived and worked? What sorts of problems were faced in the establishment of Jewish status in Canadian civil society? In what way did the fact that Jews were not Christians affect their civil and political status, and how did it impinge upon their relationships with Canadian societies, both French and English?

Goldwin Smith, a leading intellectual of his day, was Canada's best-known Jew-hater in the late nineteenth century. Although widely recognized as a liberal spirit, Smith was nevertheless so virulent an antisemite that he gained notoriety for it throughout the English-speaking world. Among his many tirades were claims that the cause of the Boer War was Britain's demand that the franchise be extended to "the Jews and gamblers of Johannesburg"; that Jews were gaining greater control over the world's press and influencing public opinion; that "the Jews have one code of ethics for themselves, another for the Gentile"; that Disraeli was a "contemptible trickster and adventurer, who could not help himself because he was a Jew. Jews are no good anyhow"; that "the Jew is a Russophobe"; and so on.[1]

These were not merely the ruminations of an elderly and increasingly bitter social critic who despaired of modern ideas and trends; Smith had embraced antisemitic views at least since the late 1870s, expressing them often in print with force, conviction, persuasiveness, and skill. His anti-Jewish articles were published in some of the most highly regarded journals of the English-speaking world, such as the *Nineteenth Century*, the *Contemporary Review*, and the *Independent*, as well as in his own Toronto papers, the *Bystander*, the *Week*, and the *Weekly Sun*. While he had an astonishingly wide range of interests (and several other long-standing hatreds), antisemitism was a major preoccupation.[2] In Smith's mind, the very presence of Jews in society posed serious problems that required urgent resolution. Their removal from Europe, he asserted ominously in 1878, would remove a "danger from Western civilization."[3] And he prophesied that unless Jews turned to "the grand remedy" of assimilation, "there is further trouble in store . . . collisions which no philanthropic lecturing will avert . . . [the Jews'] end will come."[4]

Antisemitism, as distinct from the scorn generally felt for immigrants, is not always easy to detect. In the view of journalists, members of the House of Commons, and many other Canadians preceding the First World War, Jews were usually seen as undesirable settlers, but Ukrainians also frequently received unfavourable mention on the grounds of their racial "inferiority," dress, or habits.[5] Methodist minister and Social Gospeller J.S. Woodsworth, whose book about immigrants, *Strangers within Our Gates*, was suffused by the racism characteristic of some turn-of-the-century social commentators, seems to have regarded Jews as more adaptable, assimilable, and culturally suitable to Canada than Ukrainians, Italians, Chinese, or blacks.[6] The Winnipeg general strike of 1919 witnessed more anti-Ukrainian than anti-Jewish sentiment, despite the fact that the strike probably had as much support among the Jewish working class as among Ukrainians, and the fact that Abraham Heaps – an English Jew – was among its major leaders.[7]

Moreover, notwithstanding popular prejudices, Jewish immigrants found entry into the country comparatively easy before 1914, whereas only a trickle of East Asians, Japanese, and Chinese managed to enter during the same period. Riots and bloodshed against Orientals occurred on the west coast, but nothing comparable happened to Jews.[8] The latter, in fact, may have enjoyed certain advantages over other immigrants during the early 1900s. After all, the Canadian Jewish community was an old one, and by the early twentieth century it had established an evident economic, social, and political presence. Whereas the nation's Jewish population was only 6,501 in 1891, ten years later it was 16,401, and by 1911 it numbered 74,564.[9] Also, the Canadian response to Jewish sufferings at various times during the late nineteenth century had been empathetic and generous.[10] Jewish organizations had, with varying success, interceded with political authorities to facilitate immigration and settlement.[11]

Recent scholarly investigations suggest that other immigrants before the First World War had fewer political and social mechanisms of support than Canada's Jews possessed.[12] By 1917 Canadian Jewry had a representative in the House of Commons, Sam Jacobs from Montreal, as well as aldermen on the Montreal and Toronto municipal councils.[13] A small number of Jews with sufficient wealth and political connections succeeded in exerting some influence in federal and provincial affairs on issues directly affecting the Jewish community; most other ethnic communities had no such power. Hence, during the late nineteenth- and early twentieth-century period, Jews probably suffered less from serious discrimination than most ethnic groups in Canada. Antisemitism, therefore, cannot be abstracted entirely from the fairly generalized distrust of and dislike for foreigners at that time.

Yet, in certain respects, antisemitism remains significantly different from xenophobic nativism. Before 1914, Canada's Jews were the only sizeable immigrant community outside the Christian communion. Furthermore, they continued to suffer from that self-imposed exclusion even after the secularization of western societies and states during the nineteenth century. There is no better proof of this liability and of the perpetuation of ancient prejudices in the modern world than that provided by Goldwin Smith.

While the origins of Smith's antisemitism are not entirely clear, some of his diatribes indicate that he shared popular medieval notions about Jews that persisted in early-nineteenth-century England.[14] In the 1840s, while serving as a young correspondent for London's *Morning Chronicle*, Smith wrote a series of articles attacking Benjamin Disraeli, and from that time on a bitter feud ensued between the two. In his later years, Smith wrote: "It is surprising that [Disraeli's] Hebrew flashiness should have so dazzled a practical nation,"[15] and accused Disraeli of using England as a "gaming table" for Jewish interests. By the end of the 1870s Smith's antisemitism had begun to develop into a broad belief that Judaism posed a danger to the kind of civilization Smith aspired to achieve.

Early in 1878 Smith described Judaism and the Jews as "another element originally Eastern [which] has, in the course of these events, made us sensible of its presence in the West."[16] During the debate over possible British intervention in the Turkish–Bulgarian war, in which Jewish financial interests were allegedly involved, he contended that "for the first time perhaps Europe has had occasion to note the political position and tendencies of Judaism. . . . In fact, had England been drawn into this conflict it would have been in some measure a Jewish war, a war waged with British blood to uphold the objects of Jewish sympathy, or to avenge Jewish wrongs."[17] The nations of Europe "have acted on the supposition that by extending the principle of religious liberty they could make a Jew a citizen, as by the same policy citizens have been made of ordinary Nonconformists," but they were in error. Jewish monotheism was "unreal" because the Jewish God "is not the Father of all, but the deity of His chosen race." After "the nobler part of the Jewish nation, the real heirs of David and the Prophets, heard the Gospel, and became the founders of a human religion: the less nobler part . . . rejected Humanity, and . . . fell back into a narrower and harder tribalism than before . . . bereft of the softening, elevating, and hallowing influences which . . . link patriotism with the service of mankind."

Jews, Smith contended, could not yield undivided political allegiance because their highest loyalty was to their own people, "the religion being identified with the race, as is the case in the whole group of primeval and tribal religions, of which Judaism is a survival. A Jew is not an Englishman or Frenchman holding particular tenets: He is a Jew, with a special deity for his own race. The rest of mankind are to him not merely people holding a different creed, but aliens in blood."[18]

Jews were "Christ-killers," and "plutopolitans." They were guilty of "wealth-worship, stock-jobbing, or any acts by which wealth is appropriated without honest labour."[19]

> Among the great calamities of history must be numbered the expatriation of the Jews and their dispersion through the world as a race without a country, under circumstances which intensified their antagonism to mankind and forced them more and more as objects of aversion and proscription to live by arts such as were sure at once to sharpen the commercial instinct and to blunt the conscience, the more so as they were placed beyond the healthy pale of public opinion and could look to no moral judgment but that of their tribe.[20]

In uttering these accusations, Smith was echoing the latest wave of antisemitism in Central and Western Europe. All the way from Canada, where there was no public perception of a "Jewish problem," Goldwin Smith began his entry into the international brotherhood of antisemitic propagandists. Heralded in Germany in 1879 by the publication of Wilhelm Marr's *Der Sieg des Judenthums uber das Germanenthum* (*The Triumph of Jewry over the Teutons*), a series of articles by University of Berlin history professor Heinrich von Treitschke, and the establishment of Pastor Adolf Stocker's Christian Socialist Workers' Party, this movement alleged that the German economy, judiciary, legislature, and press were controlled by Jews.[21] In spite of occasional religious overtones, this renewed antisemitism was secular in mood, repudiating Jews not for traditional Christian reasons but because they were politically, socially, and culturally alien. While reviving old images of the foes of Christendom, it also possessed a new and radical national-istic dimension.[22] The German economist Eugen Dühring went a significant step further by arguing that the Jews were a unique human species with dis-tinctive physical and moral qualities–all of them negative.

Smith was also indebted to Ernest Renan, a leading French intellectual who disparaged what he regarded as the "fanatical spirit of prophetic Judaism." Smith referred often to Renan's critique of the modern Jew, particularly his claim that "He who overturned the worldly by his faith in the Kingdom of God believes now in wealth only."[23] Smith also drew from contemporary German and Russian antisemitism, and actively solicited fashionable new anti-Jewish ideas.[24] He absorbed these notions, and propagated them throughout Britain, the United States, and Canada in some of the most potent antisemitic compo-sitions in the English language. He was not simply a critic of Jewish "tribalism"; he challenged the legitimacy of Judaism and the right of the Jewish people to survive as a distinct cultural group in the modern world. This was antisemitism of the most fundamental and dangerous kind.

During the late 1870s and the 1880s Smith nurtured his anti-Jewish pas-sions by means of a long personal association with a publicist in London, Joseph Laister, who wrote to him regularly. Laister informed Smith about the "differences between Talmud Jews and Bible Jews," the "real" reasons for the outbreak of anti-Jewish rioting in Russia during the early 1880s, the "barbaric rites" of the Jews, various aspects of Jewish sexuality, and any number of other related matters. He was probably Smith's most important source of antisemitic material, sending him countless pamphlets and articles from all over Europe, as well as his chief avenue of contact with the leading European antisemites of the day. Smith wrote frequently to offer advice, ask questions, and remit cheques–sometimes referred to by Laister as "encouragement"–in payment for services rendered.[25] He incorporated much of Laister's material into his own articles.

In almost every piece he composed on these matters, Smith alleged Jewish control over the press to explain why the truth could not reach the public. "What organs can they not command," he asked rhetorically in July 1883, when dealing with Jewish claims of persecution in Europe.[26] In July 1897 he informed the readers of the *Weekly Sun* that "the Jews control the European press. They are sometimes found behind even Christian religious journals."[27] Whenever the London papers were less than favourable to Jewish complaints of persecution in Russia, or whenever "Jewish domination" of the fourth estate was being resisted, Laister passed the news to Smith, who passed it on. "Is there such a thing as a paper or periodical which is not controlled by Jews or afraid to print the truth . . . about them?" Smith lamented to a friend in May 1906. "They seem to be behind the press everywhere, or at least be able to muzzle it."[28]

The Talmud, the great storehouse of Jewish law and commentary, held for Smith, as for many antisemites, an enormous fascination. The Talmud and "Talmud Jews" were frequent objects of his derision, and he repeated old myths about biblical Judaism, which he regarded as legitimate, and Talmudic Judaism, which he excoriated as evil.[29] In a lengthy article for the *Nineteenth Century* of November 1882, he wrote:

> Talmudism is the matter from which the spirit has soared away, the lees from which the wine has been drawn off. It is a recoil from the Universal Brotherhood of the Gospel in a Tribalism . . . which . . . built up ramparts of hatred. . . . It is a recoil from the moral liberty of the Gospel in a legalism which buries conscience under a mountain of formality, ceremony and casuistry. . . . It is a recoil from the spirituality of the Gospel . . . to a religious philosophy which . . . makes the chief end of man consist in the pursuit of wealth, as the means of worldly enjoyment.[30]

The Talmud, he informed the readers of the *Bystander* in 1883, was "a code of casuistical legalism [and] . . . of all reactionary productions the most debased, arid, and wretched."[31]

Still, some Jews, to Smith, were better than others. He regarded the religion as the source of the offence, arguing that Jews would be acceptable if they assimilated into the surrounding cultures.[32] Yet, in demanding the eradication of all religious and cultural traces of Judaism, he was really demanding the eradication of the Jewish people as a distinctive entity. This was tantamount to calling for an anti-Jewish crusade.

While Smith seems to have avoided explicit sexual allusions, he repeated canards current among Russian antisemites that Jews lacked "civic honesty," exploited their female servants sexually, corrupted the Russian peasants with drink, abused Christian burgesses, raised prices of food unjustly, mixed vodka with impure substances, traded on the Christian Sabbath and holidays, and put peasants into debt.[33] He made frequent oblique references to "facts" such as "the fact that the Oriental character, in its leading features, is inferior to the European . . . race."[34] Jews who wished to remain fully Jewish should emigrate to Palestine; however, "those who refuse to mingle with humanity must take the consequences of their refusal. They cannot expect to enjoy at once the pride of exclusiveness, and the sympathies of brotherhood."[35] In a viciously humorous piece for the *Weekly Sun* in July of 1897, he wrote: "The discovery of the Ten Lost Tribes is another religious fancy of which we ought to have heard the last. 'I am very much out of funds,' was the reply of one who had been asked to subscribe for that object, 'and I really cannot afford at present to give any thing to your association for finding the Ten Tribes, but if you have an association for losing the Two Tribes, poor as I am, I will try to contribute.' "[36]

To Smith the major threat was Jewish financial power. "Their usurious oppression of the people" would have to be given up before they could be absorbed into their host societies.[37] Fearing the effects of public sympathy because of the Russian atrocities, he gave the consular reports large play in Britain and Canada, claiming that Jewish losses "were in most cases exaggerated, and in some to an extravagant extent."[38] In any event, he said, the troubles started over "bitterness produced by the exactions of the Jew, envy of his wealth, jealousy of his ascendancy, combined in the lowest of the mob with the love of plunder."[39] He repeated these allegations over twenty years later, after anti-Jewish pogroms broke out in Romania in 1907: "Any race, let its religion and its historical record be what they might, which did what the Jews have done would have provoked the same antipathies with the same deplorable results."[40]

If antisemitism existed, Jews had invited it by persecuting others. "To pronounce the antipathy to the Jews utterly groundless is in fact to frame an indictment against humanity." Had not Tacitus and Juvenal written about Jew-hatred in the ancient world, and did not Gibbon find evidence of it in his research? In medieval times, Smith averred, Jews "provoked the hatred of the people by acting as the regular and recognized instrument of royal extortion";[41] they avoided military service; they bought land and thereby undermined the feudal system; they attacked Christian religious processions; they lent money at high interest; they sympathized with and supported the forces of Islam, notably in medieval Spain; they showed themselves to be intolerant of religious dissenters in their own ranks, like Spinoza and Acosta. Jews like Disraeli and the merchants of Johannesburg fostered war for their own financial gain. In Russia, Jews were "eating into the core of her Muscovite nationality," while in Germany they "lie in wait for the failing Bauer" and in the southern United States "a swarm of Jews" had engaged in "an unlawful trade with the simple negroes . . . [thus] driving out of business many of the old retailers."[42]

Coming from a person of Smith's intellectual stature, these charges must have inflicted considerable damage, although it is impossible to estimate the true effect of his declarations on Canadian public opinion or public policy.

Outside of the Jewish community, there appears to have been little reaction. One prominent Canadian did respond strongly, however. In a review of Smith's *Essays on Questions of the Day*, George Monro Grant, principal of Queen's University, pointed out that Smith's explanation for the rise of antisemitism amounted to blaming the victims: "The fault is thrown wholly upon the Jews and not upon those who treat them with brutal violence."[43] While Smith's views do not appear to have had any discernible influence on Canadian immigration policy during his life, his disparagement of Jews (and other Europeans) may have contributed to the general tensions over immigrant issues during the 1890s and 1900s.[44] However, he wrote only sporadically and without much fervour in criticism of existing policies. "What is the use of excluding the Chinaman when we freely admit the Russian Jew?" he asked despondently in July 1897. Ten years later he lamented: "we have been welcoming a crowd of . . . Russian and Polish Jews, the least desirable of all possible elements of population."[45] Nor did Smith, a prolific writer of letters to prime ministers Sir John A. Macdonald and Sir Wilfrid Laurier, even raise this question with them.

Still, Smith's fulminations amounted to nothing less than an outright assault on the right of people to live as Jews in civil society. He sought out and paid for professional assistance on this subject, and pursued a vigorous literary campaign across the English-speaking world for over thirty years. He served as a leading conduit for some of the worst forms of European antisemitism to North America and provided these prejudices with his personal endorsement.[46] Most likely, he would not have wished to lead an overt antisemitic political party or movement, even if this had been possible. He was ultimately too much of a mid-Victorian believer in the British party system to advocate such measures, and he might have sensed the revolutionary dangers of a single-interest party. But he declaimed his views to all who would listen, and his influence on at least one young student at the University of Toronto in the 1890s was profound. Writing in his diary in February of 1946 about the threat of Communism, Prime Minister William Lyon Mackenzie King confided:

> I recall Goldwin Smith feeling so strongly about the Jews. He expressed it at one time as follows: that they were poison in the veins of a community . . . the evidence is very strong, not against all Jews . . . that in a large percentage of the race there are tendencies and trends which are dangerous indeed."[47]

Antisemitism was part of Canada's general culture in the late nineteenth and early twentieth century. Politicians made remarks that associated Jews with unscrupulous business practices, as the Honourable John Thompson did in Antigonish in December 1878, when he said that Nova Scotia "was getting into the hands of the 'Jews and shavers of [Halifax's] Hollis Street'."[48] Phyllis Senese points to this phenomenon in her study of the reaction to the Dreyfus case in the western Canadian press, where she discovered "that a habitual, unthinking, unarticulated, but very real antisemitism was for many [Western Canadians] a part of their way of thinking."[49] There were distinctly antisemitic overtones to a riot in early August 1903 at Inverness, Nova Scotia, and a possibility of the same sentiments in the smashing up of a Jewish-owned liquor store at Londonderry, Nova Scotia, in late June of 1904.[50]

In 1904 the Lord's Day Alliance, an organization devoted "to establishing what they called the 'English Sunday' as an invented Canadian tradition," viciously attacked Orthodox Jews who had complained about Sunday observance laws.[51] Jews, one of the organization's pamphlets contended, "had sought out our land FOR THEIR OWN GOOD" and should conform to Canada's "civil customs." Jews were among the groups who, in the mind of Reverend S.D. Chown, head of the Canadian Methodist church in the early 1900s, were parasites in the national bloodstream.[52] As late as 1920, Dr. C.K. Clarke, the Dominion's leading psychiatrist, argued strenuously against allowing the immigration of refugee Jewish children from the Ukrainian famine on the grounds that they ". . . belong to a *very neurotic* race . . ." while Reverend John Chisholm pointed out that "Jews have much to do with commercialized vice."

Sentiments such as these may not indicate more than simple momentary discontent, but the fact that this discontent was so often directed against Jews does suggest the existence of deep antipathies towards them. In 1913 Halifax was the scene of an interesting controversy over the Jewish method of slaughtering cattle. A police court magistrate had found an individual, who claimed to be a rabbi and had slaughtered a heifer according to the Jewish mode, guilty of cruelty to an animal, implying that Jewish practices were inhuman.[53] An eloquent response to these charges published in the Halifax *Herald*, which was evidently repeated in other Canadian newspapers, reflected increasing Jewish sensitivity to such attacks, which held them up to hatred or ridicule.

In his 1909 novel, the *Foreigner*, the popular Canadian writer Ralph Connor depicted the Jew in starkly negative terms as the "middle-man acting dishonestly as interpreters and business agents for less educated immigrants," and as a powerful metaphor for greed, conniving, immorality, and oppression – the very antithesis of individual freedom, democracy, and Christian decency.[54]

Universities were rife with antisemitism. Assertions of Christian supremacy surfaced during the 1912 controversy at Queen's over the new provincial act which defined the constitution of the university. One member of the board of trustees insisted that a phrase be added affirming that "the University shall continue distinctively Christian and the trustees shall satisfy themselves of the Christian character of those appointed to the teaching staff."[55] Although some elements of the Jewish community protested strongly against this provision, it was nevertheless included in the act. Seven years later a serious antisemitic incident arose as a result of remarks by the new principal of Queen's, Dr. R. Bruce Taylor, at a luncheon meeting of the newly formed association of the university's Montreal alumni. Dr. Taylor congratulated himself "that Queen's unlike McGill was not situated in a great centre of population (mostly Jews) and of wealth (mostly held by Jews)."[56] When asked to explain his meaning, Dr. Taylor warmed to his subject. "He was rather proud of the fact that there were only five Jews at Queen's," recalled one member of his audience. "The presence of many Jews tended to lower the tone of Canadian Universities," Taylor continued, and he claimed to have been told by Dean Moyse of McGill that he "deplored the presence of so many Russian Jews in his English classes – 'These Jews he said, when they came to him, were not even conversant with Shakespeare' ":

> Speaking frankly, and among ourselves, we should do our best to keep their numbers [the Jews] from increasing in our Universities.
>
> No wonder they did so well in school, they stayed at home and studied when their place was at the front [during the war].

In a letter to Sir Edward Beatty, chancellor of Queen's, Lazarus P. Silver, a Queen's graduate and an elected member of the Montreal alumni group, pointed out that of the four Jews at Queen's when war broke out, two had enlisted immediately, and asked whether "it will be your policy to offer both Jew and Christian of all classes every facility to avail themselves of the knowledge and traditions of that University." Deeply embarrassed by the incident, Beatty replied lamely that "Principal Taylor's remarks were, I think, phrased in such a way as to be misunderstood and did not convey his meaning."[57]

A few years earlier, Lewis Namier's application for a lectureship at the University of Toronto had been turned down despite the opinion of his Oxford tutor, who wrote: "I started on him with the normal prejudice about Jews, but now I can not speak too highly of him."[58] Namier was regarded by all as a brilliant prospect, but the Toronto professors who interviewed him found his accent to be undesirable[59] – or, as Professor James Mavor put it: "the major drawback about [Namier] evidently is that he has the misfortune to have the

Jewish characteristic of indistinct articulation strongly developed."[60] Yet even a Jew with impeccable articulation, Ontario-born Abraham I. Willinsky, had a tough time finding an internship at a local hospital when he graduated from the University of Toronto medical school in 1908.[61]

At McGill, steps were taken to reduce the number of Jews. While they constituted 25 per cent of arts students, 15 per cent of medical students and 40 per cent of law students in 1920, university officials imposed stiff quotas that would severely reduce those percentages during the interwar years.[62]

Meanwhile, the Jewish presence in Quebec elicited a French Canadian response, marked by the desecration of the Jewish cemetery in Trois-Rivières and the reemergence of the school question in 1901, local Sunday closing legislation in 1904, and the Plamondon libel of 1910. The Jews of Montreal believed they were faced with threats to their honour, freedom of religion, civil rights, and livelihoods, and their reactions to these threats impacted significantly on the social politics of the community, which was undergoing important transformations in the first two decades of the twentieth century. Jew and non-Jews met, in the Montreal Board of Trade and, inevitably, in business, schools, university, and the professions. And while the orientation of the Jews was almost exclusively towards the Anglophone community, both for business reasons and because the Protestant school system they attended was English-speaking, Jews were not totally excluded from contact with French Canadians; a few attended the law school at Université Laval à Montréal or the medical school at the Université de Montréal. While the atmosphere was generally tolerant in both Anglophone and Francophone Quebec, efforts to convert the Jews—undertaken by both Protestant and Catholic organizations—served as a constantly irritating reminder that their religion was viewed with hostility and contempt.

The Presbyterians were particularly zealous in this endeavour. Back in the mid-nineteenth century they had sent a Jewish convert to proselytize in Palestine, and in the 1890s they had set up conversion missions in both Toronto and Montreal.[63] The Toronto Presbytery reactivated its missionary efforts in 1907 under the supervision of a former rabbinical student, Shabbatai Benjamin Rohold, whose efforts aroused powerful opposition in the local Jewish community.[64] Rohold nevertheless insisted that his "unconditional, whole-hearted, sincere love without interest" had paid off.[65] In 1910 he reported that large numbers of Toronto's poor Jews had taken advantage of his Christian charity: 8,234 had visited his Terauley Street reading room, 292 had enrolled in English-language classes, 58 in sewing classes, and 3,142 had been treated in the dispensary. Still, although 9,000 Christian tracts had been distributed, only seventeen Jews had converted. Rohold soldiered on, however, until in 1921 he departed Toronto for Palestine, still contending that he had planted the seeds of Christian beliefs among many more Jews who feared to openly profess them.[66]

The situation in Quebec changed drastically towards the end of the nineteenth century. By 1901 Jews had become the largest single ethnic group in the province after French, British, and Native Canadians.[67] Some 6,000 of the Jews were of Russian origin, mostly poor, and heavily concentrated in the central core of downtown Montreal.[68] The Catholic church, strongly ultramontane in spirit and drawing inspiration from Rome and France, began to perceive the Jews as even more dangerous aliens than before. Accused of being allied with the anti-clericals, socialists, and freemasons, they were seen as threats to the preservation of a Catholic Quebec, while some young nationalists viewed them, along with the English, as an entirely foreign and dangerously disruptive element. The publication in 1886 of Edouard Drumont's virulently antisemitic book *La France Juive* was warmly received by part of the French Canadian press,[69] and among Quebec church leaders and laymen who, like Drumont, believed that modern civilization, "which had impoverished and degraded man and robbed life of its poetry and truth,"[70] held out special dangers for the survival of French Canadian civilization. As the "spearhead" of modern capitalism, the Jews were perceived by some as exploiters and destroyers of the purity and sacredness of Quebec's rural way of life. Leading intellectual and newspaper editor Henri Bourassa had only contempt for the poor ghetto-dwellers he saw in the Montreal Jewish quarter, and in his remarks to the Commons on the proposed Lord's Day legislation in 1906 he displayed utter lack of concern for the bill's effect on observant Jews.[71] Bourassa objected to provisions of the bill which would exempt Jews. These were added, he charged, "in order to pander to the Jewish vote."[72] Citing the views of Goldwin Smith, he stated that Jews "are the least remunerative class [of immigrants] that we can get – that class which sucks the most from other people and gives back the least . . . they are the most undesirable class that can be brought into the country." To Bourassa Jews were "vampires on the community instead of being contributors to the general welfare of the people" and are "detrimental to the public welfare." According to Pierre Anctil: "the founder of *Le Devoir* believed it was necessary to construct a coherent and striking response to this massive and unprecedented presence of immigrants in a society born, in practice and in law, from the encounter of two competing colonial empires on a new continent."[73]

But aside from an article critical of Clarence de Sola (reported in the *Jewish Times* in its September 30th, 1910 issue) in which it was suggested that "Jews had no place in the high offices of a Christian society," in Bourassa's own newspaper, *Le Devoir*, there were no editorial attacks on Jews. There were, however, numerous impartial reports before 1920 on many aspects of Jewish communal activity. Indeed, one lengthy editorial in April of 1914 — possibly written by Bourassa himself — argued constructively that the solution to the continuing tensions between the Montreal Jewish community and the Protestant school commission would be to allow Jews to set up their own school system: "Le moyen de profiter du principe général de liberté qui est à la base de notre loi."[74] His co-editor, Armand Lavergne — every bit as much the nationalist as Bourassa — and also an M.P., was sympathetic to Jews and during the 1906 debate said: "we should treat them as Canadians . . . I should [not] want another minority to be deprived of what they have a right to do."[75] While the newspaper frequently published accounts of local Jews being tried in court for infractions of various kinds, *Le Devoir* also included several articles highly favourable to Jews by columnist Omer Heroux. One of them entitled "L'exemple des Juifs," was a highly laudatory account of the operations of Montreal's Hebrew Free Loan Association; "la chose ne vaudrait-elle pas la peine d'être étudier par les chrétiens," Heroux asked.[76] A few years later, *Le Devoir* published the full translated text of a lengthy appreciative article that had appeared in the *Keneder Adler* on the fiftieth anniversary of the newspaper *Le Pays*, which, along with other progressive positions, had battled vigorously and for many years against antisemitism in Quebec.[77] In March of 1919, *Le Devoir* carried substantial and impartial accounts of the proceedings in Montreal of the Canadian Jewish Congress. Thus, throughout its first decade of existence, *Le Devoir* — the premier journal of French Canada's rising spirit of nationalism — was not spreading antisemitism among its readers.

After 1900, there were many more threats to Jews from within Quebec than there had ever been before. The desecration of the ancient Jewish cemetery at Trois-Rivières, which had been judicially sanctioned to enforce the expropriation of the property — and the removal of bodies and reinterment without religious services — was a reminder of the vulnerability of Jews in an environment which could become very hostile.[78] An issue of even greater significance was the reemergence of the school question, which not only bedevilled Jewish–Protestant relations for the next thirty years, but caused serious divisions among Jews themselves. In 1894 the Protestant school board of Montreal had accepted responsibility for providing elementary schooling for the city's Jewish pupils in return for Jewish school taxes, and had agreed to pay a salary of $800 annually to a teacher who would provide religious and Hebrew-language instruction to the Jewish pupils. The Protestants had also assumed responsibility for supporting the "Baron de Hirsch" school to provide the first few grades of elementary schooling for immigrant Jewish children who could not cope with the English instruction in the Protestant schools. However, by 1900 the Protestants faced serious financial difficulties. The proceeds from Jewish school taxes did not cover the entire cost of educating these children. In the late 1890s, as Jewish immigration increased, the Protestant board began to contemplate action to precipitate a public debate on the whole issue. With the start of the 1900–01 school year, the number of Jewish pupils in the Protestant schools reached 1,153. According to the board, they cost $34,351.35 to educate, while only $11,016.24 was received from Jewish school taxes and fees.[79] The Protestants were therefore losing over $20 on every student. As if to emphasize the precarious status of the Jews in their schools, the commissioners served notice that Jewish pupils would not be eligible for prizes and scholarships awarded for academic achievement.

In 1901, Jacob Pinsler—a ten-year-old pupil at Dufferin School, in the heart of the Jewish quarter—was accordingly refused a prize for free tuition which he had won with an average of 83 per cent[80] Jacob Pinsler's case became a *cause célèbre* around which this whole issue was publicly debated. It was clear to all concerned that the quarrel involved not only Jews and Protestants, but the government of Quebec as well. While the Jews had been semi-officially part of the Protestant community, for educational purposes, since 1894, this was not taken into account by the government when it divided up the provincial education grant, or by the City of Montreal in its allocation of proceeds from the Neutral Panel, into which school taxes paid by corporations were deposited.[81] Hence, the Protestant schools derived no funding for their Jewish pupils from these substantial sources. By forcing the issue of Jewish rights in the schools, the Protestant board hoped to ensure a final resolution of this pressing financial question. It should be noted that Jewish children were never actually barred from the Protestant schools; they were not forced to accept instruction in the Christian faith, nor was it ever proven that they were in any way penalized for not accepting religious instruction.[82] While they were, in certain ways, made to feel unwelcome, and while Jewish teachers were not employed, all Jewish pupils who presented themselves were accepted, received instruction, and enjoyed other facilities.

So the Protestant school commissioners did not believe that they needed to apologize to the Jewish community. The Jews were simply the odd men out, who did not fit into either of the established school systems. They had no clear legal right to require either the Protestant or the Catholic board to educate their children, unless they were property-owners and assigned their school taxes to either board. (Protestants, on the other hand, were guaranteed education whether their families paid taxes or not.) As the Protestant board declared in 1901:

> A resident of the Jewish religion who, although an owner of real estate, has not adopted as to his school tax, or who does not own real estate, cannot claim as of right to have his children admitted to the public schools . . . such admission is given by grace and subject to whatever conditions the commissioners choose to impose, inclusive of non-eligibility for the scholarship in question.[83]

Such second-class citizenship was not acceptable, because it placed all Jews — taxpayers and tenants — in a tenuous position, and the Jewish leadership of Montreal rose to challenge the Protestant commissioners by taking up the Pinsler case in the courts. In his reluctant judgement against Jacob Pinsler in 1903, Justice Davidson urged the law makers to change the existing situation:

> There are now over 10,000 Jews in the city, and besides a great many property owning taxpayers, who are neither Protestants nor Roman Catholics. These numerous and important groups of our population create problems which did not exist when the foundations of our present educational system were laid. Their solution by the Legislature, if this judgement correctly interprets the law, has become of pressing importance.[84]

The judicial decision in the Pinsler case threatened both segments of the community: the downtowners because of the possibility that their children would be denied places in the schools, and the uptowners because of the implication that the civil rights of Jews were intrinsically less than complete. Already alarmed by local reaction to the Dreyfus affair and by the desecration of the Trois-Rivières cemetery, both sides were determined to insist on full social equality. The uptown Jews, with their university degrees, legal advisers, facility with the English language, comparative wealth, and leisure, immediately became the spokesmen of the action. They were supported by vocal demonstrations and protests from downtown, and a formidable (if temporary) force was created.

At a mass meeting held on February 24, 1903 to inform the Jewish community of the situation, a committee was appointed to discuss the entire school question with the Protestant board. Maxwell Goldstein, KC, a Quebec-born lawyer prominent in Montreal Jewish affairs, was chosen as head of this delegation. Goldstein had important connections outside the Jewish community – he was active in civic affairs such as the Montreal General and Western hospitals, and the Victorian Order of Nurses – and enjoyed the support of virtually the entire community itself. In a series of meetings with the Protestant board, he reached an agreement providing that "the Jewish population shall, if so provided by law, be identified with the Protestant system of Montreal."[85]

The commissioners and the Jewish delegation also agreed that, while "this system shall as heretofore be distinctly Protestant, and therefore Christian, . . . the regulations shall contain a conscience clause protecting the religious convictions of Jewish scholars."[86] The 1903 provincial act[87] that legalized this agreement provided that all Jewish proprietors would pay school taxes to the Protestant board, and that Jews would be counted as Protestants in the per capita allocation of school taxes from the Neutral Panel and from legislative grants.[88] The act also provided that "the children of persons professing the Jewish religion shall have the same right to be educated in the public schools of the province as the Protestant children, and shall be treated in the same manner as Protestants for all school purposes." Although the act made no specific reference to the agreement that the schools would remain "Christian and Protestant," a conscience clause which provided that "no pupil of the Jewish religion can, however, be compelled to read or study any religious or devotional books or to take part in any religious exercises or devotions" was generally understood to mean that the school system would retain its exclusively Protestant orientation.[89]

This last point was the object of an assault mounted three years later by those proposing a bill which would provide for the election of commissioners for the Protestant schools by ratepayers, both Protestant and Jewish, on a ward basis. While Maxwell Goldstein claimed that this proposed liberalization was supported by "numerous non-Jews," there is no evidence that it had any broad support among non-Jews.[90] The initiative was largely Jewish[91] in origin, and represented a further drive by a militant group to secure full civil rights, to eliminate all barriers to Jewish participation in the civic and political life of the community. Eligibility for election to the management of a body in which, by law, Jews were now full and equal members seemed logical and desirable. From the standpoint of the Protestant board, however, the election of Jewish school commissioners threatened to undermine the very character of their school system.

Reacting to the "serious consequences which may ensue" from this change, the Protestant board publicly attacked the bill, and reminded Montreal's Jews and Protestants of their 1903 agreement that the school system was to remain distinctly Protestant and Christian.[92] In 1909, when the Jews revived the issue with a similar bill, it received an even stronger rebuke from the adamant Protestants. Jews were still, at best, guests in the house–it was not their place to rearrange the furniture. In a circular distributed to Montreal Protestants, H.J. Silver, secretary-superintendent of the Protestant board of school commissioners, announced that "Admission of Jewish Citizens to the Electorate, And as a Consequence, of Jewish Representatives to the Membership of the Board, would Immediately involve the destruction of the Christian character of the administration." He warned that "The employment of Jewish teachers would logically follow, and as a result the religious instruction of Protestant children would, in certain cases, be placed in non-Christian hands. It seems scarcely necessary to characterize such an innovation as undesirable."

By 1909 the Jewish student component was 4,374 pupils, more than one-third of the total enrolment of 11,956, and immigration patterns gave every indication that the proportion would continue to increase. Even Jewish leaders expressed concern. In an interview published in Britain's *Jewish Chronicle,* Maxwell Goldstein explained that among the "problems" facing Canadian Jewry was the difficulty posed by an influx of "foreign Jews" who formed ghettos and fostered prejudice among the French Canadians[93]–a curiously one-sided idea coming from a community leader. He did not indicate precisely how these Jews were responsible for this prejudice, but presumably he meant that the concentrated presence of their increasing population, and the petty commerce they engaged in, were key causes of French Canadian antisemitism.

"These foreign Jews," Goldstein continued, "form their own synagogues . . . and have had the temerity to select their own chief rabbi [probably a reference to Rabbi Simon Glazer, known as 'the people's rabbi'] whom the uptown Jews refused to recognize." These immigrants, he warned, had to be taken by the hand and persuaded to "recognize their duties to the community"; the real problem lay in consolidating and assimilating the newcomers, and Goldstein even argued that it would be well for Jewish immigration to be restricted for another couple of years, until this had been achieved. Thus the pain and anguish of East European Jewry counted for less, in his view, than the embarrassment he and his fellow West Enders felt when these rather bedraggled immigrants arrived at the Montreal docks and proceeded up St. Lawrence Street to take their precarious place in the crowded Jewish quarter. While the West Enders were striving for dignity, propriety, and acceptance, the continuing arrival of large numbers of their co-religionists, unkempt and poor, radicals, nationalists, or Orthodox, speaking a Yiddish whose sharp accents the uptowners were trying hard to erase from their own speech, made it difficult for that goal to be reached.

The *Jewish Times* perhaps best represented the views of Anglophile Jews like Goldstein when it editorialized in April of 1905 that sectarian education was "entirely out of harmony with the times and genius of democracy."[94] But for the Protestants to yield on the religious character of their educational system would be to deny its whole reason for existence; in the sectarian atmosphere of Quebec such a concession would drastically weaken the coherence and survival of the whole minority Protestant community. The Protestant board therefore saw every reason to resist the changes being demanded. After all, the Jews were newcomers to the scene; if they were unwilling to accept the existing system, perhaps they should set up their own. Certainly the prospect of employing Jewish teachers in the schools of the existing sectarian system was totally unacceptable.

The issue was bound to become a bitter and protracted struggle because, while the Protestants adopted a rigid posture of "no surrender," the Jewish leaders were determined to achieve full civil rights. Since Jewish children constituted virtually the entire population in some schools, the fact that no Jewish teachers were hired meant that Jewish children would receive no moral instruction in school, as Protestant teachers were debarred by the 1903 law from trying to teach religion to Jewish pupils, who could excuse themselves from these classes under the "conscience clause." Equally serious was the limitation on employment opportunities for qualified Jewish teachers. A letter headlined "No Jewish Teachers Need Apply" to the *Jewish Times* in January of 1910 angrily asserted that "Until something is done by . . . the set of so-called leaders who claim to represent public Jewish opinion . . . to endeavour to rectify the glaring abuse, our self constituted leaders cannot hope to have the confidence of the rank and file of Montreal Jewry."[95] Even though the Protestant board decided in June 1913 to permit the hiring of Jewish teachers, very few of them were employed and for some years thereafter the issue continued to fester as part of the contest between the Jewish community and the Protestant school board.[96]

For all the commotion over education and civil rights, the most blatant threats to the Jews in Montreal were the attacks on their religion and on their persons. Such attacks served to remind them of the kind of antisemitism they were all too familiar with in Eastern Europe. Catholic clergymen frequently reviled Jews, as did journalists and intellectuals—one Monsignor Clouthier declared at a meeting in Trois-Rivières that the Jews were a tragedy for Canada[97]—and occasional dust-ups occured in the streets. While Quebec at its worst was hardly comparable to Ukraine, where murderous pogroms against

Jews took a heavy toll, the many Jews who came from Ukraine from time to time saw reminders of their old hometowns in the Jew-baiting on the streets, and the small-scale riots down in the Jewish quarter, when gangs of French Canadian ruffians came in looking for action – and found it. During one such punch-up in late August of 1909, a running battle between French Canadians and Jews raged up and down St. Lawrence Main for several hours before police were able to separate the combatants; they arrested three Jews.[98] At times, Jewish pedlars going through the tough Point-St-Charles section were beaten up and robbed by Polish hooligans.[99]

Borrowing from his experience in Europe, where self-defence groups sometimes succeeded in fighting off *pogromchiks*, an activist named Rosenberger organized a large "vigilance committee" to protect Jewish lives, honour, and property in the quarter. This initiative attracted criticism from the *Jewish Times* and from Lyon Cohen, who argued that the formation of such strong-arm squads would only provoke more incidents; Cohen preferred instead to ignore the August 1909 brawl and to rely on the police for protection.[100] Only the most serious of these incidents attracted the attention of the local Jewish press, but the potential for anti-Jewish violence, which was always believed to be present, added a certain degree of uncertainty to Jewish life in Montreal.

Ultimately, however, the most sinister threat was not religious disapprobation or even physical violence; it was the open support at least some segments of the Quebec Catholic community gave to the most obscene medieval myths and superstitions about Jews. A tide of vicious antisemitic propaganda pervaded many of Quebec's nationalist and clerical newspapers. Antisemitic articles had appeared in several minor French Canadian newspapers since the early 1900s.[101] A major complaint was the increasing Jewish purchases of houses and businesses in the areas where both communities lived side by side: in the Quebec City suburb of St-Roch and in Montreal's St-Laurent and St-Louis quarters, especially on St-Laurent Boulevard and on Ste-Catherine and Ontario streets.[96] After 1910, much of this hate literature circulated in the clubs of the newly organized Association Canadienne de la Jeunesse Catholique, an association of French Canadian youth for nationalist and religious action.

Some of this literature was pretty virulent stuff. In the summer of 1909, *La Libre Parole* described Jewish and Syrian pedlars as "une épidémie . . . qui passent par les paroisses. . . ."[102] In October the same newspaper featured an article with the headline "La Gangrène Juive" in which "Youpins" – a contemptuous reference to Jews – were spreading "dans notre bonne ville de Québec."[103] The Quebec suburb of St. Roch was becoming especially "gangrené" and within ten years, *La Libre Parole* predicted "la plus grande partie de St. Roch sera juive."

Readers were implored not to purchase anything from these "youpins" but to buy what they needed instead from their own kind. These writings referred to French Canadian young women, "petites Canadiennes," as being somehow especially susceptible to the blandishments of Jewish pedlars, a suggestion, perhaps, of dangers which could not be discussed openly. "La Juiverie à Montréal. Elle S'Impose de Jour en Jour," announced a minor headline in one December 1909 issue of *La Libre Parole* concerning Montreal Jews getting their names on voter's lists, while other entries such as, "La Race Juive" and "La Presse et les Juifs" seem intended to arouse fears of the spread of a "Jewish peril" and Jewish control of the American press.[104] Soon *La Libre Parole* was including Jews among the other enemies of French Canada, the Freemasons and the Orangemen, but the descriptions of Jews as parasites and filthy vermin, as the forces behind every villainy and scandal, and as "seducing" girls into buying things they don't need were apparently intended to invoke powerful emotions. In its 1910 new year's day issue, *La Parole's* editors published a veritable cornucopia of antisemitic writings. In one piece, the writer's eloquence soared:

> "Oh, si Papineau, Chénier, Mercier, Chapleau et tous nos grandes patriotes passés, . . . , sortaient de leurs tombeaux, ce seraient certainement pour nous trancer [scold] d'importance et mettre les Juifs au ban de la société."[105]

Readers were then told to turn the Jews loose, to apply the whip ("allons donc! fouetter les Juifs") and drive them out of Quebec. The same issue contained a lengthy denunciation of "Jewish trusts," a report on alleged Jewish brothelkeepers in Toronto, and a joke about Jews.

Jews were among French Canada's most serious enemies, along with Free Masonry, alcohol, cigarettes, novels and magazines and candy stores[106] and what was needed were "des ligues antisémites" to keep out Jews who were "plus sale que ces parasites," the leaders of revolutionary movements, strikers, and Free Masons.[107] One of the reasons for supporting the nascent Caisses Populaires movement was the need in Quebec to stop "la cooperation universelle de la juiverie pour étrangler [strangle] le peuple chrétien."[108]

While not a major newspaper, *La Libre Parole* and another contemporary antisemitic journal, *L'Action sociale* (which printed virulent attacks on Jews in 1910), nevertheless can be assumed to have had some effect on readers. Moreover, the existence of such publications were indications of an antisemitic movement — however limited its support — in Quebec.

On March 30, 1910, Quebec City notary Joseph Edouard Plamondon delivered a lecture at Jeunesse Catholique which contained some of the foulest lies about Judaism, including the old calumny of ritual murder. Plamondon's charges became a major issue in the Jewish community, where, as we have seen, the accumulation of antisemitic incidents had already inspired considerable apprehension. Both the West End and the downtown were fearful of the larger influences and broader attitudes that had inspired this lecture. Rabbi Simon Glazer wired the federal Minister of Justice asking him to "direct [the] attorney general of Quebec to stop antisemitic agitation and [calls] for massacre against the Jews of Quebec. Large meetings to plan riots against Jews take place Wednesday night Quebec city."[110] The Jewish community sued Plamondon for libel.

Plamondon had repeated many of the allegations and dark "truths" about Judaism contained in the writings of Edouard Drumont and other nineteenth-century French antisemites, such as Abbé Lamarque, Abbé Draceq, Abbé Demossot, and Abbé Delassue. The allegations were summed up by Samuel Jacobs, KC, one of the community's lawyers, in a letter to an enquiry from the United States:

[the] defendant . . . has circulated statements to the effect that Jews are enemies of the faith, honor, lives and well-being of their Christian fellow-citizens; that Jews are thieves, corrupters of women, assassins of Christian children, instigators of revolutions; and that they have done these things wherever they lived, and will attempt to do the same in the Province of Quebec, as soon as they are sufficiently powerful; also that Jews offer sacrifice to God by shedding blood of non-Jews.[111]

Plamondon also asserted that, being a menace to the country, Jews should not be given the same rights as other citizens;[112] rather, they should be governed under special laws similar to those enacted by medieval popes and potentates in order to establish and give legal sanction to their inferiority. Better still, they should be excluded from the country.[113]

The case came to trial at Quebec City on May 19, 1913, in Superior Court, before Mr. Justice Malouin. Plamondon was represented by J. Bédard, E. Beloeil, and J.A. Lane, all KCs from Quebec City. Representing the plaintiffs, Lazarowitz and Ortenberg of Quebec City, were two of Montreal's brilliant young Jewish lawyers, Sam Jacobs, and Louis Fitch, who worked with L.A. Cannon, KC, of Quebec City. As witnesses on his behalf, Plamondon summoned Abbé Grandbois, professor of theology at Laval, Abbé Damours, editor of L'Action Sociale, and Abbé Nadeau, professor of Greek history at the Collège de Lévis. The community's witnesses included Dr. Herman Abramowitz, rabbi of Montreal's Sha'ar Hashomayim synagogue, Montefiore Joseph, a

Quebec City merchant, Canon Scott, rector of Saint Matthew's Church in Quebec City, and Dr. Ainslie Young, principal of the high school in Quebec City.

While the plaintiffs alleged that, as a result of Plamondon's charges, they had suffered financial losses and personal physical harassment, the case obviously had far wider implications. The whole Jewish people were being slandered, and their tradition – including the Talmud, which Plamondon referred to repeatedly as the text which justified these abominations against non-Jews – was being held up to ridicule and contempt. Since these charges were precisely the kind of myths spread by antisemites in Eastern Europe and elsewhere, Jews were well aware that the consequences were intense hatred, fear, and suspicion – which sometimes erupted in pogroms of pillage, rape, arson, torture, and murder. In April of 1903 a savage pogrom in Kishinev had taken a toll of at least fifty Jewish lives, and in Odessa in 1905 a four-day pogrom had resulted in over 300 Jewish deaths; a year later, bloody pogroms had erupted in Bialystok and Siedlce.[114] In 1911, at a conference of associations of Russian nobles, several "experts" had testified that Jews needed Christian blood for their religious observances;[115] shortly thereafter, a Kiev carpenter, Mendel Beilis, had been accused of murdering a Christian boy for ritual purposes.

The Jews knew that the distance from Kiev to Montreal was a long one, and that the cultural and political differences between the Russian Empire and the Dominion of Canada were fortunately vast. But they also understood that belief in lies such as the blood libel knew no national boundaries, and that, while pogroms were unlikely in Canada, deep-seated Christian antisemitism could be reinvigorated by the repetition of such horrendous lies, and might lead to highly unpleasant manifestations. Louis Fitch, in summing up for the plaintiff, put it succinctly:

> Fortunately we live in a civilized country here: I do not expect that the adherents of Mr. Plamondon will murder us, or rape our women, or rob us of our property. . . . But I say the effect is to excite hatred among the people with whom we live, and, though perhaps to a lesser extent, bring disastrous results.[116]

Concentrating his remarks on the blood libel so recently revived during the Beilis case in Kiev, Sam Jacobs put his case this way:

> If the Christian inhabitants of St. Roch's believed these charges to be true, and were convinced that Jews practised a religion which ordered them to commit such offences, is it not reasonable to conclude that they

would and ought to take the most stringent means of ridding themselves
of such a danger lurking in their midst? History, unfortunately, has shown
what happens when an ignorant mob, whose feelings have been worked
upon by demagogues, rises in fury against a handful of people who may
not partake of the religious views of the majority, especially when the
rabble are told that the work of putting to the sword those who are helpless, is a holy work and one which is bound to bring its reward.[117]

Despite such argumentation, the libel action was lost. It was not enough for
Jacobs and Fitch to brilliantly demonstrate that Plamondon and the witnesses who
appeared on his behalf were totally ignorant of the Talmud – which they cited as
the source of their allegations – nor was it enough for Dr. Abramowitz, who had
studied the Talmud for twenty-five years, to categorically deny the blood libel and
other charges and demonstrate that Plamondon's witnesses had no evidence from
the Talmud or any other source. Even calling the two prominent Christians,
Canon Scott and Dr. Ainslie Young, to testify that Jews were decent, upstanding,
and law-abiding citizens did not help. The problem was a technicality: the law of
libel did not cover group defamation, and, since Plamondon was not accusing any
particular Jew of these abominations, the court found for the defendant. Quebec's
Jews were deprived of an important legal victory, however impressive a moral
victory they had won by disproving all of Plamondon's charges.[118]

Coming so close on the heels of the Beilis outrage in Kiev, the Plamondon
libel had a galvanic impact upon the Jews of Quebec. The repetition of the
ancient charges, no matter how often or by whom they were denied and dis-
proved, brought a collective shudder of disgust and fear to all Jews. Thus, when
Justice Malouin's judgement went against the plaintiffs, a number of Montreal's
Jews decided to appeal, and a fund was collected for this purpose by the "Baron
de Hirsch" legislative committee.

In the meantime, the *Jewish Times*, the voice of Montreal's Anglo Jews –
perhaps still in shock – refrained from commenting extensively on the case, and
dealt instead with the Beilis trial, reporting triumphantly and inaccurately on
November 14, 1913, that Beilis had been acquitted. (He was not. The charges
against him were dropped.) The *Times* did warn of probable antisemitic outbreaks in Quebec because of the Plamondon judgement, but the warning was
strangely brief, matter of fact, and colourless. The *Keneder Adler* gave even less
prominence to the Quebec case than the *Times*; aside from brief mention of
Plamondon's charges in May and a comment on Sam Jacob's remarks in court,
the *Adler* devoted little attention to the case.[119] Though not unaware of its

importance, the *Adler* was far more interested in the Beilis case, even in local reaction to it, taking note that both Armand Lavergne and *L'Action Sociale* had publicly condemned protest against the Beilis trial.[120] Montreal's Yiddish readers were invited to rejoice by a banner headline in the *Adler* on November 10, 1913, which announced the withdrawal of charges against Beilis.

To demonstrate their concern over the fate of Mendel Beilis in Kiev, the Jews of Montreal had held a huge rally at the Gaiety Theatre in October of 1913. All of the West End "prominents" had been present, as well as many representatives of the East End, while the battery of speakers included Sam Jacobs, Rabbi Abramowitz, Rabbi Nathan Gordon, Peter Bercovitch, and Louis Fitch — along with Montreal's mayor, Louis Arsène Lavallée. All of them had denounced the tyranny and antisemitism of the Russian authorities, to the applause of 5,000 Jews inside and outside the theatre.[121] The blood libel was still not dead in Quebec. In July of 1914 Abbé Antonio Huot, a prominent Catholic priest, would publish an inflammatory pamphlet with allegations that, while the accusation could not be made against Jews in general, "certain dark and secret (Jewish) sects . . . used Christian blood for ritual purposes."[122] Still this event, and many others like it over the years, symbolized the degree of unity that had been reached among Montreal Jews by 1913. A certain amount of co-operation was forthcoming from all segments of the community on perceived threats, whether Canadian or European in origin. Though there were subtle differences in the way Anglo-Jews and immigrants assessed these threats, as was demonstrated by the differing responses of the *Times* and the *Adler* in the Quebec libel action, they all nevertheless possessed a clear perception of danger. Though there might be disagreement on the degree of danger, some apprehended no better than a qualified answer to the eternal question that stemmed from centuries of insecurity — "Is it good for the Jews?"

At the same time, however, relative to the conditions in Eastern Europe, there could be little serious doubt that, generally speaking, life in Canada was good for most Jews, even for the majority of newly-arrived and struggling immigrants. The existence of these and other manifestations of antisemitism — however nasty and frightening they might be — was only one reality, and on the whole not a very dangerous one. Despite antisemitism, Jewish men (and a few women) attended universities, Jewish storekeepers and pedlars plied their trade, Jewish workers laboured alongside non-Jews and walked the same picket lines, and Jewish householders shared neighbourhoods with Christians. The Dominion of Canada allowed these and other possibilities for the blessings of peace, freedom, and opportunity.

13

Enlightenment, Protest, and Reform

Between 1900 and 1920, Canadian Jewry experienced major transformations. The first of these involved the arrival of unprecedented numbers of immigrants whose ideas, cultures, language, and approach to Jewishness not only differed substantially from, but also conflicted with, the outlook of most of those in the established communities. The second was economic, as Jewish society greatly diversified, occupationally, and broadened in national and religious identifications. A third change involved politics – chiefly domestic political issues which intruded into Jewish life, both from the local non-Jewish environment and from Europe and Palestine, where the crisis of the First World War raised serious questions concerning the future of Jewish communities. What emerged by about 1920 was a Canadian Jewry divided in many ways as its internal structure became more complex, confused about its Canadian identity as the issues proliferated and crystallized, and increasingly involved in world Jewish problems as the threats and challenges became clearer.

The transformation in the intellectual life of East European Jewry between about 1870 and 1920 helped to set a rapidly increasing part of the agenda for Canadian Jewry during the same era. In the process, Canadian Jewish organizational life was at least partly affected by East European Jewish culture. The ideas that brought this about were conveyed to Canada by the immigrants, and the literature they carried and continued to receive from Europe. This East European intellectual ferment might be described as enlightenment, protest, and reform. In the transposition of these broad categories of thought to the

Canada of Wilfrid Laurier, the debates within them helped to establish the contours of a Canadian Jewish identity.

While Canadian Jewry spread across the land in communities where Jewish life thrived and began to take on the characteristics unique to small places, the most vibrant centres were located in Montreal, Toronto, and Winnipeg. It was simply a matter of numbers. In each of these cities – in contrast to the small towns – lived sufficient Jews to form political, social, and religious groupings to cater to almost all tastes and varieties of opinion. The intellectual ferment that was carried across the Atlantic to Winnipeg's Main Street, Toronto's Ward, and Montreal's St. Lawrence Boulevard took root among the masses and flourished. And the issues around which new institutional formations would develop began to coalesce.

Transformations in Jewish self-awareness within the British and American context of Canadian life and the socialist, nationalist context of Eastern Europe were accompanied by continuities of Jewish religious observance. For many Jews, neither Karl Marx nor Theodor Herzl heralded the messianic age. To them, the synagogue and religious observances in the home were continuing verities – altered, to be sure, by the necessity of re-establishing the structures that would make them possible in this new land, but as commanding require-ments of Jewishness as they had been in the old home. Thus, on arrival in Canada, many immigrants promptly attempted to form religious institutions like synagogues, ritual baths, and burial societies, while seeking ways of pro-viding for the regulation of kosher meat and religious education. In Montreal some dozens of new congregations with fixed, though often very humble, premises were set up between 1900 and 1920, while numerous associations – some of them self-help societies like the *landsmanshaften* – were formed. Toronto saw the emergence of about ten new congregations, and Winnipeg several more, during the same period.

Rabbis were brought over from the old country, while others came from the United States and Britain, especially for the older congregations, whose members – many of them Canadian-born – insisted on having sermons deliv-ered in impeccable English. Nathan Gordon, a recent graduate of Hebrew Union College in Cincinnati, came to Temple Emanu-el in Montreal in 1906. Toronto's Holy Blossom enjoyed a succession of British-born rabbis: Dr. Barnett A. Elzas, who served the congregation between 1890 and 1893, and Abraham Lazarus, who served from 1894 to 1900, were both graduates of London's Jews' College; Rabbi Solomon Jacobs had been born in Sheffield and was brought from his post in Kingston, Jamaica, to be spiritual leader in 1901, serving until 1920.[1] From 1882 to 1918 Montreal's Spanish and Portuguese congregation was led by Meldola de Sola, who, though not formally trained in Britain, looked to London rabbis for religious guidance and inspiration.[2] Montreal's Sha'ar Hashomayim congregation hired Herman Abramowitz, a graduate of New York's Jewish Theological Seminary, in 1903, shifting from Orthodoxy to a more "modern" form of Judaism.[3] In 1914 Winnipeg's Sha'arey Zedek hired Herbert J. Samuels, a graduate of Jews' College, London, from his post in Swansea, Wales.[4]

Not all of the leading Canadian rabbis of the early twentieth century were of American or British origin, however. Perhaps the foremost Toronto rabbi was Jacob Gordon, a graduate of talmudic academies in Volozhin, Minsk, and Kounas. Widely known for his scholarly publications and for his oratory, Gordon achieved eminence during the 1920s from his pulpit in the city's largest synagogue, the Goel Tzedec, on University Avenue.[5] Israel Kahanovitch, who became rabbi of Sha-arey Zedek in Winnipeg in 1907, and later chief rabbi of Western Canada – an unofficial but highly-respected position – was a graduate of the talmudic academies of Grodno and Slabodka. Hamilton's Anshe Sholom congregation seems to have employed a series of German rabbis in the nineteenth and early twentieth century, until, in 1917, they hired Julius Berger, a graduate of the Jewish Theological Seminary in New York.[6] Montreal's leading rabbinical leader of this era was Hirsch Cohen, a graduate of the Vilnius and Volozhin academies, and such a widely recognized authority on religious questions that he served as chairman of the Montreal Council of Orthodox Rabbis for many years, and as spokesman for the city's Orthodox Jews.[7]

Thus the rabbinical influence in Canada's major cities during the early twentieth century was mixed, reflecting both the growing importance of the United States, where the Reform and Conservative academies were in the ascendant, and the continuing associations with British rabbinical leadership, especially with London's Jews' College. Equally significant is the fact that Lithuania and White Russia, whose graduates were renowned throughout the Jewish world as the most learned and rigorously trained, still dominated in several of the major synagogues, retained leadership of Orthodox Jewry in Canada, and spearheaded the movement for the improvement of traditional Jewish education, especially in the big cities.

Everywhere, education was given a high priority by the new arrivals, and it is important to note that the institutions they established – usually called Talmud Torahs, and, following Old World tradition, open to all regardless of ability to pay, employed curricula stressing traditional subjects like history, Hebrew, Yiddish, religious holidays, prayers, and, often, Talmud and Mishnah (the written law), or other texts. While the religious influences were strong, especially at the United Talmud Torah of Montreal and the Toronto Hebrew Free School (later known as the Brunswick Street Talmud Torah), certain "modern" ideals made their appearance, such as the importance placed on modern Hebrew. In the Winnipeg Hebrew Free Schools, which began in 1905 and moved to large new premises in 1912, an especially strong emphasis was put on Hebrew, not only as a subject but as a living language in which most subjects were taught.[8]

This emphasis on Hebrew reflected the influence of the Haskalah, the movement among many East European Jewish intellectuals for reform, modernization, and a redefinition of the nature of Jewish identity. Among the Maskilim ("enlightened ones") or promoters of the Haskalah, a major vehicle of expression was Hebrew, the national language of the Jewish people. Thus the stress given to it in Canada is indicative of the strength of these ideas, as well as the influence of Zionism, which also emphasized the importance of Hebrew. Winnipeg, Toronto, Montreal, and other Jewish centres where schools with the same orientation were established were, in a real sense, outposts of the Haskalah.[9] Winnipeg's Talmud Torah earned a reputation as one of three best schools of its kind in North America, and provided a model for similar institutions in Regina, Edmonton, and Calgary. In this sense, Winnipeg was the Jewish educational metropolis of Western Canada.

The traditional Talmud Torah, even though "modernized" and increasingly infused with Zionism, did not have the support of all sectors of the community. Indeed, the most remarkable and significant development in the field of Jewish education was the emergence of school systems based on new concepts of Jewish identity, shaped by the revolutionary ideas then transforming the outlook of many Jews, especially the urban youth in Poland, Russia, and Lithuania. Many forms of socialism and nationalism current among East Europe's Jewish youth were conveyed by immigrants to North America. While adding a new body of ideas to Canadian Jewish life through the means of trade unions, those who adhered to these ideas were also determined that their children should receive an education different in form and content from what traditional religious schools offered.

In all three major cities, the movement to establish these schools was well under way by 1910. The Poale Zion clubs of Montreal began a drive to organize what came to be called the People's Schools, which Hananiah Meir

Caiserman proclaimed would "stand for more, not for less Judaism; for maximum, not minimum Jewish education; for Jewish nationalism and aggressive Zionism, not luke-warm Reform Judaism clothed in semi-ortho-doxy. The Jewish People's Schools stand for proud, progressive Judaism, for a living Hebrew and Yiddish culture."[10] Caiserman's statement captured all the motifs of these schools, though not all the schools gave them this same order of priority.

In Winnipeg, as noted above, the young immigrants who established the Yiddisher Yugend Farein (Jewish Youth Organization) in 1905 began prepara-tion for a Yiddish school devoted to secular, national, and socialist ideals.[11] Soon after the National Radical School opened in 1914, a group believing in a more leftist and internationalist perspective split off to form its own school. But the National Radical School thrived, changed its name to the Peretz School in honour of that great literary figure, and became another of Winnipeg's major Jewish institutions. With a curriculum devoted mainly to Yiddish literature, Jewish history, Hebrew, songs, and dances, this school operated first in the evening, but within a few years began to convert to a full-time elementary school offering secular as well as Jewish subjects.

The first of these emphatically non-religious schools had opened in Toronto in 1911 as the Jewish National Radical School, under the inspiration of labour leader Isaac Matenko and writer Abraham Rhinewine, later editor of Toronto's *Hebrew Journal*. It had essentially the same emphasis on Jewish national history and Yiddish culture as the other schools of its type. It experienced stormier weather than its Winnipeg counterpart, not so much from internal dissension over its curriculum as from the opposition of Toronto's militant religious Jewish establishment.[12] The school's radical spirit was too much even for some of its own supporters, and in 1917 the Labour Zionists and Socialist Territorialists withdrew their support and established the Folks Shule, which was also secular but maintained a curriculum that was closer to their movement's ideologies,[13] including modern Hebrew literature along with a Zionist orientation.

The distinctions between the schools reflected fundamental differences in the ways various groups defined themselves as Jews, and envisioned the Jewish future. And this concern for passing on their culture to the younger generation was by no means unique to Jewish immigrants in that era, as work on private education among non-Jewish Ukrainians makes clear.[14] But Jews were perhaps unique among Canadian immigrant groups in being intensely committed to political ideologies.[15]

What is significant about these schools, and their support organizations and cultural spinoffs, is that they reflected the presence – and not only in the three major cities – of alternatives to traditional Judaism. The socialists and nationalists adhered to views which not only proposed secular solutions to the "Jewish problem," however defined, but also supported secular educational and other cultural institutions. These associations fostered amateur theatre and choral presentations, and sponsored appearances of professional companies from the United States. Classics in Yiddish translation (some of Shakespeare's works, like *King Lear*, were favourites), as well as growing numbers of dramatizations and songs about Jewish life in the old home and the pain and anguish of adjustment in the New World, drew large, enthusiastic, and, at times, highly emotional audiences.

The life of the mind was at the centre of existence. To immigrant Jews it was important to foster serious literary expression. Yiddish newspapers had made their appearance in all three cities in the early 1900s: Montreal's *Keneder Adler*, Toronto's *Yiddisher Zhurnal*, and Winnipeg's *Dos Yiddishe Vort*. Newspapers from the United States and even from Europe had been available for many years previously, and continued to attract substantial numbers of readers in Canada.

The journals were important outlets for Yiddish literary expression in Canada, and a considerable number of poets and writers, like Jacob Segal in Montreal and Abraham Rhinewine in Toronto, first reached large readership through the medium of the *Adler* and the *Zhurnal*. These forums of debate and self-expression included literary and historical essays, stories by "greats" like Sholem Aleichem and Judah Leib Peretz, book reviews, synopses of plays, and helpful advice to immigrants. Editorials attempted to analyse trends in world and local affairs, especially as they affected Jews, and some letters to the editor – many of them showing the frustration and heartbreak of recent immigrants – elicited advice and counselling. The Yiddish press provided a window on the world of events and ideas; it was the university for the Jewish common man and woman in their own beloved first language.

By the end of the 1910s, some of the literary compositions that had first appeared in these newspapers had been republished in an anthology, *Kanada: A Zamelbuch*, edited by Lazar Rosenberg, a local Yiddish poet who collected the poetry of Canadian Yiddish poets and essayists.[16] This was a modest effort, to be sure, but it represented an important benchmark of self-expression by a significant segment of the newest part of the community. Here, in poetry, short stories, and essays, appeared the anguish and hopes of the immigrant. Jacob Segal celebrated the country in his poem entitled "Oif Frieye Vegn" ("On Free Roads"). Of Toronto's Yiddish poets, Shimon Nepom was the most renowned;

a streetcar conductor, he wrote prolifically, though he published only three slim volumes of poetry—the last was entitled *Tramvai Lider* (*Streetcar Poems*).[17] Yiddish culture also thrived in the smaller centres. In London, for example, Dr. Isidore Goldstick, a high school language teacher, published translations of Yiddish literature in English, while Melech Grafstein published various Yiddish works, and two major English anthologies devoted to the Yiddish writers Judah Leib Peretz and Sholem Aleichem.[18]

Thus the East Europeans who arrived prior to 1920 wrought far-reaching changes in Canadian Jewish life, with effects that lasted for at least another generation. Not only did they create a parallel set of cultural, religious, and welfare institutions, with their *vereins*, makeshift *shuls*, *landsmanshaften*, newspapers, unions, and clubs, they also revolutionized Jewish political life on several different levels. They demanded democratic governance of the national community and expression of its concerns, and they insisted on the recognition of Jewish constituencies in municipal, provincial, and federal affairs, while they battled for a national solution to the bitterly contested school question in Quebec. Although in some senses these endeavours were separate battles, they were all related aspects of a common struggle for the emancipation of Jews from the bonds of intra-communal elite control and from political and social inferiority, and for the liberation of the Jewish creative spirit to develop its cultural and linguistic uniqueness in Canada.

This energy peaked during the First World War and coalesced in the movement to establish a Canadian Jewish Congress. When the congress first convened on March 16, 1919, it marked a major watershed in Canadian Jewish history and a veritable revolution in the power structure within the community. In the congress, the East Europeans served notice that they had arrived and that they intended to be an important force in the community thereafter.

It must be emphasized that the East Europeans had a fundamentally different experience of political activism than the established Canadian community. The latter had, of course, already been engaged in political activity. But it was of a kind the East Europeans abhorred because it smacked of old-style *shtadlanut* (political influence by Jewish elite). The deliberations over Jewish rights in the school system had taken place largely in private, with the Jewish masses of Montreal having little say in determining the community's position. The East Europeans strongly favoured a more democratic method of determining and expressing Jewish positions, on the school question or any other issue that might arise.

The idea of a "parliament" of Canada's Jews had first been raised in 1908 by

S. Shneour, editor of the newly established *Keneder Adler*. He called upon all Jews who wished to push for the summoning of such a parliament to write him at the *Adler;* he lectured on the subject and occasionally publicized the idea in the newspaper's columns. In February 1909, the question of establishing a Canadian Jewish board of deputies – modelled perhaps on the British board – was raised. But the proposal ran into opposition from the directors of the "Baron de Hirsch," who resisted sharing their power in the community with new immigrants, and the idea was allowed to die.[19] The congress idea was revived in 1912, in connection with European proposals for establishing a world Jewish parliament, but the impetus for a Canadian congress aroused broad support across the Dominion only after the outbreak of the First World War. Inspired by the American Poale Zion groups, who had summoned Jews in the United States to establish a democratic American Jewish Congress in 1914, Reuben Brainin began agitating for a Canadian congress to facilitate relief efforts and post-war planning.[20]

The war had a catalytic effect on Canadian Jewry – particularly on the relatively recently arrived East Europeans, who were so alarmed at the fate of their families in the war zones that they undertook massive campaigns to raise funds for relief. In Montreal, for example, some 200 representatives of seventy synagogues, organizations, and *vereins* came together for this purpose, as early as November 1914.[21] Simon Belkin discovered that a committee of twenty-one individuals – fifteen "uptowners" and six "downtowners" – was selected to oversee the collection and distribution of relief funds. But when the committee reported its activities in early 1915, it was revealed that, of $24,000 collected, only $6,000 had been sent for European relief; the rest had been used for local welfare. Believing that the purposes of the campaign had been subverted by the "uptowners," the "downtowners" now moved to establish a War Relief Conference on a democratic basis that would, presumably, express the wishes of the majority of Canadian Jewry to give priority to overseas relief funding. "We were absolutely ignored in the distribution of the Assistance Fund to which each of us has contributed his share," began the invitation to attend the conference, called for February 21, 1915. "It is our obligation to ensure that the cry of the hungry and of the suffering shall not be a voice calling in the desert."[22] "It was at this conference that the Canadian Jewish Congress was born."[23] The conference laid down three essential principles on which the congress was later founded: the immediate mobilization of relief for war-stricken European Jews, the affirmation of democratic principles, and a concern with immigration problems. Calling itself the Canadian Jewish Alliance, the group issued a summons to Jewish organizations to attend a meeting on March 7 to discuss these issues, among many others. The alliance would take the lead in the drive to establish a nationwide conference.

The alliance met again on March 28 to draft a "Declaration of Principles" in which the solution of the sufferings of Jews in the European war zones, "must derive from the will of the awakened awareness of the entire Jewish people."[24] Representatives of 71 Montreal organizations were present: 16 synagogues, 6 labour unions, 10 sick benefit societies, 18 loan syndicates, 8 cultural and 5 political organizations, and 8 charitable societies, representing the vast majority of the city's Jewry.[25] The Congress idea was obviously very popular. Branches were organized in Toronto, Hamilton, London, Chatham, Calgary, Glace Bay, North Bay, Quebec City, Saskatoon, and Edenbridge.

Yehuda Kaufman, a leading left-wing Montreal Zionist, attempted to establish some of its agenda by making several major points at the March 28 meeting. First, he urged the community to press Britain to insist that Russia, its ally in the war, protect its Jews, who were suffering under official persecution. He stressed, secondly, that Canada was a pioneer country with great colonization possibilities, a clear reference to concerns about possible limitations on Jewish immigration.[26] Kaufman argued further that the Jews of Canada, like those in the United States, needed to establish a political body which would be in a position to express what he called "our national revindications" at a postwar peace conference.[27]

Hananiah Caiserman, an active participant in these Montreal initiatives, wrote in his account of the first Canadian Jewish Congress that "the appeals of the Montreal Committee [the War Relief Conference] made an impression all over the country." In response to them, local committees were organized, although in both cities and small towns efforts were already under-way to collect money for war relief,[28] under the umbrella of the Canadian Jewish Alliance.

But the first push for a congress was delayed, largely because of opposition from the Federation of Zionist Societies of Canada, which took the position that the time was not "opportune."[29] The federation's president, Clarence de Sola, believed that a congress was not needed since there was already a national organization, the federation itself, and that another such body would only weaken Canadian Jews' contributions to Palestinian colonization as well as war relief efforts in Europe. A congress, said de Sola, would fragment communal unity and frustrate the federation's claims of representing Canadian Jewry, defining its goals, and ordering its priorities.[30] Over the protests and opposition of the Montreal forces in the alliance, the Zionist federation summoned its own national conclave – known as the Canadian Jewish Conference – which assembled on November 14, 1915. Because it was dominated by the federation, in Caiserman's eyes "it was certainly not representative . . . of the Jewish masses in the Dominion."[31]

But while they had different priorities, the federation's agenda was much the same as that being proposed by the alliance. The most crucial differences were their views on who should be empowered to prioritize the agenda and how leaders should be selected. Otherwise, as Caiserman shrewdly observed, there "existed a striking similarity of purpose" between the two parties. Despite the rhetoric – and personal rivalries – the mounting crisis among world Jewry forced Zionists, Bundists, socialists, and those with other political agendas to concentrate on the importance of presenting Jewish national priorities for Palestine and for Jewish civil rights in the nations of Eastern Europe at a peace conference after the war. Thus, while the alliance wanted to consider "how together with World Jewry to secure representation to the Peace Conference," de Sola spoke guardedly of the need to "organize and have representatives appointed who will be able to plead on our behalf when the great conference of the nations is held."[32]

One issue that arose early in September 1915 momentarily confused the whole question. This was the invitation, received in Montreal, for Canadian Jews to be represented at the American Jewish Congress. This was a delicate issue because the United States was not yet a belligerent in the war, and the participation of Canadians might cause an embarrassment when international questions arose on which the governments of the United States and Great Britain might differ.[33] The *Adler* called for a special conference of representatives to discuss the issue before the forthcoming convention of the federation in November. While pronouncing the Canadian congress desirable, "indeed a necessity," the *Adler* emphasized that it was vital "to be extremely circumspect and to act with every reserve" because "it is . . . a very debatable point if, under such circumstances, Canadian Jews may be represented in this [American] Congress, ignorant as we are of what the Congress may do and how its measures may react upon ourselves living here on British soil."[34] Louis Brandeis, the prominent U.S. Zionist leader and advocate of the American Jewish Congress, was invited to address the special conference.

In editorials over the next few weeks, both the *Adler* and the *Chronicle* emphasized that the forthcoming conference to formulate an answer to the American Jews would benefit both the Zionist federation and all of Canadian Jewry, which "will acquire an experience of solidarity" – a subtle reminder to the federation that they did not speak for all the Jews in the country.[35] It was clear, moreover, that the federation's agenda – the building of Jewish settlement in Palestine – was much too narrow for most Canadians. In September a mass meeting of the community in Winnipeg approved sending a telegram to Lord Reading, a prominent English Jew, asking him

> for that powerful influence which you can bring to bear upon the imperial government for its active sympathy at the time of negotiations for peace, so as to insure the inclusion in all treaties of clauses, providing for and enforcing the extension to Jews in all lands, of the fundamental rights of human beings, the bestowal of civil and political equality, and the establishment of the principle that the differences in religious belief, should not preclude anyone from the enjoyment of full liberty, admission to public offices and honors, and the free exercise of all professions and industries.[36]

The meeting called also for "the recognition of the claim of the Jewish people [for] unrestricted settlement in Palestine," but this was a far less important demand than that for civil rights for the Jewish minorities in Europe. In Toronto, similar enthusiasm was expressed by both Zionists and others at meetings convened to explain the purposes of the conference.

But some differences of opinion had begun to surface. At one meeting in Toronto, Rabbi Dr. Price denounced the attempts of certain self-appointed "leaders" to create factions in the community, saying that they were "a curse to Canadian Judaism." He may have been referring to Clarence de Sola, who was absolutely opposed to the proposals for establishing a congress, which implied a permanency and purpose that could well detract from the importance and strength of the federation. The federation did – at least officially – support the idea of a special conference. Leon Goldman, its executive secretary, toured the country together with Louis Fitch, pumping up enthusiasm for the idea.[37] In Ottawa, however, Fitch made it clear that he saw the conference as a prelude to a congress which must be "an organized Jewish representative body in Canada."[38] The *Chronicle's* editor, Hyman Edelstein, picked up on this point in his editorial on October 29: "It is the first time in the history of Canadian Jewry that a body of new representatives of our entire community will assemble."[39]

Edelstein went on to articulate a broad agenda for the conference. The first was immigration; assuming the resumption of an "inevitable vast influx of immigrants into this country on the conclusion of that war," the fact that "none of the large organizations is in a position to undertake any preparation for this contingency" required serious attention from local charities "and the best instrument to accomplish this happy end is the Conference." Next on his agenda was the appointment of an observer, rather than a representative, to the American Jewish Congress, to attend and report back. Third was the need to attend to "domestic questions" – but, since "the Jewish people has no home," Jewish suffering elsewhere required that "the Conference will seek to establish solidarity of the Jews of Canada, not merely as a means of regulating and bettering our own domestic affairs, but of being of greater service, efficient through organization, to our people in whatever part of the globe they are afflicted."[40] The *Chronicle* did not explicitly endorse the congress idea, but in an editorial published on the eve of the conference it stated that "the Conference will have justified its calling if it appoints a Canadian Jewish Board of Deputies on a democratic basis . . . to hold the reins of communal administration for the entire Jewry of this dominion."

When the conference met on November 14, 1915, in Montreal, it appeared to have virtually unanimous public support, including that of the Zionist federation. An executive committee was elected to carry its efforts forward and to work with organizations not represented at the conference, "with the object of calling a Congress of all Canadian Jews if necessary."[41] But even with that enthusiasm and the endorsement of the federation, which met a day later, plans for a congress did not go forward. Called at the instigation of the Zionists and enjoying their official support, the Congress did not have their heartfelt endorsement. Clarence de Sola would have no congress as long as he controlled the federation, and although he had agreed to serve on the committee to move it forward, he was clearly opposed to the whole project. "The Zionists alone," he told delegates, "have an international Jewish organization representative of a large portion of our people, they alone are ready to place before [the Peace Conference] a clearly defined plan for putting an end to Israel's woes. All others have yet no plan, no organization."[42] While the ordinary Jew, "the rank and file, the men who knew suffering," did support Zionism,

> many [others] whose co-operation would have been invaluable, whose assistance would have made success assured, utterly failed us. . . . They made the unfortunate blunder of treating a big political problem like the Jewish question as though it were merely a philanthropic problem, requiring but temporary expedients and but local palliatives. . . . They were incapable of seeing that . . . a plan that would put an end of the Goluth [exile], that would realize our racial individuality, a plan that would enable us to develop to the utmost limit our religious teachings,

our spiritual aspirations, our philosophy and our sacred Hebrew language could meet our requirements.

With such historic aspirations and single-minded perspectives, Clarence de Sola could find little interest in the post-war concerns of a congress: poverty in Montreal, starvation in Eastern Europe, civil and political rights for Jewish minorities, the school question in Montreal. He saw only one solution to the "Jewish problem": Zionism. No wonder, then, that the congress idea, as long as he and other Zionists controlled the executive of the Canadian Jewish Conference which was supposed to promote the matter, went nowhere.

The difference between the two sides reflected the divided state of Canadian Jewry at this critical juncture of its history; the alliance was eclectic and feisty, democratic and socialist, while the federation was cautious and conservative, paternalistic and traditional. And while both camps believed in the same causes – the presentation of Jewish minority rights to the peace conference, the relief of war sufferers in Eastern Europe, and the future of Jewish settlement in Palestine – there were wide gulfs over the order of priorities and methods of presentation.

Here the Canadian experience differed sharply from that of American Jewry, where the Zionists, led by Louis D. Brandeis, had pushed strongly for the establishment of an American Jewish congress. An organization with a broad emotional appeal to the East European immigrants would allow Zionists to direct more substantial relief funds to Palestine than they could raise through their own efforts. Moreover, a congress would provide them with a vehicle for establishing their leadership over American Jewry. Thus they would outflank the "establishment" in the American Jewish Committee, which consisted of the aristocratic and rich *yahudim*, Jews of German origin who resented the upstart East Europeans' attempt to form a new organization tinged with a strong nationalist flavour that conflicted directly with their own conservative outlook.[43] Realizing that the East Europeans wanted a voice in American Jewish affairs, Zionists there led the fight to establish the American Jewish Congress.

While the federation's philosophy was a far cry from that of the American Jewish Committee, its leader, Clarence de Sola, was equally an establishment figure. He had an uneasy relationship with some of the downtown East Europeans and, though he made efforts to keep them within the ambit of the federation,[44] he was only partly successful. The Poale Zion clubs had their own national organization and their own fund-raising campaigns. Their intellectuals and leaders had relatively little to do with the federation. The Zionists felt threatened in several ways. First, an organization with the broad scope and emotional appeal of a national congress would diminish the importance of the federation, and its role as a conduit to the non-Jewish world. Secondly, it would lay claim to control of all Jewish relief efforts, including those directed towards Palestine, and establish priorities with which the Zionists might not agree. And thirdly, the program of such a congress would include items like representation at a peace conference that the Zionists wished to dominate, or, possibly, radical solutions to contentious issues like the school question.

During the war, the tide of Canadian Jewish opinion, however, swung gradually in favour of the alliance. The democratic elections to the newly formed American Jewish Congress in 1918 influenced Canadians to demand the same system, especially in the west. The alliance mounted a vigorous campaign in Winnipeg and in the prairie farm colonies and villages where Winnipeg's *Dos Yiddishe Vort* circulated; its powerful editorials through 1917 and 1918 had demanded openness and democracy in the formation of the congress. In Toronto, as well, the Jewish press had become strongly favourable to the establishment of a Canadian congress on broad democratic principles, while in Montreal Reuben Brainin's short-lived daily *Der Veg* (The Way) tried to mobilize the Jewish population to support the proposal. At last, then, a provisional congress committee under Hananiah Caiserman had been struck in December of 1918, with the mandate of convening all Jewish organizations – including the Zionist federation – to send representatives to the congress.[45]

Though still harbouring reservations, the federation – headed from 1919 on by the genial and pliable Archie Freiman, who had succeeded the ailing Clarence de Sola – had agreed to participate in the movement. Canadian Jewish newspapers had been ecstatic over the revival of congress proposals and the Zionists' co-operation. The *Chronicle* thanked them "for having kept the Jewish national idea alive" and continued: "now that the idea is to become realized [through the Balfour Declaration of 1917], it can no longer remain in the hands of the few. It has become the personal problem of every Jew and Jewess the world over."[46]

Thus the conclave which assembled in Montreal in January 1919 included 125 Montreal organizations representing virtually all shades of opinion in the city. A committee was selected to organize the congress on a democratic basis, with an agenda that included the most burning issues of the day: the establishment of a Jewish national home in Palestine, the recognition and legalization of Jewish national rights "where they live in compact masses," "equal rights" with other minorities in Canada, affiliation with a world Jewish congress, relief

of war-sufferers, assistance to Jewish immigration to Canada, and "co-operation with the Canadian labour movement."[47]

District conferences in Montreal, Toronto, and Winnipeg were assembled
in early March of 1919 to discuss these issues and establish procedures for the
election of delegates. Nearly 25,000 ballots were cast in these elections, an
astonishingly high figure considering the fact that the total Jewish population of
Canada was only about 125,000. When the Canadian Jewish Congress (CJC)
finally convened on March 16 at Montreal's Monument Nationale (a site symbolically important in the emergence of French Canadian nationalism), the community had reached a major milestone. After a long struggle, the immigrants had
apparently won over the establishment by setting up a democratically elected
body that was widely representative of virtually all sectors of the community,
from all across the Dominion. The East European era had apparently arrived.
From all across the Dominion the delegates came, from Sault Ste Marie, Birch
Hills and Plum Coulee to Glace Bay and from all the other cities and towns
where Canada's Jews lived they came to debate the momentous issues then facing
the Jewish people in Canada, in Eastern Europe, and in Palestine.

The deliberations at the CJC supplied evidence of remarkable energy,
vision, organizational skill, and understanding of Jewish interests among the
leaders of the East Europeans. What was also interesting was the fact that
several establishment figures were recruited to the leadership. The most
notable was Lyon Cohen, president of the Baron de Hirsch Institute and of
Sha'ar Hashomayim, as well as head of the Montreal Men's Clothing Manufacturers' Association. That he could be elected unopposed to head the congress deliberations, and, at its close, to the presidency of its permanent
organization, is evidence of the wide respect he enjoyed throughout the community, notwithstanding his controversial role in the 1916-17 strike. Cohen's
exemplary handling of the agenda over the next few days of heated deliberations fully vindicated the trust that had been placed in him.

What came out of these discussions, and the sometimes tempestuous
debates, was a remarkably clear statement of concern about the community's
self-image and future, as well as about the pressing issues of Jewish minority
rights in Eastern Europe, the future of the Jewish national home in Palestine,
and, above all, the recognition due to the "Jewish nation," which should be
"admitted as a partner in the League of Nations" in order to protect these rights
and claims.[48]

In several other resolutions, the congress addressed the problems of the
recent arrivals, including the long-standing dispute over the school question.

After much debate on the latter, Louis Fitch and Hananiah Caiserman's resolution instructing the congress executive "to promote a system of separate Jewish schools . . . wherever such is possible" was passed. Overwhelming support was given to a resolution favouring the five-day work week, indicating the strength of labour sentiment among the delegates. Protest was lodged against the recent massacres of Jews in Ukraine, Hungary, Poland, and Romania; the congress directed its representatives at the Versailles Peace Conference to recommend that the countries in which these massacres were perpetrated be forced to grant minority rights.[49]

Thus, when the congress adjourned late in the evening of March 19 after final words of assessment from Yehuda Kaufman and the distinguished Yiddish philosopher and writer Chaim Zhitlowsky, it had not only made major achievements but it had also established for itself a most formidable agenda.

The *Chronicle* had argued in January 1919, before the CJC was established, that the old Zionist priority of a Jewish state in Palestine must be modified to suit present-day realities. Instead of demanding a state immediately, Jews, it said, must press the Great Powers for "opportunities and conditions to enable them to bring the Jews back to Palestine" in order to establish a Jewish majority – in time – under British trusteeship. But "the Palestine question is [not] the only question [for] world Jewry to solve," the *Chronicle* had continued. The Jewish question did not involve Palestine only, and therefore the Zionist answer was incomplete. There were specifically Canadian problems, like immigration "and the enactment of such laws as will insure the future of the Jewish immigrant to this great Canada of ours." There was as well a need for "compulsory education throughout the provinces . . . that will enable the Jewish immigrant to imbibe the ideals of Canadian citizenship in the least possible time." And the congress must have the co-operation of Canadian Jewry's communal leaders to establish an organization "representative of all classes."[50]

But this appeal to Canadian Jewry's communal leaders had yielded only disappointing results. At the meeting held in Montreal in January 1918 to set the congress going, few Montrealers had attended. "So far the balance of power seems to be with the working classes rather than with the recognized leaders of the community," the *Chronicle* had commented, lamenting that in comparison with other Jewish communities Montreal's Jews were apathetic "and indifferent to all matters that do not affect our own personal welfare. . . . The Jewish community of Montreal is sufficient unto itself and each little group into which it is divided worships its own particular "ism" and refuses to be drawn into a discussion of the "isms" of any other group."[51] Essentially, then, Montreal's West End Jews had chosen to opt out of the congress. Even when the congress was an "established fact," as the *Chronicle* had called it on the eve of elections in late February 1919, "certain classes in the community have been peculiarly apathetic." The weekly pleaded with them to accept the inevitable and participate, or have the congress, which would speak for all of Canadian Jewry, dominated by the classes that were actively participating in the elections. "We must see to it," one editorial exhorted, "that the voice of the Canadian Jewish Congress is not the voice of the radical, the reactionary or the extremists."[52] A week later the *Chronicle* was more optimistic: "the nominations for the . . . Congress inspire us with hope. Those, so far chosen, are splendidly representative of the best in Montreal Jewry."

When the congress finally met in March 1919, the *Chronicle* hailed it as a most significant event. "We are a peculiar people, all the more peculiar in that each one of us is an individualist in thought and in action, but WE CAN MEET on common ground and that ground is the welfare of the Jew."[53] It attributed this success partly to Lyon Cohen, and to the fact that "every shade of opinion [was] represented except that of the assimilationists."

Soon after the termination of the first Canadian Jewish Congress, it was clear that immigration would become the central focus of activities, because it was the one issue on which the CJC could hope to have real impact. Sam Jacobs became the chief spokesman on this issue; elected MP for Montreal's Cartier riding in 1917, Jacobs was Canada's most important Jew in federal politics and in the ranks of the Liberal Party.[54] At one congress session he gave a speech in which he predicted that "Jewish immigration is bound . . . to occur in large numbers" now that the war was over.[55] Because "These [people] will shortly be knocking at our doors for entry, and it behooves us to see that they are not turned away from our shores indiscriminately . . . ," a committee of congress ought to contact the government of Canada "to ascertain how far restrictions will be made to prevent these people from coming into the country. . . ." One measure he suspected the government might introduce was a literacy test. To this he argued that

> illiteracy of the immigrant does not affect his capacity for the work for which he is intended in this country . . . it is our experience that illiterate Italians, Belgians, Jews or Russians can work just as well in the construction of railroads, dig sewers, blast rocks, make roads, mine coal, cut trees, lay bricks, paint houses, load freight trains, and that, even where skilled labour is necessary, the ability to read and write does not necessarily add to his powers.[56]

Jacobs was just as concerned about proposed changes to the immigration act to debar persons of questionable political ideas. He pointed out that "it is at best extremely difficult to ascertain the political past of any immigrant" and noted the problems involved in trusting officials not to abuse their discretionary powers of determining an individual's political views. In any event, he added, Jews in Europe had suffered conditions which caused them to "feel a natural resentment for the countries of their origin, and the political past of some of these men is easily understandable." Most Jews belonged "to the moderate parties in the countries from which they come, and these men after a short residence in Canada, enjoying Canadian treatment, eventually give to Canada a high type of citizen, conscious of his obligations, law-abiding and hard working."

Caiserman, who had been selected as the general secretary of the CJC, performed veritable prodigies of organization in the face of problems which, in a few short years, would bring all CJC activities to a premature halt. But when he reported on his first year of activities, he was able to record some truly impressive achievements. He had established contact with the Jewish delegation at the Paris Peace Conference and put the CJC behind their efforts to secure recognition for Jewish minority rights in the new nations of Eastern Europe. The congress had also supported recognition for Jewish national representation to the League of Nations.

The main orientation of congress activity, however, was domestic. The government of Canada had been subjected to a number of strong anti-alien pressures during and after the war. The Winnipeg general strike of May and June 1919 was attributed to the presence of "foreigners," the Austrians, Galicians, and Jews who lived in the city's North End. The emergence of the Social Democratic Party and, in 1921, the Communist Party of Canada lent strength to nativist and anti-immigrant sentiments. In an atmosphere of suspicion and rising hatred of immigrants in general, Jews were the object of special resentment. A more immediate concern, however, was that regulations against the immigration of "enemy aliens" implemented in 1919 would prohibit the landing of Austrian, German, Bulgarian, and Turkish Jews.[57] Jews were later exempted from this order, but the congress remained deeply concerned about other orders concerning proper papers, minimum landing money, and continuous voyages, as well as November 1919 revisions to the Dominion's immigration act that allowed wide discretionary powers to admitting officers.[58] Restrictions on Doukhobors, Mennonites, and Hutterites also gave rise to serious concern, especially when, in November of 1920, a new order-in-council raised the required amount needed by each immigrant to $250.[59] In addition to being concerned with broad Jewish interests, the CJC understood that a large percentage of Canadian Jews were themselves immigrants hoping for family reunification, and thus it was compelled to emphasize the importance of Canada as a haven for Jewish refugees from the war.

The conditions of these displaced persons were especially serious in Ukraine, where terrible pogroms had broken out in 1918 and 1919 in the wake of the Russian Revolution and the ensuing civil war. Tens of thousands of Jews had been murdered, some of them in the most bestial fashion, by the armed forces of Simon Petlyura, leader of the short-lived Ukrainian republic and by other pogromists,[60] while many thousands of others were dwelling as refugees in abominable conditions there and, in increasing numbers, in the eastern sectors of Romania. On November 24, 1919, a huge demonstration of "mourning and protest" of 30,000 Jews took place in Montreal, while in Winnipeg and Toronto similar demonstrations were held. Several days later the *Adler* carried detailed reports on the pogroms in Kiev, where in one day some four hundred Jews were murdered amid mayhem and widespread destruction.[61] On November 19, CJC officials submitted a memorandum to the Dominion government asking that an official commission, composed of Jewish Canadians, be sent to investigate the condition of dependants of Canadian citizens in Ukraine, take them relief supplies, and begin bringing them to Canada.[62] As Simon Belkin, a close observer of contemporary events, put it, "it was no more a question of . . . relief for stricken brethren overseas; it became a question of rescuing tens of thousands of homeless refugees. . . ."[63]

Belkin headed the Ukrainian Farband, a Dominion-wide organization of Jewish immigrants from Ukraine, which raised funds to send Caiserman to survey the situation there. Meanwhile, the government requested the congress to supply the names of all Ukrainian dependants whom Canadian families intended to bring to Canada. Eight thousand persons across the country responded to a survey. The information was tabulated and presented to the government, and the congress awaited its reaction.[64]

The CJC also addressed the Montreal school question. At the plenum, delegates like Louis Fitch had made this a congress issue, even though non-Montreal delegates had expressed serious reservations concerning the proposal to set up a Jewish separate school system there. In any case, the congress could do little more than encourage unity in the badly divided Montreal community.[65] The CJC proposed to canvass the city's entire Jewish population in order to determine the aggregate Jewish school taxes – presumably to prove that the Jews were not sponging off the Protestants, who repeatedly alleged that Jewish school taxes did not cover the cost of educating Jewish children in Protestant schools. The CJC's efforts to bring representatives of the three Jewish schools set up by local organizations together under a congress school committee failed.

The congress also attempted to remedy problems with some steamship agents and bankers who, though entrusted with money to send to relations in Europe, were alleged to be dishonest. Caiserman took special interest in establishing an immigrant aid society to handle policy questions and problems of Jewish immigrants, especially those involving the Dominion government. He was successful in bringing several organizations together in 1919, and over the next several years the Jewish Immigrant Aid Society was established, with its head office in Montreal and branch offices in Toronto and Winnipeg.[66]

But after such an auspicious beginning in 1919–20, congress activities faltered, and in a few years the organization was virtually defunct. Caiserman, who had apparently served without salary, warned at the end of his first year in office that, despite immense enthusiasm at the first plenum, "one very important matter escaped the attention of the delegates, namely, to secure the necessary money in order to install an office and conduct it in a businesslike manner."[67] Lack of adequate finances thereafter proved to be "a very serious handicap and at times paralyzed [congress] activities." But sufficient financial support was not forthcoming, and Canadian Jewry was on the whole apathetic to the congress agenda – such as immigration questions, organizing Jewish communities, monitoring the Montreal school question, and minor matters like the establishment of a press bureau and a statistics department. Why had a movement that had started with such enthusiasm in 1915 and convened such an impressive gathering in 1919 faltered badly just a year later?

There are several possible explanations. The war had ended and within a year or two the worst of the Ukrainian, Polish, and Romanian anti-Jewish outrages had abated. There may also have been a fairly serious leadership problem; while Caiserman was certainly willing to do the executive work, the organization needed a cadre of community leaders who could mobilize support from all sectors of Canadian Jewry, and represent the organization to the Canadian public and to federal and provincial governments. Lyon Cohen was undoubtedly such an individual, but he seems to have lost interest in the movement after chairing most of the sessions at its first plenum. Perhaps he was too narrowly focused on the serious communal needs and internal divisions in Montreal itself to take the organization in hand and develop it. Mark Workman had been involved at the outset but he was not interested, apparently, in carrying the congress forward. Also, leaders like Cohen and Workman, and many lesser figures, may have been seriously affected by the business recession of the early 1920s; the clothing industry was undergoing a very serious shakeout. What the CJC needed was someone with Clarence de Sola's drive, single-mindedness, and financial resources. But de Sola was now dead.

The CJC itself, though not exactly dead, was by 1921 crippled by the lack of leadership and funding. It languished for a year or two and then virtually disappeared as a force in Canadian Jewish life; it would not be revived until 1933. Through the twenties, Canadian Jewry was without its parliament, without its forum of opinions from across the intellectual spectrum, and without a voice for its collective concerns. But while Canadian Jewry was weaker without an active congress, it would be wrong to assume that even a stronger organization could have affected public policy on immigration. The exclusionist policies followed in the 1930s were pursued even after the CJC was reestablished. A continuing congress might, however, have achieved a further community consolidation of the sort envisioned by Caiserman, who would have carried it forward with his accustomed humanity, energy, and brilliance.

Even so, with the realization of the congress ideal, Canadian Jewry had reached a watershed in its evolution within the fences of its communal life. The war had brought the community prolonged crisis, terrible disaster, and apparent triumph in perhaps equal measure, and had changed its structure in important ways. The East European immigrants had proved that they could circumvent old organizations like the federation, and create new ones that served their specific needs. This process had not originated with the war, but the compelling exigencies of wartime were so powerful that the immigrants had swept aside virtually all resistance.

By 1920, it was clear that Canadian Jewry had become so diversified and so complex that it was remarkable that a truly representative, democratic congress could ever have been created. But behind all the divisions and dissensions lay a vital and—considering the war and the pogroms—remarkable common ground. It was hope, even optimism, for the Jewish future. The Bolshevik Revolution, still being tested in 1920, promised reform and reconstruction for Jewish life in Russia. The Balfour Declaration promised a Jewish national home in Palestine. The freedom offered by North America promised material improvement and social equality. The Treaty of Versailles, with its provisions for minority rights in the new nations of Eastern Europe, promised equality for the Jews of Poland, Romania, and Hungary. Most of these promises were yet to be realized. But enough had been tasted and enjoyed to give substance to an optimism that, in years before, had been little more than a dream.

Conclusion

"Spaceless Boundaries of Loss"

Canadian Jewry was an integral part of the Jewish world that had fully entered modern history by the end of the First World War. The Zionist agenda was on the road to fulfilment, as a Jewish homeland in Palestine seemed now assured of international approval and British support. A new era was dawning for the Jewish people – the realization of the dream of a return to Zion – and it is significant that Canada's first nationwide Jewish organization was dedicated to achieving this goal. And while the Canadian Jewish Congress, whose agenda was really more diffuse, faltered and failed in the 1920s, the Zionist Organization of Canada would continue and grow stronger, along with Poale Zion and Mizrachi, in support of practical projects that would bring the great goal closer. Though that story is part of another book, it nevertheless has its roots in the community's history before that time. For, if Zionism became in some ways the most predominant, enduring, and identifying feature of Canadian Jewish life, its origins lie in the nineteenth century, when the community was being formed, when the Canadian context permitted – perhaps encouraged – the expression of this and other ethnic identities. Orangeism among Protestant Irish immigrants, ultramontanism among Roman Catholic French Canadians, may have been expressions of the same, peculiarly Canadian, social context, without real parallel in the United States.

Canada's social and political environment not only permitted and encouraged the expression of an articulated ethnic identity, it also shaped the agenda of Jewish social politics. To be sure, much of this activity was centred in

Quebec, where some of the most overt – but not the only – forms of anti-semitism surfaced as manifestations of extreme French Canadian xenophobia as well as Anglophone Protestant supremacism. But while the bulk of the problems transpired in Montreal, the Toronto of Goldwin Smith provided both a British and an international connection for the expression of an even more virulent and widely published antisemitism.

The fact that agriculturalism became (and remained, well after 1920) one of the significant concerns of the Canadian Jewish community – long after the vitality of the Jewish farming colonies had departed – illustrates the continuing importance of the Canadian west in the community's imagination. This was a source of some highly interesting social and political ideas, and a place where many of the nation's hopes for the future were invested in this expanding nation of new transcontinental railways, rapidly rising wheat production, massive immigration, and burgeoning cities. Much like the Argentinian pampas, where numerous Jews were likewise settled in quest of the reconstruction of the Jewish people, the prairie west was also a region of the Jewish mind.

And what, finally, of the identity of Canada's Jews? In this northern land of "limited identities," where region, culture, and class differ so significantly, what was to signify a Canadian Jewish identity? It is clear that as early as the American Revolution, when loyalty to the Crown became a hallmark of British North American identity, the Jewish community was divided – as were the non-Jews in both Quebec and Nova Scotia – and that Britishness among Jews was just as pronounced as it was in the general population – perhaps even more so. In view of their minority status, most Jews likely would have been reluctant to utter dissent and thus attract attention (and even antisemitism) on the grounds of disloyalty. Yet it was not only fear that inspired their Britishness; it was also pride in Britain's accomplishments, and the borrowed prestige of its imperial stature. In the mid-nineteenth century, Abraham de Sola noted the differences between his political context and those of his American counterparts, while his sons, Clarence and Meldola, were by 1900 fully fledged Canadian nationalists. To them, Zion's heritage would be redeemed through Albion's magnanimity and tolerance.

As well, the Canadian Jewish identity was imprinted by the crude rawness of this enormous land, which stamped itself on those who struggled to make the living which conditions in their European homeland denied them. Intellectuals like Reuben Brainin noticed such rawness immediately on reaching these shores. In Montreal, in the early 1900s, he noted, "No one asks whence or whither? why or wherefore? There are no wayfarers on the paths of the mind and no one turns the vessel to see its nether side. All but count and account, and merely pose the question, how much? . . . There is much laboring and little of the song of labor."[1] Brainin and other intellectuals, and Montreal Yiddish poets of the 1920s like Jacob I. Segal, understood instinctively the problem of maintaining a Jewish identity in Canada. Segal's haunting poem "Fremd" ("Strange") expressed his sense of ambivalence upon witnessing the transformations in the Jews around him, caught between rejoicing for the opportunity and freedom Canadian life offered and mourning the loss of a culture which had not fully survived the migration to the New World:

> And sometimes – a Sunday morning,
> When the houses are still sleeping here,
> It seems to me the spirit of the neighbourhood
> Is like a world of very long ago.
> Here lives another generation,
> That has nothing at all to do with Montreal.[2]
> (Translated by Miriam Waddington)

Longing for that "other generation" of the past, Segal, in his poem "A Jew," becomes the quintessential Canadian Jew caught between the fading tradition of the past and the confusing modernity of the present and future:

> It's no use my turning east
> and it's no use my praying west,
> I'm forever on the road, in transit,
> dragging my baggage of exile.
>
> . . . .
>
> But it survives, my Jewish tree,
> like a talisman of homecoming
> and it longs to gather all us Jews
> from our spaceless boundaries of loss.[3]
> (Translated by Miriam Waddington)

The "baggage of exile" was the past, the very burden of Jewish history: the challenge, on the one hand, of repairing the world, and the responsibility, on the other, of building a rampart around the Torah.

Modernity also threatened the continuity of Jewish religious tradition, the *halakha*, which embodied the hallowed principles and practices of observant Jews. The openness and materialism of North American culture robbed those Jews who were drawn into its vortex of their own rich tradition. Rabbi Yudel

Rosenberg, a Chassid known as the Skaryszewer Ilui (the Genius of Skaryszew), who had moved from his native Poland to Toronto in 1913 and to Montreal in 1919, lamented the widespread violation of the Sabbath among Canada's Jews, and concluded that Torah Judaism was in a state of siege.[4] In 1923 he published an eloquent plea, *A Brivele fun di Zisse Mamme Shabbes Malkese zu Ihre Zihn un Tekhter fun Idishn Folk* (*A Letter from the Sweet Mother Sabbath Queen to her Sons and Daughters of the Jewish People*), in which he implored Canada's traditional Jews to return to Sabbath observance. Failure to do so, he implied, would prolong the already overlong exile of the Jewish people, and delay the coming of the Messiah. But who would hear the rabbi's urgent appeal amid the buzz of sweatshop sewing machines and the noise of the "jargoning city"? And who would heed his call for Torah observance, forsaking the blandishments of North American culture? Indeed, how could Canadian modernity accommodate such a tradition as that of Eastern European Jews? Such questions cried out for answers, but the formulation of those answers had not yet begun.

History's message was at best ambiguous for Canadian Jewry in 1920. Their history was marked by massive migration, mainly from Eastern Europe, to cities, towns, and farms, and by a European Judaic ghetto culture then being transformed amid revolution, nationalism, and modernization. By 1920 these forces were already radically altering the co-ordinates of East European Jewish existence. Thus the "baggage of exile" brought to Canada by the Jewish immigrants to be admitted during the 1920s would typically be somewhat different from that of their pre-1914 counterparts. The newcomers had experienced first-hand a war of unparalleled bloodshed and destruction, the massive upheaval of the Russian Revolution, the ensuing devastating Russian civil war, the emergence of Polish and Romanian independence, and the terrible Ukrainian pogroms.

If the past was ambiguous, so was the present, and the future was an enigma. Canada's Jews were linked to Europe and the past while they built new lives in Canada and contributed to the reconstruction of the old-new land in Palestine, thereby investing in the present and the future. Canadian Jewish history to 1920—and well beyond—was shaped by a set of co-ordinates which were unique to the northern half of this continent, and which resulted in the evolution of a distinctive community. Canada's political structure and dual "founding peoples," its economic dependency and long-lasting constitutional colonial status, its own immigration patterns and urbanization processes, had together shaped a historical experience different from that of American Jewry. But these were not the only elements that had moulded Canadian Jewish history, important though they were. There was also the past beyond Canada. Canada's Jews were not like Ireland's "exiles" in the New World, who were "involuntary" emigrants to America.[5] Jews were generally willing emigrants from their most recent sojourning places, though some of them may have seen themselves as exiles from an ancient home. Now taking root in the northern half of North America, they continued to exist—with still-worried glances over their shoulders—in both parochial and secular time, as well as in Canadian space.

List of Abbreviations

The following abbreviations appear in the notes.

PUBLICATIONS

AJA	*American Jewish Archives*
AJH	*American Jewish Historical Society*
CJA	*Canadian Jewish Archives*
CJC	*Canadian Jewish Chronicle*
CJHSJ	*Canadian Jewish Historical Society Journal*
DCB	*Dictionary of Canadian Biography*
EJ	*Encyclopedia Judaica*
JSS	*Jewish Social Studies*
JT	*Jewish Times*
JWB	*Jewish Western Bulletin*
KA	*Keneder Adler*
TJHSE	*Transactions of the Jewish Historical Society of England*

ARCHIVES AND INSTITUTIONS

AJHSA	American Jewish Historical Society Archives, Waltham, Mass.
CHA	Canadian Historical Association
CJC	Canadian Jewish Congress
CJCAM	Canadian Jewish Congress Archives, Montreal
CZA	Canadian Zionist Archives, Jerusalem
JCA	Jewish Colonization Association
JPLM	Jewish Public Library of Montreal
JPSA	Jewish Publication Society of America
NAC	National Archives of Canada
PABC	Public Archives of British Columbia
PAM	Public Archives of Manitoba
PANS	Public Archives of Nova Scotia

Notes

PREFACE

1. Binyamin G. Zak, *Geschichte fun Yidn in Kanada, Fun di Friste Onhoib Biz Der Letster Tseit* (Montreal: Northern Printing and Stationery Co., 1948. Ershter Band: Fun Frantsoizishn Reshym Biz Soif Ninetsn Yorhundert). The book was translated into English in 1965. Benjamin G. Sack, *History of the Jews in Canada* (Montreal: Harvest House, 1965). See Saul Hayes, "Benjamin Gutl Sack," Benjamin G. Sack, *Canadian Jews – Early in This Century* (Montreal: CJC, 1975), pp. i–iii.

2. Simon I. Belkin, *Die Poale Zion Bavegung in Kanada: 1904–1920* (Montreal: Actions Committee of the Labour Zionist Movement in Canada, 1956).

3. Simon I. Belkin, *Through Narrow Gates: A Review of Jewish Immigration, Colonization and Immigrant Aid Work in Canada (1840–1940)* (Montreal: CJC and JCA, 1966).

4. Louis Rosenberg, *Canada's Jews: A Social and Economic Study of the Jews in Canada* (Montreal: CJC. Bureau of Social and Economic Research, 1939).

5. David Rome (comp.), *A Selected Bibliography of Jewish Canadiana* (Montreal: CJC and JPLM, 1959); Bernard Figler and David Rome, *Hananiah Meir Caiserman: A Biography* (Montreal: Northern Printing and Lithographing Co., 1962). The latter includes David Rome, "An Essay on Modern Jewish Times."

6. There are some 45 volumes in this series: *Canadian Jewish Archives, New Series*, published since 1974 by the National Archives of the Canadian Jewish Congress, Montreal.

7. See William Kurelek and Abraham Arnold, *Jewish Life in Canada* (Edmonton: Hurtig Publishers, 1976); Cyril E. Leonoff, *Pioneers, Pedlars and Prayer Shawls: The Jewish Communities in British Columbia and the Yukon* (Vancouver: Sono Nis Press, 1978).

8. Stuart Rosenberg, *The Jewish Community in Canada* (Toronto: McClelland and Stewart, 1970, 2 volumes); Irving Abella, *A Coat of Many Colours* (Toronto: Lester & Orpen Dennys, 1990).

9. Bernard L. Vigod, *The Jews in Canada* (Ottawa: Canadian Historical Association, 1984).

10. Michael Brown, *Jew or Juif? Jews, French Canadians, and Anglo-Canadians, 1759–1914* (Philadelphia: Jewish Publication Society, 1987).

11. Stephen A. Speisman, *The Jews of Toronto: A History to 1937* (Toronto: McClelland and Stewart, 1979); David J. Bercuson, *Canada and the Birth of Israel: A Study in Canadian Foreign Policy* (Toronto: University of Toronto Press, 1985); Pierre Anctil, *Le Devoir, les Juifs et l'Immigration, de Bourassa à Laurendeau* (Montreal: Institut Québécois de Recherche sur la Culture, 1988); *Le Rendez-Vous Manqué: Les Juifs de Montréal face au Québec de l'entre-deux-guerres* (Montreal: Institut Québécois de Recherche sur la Culture, 1988).

12. Jonathan Sarna, "The Value of Canadian Jewish History to the American Jewish Historian and Vice-Versa," *CJHSJ* 5, No. 1, Spring 1981, 17–22.

13. See Bram de Sola, "The Jewish School Question," *The University Magazine*, December 1909, 533–560; David Rome, "On the Jewish School Question in Montreal: 1903–1931" (Montreal: CJCAM, CJA, New Series, No. 3, 1975).

14. Maxwell Goldstein, "The Status of the Jew in the Schools of Canada," Arthur D. Hart (ed.), *The Jew in Canada* (Montreal: Canadian Jewish Publications Limited, 1926),

497–98; NAC, MG 27, III, C23, Peter Bercovitch Collection; William Nadler, "The Jewish-Protestant School Problem," typescript, CJCAM, 1925; David Rome, "On the Jewish School Question."

15. Michel Brunet, "Trois Dominantes de la Pensée Canadienne-Française," La Présence Anglaise et les Canadiennes (Montreal: Beauchemin, 1964), 113–166; Denis Monière, Ideologies in Quebec: the Historical Development (Toronto: University of Toronto Press, 1981), 175.

16. Susan Mann Trofimenkoff, Action Française: French Canadian Nationalism in the Twenties (Toronto: University of Toronto Press, 1975), 76–77, 78.

17. La Patrie, 14, 23 Nov.; 14, 27 Dec., 1894. See Arthur I. Silver, The French Canadian Idea of Confederation, 1864–1900 (Toronto: University of Toronto Press, 1981), 232.

18. Report of the Royal Commission upon the Sweating System in Canada, Canada, Sessional papers (1896), No. 61, 10–11.

19. Trofimenkoff, Action Française, 78–79; Labour Gazette (1933), 1183; Les Midinettes 1937–1962: Union des Ouvriers de la Robe (Montreal: Bureau Conjoint, Montréal Union Internationale des Ouvriers du Vêtement pour Dames [FAT-C10-CTC], 1962), 18, 80; CJC, 6 July 1934.

20. See Louis Rosenberg, "A Study of the Growth and Changes in the Distribution of the Jewish Population of Montreal" (Montreal: Canadian Jewish Population Studies, Canadian Jewish Community Series, No. 4, Bureau of Social and Economic Research, CJC, 1955), 8–14.

21. See Elson I. Rexford, Our Educational Problem: The Jewish Population and the Protestant Schools (Montreal: Renouf, n.d.)

22. See Howard Palmer (ed.), Immigration and the Rise of Multiculturalism (Toronto: Copp Clark, 1975), 44–53; W. Peter Ward, White Canada Forever: Popular Attitudes and Public Policy toward Orientals in British Columbia (Montreal: McGill-Queen's University Press, 1978).

23. Rosenberg, Canada's Jews, 9–16.

24. Bertram W. Korn, American Jewry and the Civil War (New York: Atheneum, 1970), 1.

25. See Leon Goldman, "History of Zionism in Canada," Hart, The Jew in Canada, 291–320; CZA.Z1/244, Jacob de Haas to Dr. Theodor Herzl, 14 Apr. 1903.

26. See Daniel J. Elazar, Community and Polity: The Organizational Dynamics of American Jewry (Philadelphia: JPSA, 1980), Chapter 5.

27. Harry Gutkin, Journey into Our Heritage (Toronto: Lester & Orpen Dennys, 1980), 195–196.

28. Nathan Glazer, American Judaism (Chicago: University of Chicago Press, 1972, 2nd Edition), Chapter 3.

29. Bertram W. Korn, German-Jewish Intellectual Influences on American Jewish Life (Syracuse, 1972, B.G. Rudolph Lectures in Judaic Studies), 1, 6.

30. Glazer, American Judaism, 44, 60.

31. See Stephen Birmingham, "Our Crowd": The Great Jewish Families of New York (New York: Dell, 1967), Part 4; Arthur Mann, Yankee Reformers in the Urban Age: Social Reform in Boston, 1880–1900 (New York, Harper & Row, 1966), Chapter 3.

32. Sack, Jews in Canada, Chapter 14.

33. Speisman, The Jews of Toronto, 32.

34. Michael Brown, "The Beginnings of Reform Judaism in Canada," *JSS* 34, No. 4 (1972), October, 322–342, 323, 330–31.

35. Will Herberg, *Protestant–Catholic–Jew: An Essay in American Religious Sociology* (New York: Doubleday, Anchor Books, 1960), Chapter 7.

36. See Jonathan D. Sarna, "Jewish Immigration to North America: The Canadian Experience (1870–1900)," *Jewish Journal of Sociology* 17, No. 1 (1976) June, 31–42. Sarna argues that Canadian Jews were more receptive to East European Jewish immigrants than contemporary U.S. Jews, 35.

37. Goldman, "Zionist Organization of Canada," 291–313. See Bernard Figler, *Lillian and Archie Freiman* (Montreal: Northern Printing and Lithographing Co., 1962).

38. Melvin I. Urofsky, *American Zionism from Herzl to the Holocaust* (New York: Doubleday, Anchor Books, 1976), 85–91.

39. See Allon Gal, *Brandeis of Boston* (Cambridge: Harvard University Press, 1980).

40. Kenneth I. Cleator and Harry J. Stern, *A Rabbi's Journey* (New York: Block, 1981), 9.

41. Speisman, *The Jews of Toronto*, 242; see Maurice Eisendrath, *The Never Failing Stream* (Toronto: Macmillan, 1939), 224–242, for his sermon "Nation, Race or Religion," in which he attacked the Zionist cause as "ridiculous and . . . symptomatic of the blind conceit which afflicts every nationalist!", 236.

42. Carl Berger, *The Sense of Power: Studies in the Ideas of Canadian Imperialism, 1867–1914* (Toronto: University of Toronto Press, 1970), 9; John Farthing, *Freedom Wears a Crown* (Toronto: Kingswood House, 1957).

43. James S. Woodsworth, *Strangers within Our Gates, or Coming Canadians* (Toronto: Missionary Society of the Methodist Church, Canada, The Young People's Forward Movement Dept., 1909), 150–159, 279–289.

44. Goldman, "Zionist Organization of Canada," *passim*.

45. Rosenberg, *Canada's Jews*, 4.

46. Ibid., 134.

47. JT, 17 Aug. 1900. See also *The Maccabean* (1903) Dec., 363–5; Goldman, "Zionist Organization of Canada," 302.

48. Rosenberg, *Canada's Jews*, 134.

49. Belkin, *Through Narrow Gates*, Chapters 9–13; Joseph Kage, *With Faith and Thanksgiving: The Story of Two Hundred Years of Jewish Immigration and Immigrant Aid Work in Canada (1760–1960)* (Montreal: Eagle Publishing Co., 1962), 87.

50. Abraham M. Klein, *The Second Scroll* (Toronto: McClelland and Stewart, 1961, New Canadian Library, No. 22), 138.

51. Ibid., 95, 97.

52. Henry Feingold, *Zion in America: The Jewish Experience from Colonial Times to the Present* (New York: Hippocrene Books, 1974).

53. See Lubomyr Luciuk and Stella Hryniuk (eds.), *Canada's Ukrainians: Negotiating an Identity* (Toronto: University of Toronto Press, 1991), xxi.

INTRODUCTION

1. Robert Harney, "Ethnic Studies: Handmaiden of Multiculturalism," (unpublished paper delivered to Canadian Historical Association, June, 1984).

CHAPTER ONE

1. Jonathan I. Israel, *European Jewry in the Age of Mercantilism 1550–1750* (Oxford: Clarendon Press, 1989), 106–07, 155.

2. See Simon Wiesenthal, *Sails of Hope: The Secret Mission of Christopher Columbus* (New York: Macmillan, 1973), 172.

3. See Henry Feingold, *Zion in America: The Jewish Experience from Colonial Times to the Present* (New York: Hippocrene Books, 1974), Chapter III.

4. Louis Rosenberg, "Some Aspects of the Historical Development of the Canadian Jewish Community," *AJH* 50, No. 2, 1960, 121–42, 122.

5. Benjamin G. Sack, *History of the Jews in Canada* (Montreal: Harvest House, 1965), 70.

6. Letter from Jonathan Sarna to G. Tulchinsky, 6 Feb. 1992.

7. See Jacob R. Marcus, *American Jewry – Documents Eighteenth Century* (Cincinnati: Hebrew Union College, 1959), 90.

8. Jacob R. Marcus, *The Colonial American Jew, 1492–1776*, 3 volumes (Detroit: Wayne State University Press, 1970), II: 632, 733–37, III: 1054–55.

9. Frances Dublin, "Jewish Colonial Enterprise in the Light of the Amherst Papers (1758–1763)," *AJH* 29, 1939, No. 35, 1–25.

10. Marcus, *Colonial American Jew*, I: 381.

11. See José Igartua, "A Change of Climate: The Conquest and the Marchands of Montreal," *CHA*, Annual Report (1974).

12. Marcus, *Colonial American Jew*, I: 311, II: 727–28; Walter Dunn, Jr., "Ezekiel Solomons," *DCB* IV: 718–19.

13. Robert A. Rockway, *The Jews of Detroit: From the Beginning, 1762–1914* (Detroit: Wayne State University Press, 1986), 3–4.

14. Jacob R. Marcus, *Early American Jewry: The Jews of New York, New England and Canada, 1649–1794*, 2 volumes (Philadelphia: Jewish Publication Society, 1951), I: 230; see also Marcus, *Documents – Eighteenth Century*, 464–65, 474–75.

15. Marcus, *Documents – Eighteenth Century*, 227–32, 457–59.

16. Allan Greer, *Peasant, Lord and Merchant: Rural Society in Three Quebec Parishes, 1740–1840* (Toronto: University of Toronto Press, 1985), Chapter six.

17. Denis Vaugeois, "Aaron Hart," *DCB* IV: 331–33.

18. Raymond Douville, *Aaron Hart, Récit Historique* (Trois Rivières: Edition du Bien Public, 1938), 30.

19. Marcus, *Colonial American Jew*, I: 382.

20. Ibid., 377.

21. Ibid., 379.

22. Sack, *Jews in Canada*, 7–11; Irving Abella, *A Coat of Many Colours* (Toronto: Lester & Orpen Dennys, 1990); Louis Rosenberg, "The Earliest Jewish Settlers in Canada: Facts vs. Myths," 2 (Unpublished manuscript, JPLM, Louis Rosenberg Manuscripts).

23. The most recent and thorough work on this subject is Richard Menkis, "The Gradis Family of Eighteenth-Century Bordeaux: A Social and Economic Study" (Brandeis University, Ph.D. thesis, 1988).

24. Marcus, *Colonial American Jew*, I: 381–82.

25. Gérard Malchelosse, "Les Juifs dans l'histoire canadienne," *Les Cahiers des Dix* (Montreal: Fides, 1939), 170; Rosenberg, "Some Aspects," 123–24; Solomon Frank *Two Centuries in the Life of a Synagogue* (Montreal: 1968), 40.

26. See Marcus, *Documents – Eighteenth Century*, 106; *CJA*, 1, No. 4 (1959), "Minutes of the Shearith Israel Congregation in Montreal, 1778 to 1780," 10.

27. Jacob Neusner, "Anglo-Jewry and the Development of American Jewish Life, 1775–1850," *TJHSE*, 18 (1958), 231–42.

28. Marcus, *Early American Jewry*, I: 224.

29. *CJA*, 1959, "Minutes," 12.

30. Ibid., 14.

31. Ibid., 16.

32. *CJA*, 1, No. 5 (1959), Documents 1–10.

33. Frank, *Two Centuries*, 40.

34. Ibid., 41.

35. Doris G. Daniels, "Colonial Jewry: Religion, Domestic and Social Relations," *AJH* 66, March 1977, 385.

36. See Steven Singer, "Jewish Religious Observance in Early Victorian London, 1840–1860," *Jewish Journal of Sociology*, 28, No. 2 (1986), 117–37.

37. *Colonial American Jew* II:711; III:1267–78, 1287. For fascinating documents on Franks' later career see *Documents – Eighteenth Century*, 274–77, and Jacob R. Marcus, *Memoirs of American Jews*, 3 volumes (Philadelphia: JPSA, 1955), I:45–49.

38. There was at least one Jewish Loyalist who fled from New York to Nova Scotia in 1782. *Documents – Eighteenth Century*, 282–83; *Colonial American Jew* III:1294–95.

39. Sylvia Van Kirk, "'Women in Between': Women in Fur Trade Society in Western Canada," M. Cross and G. Kealey (eds.), *Readings in Canadian Social History* (Toronto: McClelland and Stewart, 1982), 191–211.

40. Malcolm H. Stern, "Jewish Marriage and Intermarriage in the Federal Period, 1776–1840," *AJA*, 19, No. 2 (1967).

41. *Le Bien Public*, 23 Mar. 1939.

42. *Documents – Eighteenth Century*, 429–31.

43. Robert Cohen, "The Demography of the Jews in Early America," Paul Rittenband (ed.), *Modern Jewish Fertility* (Leiden: E.J. Brill, 1981, Studies in Judaism in Modern Times, ed. Jacob Neusner), 144–59, 145.

44. Alfred L. Burt, *The Old Province of Quebec* (Toronto: Ryerson Press, 1933), 194.

45. Hilda Neatby, *Quebec: The Revolutionary Age, 1760–1791* (Toronto: McClelland and Stewart, 1966), 140.

46. Bernard Blumenkranz, "From the Expulsion from Provence to the Eve of the Revolution," "France", *EJ* VII:21–22.

47. *Colonial American Jew* I:388.

48. Ibid., 478.

49. Nathan Glazer, *American Judaism* (Chicago: University of Chicago Press, 1972, 2nd Edition), Chapter 3.

CHAPTER TWO

1. Gerald M. Craig, *Upper Canada: The Formative Years, 1784–1841* (Toronto: McClelland and Stewart, 1963), 199.

2. Susan Trofimenkoff, *The Dream of Nation: A Social and Intellectual History of Quebec* (Toronto: Gage, 1983), 60.

3. Fernand Ouellet, "Pierre-Stanislas Bédard," *DCB* VI: 41–49, 46.

4. Denis Vaugeois, "Ezekiel Hart," *DCB* VII: 386–89, 386.

5. Benjamin Sulte, "Les Miettes de l'histoire," *Revue Canadienne* (Montreal: E. Senécal, 1870), 427–43, 433.

6. W. Stewart Wallace, *The Macmillan Dictionary of Canadian Biography* (Toronto: Macmillan, 1963), 242.

7. *Quebec Mercury*, 20 Apr. 1807.

8. Abraham J. Arnold, "Ezekiel Hart and the Oath Problem in the Assembly of Lower Canada," *CJHSJ* 3, No. 1 (1979), 10–26, 13. This article offers a scholarly account of the 1807–1808 confrontation. Abraham Rhinewine, *Looking Back a Century on the Centennial of Jewish Political Equality in Canada* (Toronto: Kraft Press, 1932), contains much useful detail.

9. *Le Canadien*, 18 Apr. 1807.

10. Ibid.

11. Ibid.

12. *Quebec Mercury*, 11 May 1807.

13. *Le Canadien*, 13 Feb. 1808. Coffin petitioned the House that "*Ezekiel Hart, étant Juif, ne pourrait prêter le serment requis de la part des membres et par conséquent ne pourrait être admis à la Chambre*" – that Hart, being a Jew, was unable to take the prescribed oath and was thus ineligible.

14. *Le Canadien*, 15, 16 Feb. 1808.

15. Ibid., 17 Feb. 1808.

16. Ibid., 20 Feb. 1808.

17. *Quebec Mercury*, 15 Feb. 1808.

18. Ibid., 22 Feb. 1808.

19. *Le Canadien*, 2 Mar. 1808.

20. Ibid., 21 May 1808.

21. *Quebec Mercury*, 21 Mar. 1808.

22. *Le Canadien*, 20 May 1808.

23. Quoted in Joseph Tassé, "Droits Politiques des Juifs en Canada," *Revue Canadienne*, June (1870), 411, 416.

24. Cited in Arnold, "Ezekiel Hart," 25.

25. *Quebec Mercury*, 11 May 1809.

26. Ibid., 15 May 1809.

27. See Jean-Pierre Wallot, "Les Canadiens français et les Juifs (1808–1809). L'Affaire Hart," Naim Kattan (ed.), *Juifs et Canadiens: Deuxième Cahier du Cercle Juif de la Langue Française* (Montreal: Editions du Jour, 1967), 113–21.

28. Ibid., 121.

29. Helen T. Manning, *The Revolt of French Canada 1700–1835: A Chapter in the History of the British Commonwealth* (Toronto: Macmillan, 1962), 84.

30. David Rome, "Adolphus Mordecai Hart," *DCB* X: 337.

31. *CJA* 1, No. 3 (1957), 8. See also Rhinewine, *Looking Back a Century*, 80–81.

32. Richard Menkis, "Antisemitism and Anti-Judaism in Pre-Confederation Canada" (manuscript), 11.

33. Letter from Fernand Ouellet to G. Tulchinsky, 1 Oct. 1990.

34. Menkis, "Antisemitism Pre-Confederation," 11.

35. Rome, "Adolphus Mordecai Hart," 337.
36. See Israel Feinstein, "Anglo Jewish Opinion during the Struggle for Emancipation (1828–1858)," *TJHSE* 20 (1964), 113–43.
37. Queen's University Archives, Hart Papers, microfilm, 15 reels.
38. Denis Vaugeois, "Bécancour et les Hart," Naim Kattan (ed.), *Les Juifs et la Communauté Française* (Montreal: Les Editions du Jour, 1965), 108–09; Denis Vaugeois, "Moses Hart," *DCB* VIII: 367–70.
39. Denis Vaugeois, "Moses Hart," 368–69.
40. Elinor K. Senior and James H. Lambert, "David David," *DCB* VI: 179–81.
41. Ibid., 180.
42. MBHP. Assignment of David David. Notary Griffin, 25 Jan. 1825, No. 5538.
43. Carman Miller, "Moses Judah Hayes," *DCB* VI: 379–81.
44. MBHP, N.B. Doucet, No. 10275, 10055, 11136, 11529, 8728, 13015, 13404; Crawford, No. 147.
45. Paul-André Linteau and Jean-Claude Robert, "Propriété foncière et société à Montréal: Une hypothèse," *Revue d'histoire de l'amérique française* 28, No. 1 (1974), 45–46.
46. Michel De Lorimier, "Louis Marchand," *DCB* XI: 585–87, 585.
47. Elinor K. Senior, "Eleazar David David," *DCB* XI: 234–35.
48. *CJA* 1, No. 1 (1955), "Extract from the Register Kept by the Prothonotary of His Majesty's Court of King's Bench for the District of Montreal under the Provincial Statutes 9 & 10 Geo. IV chap: 75," p. 3; No. 11, "Sale of Seats in New Synagogue 31st August 1838."
49. Solomon Frank, *Two Centuries in the Life of a Synagogue* (Montreal, 1968), 42.
50. Esther I. Blaustein, Rachel A. Esar, and Evelyn Miller, "Spanish and Portuguese Synagogue (Shearith Israel) Montreal, 1768–1968," *TJHSE* 23, 1969–70, 111.
51. *CJA* 1, No. 1 (1955), Abraham Hart, Jr., London, to the trustees of the Montreal Synagogue, Montreal, Lower Canada, 13 Dec., 1838. In June of 1835 a lot on Chenneville Street was purchased for a new synagogue. Frank, *Two Centuries*, 43; *CJA* 1, No. 2 (1956), "Deed of Sale of Lot for Synagogue on Chenneville Street from Representatives of M. Gabriel Cotte to the Trustees of the Israelitish Congregation in Montreal, dated June 30th, 1835," 6–8.
52. MBHP, Notary G.D. Arnoldi, No. 4040, 4041, 4, 9 Mar. 1835.
53. Newton Bosworth, *Hochelaga Depicta, The Early History and Present State of the City and Island of Montreal* (Montreal: William Greig, 1839), 112–13.
54. *CJA* 1, No. 2 (1956), 12–13.
55. *CJA* 1, No. 1 (1955), 6.
56. Ibid., 6–7.
57. Ibid., Chapter 2, article 1.
58. *CJA* 1, No. 1 (1955), H.B. Doucet, notary public, to Benjamin Hart and Aaron H. David, 2 Sept. 1839.
59. Ibid.
60. Ibid., 13.
61. *CJA* 1, No. 6 (1962), "An Act to amend the Act of Lower Canada therein mentioned, extending certain privileges to persons of the Jewish persuasion." Chapter 96, 9 June 1846.
62. *The Occident*, 1 July 1843, No. 4.

63. Moses Hart, *Modern Religion* (New York: 1816). The JPLM possesses a photocopy of this rare book.

64. Jacob R. Marcus, "The Modern Religion of Moses Hart," *Hebrew Union College Annual* 20 (1947), 585–616, 612.

65. Hart also wrote diatribes against Roman Catholicism. Denis Vaugeois, "Les Positions Religieuses de Moses Hart," *Canadian Catholic Historical Association* (1966), 41–46.

66. Malcolm H. Stern, "The 1820s: American Jewry Comes of Age," Jonathan Sarna (ed.), *The American Jewish Experience* (New York: Holmes & Meier, 1986), 34–35.

67. Mason Wade, *The French Canadians, 1760–1945* (Toronto: Macmillan, 1956), 189–190.

CHAPTER THREE

1. Henry Feingold, *Zion in America: The Jewish Experience from Colonial Times to the Present* (New York: Hippocrene Books, 1974), 101–05; Arthur Hertzberg, *The Jews in America: Four Centuries of an Uneasy Encounter* (New York: Simon & Schuster, 1989), 91–92.

2. John I. Cooper, *History of St. George's Lodge*, No. 1, G.R.Q. (Montreal: 1955); See Benjamin G. Sack, *History of the Jews in Canada* (Montreal: Harvest House, 1965), ch. 9, 10.

3. Carman Miller, "Abraham de Sola," *DCB* XI: 253–56. See also Evelyn Miller, "The 'Learned Hazan' of Montreal: Reverend Abraham de Sola, LL.D.: 1825–1882," *American Sephardi*, 7–8, 1975, 23–42.

4. *The Occident* IV, Feb. 1847, No. 11

5. Edwin Wolf and Maxwell Whiteman, *The History of the Jews of Philadelphia* (Philadelphia: JPSA, 1975), 373; Leonardo Hellemberg, "Rebecca Gratz," *EJ* VII: 860.

6. Stanley B. Frost, *McGill University For the Advancement of Learning*, Vol. 1, 1801–1895 (Montreal: McGill-Queen's University Press, 1980), 118.

7. Isidore S. Meyer, "Jacques Judah Lyons," *EJ* XI: 626.

8. Susan M. Trofimenkoff, *A Dream of Nation: A Social and Intellectual History of Quebec* (Toronto: Gage, 1983), 93.

9. H. Blair Neatby, *Laurier and A Liberal Quebec: A Study in Political Management* (Toronto: McClelland and Stewart, 1973).

10. Jacques J. Lyons and Abraham de Sola, *A Jewish Calendar for Fifty Years . . . From A.M. 5614 to A.M. 5664. Together with an Introductory Essay on the Jewish Calendar System, etc.* (Cincinnati: Block Publishing Company, 1854). Besides a small income, these literary efforts brought de Sola a considerable reputation as one of North America's leading Jewish scholars. On Lyons see Hyman G. Grinstein, *The Rise of the Jewish Community of New York, 1654–1860* (Philadelphia: JPS, 1945), passim; Isidore S. Meyer, "Jacques-Judah Lyons," *EJ*1, 626.

11. See Carl Berger, *Science God and Nature in Victorian Canada* (Toronto: University of Toronto Press, 1983, The 1982 Joanne Goodman Lectures).

12. British American Journal of Medical and Physical Science, 1849–50: 227–29, 259–62, 290–93.

13. *Canadian Medical Journal and Monthly Record of Medical and Surgical Science*, 1852–53: 135–54, 203–11, 325–40, 464–68, 529–32, 589–99, 654–56, 728–41, later published as *The Sanatory Institutions of the Hebrews . . .* (Montreal: 1861).

14. Dropsie College, Philadelphia. Isaac Leeser Papers. Letter from de Sola to Leeser, 6 Dec. 1848.

15. Ibid., 11 May 1856.
16. See Walter J. Fischel, "Persia," *EJ* XIII: 301–19, 316.
17. Leeser Papers, de Sola to Leeser, 29 Oct. 1848, 16 Apr. 1849.
18. Ibid., 7 Dec. 1848.
19. Peter R. Eakins and Jean Sinnamon Eakins, "Sir John William Dawson," *DCB* XII: 230–37.
20. Leeser Papers, de Sola to Leeser, 10 Jan. 1860.
21. Ibid., 19 Apr. 1864.
22. Frost, *McGill University*, 118.
23. Leeser Papers, de Sola to Leeser, 12 May 1864.
24. Ibid., 8 May 1865.
25. Ramsay Cook, *The Regenerators, Social Criticism in Late Victorian English Canada* (Toronto: University of Toronto Press, 1985), 58–59, 245.
26. See Jack Riemer, "Isaac Leeser," *EJ* X: 1561–62.
27. Feingold, *Zion in America*, 66.
28. Leeser Papers, de Sola to Leeser, 24 Nov. 1847.
29. Ibid., 12 June 1855.
30. Ibid., 10 Jan. 1860.
31. Ibid., 24 June 1866.
32. Ibid., 15 Aug. 1865.
33. See Ms Evelyn Miller (ed.), *Abraham de Sola Papers, A Guide to the Microfilm* (Montreal: McGill University Archives, 1970).
34. Leeser Papers, de Sola to Leeser, 15 Aug. 1865.
35. Ibid., 17 Aug. 1857.
36. Ibid., 1854. No date.
37. Ibid., 8 Aug. 1865.
38. Ibid., 15 Aug. 1865.
39. Ibid., 22 Feb. 1848.
40. Ibid., 3 Nov. 1862.
41. Ibid., 12 May 1864.
42. *The Occident* VI, October 1848, 368–70, quoted in Sack, *Jews in Canada*, 139–40. "Baron de Hirsch Institute," Arthur D. Hart (ed.), *The Jew in Canada* (Montreal: Canadian Jewish Publications Ltd, 1926), 201–05, 201.
43. Hart, *Jew in Canada*, 201.
44. One of the most eminent Canadian Jews of his time, Dr. Hart was born in Trois Rivières in 1844. He was the second Jewish doctor to graduate in Canada. As an officer in the Militia, he saw active service during the 1870 Fenian raids. Dr. Hart took a lifelong interest in many aspects of Jewish life in Montreal, served as medical adviser to the Baron de Hirsch Institute, founded the Jewish Dispensary, remained a member of the Spanish and Portuguese congregation, and helped to establish the first Zionist society in Canada. Hart, *Jew in Canada*, 411.
45. Leeser Papers, de Sola to Leeser, 24 Nov. 1847.
46. *Montreal Gazette*, 8 Jan. 1856.
47. David A. Ansell's reminiscences, quoted in Sack, *Jews in Canada*, 169.
48. NAC, MG 28, v86, Jewish Family Services of the Baron de Hirsch Institute (est. 1863),

Montreal. Minutes of the Board, Baron de Hirsch Institute of Montreal 1863–1914; Vol 1, 23 July 1863 (hereafter cited as Minutes). The qualification that Members be unmarried was changed in Nov. 1864 to allow "any member of the Hebrew faith over the age of 13 years and unmarried[,] of good reputation . . . but in the event of their marrying while members, they still retain their membership." Ibid., 27 Nov. 1864.

49. The religious affiliations of most original members can be established from the histories of the synagogues in Hart, *Jew in Canada*, and the published congregational histories by Bernstein and Frank.

50. Minutes I, 23 July 1863.

51. Minutes I, 14 Apr. 1867.

52. Louis Rosenberg, *Canada's Jews: A Social and Economic Study of the Jews in Canada* (Montreal: CJC. Bureau of Social and Economic Research, 1939), 308.

53. Minutes I, 18 Oct. 1874; Montreal *Gazette*, 7 Jan. 1875.

54. For one such instance, see Minutes I, 17 Nov. 1867.

55. Ibid., 25 Mar. 1876.

56. Ibid., 4 Jan. 1864; 25 Feb. 1872; see also Montreal *Gazette*, Feb. 4 and 11, 1873 for a lengthy description of one of these entertainments.

57. Dr. David was Dean of Medicine at the University of Bishop's College from 1871 to 1882. Elizabeth H. Milner, "Bishop's Medical Faculty 1871–1905: Its Jewish Dean, Aaron Hart David, and Its Jewish Students," *CJHSJ* 6, No. 2, Fall 1982, 73–86. The Montreal General Hospital later received a financial contribution from the society in return for its services.

58. Minutes I, 1862. Levey persisted in his efforts to limit the society's relief activities by giving notice of a motion in 1868 – which he apparently did not push any further – that would have limited annual relief payments to a maximum of $15 per applicant; Minutes I, 12 July 1868.

59. "The Young Men's Hebrew Benevolent Society of Montreal," Revised By-Laws, Art. II, Object, Section 1, included in Minutes I, 13 Aug. 1871.

60. Ibid., 1 Feb. 1864.

61. The problem of poverty in Canadian cities due to the economic slowdown caused by winter conditions receives perceptive discussion in Judith Fingard, "The Winter's Tale: The Seasonal Contours of Pre-industrial Poverty in British North America," CHA, *Historical Papers* (1974), 65–94.

62. Minutes I, 25 Mar. 1876.

63. Ibid., 14 July 1867.

64. Ibid., Mar. 1878.

65. *London Jewish Chronicle*, 22 Oct. 1875. See also Minutes I, 14 Nov. 1875.

66. Ibid., 4 Nov. 1877.

67. See Lloyd Gartner, *The Jewish Immigrant in England 1870–1914* (Detroit: Wayne State University Press, 1960), 49–50.

68. Minutes I, 17 Nov. 1878.

69. Ibid., 12 Dec. 1874. Gutman then pointed out that the YMHBS "should be a general one, open to all Israelites in the city."

70. Ansell, "Reminiscences", quoted in Sack, *Jews in Canada*, 169.

71. Hart, *Jew in Canada*, 83–85, 93–95, 121–22.

72. NAC. M.G. 29C95, Microfilm Reel A913. Clarence de Sola Diaries, 23 July 1874.

73. *The Occident* VII, Apr. 1849.

74. *The Occident* VII, Sept. 1849.

75. Stephen Birmingham, *"Our Crowd": the Great Jewish Families of New York* (New York: Dell, 1967) and *The Grandees: The Story of America's Sephardic Elite* (New York: Dell, 1971); Annette Wolff, "Abraham Joseph," *DCB* XI: 454–56; Hart, *Jew in Canada*, 331.

76. Rosenberg, *Canada's Jews*, 12.

77. NAC, Microfilm Reel A913: Clarence de Sola Diaries, 21 Apr., 13 Dec. 1882.

78. Ibid., Reel A913, 12 Oct. 1880; Reel A915, 31 Mar. 1906, 13 May 1913.

79. Cecil Roth, "Anglo-Jewish Association," *EJ* II: 977–78. See also Eugene C. Black, *The Social Politics of Anglo-Jewry, 1880–1920* (London: Basil Blackwell, 1988), 44–50.

80. Todd Endelman, "Communal Solidarity among the Jewish Elite of Victorian London," *Victorian Studies* (1985), Spring, 491–526.

81. Bertram Korn, *American Jewry and the Civil War* (New York: Atheneum, 1979), 2.

82. Michael Brown, "The Beginnings of Reform Judaism in Canada," *JSS* 34 (Oct. 1972), 322–42.

83. Rosenberg, *Canada's Jews*, 10.

84. Hertzberg, *Jews in America*, chapter 7.

85. Ibid., 103.

86. See Jacques Monet, *The Last Cannon Shot, A Study of French-Canadian Nationalism, 1837 to 1850* (Toronto: University of Toronto Press, 1969), and Brian Young, *In Its Corporate Capacity: The Seminary of Montreal As a Business Institution 1816–1876* (Montreal: McGill-Queen's Press, 1986).

87. W.P.M. Kennedy, *Documents of the Canadian Constitution 1759–1915* (Toronto: Oxford University Press, 1917), 665.

88. Carl Berger, *The Sense of Power: Studies in the Ideas of Canadian Imperialism 1867–1914* (Toronto: University of Toronto Press, 1970), *passim*.

89. Charles Cole, "The Montreal Jewish Community in 1861 and 1871." McGill University, Dept. of Geography, honours undergraduate thesis, 1983, 12–13.

90. Ibid., 20.

CHAPTER FOUR

1. Harvard University. Baker Library. R.G. Dun and Company. Credit Ledgers. Montreal 1846–76, 3 volumes.

2. Ibid., I, 251.

3. Charles Cole, "The Montreal Jewish Community in 1861 and 1871" (McGill University, Dept. of Geography, Honours undergraduate thesis, 1983), Appendices A (1861) and B (1871).

4. Elinor K. Senior and James H. Lambert, "David David," *DCB* VI: 179–81; Gerald Tulchinsky, "The Construction of the First Lachine Canal, 1815–26" (McGill University, M.A. thesis, 1960), 36.

5. Carman Miller, "Moses Judah Hayes," *DCB* IX: 379–81. See also Christopher Armstrong and H.V. Nelles, *Monopoly's Moment: The Organization and Regulation of Canadian Utilities, 1830–1930* (Philadelphia: Temple University Press, 1986) 13, 14, 15.

6. Miller, "Hayes," 380; Gerald Tulchinsky, "Studies of Businessmen in the Development of Transportation and Industry in Montreal, 1837 to 1853" (University of Toronto, Ph.D. thesis, 1971), 465.

7. Armstrong and Nelles, *Monopoly's Moment*, 78.

8. Steven Hertzberg, *Strangers within the City: The Jews of Atlanta, 1845–1915* (Philadelphia: JPSA, 1978). Elliott Ashkenazi, *The Business of Jews in Louisiana 1840–1875* (Tuscaloosa: University of Alabama Press, 1988). William Toll, *The Making of an Ethnic Middle Class: Portland Jewry over Four Generations* (Albany: State University of New York, 1982).

9. David A. Gerber, "Cutting Out Shylock: Elite Anti-Semitism and the Quest for Moral Order in the Mid-Nineteenth Century American Marketplace," David A. Gerber (ed.), *Anti-Semitism in American History* (Urbana: University of Illinois Press, 1986), 201–32.

10. Ashkenazi, *Jews in Louisiana*, 160.

11. D. McCalla, *The Upper Canada Trade, 1834–1872: A Study of the Buchanans' Business* (Toronto: University of Toronto Press, 1979). Gerald J.J. Tulchinsky, *The River Barons: Montreal Businessmen and the Growth of Industry and Transportation 1837–53* (Toronto: University of Toronto Press, 1977).

12. Cole, "Montreal Jewish Community," *passim*.

13. Dun, Montreal, I, 193.

14. Ibid., 262.

15. Benjamin G. Sack, *History of the Jews in Canada* (Montreal: Harvest House, 1965), 154, 156.

16. Dun, Montreal, I, 232.

17. Ibid., 231.

18. Ibid., 255.

19. Ibid., 125.

20. Ibid., II, 105.

21. Ibid., I, 138, 256.

22. Ibid., II, 217.

23. Sack, *Jews in Canada*, *passim*.

24. Arthur D. Hart (ed.), *The Jew in Canada* (Montreal: Canadian Jewish Publications Limited, 1926).

25. Dun, Montreal, I, 192.

26. Hart, *Jew in Canada*, 330.

27. J.D. Borthwick, *History and Biographical Gazetteer of Montreal to the Year 1892* (Montreal: 1892), 471–72.

28. Dun, Montreal, I, 192.

29. Ibid., II, 33.

30. Hart, *Jew in Canada*, 133.

31. Dun, Montreal, II, 84.

32. Ibid., I, 409.

33. Ibid., 12.

34. Ibid., 177.

35. Ibid., 434.

36. Ibid., II, 84.

37. Ibid., I, 28, 137; II 38. See also Sack, *Jews in Canada*, 115–16.

38. Tulchinsky, *River Barons*, 219–20.

39. *Montreal in 1856: A Sketch Prepared for the Opening of the Grand Trunk Railway of Canada* (Montreal: 1856), 46.

40. Dun, Montreal, I, 84.

41. Dun, Montreal, II, 70.

42. Gerald Tulchinsky, "Aspects of the Clothing Manufacturing Industry in Canada, 1850s–1914" (unpublished paper delivered to Business History Conference, Trent University, 1984), 18–20.

43. Gerald Tulchinsky, "Hollis Shorey," *DCB* XII: 968–70.

44. J.M.S. Careless, *Toronto to 1918: An Illustrated History* (Toronto: James S. Lorimer & Company, 1984), 71–108.

45. John C. Weaver, *Hamilton: An Illustrated History* (Toronto: James Lorimer & Company, 1982), 41–78.

46. NAC, R.G. Dun and Company Credit Ledgers, XXVI, Microfilm Reel M–7760, 258. Hereafter cited as "Dun, Toronto."

47. Dun, Montreal, I, 261.

48. Dun, Toronto, 127.

49. Ibid., 231.

50. Ibid., 332.

51. Stephen Speisman, *The Jews of Toronto: A History to 1937* (Toronto: McClelland and Stewart, 1979), 12.

52. Dun, Toronto, 202.

53. Ibid., 339.

54. Ibid. Altogether, the Rossins owned 27 properties in Toronto in 1860. City of Toronto Archives, Assessment Rolls, 1860. St. George Ward, 6, 17, 12, 36; St. James Ward, 25, 26. I am grateful to Dr. Peter Goheen of the Queen's Dept. of Geography for this information.

55. Speisman, *Jews of Toronto*, 14.

56. Hugh Grant, "The Mysterious Jacob L. Englehart and the Secret of Accumulation in the Early Ontario Petroleum Industry" (University of Winnipeg, Dept. of Economics, *unpublished paper*, 1990), 6.

57. Speisman, *Jews of Toronto*, 21.

58. Sigmund Samuel, *In Return: The Autobiography of Sigmund Samuel* (Toronto: University of Toronto Press, 1963), 7–9.

59. Dun, Toronto, 136.

60. See Joy L. Santink, *Timothy Eaton and the Rise of His Department Store* (Toronto: University of Toronto Press, 1990), 58–89.

61. Samuel, *In Return*, 17; McCalla, *Buchanans, passim.*

62. Samuel, *In Return*, 24.

63. Ibid., 18.

64. Ibid., 24.

65. NAC, Dun, XXV, Ibid. Microfilm Reel M-775 9, 115.

66. Ibid.

67. Ibid., 220.

68. Brian S. Osborne, "Trading on a Frontier: The Function of Peddlers, Markets, and Fairs

in Nineteenth Century Ontario," Donald H. Akenson (ed.), *Canadian Papers in Rural History*, II (Gananoque: Langdale Press, 1980), 60.

69. NAC, Dun, XIII, 73.

70. Ibid. XV, 111.

71. Ibid. XIX, 35, Microfilm Reel M-7758.

72. Ibid., 36.

73. Ibid., 100.

74. Ibid. XXII, 50; XVIII, 106; Dun Montreal, I, 402, 457.

75. See Sheldon and Judith Godfrey, *"Burn This Gossip," The True Story of George Benjamin of Belleville, Canada's First Jewish Member of Parliament 1857–1863* (Toronto: The Duke & George Press, 1991).

76. Helmut Kallman, "Abraham Nordheimer," *DCB* IX: 600–01.

77. Marian E. Meyer, *The Jews of Kingston: A Microcosm of Canadian Jewry* (Kingston: Limestone Press, 1983), 15.

78. Hart, *Jew in Canada*, 96.

79. Ibid., 102.

80. Ibid., 98. Solomon Levinson and Jacob Cohen (in 1869) and Harris Vineberg (ibid., 342).

81. Dun, Montreal, 4076.

82. Michael Bliss, *Northern Enterprise, Five Centuries of Canadian Business* (Toronto: McClelland and Stewart, 1987), 156.

83. Ibid., 187.

84. Shmuel Ettinger, "The Modern Period," H.H. Ben Sasson (ed.), *A History of the Jewish People* (Cambridge, Mass.: Harvard University Press, 1976), 727–1096, 807.

85. Ashkenazi, *Jews in Louisiana*, 160.

CHAPTER FIVE

1. Leo Hershkowitz and Isidore S. Meyer (eds.), *The Lee Max Friedman Collection of American Jewish Colonial Correspondence. Letters of the Franks Family (1733–1748)* (Waltham, Mass.: American Jewish Historical Society, 1968), 124, 136.

2. Jacob R. Marcus, *The Colonial American Jew, 1492–1776*, 3 volumes (Detroit: Wayne State University Press, 1970), I: 363; II: 752.

3. Quoted in Jan Goeb, "The Maritimes," *Viewpoints* 7, Nos. 3 and 4 (1973), 9–23, 13.

4. JPLM, Louis Rosenberg, "The Earliest Jewish Settlers in Canada – Facts vs. Myths", (unpublished manuscript), 1. All of them were merchants who dealt in New England colonial goods, manufactured articles from England, and staples from Nova Scotia. Isaac Levy even applied for the right to mine coal in Cape Breton.

5. Jacob R. Marcus, *Early American Jewry: The Jews of New York, New England and Canada, 1649–1794*, 2 volumes (Philadelphia: Jewish Publication Society, 1951), I: 200.

6. Marcus, *Colonial American Jew*, I: 380. Surviving records indicate that some of these merchants intended to stay. Abrahams' household consisted of three males and seven females, who presumably included his wife and daughters, while Nathans' domicile included five males over sixteen. C. Bruce Fergusson, "Jewish History in Nova Scotia Dates Back to 1752," Eli Gottesman (ed.), *Canadian Jewish Reference Book and Directory*

(Ottawa: Jewish Institute of Higher Research/Central Rabbinical Seminary of Canada, 1963), 290.

7. Ibid.

8. Edwin Wolf and Maxwell Whiteman, *The History of the Jews of Philadelphia* (Philadelphia: JPSA, 1975), 68, 76.

9. Marcus, *Colonial American Jew*, I: 1380.

10. Denis Vaugeois, "Samuel Jacobs," *DCB* IV: 384–86, 384.

11. Marcus, *Colonial American Jew*, II: 681; Frances Dublin, "Jewish Colonial Enterprise in the Light of the Amherst Papers (1758–1763)," *AJH* 29, 1939, No. 35, 5.

12. Marcus, *Colonial American Jew*, II: 681. Fergusson, "Jewish History in Nova Scotia," 290.

13. Morris A. Gutstein, *The Story of the Jews of Newport: Two and a Half Centuries of Judaism, 1658–1908* (New York: Bloch Publishing Co., 1936), 163–64.

14. Stanley F. Chyet, *Lopez of Newport: Colonial American Merchant Prince* (Detroit: Wayne State University Press, 1970), 58, 82, 118, 128, 134, 213.

15. Ibid., 126, 128.

16. Fergusson, "Jewish History in Nova Scotia," 290.

17. Marcus, *Colonial American Jew*, III: 1294.

18. Goeb, "Maritimes," 13.

19. Cecil Roth, "Some Jewish Loyalists in the War of American Independence," *AJH* 38, 1936, No. 3, 99.

20. David A. Sutherland, "Samuel Hart," *DCB* V: 409–10.

21. David A. Sutherland, "Merchants of Halifax, 1815–1860: A Commercial Class in Pursuit of Metropolitan Status" (University of Toronto, Ph.D. thesis, 1975), 476–77.

22. NAC, R.G. Dun & Company Credit Ledgers, Vol. II, Microfilm reel M-7756, n.p.

23. Goeb, "Maritimes," 12.

24. James A. Fraser, *By Favorable Winds: A History of Chatham, New Brunswick* (Chatham: The Town of Chatham, 1975), 258, 289–91.

25. Goeb, "Maritimes," 13.

26. Arthur D. Hart, *The Jew in Canada* (Montreal: Canadian Jewish Publications Ltd, 1926), 552; Sheva Medjuck, *The Jews of Atlantic Canada* (St. John's: Breakwater Press, 1986), 23; Marcia Koven, *Weaving the Past into the Present: A Glimpse into the 130 Year History of the Saint John Jewish Community* (Saint John: Jewish Historical Museum, 1989), 1–3.

27. Eli Boyaner, "The Settlement and Development of the Jewish Community of Saint John," *New Brunswick Historical Society*, 1959, 79–86, 84.

28. Medjuck, *Atlantic Canada*, 23–24.

29. Ibid., 24.

30. Ibid., 23–24.

31. Louis Rosenberg, *Canada's Jews: A Social and Economic Study of the Jews in Canada* (Montreal: Canadian Jewish Congress. Bureau of Social and Economic Research, 1939), 308.

32. D.O. Carrigan, "The Immigrant Experience in Halifax, 1881–1931" (unpublished paper).

33. Quoted in David Rome, *The First Two Years: A Record of the Jewish Pioneers on Canada's Pacific Coast, 1858–1860* (Montreal: H.M. Caiserman, 1942), 3.

34. J.M.S. Careless, "The Business Community in the Early Development of Victoria, British Columbia," David S. Macmillan (ed.), *Canadian Business History: Selected Studies* (Toronto: Macmillan, 1972), 104–23.

35. Cyril E. Leonoff, *Pioneers, Pedlars and Prayer Shawls: The Jewish Communities in British Columbia and the Yukon* (Vancouver: Sono Nis Press, 1978), 15.

36. David Rome, "First Jews in Western Canada," *JWB*, 30 June 1958.

37. Ibid.

38. Rabbi Jack A. Levey, "A Message from Your Own Home Town," n.p.: D. Rome, "Jews in the Cariboo," *JWB* 30 June 1958.

39. Careless, "Business Community," 108.

40. C. Leonoff, "The Centennial of Jewish Life in Vancouver, 1886–1986" (paper presented to the CHA and Jewish Historical Society of Western Canada, Winnipeg, 8 June 1986), 3.

41. I.J. Benjamin, *Three Years in America 1859–1862*, 2 vols. (Philadelphia: JPSA, 1956).

42. David Rome, "Early British Columbia Jewry: A Reconstructed 'Census'," *Canadian Ethnic Studies/Études Ethniques du Canada* 3 (1971), No. 1, 57–62, 61.

43. Christine Wisenthal, "Insiders and Outsiders: Two Waves of Jewish Settlement in British Columbia, 1858–1914" (University of British Columbia, M.A. thesis, 1987), 17.

44. Ibid., 14.

45. Ibid., 30, 59.

46. Ibid., 41.

47. Ibid., 47.

48. Cyril E. Leonoff, "Pioneer Jewish Merchants of Vancouver Island and British Columbia," *CJHSJ* No. 1 (1984), 12–43, 12.

49. PABC, "Congregation Emanuel Victoria," guide.

50. PABC, "Constitution and By-Laws of Congregation Emanu-El of Victoria," V.I. (Victoria, B.C.: Jas. A. Cohen Printer, 1893), 2.

51. PABC, File 7b, "Documents re Hebrew Synagogue Emanuel 1862–63," Letter from Robert Bishop, 13 Nov. 1862.

52. Ibid., A. Hoffman to the board of Trustees and Members of the Congregation Emanuel, 22 Nov. 1862.

53. Ibid., Hoffman to Rev. Dr. N. Adler, 5 May 1863.

54. Alan Klenman, "British Columbia Pioneers Contribute to Build Western Canada's First Synagogue, 1862–1863," *Western States Jewish History*, 22 (1990), No. 3, 258–64.

55. J.K. Unsworth, "Victoria Synagogue Is the Second Oldest House of Worship," *JWB*, 30 June 1958.

56. Wisenthal, "Insiders and Outsiders," 21.

57. Ibid., 19.

58. PABC, File 7b, "Documents," M.R. Cohen to the President of the Congregation, 9 Nov. 1863.

59. "Constitution and By-Laws of Congregation Emanu-El," 21.

60. Leonoff, "Centennial," 5.

61. Leonoff, *Pioneers*, 168.

62. See Patricia Roy, *Vancouver: An Illustrated History* (Toronto: James Lorimer, 1980).

63. Peter Liddell and Patricia G. Roy, "David Oppenheimer," *DCB* XII: 803–06.

64. Leonoff, "Centennial," 13.

65. Wisenthal, "Insiders and Outsiders," 26.

66. See Michael B. Katz, *The People of Hamilton, Canada West: Family and Class in a*

Mid-Nineteenth-Century City (Cambridge, Mass.: Harvard University Press, 1975).

67. Barry M. Gough, "The Character of the British Columbia Frontier," W. Peter Ward and Robert A.J. McDonald (eds.), *British Columbia Historical Readings* (Vancouver: Douglas & McIntyre, 1981), 232–44, 240.

68. Robert A.J. McDonald, "Victoria, Vancouver, and Economic Development of British Columbia, 1886–1914," ibid., 369–95, 372.

CHAPTER SIX

1. Simon Kuznets, "Immigration of Russian Jews to the United States: Background and Structure," *Perspectives in American History* (Cambridge, Mass.: Harvard University Press, 1975); Charles Warren Center for Studies in American History, IX (1975), 39. See also Usiel O. Schmelz, "Migrations," *EJ* 1: 1518–29, 1519; and Mark Wischnitzer, *To Dwell in Safety, the Jewish Migration since 1800* (Philadelphia: Jewish Publication Society, 1948).

2. Yehuda Slutsky, "Pale of Settlement," *EJ* XIII: 24–28; Shmuel Ettinger, "The Modern Period," H.H. Ben-Sasson (ed.), *A History of the Jewish People* (Cambridge, Mass.: Harvard University Press, 1976), 727–1096, 757–58.

3. Slutsky, "Pale," 24.

4. Alexander Herzen, *My Past and Thoughts* I (1968), 219–20, quoted in Yehuda Slutsky, "Cantonists," *EJ* V: 130–33, 131. See also Michael Stanislawski, *Tsar Nicholas I and the Jews. The Transformation of Jewish Society in Russia. 1825-1855* (Philadelphia: JPS, 1983), chapter 1.

5. Ettinger, "The Modern Period," 819.

6. Anatole Leroy-Beaulieu, *The Empire of the Tsars and the Russians*, 3 volumes (New York: G.P. Putnam Sons, 1896), III: 573. Notwithstanding this extreme reluctance to serve in the army, there were 45,000 Jews among the conscripts of the class of 1886, "enough to form an entire army corps." Ibid., 574.

7. Salo W. Baron, *The Russian Jew under Tsars and Soviets* (New York: Macmillan, 1964), 44.

8. Ibid., 47.

9. Howard M. Sachar, *The Course of Modern Jewish History* (New York: Dell, 1958), 187.

10. Louis Greenberg, *The Jews in Russia: The Struggle for Emancipation*, 2 volumes (New York: Schocken Books, 1976), I: 87.

11. Ibid., 97.

12. Steven J. Zipperstein, *The Jews of Odessa: A Cultural History, 1794–1881* (Stanford: Stanford University Press, 1985), Chapter 5.

13. Ibid., 124.

14. See Steven M. Berk, *Year of Crisis, Year of Hope. Russian Jewry and the Pogroms of 1881-1882* (Westport, Connecticut: Greenwood Press, 1985. Contributions in Ethnic Studies, No. 11), 55.

15. Yehuda Slutsky, "Pobedonotsev," *EJ* XIII: 664–65.

16. Ettinger, "The Modern Period," 794.

17. Leroy-Beaulieu, *Empire of the Tsars*, III: 558.

18. Kuznets, "Russian Jews," 43–44.

19. Ibid., 52.

20. Leroy-Beaulieu, *Empire of the Tsars*, III: 569.

21. See Martin Gilbert, *Jewish History Atlas* (London: Weidenfeld & Nicholson, 1969), 67.

22. Zipperstein, *Jews of Odessa*, 138–39.

23. Shimshon L. Kirshenboim, "Lodz," *EJ* XI: 426.

24. Nathan M. Gelber, "Bialystok," *EJ* IV: 8, 806.

25. I.M. Rubinow, "Economic Condition of the Jews in Russia," *Bulletin of the Bureau of Labor*, No. 72 (Washington: Dept. of Commerce and Labor, Sept. 1907), 467–583, 502.

26. Ibid., 506.

27. Leroy-Beaulieu, *Empire of the Tsars*, III: 569.

28. Ibid., 533.

29. I.M. Rubinow, "Economic Condition," 534.

30. Ibid., 541.

31. Ibid., 543–44.

32. Ibid., 545.

33. Jacques Silber, "Some Demographic Characteristics of the Jewish Population in Russia at the End of the Nineteenth Century," *JSS* 42, No. 3–4, Summer–Fall 1980, 269–81, 278.

34. Ettinger, "Modern Period," 790.

35. Orest Subtelny, *Ukraine, A History* (Toronto: University of Toronto Press, 1988), 277.

36. Baer Ratner, quoted in Gilbert, *Jewish History Atlas*, 68.

37. See Edward J. Bristow, *Prostitution and Prejudice, The Jewish Fight against White Slavery 1870–1939* (Schocken Books: New York, 1983), 49–50, 54–60.

38. Gilbert, *Atlas*, 73.

39. Theodor Lavi, "Romania," *EJ* XIV: 390.

40. Mordechai Hacohen, "Israel Meir Ha-Kohen," *EJ* IX: 1068–70.

41. Ettinger, "Modern Period," 840.

42. Ibid.

43. Ibid., 843.

44. Shlomo Avineri, *The Making of Modern Zionism, the Intellectual Origins of the Jewish State* (New York: Basic Books, 1981), 38.

45. Ibid., 63.

46. Simon M. Dubnow, *History of the Jews in Russia and Poland from the Earliest Times until the Present Day* (Philadelphia: JPSA, 1916), 2 vols, II, 331.

47. Getzel Kressel, "Hameliz," *EJ* VII: 1231–32; Yehuda Slutsky, "Hashahar," ibid., 1366–67.

48. Getzel Kressel, "Bilu," *EJ* IV: 999.

49. Ezra Mendelsohn, *The Class Struggle in the Pale: The Formative Years of Jewish Workers' Movements in Tsarist Russia* (London: Cambridge University Press, 1970).

50. Moshe Mishkinsky, "Bund," *EJ* IV: 1498.

51. Hillel Halkin, "Am Olam," *EJ* I: 862.

CHAPTER SEVEN

1. Usiel O. Schmelz, "Migrations," *EJ* XVI: 1519.

2. Ibid., 1519–20.

3. Jonathan D. Sarna, "The Myth of No Return: Jewish Return Migration to Eastern Europe, 1881–1914," Dirk Hoerder (ed.), *Labor Migration in the Atlantic Economies, The*

European and North American Working Classes during the Period of Industrialization (Westport, Conn.: Greenwood Press, 1985, Contributions in Labour History, No. 16), 423–34; Simon Kuznets, "Immigration of Russian Jews to the United States: Background and Structure," *Perspectives in American History* (Harvard: Charles Warren Center for Studies in American History, IX, 1975), 40.

4. See Louis Rosenberg, *Canada's Jews: A Social and Economic Study of the Jews in Canada* (Montreal: CJC. Bureau of Social and Economic Research, 1939), 10.
5. Ibid., 13–15.
6. Marcus L. Hansen and John B. Brebner, *The Mingling of the Canadian and American Peoples* (New Haven: Yale University Press, 1940).
7. M.L. Kovacs, "The Saskatchewan Era, 1885–1914," N.F. Dreiszinger (ed.), *Struggle and Hope: The Hungarian-Canadian Experience* (Toronto: McClelland and Stewart, 1982, Generations: A History of the Canadian Peoples), 62. See also Anthony W. Rasporich, *For a Better Life, A History of the Croatians in Canada* (Toronto: McClelland and Stewart, 1982, Generations: A History of the Canadian Peoples), 44.
8. See Harold M. Troper, *Only Farmers Need Apply. Official Canadian Government Encouragement, Immigration, from the United States, 1896–1911* (Toronto: Griffin House, 1972).
9. Montreal *Gazette*, 18 Jan. 1882.
10. Ibid., 1 Feb. 1882.
11. Ibid., 13 Sept. 1882. From May to August of 1882 almost every issue of the Montreal *Gazette* included a list of contributors to the JEAS and the Citizens' Committee.
12. Ibid., 14, 22 May 1882.
13. Irving Howe, *World of Our Fathers: The Journey of the East European Jews to America and the Life They Found and Made* (New York: Harcourt, Brace, Jovanovich, 1976), 47.
14. Montreal *Gazette*, 16 May 1882.
15. Ibid., 22 May 1882.
16. Of the 180 persons who had used the home since it was opened, 80, mostly women and children, still remained, 48 of whom had been on their way to Manitoba where "they were most anxious to take up farming, with which they were acquainted." Ibid., 21 June 1882.
17. Ibid., 12 Mar. 1883.
18. Stephen Speisman, *The Jews of Toronto: A History to 1937* (Toronto: McClelland and Stewart, 1979), 58; Simon I. Belkin, *Through Narrow Gates: A Review of Jewish Immigration, Colonization and Immigrant Aid Work in Canada (1840–1940)* (Montreal: CJC and JCA, 1966), 31.
19. Doug Owram, *Promise of Eden: The Canadian Expansionist Movement and the Idea of the West* (Toronto: University of Toronto Press, 1981), *passim*; Arthur A. Chiel, "Herman Landau's Canadian Dream," *CJHSJ* 2 (1978), No. 2, 113–20.
20. Belkin, *Through Narrow Gates*, 51.
21. See chapter 8.
22. Ibid., 52.
23. Gerald Friesen, *The Canadian Prairies, A History* (Toronto: University of Toronto Press, 1984), 183.
24. Montreal *Gazette*, 18 Jan. 1882. Oscar D. Skelton, *The Life and Times of Sir Alexander Tilloch Galt* (Toronto: Oxford University Press, 1920), 544.
25. Quoted in Henry Trachtenberg, "Opportunism, Humanitarianism and Revulsion: The

'Old Clo Move' Comes to Winnipeg, 1882–3" unpublished paper, Canadian Historical Association Meetings, Winnipeg, 1986, 2.

26. Quoted in ibid.

27. Ibid., 3.

28. NAC, MG 26, John A. Macdonald Papers, A1, 524, Letterbook 21, 684–86, Macdonald to Galt, 26 Feb. 1882.

29. Quoted in Trachtenberg, "Opportunism," 3.

30. NAC, MG 27, I D8, Galt Papers, 93316, Galt to Macdonald, 25 Jan. 1882.

31. See Abraham J. Arnold, "Jewish Immigration to Western Canada in the 1880s," *CJHSJ* 1 (1977), No. 2, 82–95. In the early 1890s the Berlin (Jewish) Conference on Emigration considered Canada a suitable destination for refugee Russians; Jonathan D. Sarna, "Jewish Immigration to North America: The Canadian Experience (1870–1900)," *The Jewish Journal of Sociology* 18, No. 1 (1976), 31–41. PAM. JHSWC Collections, MG 10 F3 (MG1, E1), 31998–99.

32. Trachtenberg, "Opportunism," 3.

33. Montreal *Gazette*, 18 Jan. 1882.

34. Ibid., 23 Jan. 1882.

35. Joel Geffen, "Jewish Agricultural Colonies as Reported in the Pages of the Russian Hebrew Press *Ha-Melitz* and *Ha-Yom*: Annotated Documentary," *AJH*, June 1971, 355–81.

36. Ibid., 377. See Arthur A. Chiel, *The Jews in Manitoba: A Social History* (Toronto: University of Toronto Press, 1961), 37–38, and Benjamin G. Sack, *History of the Jews in Canada* (Montreal: Harvest House, 1965), 198–99 for fuller renditions and slightly different translations of this letter.

37. Sack, *Jews in Canada*, 200.

38. Ibid., 201.

39. Andrew A. den Otter, *Civilizing the West: The Galts and the Development of Western Canada* (Edmonton: University of Alberta Press, 1982), 11.

40. Ibid., 83–84.

41. See Eugene C. Black, *The Social Politics of Anglo-Jewry, 1880–1920* (London: Basil Blackwell, 1988), 254.

42. NAC, RG 15, Department of Interior, 318, File 73568(1), Galt to Burgess, 1 April 1884.

43. Ibid. William Van Horne of the CPR suggested a location for the colony.

44. Ibid., Hall to Galt, 7 April 1884.

45. Ibid., Galt to Burgess, 5 May 1884. See also Trachtenberg, "Opportunism," 5.

46. Abraham J. Arnold, "The Jewish Farm Settlements of Saskatchewan: From New Jerusalem to Edenbridge," *CJHSJ* 4 (1980), No. 1, 25–43, and "The Contribution of Jews to the Opening and Development of the West," *Historical and Scientific Society of Manitoba* papers, III, No. 25. (1968–69), 23–37, 36. See also Cyril E. Leonoff, *The Jewish Farmers of Western Canada* (Vancouver: Jewish Historical Society of British Columbia, 1984).

47. Belkin, *Through Narrow Gates*, 56. But see PAM, JHSWC MG 10, F 3, declaration of William A. Thompson, 13 May 1886, indicating average loans of $500.

48. Belkin, *Through Narrow Gates*, 57.

49. Norbert Macdonald, *Canada: Immigration and Colonization, 1841–1903* (Toronto: Macmillan, 1966), 222.

50. Canadian House of Commons, *Sessional Papers*, 1888, No. 4. "Report of Minister of Agriculture for 1887" (Ottawa: Maclean, Roger Co., 1888), 97.

51. PAM, JHSWC, MG 10, F 3, 6 May 1886, Galt to Hon. Thomas White, Minister of Interior.

52. Ibid., 23 Feb. 1892, H. Parke to H.H. Smith, Dominion Lands Commission, Winnipeg.

53. Belkin, *Through Narrow Gates*, 58.

54. Chiel, *Jews in Manitoba*, 47.

55. Cyril E. Leonoff, *Wapella Farm Settlement (The First Successful Jewish Farm Settlement in Canada), A Pictorial History* (Historical and Scientific Society of Manitoba and JHSWC, 1970), 2.

56. Ibid., 12–13.

57. Ibid., 16.

58. Michael R. Marrus, *Mr. Sam, the Life and Times of Samuel Bronfman* (Toronto: Viking, 1991), 37.

59. Quoted in ibid., 37–38.

60. Skelton, *Galt*, 544.

61. NAC. Department of Interior, 318, File 73568(1), Galt to Burgess, 30 Jan. 1888, p. 16751.

62. Theodore Norman, *An Outstretched Arm: A History of the Jewish Colonization Association* (London: Routledge & Kegan Paul, 1985).

63. One member of the board of directors favoured using the grant to establish a colony of some of the Russian Romanian Jewish refugees, see NAC MG 28, v86, Minutes of the Board, Baron de Hirsch Institute of Montreal 1863–1914; Vol. 1, 29 Aug. 1890. Hereafter cited as Minutes.

64. This committee was appointed by the YMHBS to supervise the spending of the grant from the Baron de Hirsch.

65. Ibid., 29 Mar. 1891.

66. Ibid., 12 Aug. 1891.

67. Ibid., 16 Aug. 1891.

68. Ibid., 29 Sept. 1891. The Colonization Committee sent a delegation to Ottawa some time between Sept. 1891 and 7 Jan. 1892, and reported to the board the result of talks held with the prime minister, Sir John Abbott. See ibid., 7 Jan. 1892.

69. See Timothy R. Neufeld, "A Study of Jewish Philanthropic Company Colonization in Canada's Northwest during the Late Nineteenth Century" (University of Saskatchewan, M.A. thesis, 1982), 46. This thesis provides the most thorough account of the Hirsch project.

70. Minutes, 16 Nov. 1891. Interest in colonization was also evinced by members of London's Mansion House Committee. In December the secretary, N.S. Joseph, wrote to the YMHBS concerning "the practicability of combining an industry with the work of agriculture." Ibid., Dec. 30, 1891. The society's reply, however, elicited another letter from Joseph, stating that the Mansion House Committee would not provide assistance for any colonization scheme; ibid., 24 Feb. 1891.

71. Ibid., 7 Jan. 1892. See also 13 Mar. 1891.

72. Ibid., 13 Dec. 1891. The delegation consisted of "Messrs. Labovitch, Frankel, Erzecovitch and two others."

73. Ibid., 11 Feb. 1892.

74. Ibid., 24 Feb. 1892.

75. Ibid., 3 Apr. 1892.

76. Ibid., 21 Mar. 1892.

77. Ibid., 7 Apr. 1892.

78. Simon Belkin, "Jewish Colonization in Canada," Arthur D. Hart (ed.), *The Jew in Canada* (Montreal: Canadian Jewish Publications Limited, 1926), 485.

79. Nine teams of horses were selected by William Jacobs "free of cost or commission . . . for about $120.00 the team," Minutes, 13 Apr. 1892.

80. "Alick Rothman – wife – 1 son; Joel Handelman – wife – 2 sons – 1 daughter; Isaac Vineberg – wife and family in Russia; Joseph Kaufman – wife – child and mother-in-law; Israel Rosner – wife and 2 daughters in Russia; Soloman Emmes – wife – 2 sons – 6 more in Russia; C. Merlstein – wife; K. Zelickson – wife; S. Goldner – wife – 5 sons – 2 daughters; M. Pfepperman – wife – 2 daughters; E. Rabin – wife – 2 sons – 3 daughters; M. Hartenstein – family in Russia; I. Barenblat – wife – 3 sons – 2 daughters; A. Singer – wife – (son-in-law of Barenblat); M. Schatzsky – wife – 1 son; L. Schatzsky – wife – 1 son – 2 daughters; I. Herson – wife – 4 sons – 4 daughters; J. Shapera – wife – 3 daughters; Eli Friedman – wife – 2 sons; N. Vineberg – family in Russia; B. Samovitch (Simon) – wife – 2 sons – 2 daughters; A. Hadis – wife – 4 sons – 2 daughters; F. Davies – wife – 2 sons; S. Rosenfeldt – wife – – 5 sons; W. Dun – wife – 4 children; L. Herzcovitch – wife – 9 children." Ibid., 10 Apr. 1892. Two more families, those of Joshua and Alkon Sher, "The former leaving his family in Russia," were added a few days later, ibid., 13 Apr. 1892. By April 17 the society decided to limit the Montreal contingent to 325 persons. Only 284 were finally sent out. (Israel Rosner was later removed from the list at his own request, since he "was earning sufficient to maintain himself and also to send some money to his family"; ibid., 27 Apr. 1892.)

81. Ibid., 24 Sept. 1893.

82. Ibid., 19 Apr. 1892.

83. Ibid., 24 Apr. 1892.

84. The prospective colonists were expected to pay whatever money they had towards the cost of their transportation. This was rigorously enforced, ibid., 27 Apr. 1894.

85. Soon after their arrival, the settlers formed a society "with a committee of five to settle minor differences," ibid., 14 Aug. 1892.

86. Ibid., 31 Oct. 1892.

87. On May 29 the society wrote to McDiarmid to take a section of land on its behalf, to cut off the supplies of any colonists who "gave trouble," to arrange about the land for Hadis, under no circumstances to send Potkoff or anyone else back to Montreal, to give no help to Bloom and not to recognize any outsider not on the list already sent, to purchase seed, to send lists of food and clothes required, to buy flour and "articles which could be procured cheaply at Winnipeg, to send prices of articles he was purchasing in the north-west, to buy a horse rake and cut as much hay as possible this year, to procure more oxen, and to build the cheapest possible kind of houses for the

colonists." (After experimenting with sod houses the colonists built frame houses.) Moreover, the president, Harris Vineberg, wrote a letter to the colonists in Yiddish "advising them to live peaceably and loyally and that Herzcovitch and Garfunkel be specially warned as to their conduct"; ibid., 29 May 1892, 14 Aug. 1892. In November it was reported that "several emigrants had found their way to the colony and were there in a helpless and starving condition." The board determined "that the colonists in question should give a mortgage upon their chattles and effects and that Mr. Roth should be empowered to give them sufficient food to prevent them from starving"; ibid., 27 Nov. 1892.

88. Ibid., 14 Aug. 1892.89. Ibid., 31 Aug. 1892; 5 Feb. 1893.

90. Ibid., 18 Feb. 1893.

91. Ibid., 15 May 1892.

92. See ibid., 14 Aug. 1892.

93. Montreal *Gazette*, 18 July 1892.

94. Minutes, Aug. 14 and Oct. 2, 1892.

95. Ibid., 14 Aug. 1892.

96. Ibid., 16 Oct. 1892. A few families were added in subsequent years. Ibid., 3 May 1893.

97. Ibid., 2 Oct. 1892.

98. Ibid., 27 Nov. 1892.

99. Ibid., 30 Nov. 1892. Upon his return, the manager of the colony was questioned by Harris Vineberg and David Friedman.

100. Ibid., 13 Feb. 1893.

101. Ibid., 7 Feb. 1893, Aaron Ness and Louis Margulies. Neither remained very long; ibid., 24 May 1893.

102. Minutes, 7 Feb. 1893.

103. Ibid., 16 Mar. 1893. One of them, Schomberg, had left his farm for five days, during which his cow and calf froze to death. He was expelled from the colony and Roth was given the "power to deal with any other colonist in the same manner if in their opinion [they] find that the [colonist] is [threatening] injury to the colony."

104. Baker was instructed to sell the land and buildings owned by the society and to require all the colonists to sign mortgages on their land, animals, and buildings which had been supplied by the society. Ibid., 2 July, 15 Aug. 1893.

105. Ibid.

106. The first synagogue at Hirsch was built during the summer and autumn of 1896.

107. Minutes, 18 Oct. 1893.

108. Ibid., 25 Oct. 1893.

109. Montreal *Gazette*, 20 Nov. 1893.

110. Minutes, 22 Jan. 1894.

111. Ibid., 21 Feb. 1894.

112. Ibid., 18 Mar. 1894.

113. Ibid., 12 Sept. 1894.

114. They had been sent from Chicago to the Territories by a group of Protestant ministers who had been under the impression that they were assisting a group of East European Christians.

115. Belkin, "Jewish Colonization in Canada," 485–86.

116. Minutes, 18 Feb. 1893.

117. Macdonald, *Immigration and Colonization*, 224.

118. Ibid., 210.

119. M.C. Urquhart and K.A.H. Buckley, *Historical Statistics of Canada* (Toronto: Macmillan, 1965), 320.

120. See C.A. Dawson, *Group Settlement, Ethnic Communities in Western Canada* (Toronto: Macmillan, 1936, Canadian Frontiers of Settlement Series, W.A. Mackintosh and W.L.G. Joerg (eds.), 9 volumes), 377.

121. Judith L. Elkin, *Jews of the Latin American Republics* (Chapel Hill: University of North Carolina Press, 1980).

122. Uri D. Herscher, *Jewish Agricultural Utopias in America, 1880–1910* (Detroit: Wayne State University Press, 1981), 109–113.

123. See Robert Weisbrot, *The Jews of Argentina: From the Inquisition to Perón* (Philadelphia: Jewish Publication Society of America, 1979), Chapter 1.

124. NAC, MG 30, H 94, Vol. 24, p. 44.

125. Neufeld, "Jewish Philanthropic Company Colonization," 132.

126. Ibid., 133.

CHAPTER EIGHT

1. Paul-André Linteau, René Durocher and Jean-Claude Robert, *Québec: A History, 1867-1929* (Toronto: James Lorimer, 1983), 130. Louis Rosenberg, "A Study of the Growth and Changes in the Distribution of the Jewish Population of Montreal," *Canadian Jewish Population Studies*, No. 4 (Montreal: CJC, 1955), 13.

2. McGill University, Department of Geography. Shared Spaces Project.

3. Abraham J. Heschel, *The Earth Is the Lord's + The Sabbath*, (New York: Harper Torchbook, 1966), 98.

4. Michael R. Weisser, *A Brotherhood of Memory: Jewish Landsmanshaftn in the New World* (New York: Basic Books, 1985).

5. John Benson, "Hawking and Peddling in Canada 1867–1914," *Histoire Sociale/Social History*, 18 May 1985, 75–83.

6. I.M. Rubinow, "Economic Condition of the Jews in Russia," Bulletin of the Bureau of Labour, No. 72 (Washington: Dept. of Commerce and Labor, Sept. 1907), 500.

7. Jean Hamelin and Yves Roby, *Histoire Economique de Québec 1851–1896* (Montreal: Fides, 1971), 267.

8. Gerald J.J. Tulchinsky, *The River Barons: Montreal Businessmen and the Growth of Industry and Transportation 1837–53* (Toronto: University of Toronto Press, 1977), 224.

9. Gerald Tulchinsky, "Hollis Shorey," DCB XII: 968–70.

10. Arthur D. Hart (ed.), *The Jew in Canada* (Montreal: Canadian Jewish Publications Ltd., 1926), 100–03.

11. Ibid., 342.

12. R.P. Sparks, "The Garment and Clothing Industries, History and Organization," *Manual of the Textile Industry in Canada* (1930), 109.

13. Hart, *Jew in Canada*, 100.

14. Canada. *Report of Royal Commission on the Relations of Labour and Capital* (Ottawa: Queen's Printer, 1889), Quebec Evidence, Part I, 295, 557–60.
15. Lorna F. Hurl, "Restricting Child Factory Labour in Late Nineteenth Century Ontario," *Labour/Le Travail* 21 (Spring 1988), 101–02.
16. NAC, MG 26, William Lyon Mackenzie King Papers, J4, XXVII, C–19161.
17. Canadian House of Commons, *Sessional Papers* (1896), No. 51, 23–25.
18. *JT*, 4 Feb. 1898.
19. King Papers, XXVII, C–19162.
20. Ibid., XXVI, C–18556.
21. Ibid., C–18558.
22. *KA*, 21 Feb. 1913.
23. Bettina Bradbury, "The Family Economy and Work in an Industrializing City: Montreal in the 1870s," Gilbert A. Stelter (ed.), *Cities and Urbanization: Historical Perspectives* (Toronto: Copp Clark Pitman, 1990), 138–40.
24. Irving Abella and David Miller (eds.), *The Canadian Worker in the Twentieth Century* (Toronto: Oxford University Press, 1978), 154–55.
25. Mercedes Steedman, "Skill and Gender in the Canadian Clothing Industry, 1890–1940," Craig Heron and Robert Storry (eds.), *On the Job: Confronting the Labour Process in Canada* (Montreal: McGill-Queen's University Press, 1986), 156.
26. *JT*, 4 Feb. 1898.
27. Ibid., 17 Feb. 1899.
28. Gerald Tulchinsky, "Clarence de Sola and Early Zionism in Canada, 1898–1920," M. Rischin (ed.), *The Jews of North America* (Detroit: Wayne State University Press, 1987), 174–93.
29. As early as 1892 a group of young men proposed forming a library there.
30. JPLM, Rosenberg Manuscripts, "Minutes of the School Committee of the Corporation of Portuguese Jews of Montreal" (typescript), 40. In March of 1891 the issue of redistributing Jewish school tax monies was raised with the Congregation, but the matter was shelved. Ibid., 49–50.
31. NAC, MG 28, v86, Jewish Family Services of the Baron de Hirsch Institute (est. 1863) Montreal, Minutes of the Board, Baron de Hirsch Institute of Montreal 1863–1914; Vol. 1, 29 Mar. 1891. Hereafter cited as Minutes.
32. Two of those who strenuously opposed the position of the majority of the congregation resigned their membership; see ibid., 15 May 1892, 17 May 1892.
33. NAC, MG28, v86, *Re Jewish School Tax, City of Montreal. Memorial of the Young Men's Hebrew Benevolent Society of Montreal, A Body Corporate,* 4 May 1892.
34. According to the board of directors' minutes books, one member of the Spanish and Portuguese Synagogue made a public statement to that effect. See *Minutes*, I, 29 May 1892.
35. CJCAM, School Question, Unnumbered file. G. de Sola to H. Vineberg, 30 May 1892. Ansell's reasons were the same as those given in the memorial, the distance the children would have to travel to get to the Spanish and Portuguese Synagogue. Ibid., D. Ansell to G. de Sola, 12 July 1892.
36. Ibid.
37. CJCAM, School Question. Louis Pelletier to Rabbi M. de Sola, 1892.

38. Ibid., G. de Sola to D. Ansell, 19 Aug. 1892.

39. Ibid., D. Ansell to G. de Sola, 25 Aug. 1892.

40. Ibid., J. Boivin to Rabbi M. de Sola, 14 Oct. 1892.

41. See Montreal *Gazette*, 18 May 1892; 1 June 1892; 10 Dec. 1892; 13 Jan. 1893; 10 Nov. 1893; 19 Dec. 1893.

42. Minutes I, 2 Oct. 1892.

43. CJCAM, School Question. J. Boivin to Rabbi M. de Sola, 30 Nov. 1892. G. de Sola replied directly to Pelletier to Boivin's letter, which he said had been "erroneously addressed to him as Secretary of our School Board." De Sola went on to inform the provincial secretary somewhat airily that "I will place your letter before the next meeting of our Board, which will be held this day week." G. de Sola to Pelletier, 5 Dec. 1892. Pelletier's reply to this was sharp – "A special meeting of your Board should have been called at once, and if I do not get a reply within a few days, we [the Government] will take energetic measures to have this question settled." Pelletier to G. de Sola 9 Dec. 1892.

44. Minutes I, 27 Nov. 1892.

45. CJCAM, G. de Sola to School Committee, Baron de Hirsch Institute, 13 Dec. 1892.

46. Ibid., J. Boivin to Rabbi de Sola, 15 Dec. 1892.

47. Ibid., D. Ansell to G. de Sola, 16 Dec. 1892.

48. Ibid., Pelletier to G. de Sola, 20 Dec. 1892.

49. Ibid., G. de Sola to Pelletier, 30 Dec. 1892.

50. Ibid., Hall to de Sola, 20 Sept. 1893.

51. Ibid., M. de Sola to Hall, 22 Sept. 1893.

52. Ibid., Hall to de Sola, 25 Sept. 1893.

53. Ibid., G. de Sola to Hall, 16 Oct. 1893.

54. Ibid., Hall to de Sola, 18 Oct. 1893.

55. Ibid., Ansell to G. de Sola, 1 Jan. 1894.

56. Translated and printed in the Montreal *Gazette*, 13 Dec. 1893.

57. CJCAM, M.S. Archambault (secretary-treasurer, Catholic Board of School Commissioners) to Rev. Meldola de Sola, 10 Apr. 1894.

58. Ibid., de Sola to Ansell, 19 Apr. 1894. Ansell to de Sola, 24 Apr. 1894.

59. Ibid., de Sola to Archambault, 2 May 1894.

60. Ibid., Archambault to G. de Sola, 12 May 1894.

61. Ibid., Minutes II, 4 Oct. 1894.

62. JPLM, "School Committee . . . Portuguese Jews," 67.

63. Louis Rosenberg, "Jewish Children in the Protestant Schools of Greater Montreal in the Period from 1878 to 1958," *Research Papers*, Series E, No. 1 (Montreal: CJC. Bureau of Social and Economic Research, 16 Mar. 1959), 6.

64. *Montreal Star*, 15 Feb. 1898.

65. P. Senese, "Antisemitism in Late Nineteenth Century Quebec and Montreal: The Catholic Militants of *La Vérité* and *La Croix*" (unpublished paper delivered to Canadian Historical Association, Victoria, 1990), 34.

66. In 1894 the society was given a small burial plot by the Temple Emanu-El. See Minutes I, 15 Sept. 1892, 7 Mar. 1894.

67. Louis Rosenberg, *Canada's Jews: A Social and Economic Study of the Jews in Canada* (Montreal: CJC. Bureau of Social and Economic Research, 1939), 135.

68. See *Annual Reports*, 1890–1900, NAC, MG 28, v86, Jewish Family Services of the Baron de Hirsch Institute.

69. In 1900 the "Baron de Hirsch" aided 426 Russians, 19 Syrians, 36 English, 34 Hungarians, 2 French, 12 Canadians (from other parts of the Dominion or from the U.S.), 27 Austrians, 29 Germans, 1 Turk, 30 Poles, 10 Galicians, and 42 Americans. *Annual Reports*, 1900, 5.

70. See *Annual Reports*, 1890–1900.

71. See *Annual Balance Sheet of Board of Directors*, 1900, 10–11.

72. Veronica J. Strong-Boag, *The Parliament of Women: The National Council of Women of Canada, 1893–1929* (Ottawa: National Museums of Canada, 1976), 101–02; Stephen Speisman, *The Jews of Toronto: A History to 1937* (Toronto: McClelland and Stewart, 1979), 60.

73. Senese, "Antisemitism," 23–24.

74. Ibid., 28.

75. Quoted in ibid., 29.

76. Ibid., 30.

77. Phyllis M. Senese, "La Croix de Montréal (1893–95): A Link to the French Radical Right," Canadian Catholic Historical Association, *Historical Studies* 53, 1986, 81–95.

78. See Jean Bredin, *The Affair: The Case of Alfred Dreyfus* (New York: George Braziller, 1986), Chapter 20.

79. Michael Brown, *Jew or Juif? Jews, French Canadians, and Anglo-Canadians, 1759–1914* (Philadelphia: JPSA, 1987), 136–37.

80. *La Presse*, 23 Aug. 1899.

81. See David Rome, "On Jules Helbronner" (Montreal: CJCAM, 1978, CJA New Series, #11.)

82. *True Witness*, 11 Dec. 1898.

83. Ibid., 22 Jan. 1898.

84. Ibid., 26 Feb. 1898.

85. Ibid., 24 Sept. 1898.

86. Ibid., 11 Sept. 1899.

87. *La Minerve*, 12 June; 16, 24 Sept.; 17, 18 Nov. 1890.

88. See Patricia E. Roy, *White Man's Province: British Columbia Politicians and Chinese and Japanese Immigrants, 1858–1914* (Vancouver: University of British Columbia Press, 1989).

89. *JT*, 10 Dec. 1897. See Lewis Levendel, *A Century of the Canadian Jewish Press: 1880s–1980s* (Ottawa: Borealis Press, 1989).

90. Ernest Nolte, *Three Faces of Fascism: Action Française, Italian Fascism, and National Socialism* (New York: New American Library, 1969), 79.

91. *JT*, 4 Jan., 16 Feb. 1900.

92. Ibid., 16 Feb. 1900.

93. Ibid., 17 Aug. 1900. See also Frances Molino and Bernard Wesserstein (eds.), *The Jews in Modern France* (Hanover: University Press of New England, 1985), 107–13.

94. *JT*, 28 Oct. 1898.

95. Ibid., 15 Sept. 1899.

96. Ibid., 20 Jan. 1899.

97. Ibid., 9 Dec. 1898.

98. Alex Bein, *Theodore Herzl, A Biography* (Philadelphia: JPSA, 1948).

99. See Dorothy Suzanne Cross, "The Irish in Montreal, 1867–1896" (McGill University M.A. thesis, 1969).

100. I Goldstick, "The Jews of London, Ontario: The First One Hundred Years," Eli Gottesman (ed.), *Canadian Jewish Reference Book and Directory* (Toronto: Jewish Institute of Higher Research, Central Rabbinical Seminary of Canada, 1963), 323.

101. Rosenberg, *Canada's Jews*, 308. See Max Bookman, "Excerpts from the History of the Jew in Canada's Capital," Gottesman, *Jewish Reference Book*, 387–405.

102. Harvey H. Herstein, "The Growth of the Winnipeg Jewish Community and the Evolution of Its Educational Institutions," *Transactions of the Historical and Scientific Society of Manitoba*, Series III, No. 22, 1965–66, 29.

103. Henry Trachtenberg, "Peddling, Politics, and Winnipeg's Jews, 1891–95: The Political Acculturation of an Urban Immigrant Community" (unpublished paper, Canadian Jewish Historical Society meetings, June 1991, Queen's University), 11.

104. Speisman, *Jews of Toronto*, 50.

105. Rosenberg, *Canada's Jews*, 308.

106. Sigmund Samuel, *In Return: The Autobiography of Sigmund Samuel* (Toronto: University of Toronto Press, 1963), 45–50.

107. Speisman, *Jews of Toronto*, 67.

108. Rosenberg, *Canada's Jews*, 10.

109. Jonathan Frankel, "The Crisis of 1881–2 as a Turning Point in Modern Jewish History," David Berger (ed.), *The Legacy of Jewish Migration: 1881 and Its Impact* (New York: Brooklyn College Studies on Society in Change, No. 24, 1983), 9–22.

110. See Uri D. Herscher, *Jewish Agricultural Utopias in America, 1880–1910* (Detroit: Wayne State University Press, 1981), *passim*.

111. Michel Brunet, "Trois dominantes de la Pensée Canadienne-Française," *La Présence Anglaise et les Canadiennes* (Montreal: Beauchemin, 1964), 113–66.

CHAPTER NINE

1. Louis Rosenberg, *Canada's Jews: A Social and Economic Study of the Jews in Canada* (Montreal: CJC. Bureau of Social and Economic Research, 1939), 136.

2. M.C. Urquhart and K.A.H. Buckley, *Historical Statistics of Canada* (Toronto: Macmillan, 1965), 23.

3. Rosenberg, *Canada's Jews*, 308.

4. See Lise C. Hansen, "The Decline of the Jewish Community in Thunder Bay: An Explanation" (University of Manitoba, M.A. thesis, 1977).

5. Rosenberg, *Canada's Jews*, 308–10.

6. Sheva Medjuck, *The Jews of Atlantic Canada* (St. John's: Breakwater Press, 1986), Chapter 2.

7. Rosenberg, *Canada's Jews*, 19.

8. Sheldon Levitt, Lynn Milstone, Sidney T. Tenenbaum, *Treasures of a People: The Synagogues of Canada* (Toronto: Lester & Orpen Dennys, 1985), 57.

9. Beth Israel Archives, Kingston, unnumbered file of early congregational documents, 15 Apr. 1902.

10. Ruth Bellan, "Growing Up in a Small Saskatchewan Town," *Jewish Life and Times, A Collection of Essays* (Winnipeg: JHSWC, 1983), 116.

11. Robert H. Babcock, "A Jewish Immigrant in the Maritimes: The Memoirs of Max Vanger," *Acadiensis* 16, No. 1, Autumn 1986, 136–48.

12. Edmund Bradwin. *The Bunkhouse Man: A Study of Work and Pay in the Camps of Canada, 1903–1914* (Toronto: University of Toronto Press, 1972), 108–09.

13. Rosenberg, *Canada's Jews*, 308.

14. Alan F.J. Artibise, *Winnipeg: A Social History of Urban Growth, 1874–1914* (Montreal: McGill-Queen's University Press, 1975), 130–31.

15. See Ruben Bellan, *Winnipeg First Century: An Economic History* (Winnipeg: Queenston House Publishing Co., 1978), Chapter VII.

16. See James S. Woodsworth, *My Neighbour: A Study of City Conditions, A Plea for Social Service* (Toronto: University of Toronto Press, 1972).

17. Harry Gutkin, *Journey into Our Heritage* (Toronto: Lester & Orpen Dennys, 1980), 179–81.

18. Woodsworth, *My Neighbour*, 66.

19. See Ol'ha Woycenko, "Community Organizations," Manoly R. Lupul (ed.), *A Heritage in Transition: Essays in the History of Ukrainians in Canada* (Toronto: McClelland and Stewart, 1982), 173–94, 174–75.

20. Louis Rosenberg, *The Jewish Community of Winnipeg* (Montreal: CJC, 1946), 12.

21. Ibid., 22.

22. Ibid., 23.

23. Henry Trachtenberg, "Unfriendly Competitors: Jews, Ukrainians, and Municipal Politics in Winnipeg's Ward 5, 1911–1914" (unpublished paper, Canadian Association of Slavists, Learned Societies Conference, 1986), 2.

24. Ibid., 4.

25. Ibid., 10–11.

26. Ibid., 14.

27. See Harvey Herstein, "The Evolution of Jewish Schools in Winnipeg," *Jewish Life and Times: A Collection of Essays* (Winnipeg: JHSWC, 1983), 8.

28. Ibid., 9.

29. Ibid., 13.

30. Ibid., 17. See also Roz Usiskin, "The Winnipeg Jewish Radical Community," ibid., 155–68.

31. Roz Usiskin, "Continuity and Change: The Jewish Experience in Winnipeg's North End, 1900–1914," *CJHSJ* 4 (1980), No. 1, 71–94, 84.

32. Rosenberg, *Winnipeg*, 41.

33. Ibid., 45.

34. Harry Gale, "The Jewish Labour Movement in Winnipeg," *JHSWC* 1, June 1970, 3–4.

35. Mel Fenson, "A History of the Jews in Alberta," and Harold Hyman, "The Jews in Saskatchewan," Eli Gottesman (ed.), *Canadian Jewish Reference Book and Directory* (Toronto: Jewish Institute of Higher Research, Central Rabbinical Seminary of Canada, 1963), 281, 293.

36. PAM, MG 10, F3 (MG1B, 3–1.) Arthur J. Field, "The Jewish Community of Saskatoon, Canada," unpublished manuscript. See also J.M. Goldenberg, "History of the Jewish Community of Saskatoon," *Agudas Israel Dedication Volume, 1905–1963* (Saskatoon: 1963).

37. Louis Rosenberg, "The History of the Regina Jewish Community" (manuscript), PAM, MG10, F3 (MG1, B1–2).
38. Anthony W. Rasporich, "Early Jewish Farm Settlements in Saskatchewan: A Utopian Perspective," *Saskatchewan History* 42, 1989, No. 1, 35.
39. Harold Troper, "Jews and Canadian Immigration Policy, 1900–1950," M. Rischin (ed.), *The Jews of North America* (Detroit: Wayne State University Press, 1987), 48.
40. Quoted in Rasporich, "Jewish Farm Settlements," 38.
41. Ibid., 36.
42. Abraham J. Arnold, "The Jewish Farm Settlements of Saskatchewan: From New Jerusalem to Edenbridge," *CJHSJ* 4, 1980, No. 1, 37.
43. Simon I. Belkin, *Through Narrow Gates: A Review of Jewish Immigration, Colonization and Immigrant Aid Work in Canada (1840–1940)* (Montreal: CJC and Jewish Colonization Association, 1966), 77.
44. Ibid.
45. See Anna Feldman, "Sonnenfeld – Elements of Survival and Success of a Jewish Community on the Prairies 1905–1939," *CJHSJ* 6, No. 1, Spring 1982, 33–53.
46. Clara Hoffer and F.H. Kahan, *Land of Hope* (Saskatoon: Modern Press, 1960), 29.
47. Ibid., 32.
48. Ibid., 91–93.
49. Michael Usiskin, *Uncle Mike's Edenbridge: Memoirs of a Jewish Pioneer Farmer*, translated from Yiddish by Marcia Usiskin Basman (Winnipeg: Peguis Publishers, 1983), 11.
50. Ibid., 27.
51. Yossi Katz and John C. Lehr, "Jewish and Mormon Agricultural Settlement in Western Canada: A Comparative Analysis," *Canadian Geographer/Géographe canadienne* 35, No. 2 (1991), 128–42.
52. Stella Hryniuk, "'Sifton's Pets': Who Were They?", Lubomyr Luciuk and Stella Hryniuk (eds.), *Canada's Ukrainians: Negotiating an Identity* (Toronto: University of Toronto Press, 1991), 15.
53. NAC, MG28, v86, Jewish Family Services of the Baron de Hirsch Institute, *Report of Baron de Hirsch Institute*, 1908.
54. Stephen A. Speisman, "St. John's Shtetl: The Ward in 1911," Robert F. Harney (ed.), *Gathering Place: Peoples and Neighbourhoods of Toronto, 1834–1945* (Toronto: Multicultural History Society of Ontario, 1985), 107–20.
55. Ibid., 108; S.B. Rohold, *The Jews in Canada* (Toronto: Board of Home Missions, Presbyterian Church in Canada, 1912), 13.
56. George Quinn, "Impact of European Immigration upon the Elementary Schools of Central Toronto, 1815–1915" (University of Toronto, M.A. thesis, 1968), 95, 108.
57. Speisman, "St. John's Shtetl," 113.
58. Lynne Marks, "Jewish Mutual Benefit Societies in Toronto, 1900–1930" (University of Toronto, Dept. of History, undergraduate paper, 1978).
59. Ibid., 2. See *The Toronto Jewish City and Information Directory* (Toronto: 1925), 8–9.
60. Marks, "Benefit Societies," 2.
61. Stephen Speisman, *The Jews of Toronto: A History to 1937* (Toronto: McClelland and Stewart, 1979), 145–51.

62. Arthur A. Chiel, *The Jews in Manitoba: A Social History* (Toronto: University of Toronto Press, 1961), 131, 135.

63. Ibid., 136.

64. See Isaac Babel, *Benya Krik, The Gangster and Other Stories* (New York: Schocken Books, 1969); Stephen D. Corrsin, *Warsaw before the First World War: Poles and Jews in the Third City of the Russian Empire, 1880–1914* (Columbia University Press: New York, East European Monographs CCLXXIV, 1989), 15–16.

65. Yakov Nash, "Crime," *EJ* 5:1091.

66. Edward J. Bristow, *Prostitution and the Jewish Fight against White Slavery, 1870–1939* (New York: Schocken Books, 1983).

67. Bernard Figler, *Lillian and Archie Freiman, Biographies* (Ottawa: Northern Printing and Lithographing Co., 1962), 45.

68. Lloyd P. Gartner, "Anglo Jewry and the International Traffic in Prostitution, 1885-1914," *Association for Jewish Studies Review* 7-8, 1982-3, 129-178, 129.

69. Bristow, *Prostitution*, 170.

70. RG 76, Vol. 542, File 804221.

71. Carolyn Strange, "From Modern Babylon to a City upon a Hill: The Toronto Social Survey Commission of 1915 and the Search for Sexual Order in the City," Roger Hall, William Westfall, and Laurel Sefton MacDowell (eds.), *Patterns of the Past: Interpreting Ontario's History* (Toronto: Dundurn Press, 1988), 265; Greg Marquis, "The Early Twentieth Century Toronto Police Institution" (PhD thesis, Queen's University, 1986), 72.

72. See Andrée Lévesque, "Putting It Out: Social Reformers' Efforts to Extinguish the Red Light in Montreal" (Simone de Beauvoir Institute, Concordia University), 8–9. This paper was published in *Urban History Review* 17, No. 3, 1989, 191–202.

73. See John McLaren, "'White Slavers': The Reform of Canada's Prostitution Laws and Patterns of Enforcement, 1900–1920s" (unpublished paper, meeting of American Society for Legal History, Toronto, 1986).

74. Henry Feingold, *Zion in America: The Jewish Experience from Colonial Times to the Present* (New York: Hippocrene Books, 1974), 139–41. Arthur A. Goren, *New York Jews and the Quest for Community: The Kehillah Experiment, 1908–1922* (New York: Columbia University Press, 1970), Chapter 7.

75. "History and Development of the Big Brother Movement, Toronto (Jewish Branch)," Arthur D. Hart (ed.), *The Jew in Canada* (Montreal: 1926), 450.

76. Peter Oliver, *Unlikely Tory: The Life and Politics of Allan Grossman* (Toronto: Lester & Orpen Dennys, 1985), 2.

77. Quoted in ibid., 3.

78. Elspeth Cameron, *Irving Layton: A Portrait* (Toronto: Stoddart Publishing Co. 1985), 17–18.

79. Ibid., 25.

80. Doug Smith, *Joe Zuken, Citizen and Socialist* (Toronto: James Lorimer, 1990), 8–9.

81. Irving Abella, "Portrait of a Jewish Professional Revolutionary: The Recollections of Joshua Gershman," *Labour/Le Travail* 2 (1977), 189–91.

82. Usher Caplan, *Like One that Dreamed: A Portrait of A.M. Klein* (Toronto: McGraw-Hill Ryerson, 1982), 18–19.

83. David Lewis, *The Good Fight: Political Memoirs 1909–1958* (Toronto: Macmillan of Canada, 1981), Chapter one.

84. Ibid., 14.

85. Ari L. Fridkis, "Desertion in the American Jewish Immigrant Family: the Work of the National Desertion Bureau in Cooperation with the Industrial Removal Office," *AJH* 1981, 293.

86. American Jewish Historical Society Archives, Waltham, Mass. (Brandeis University) IRO, Box 80, Winnipeg ICA, 1905–1913, File, Assistant Manager to Max Heppner, 3 Jan. 1913.

87. Ibid., Heppner to David Bressler, 7 Apr. 1908.

88. Ibid., Heppner to IRO, 24 Aug. 1908.

89. Ibid., Heppner to IRO, 24 Aug. 1908.

90. Ibid., A. Samuel to David Bressler, 12 Sept. 1906.

91. Ibid., A. Samuel to David Bressler, 13 Sept. 1906.

92. Ibid., Box 70, Toronto 1912–1914, Associated Hebrew Charities File. P. Shulman to D.M. Bressler, 6 Aug. 1913.

93. CJAM, JCA. L 7e, "Report of Baron de Hirsch Labor and Immigration Bureau," 11 Dec. 1907.

94. Baycrest Terrace Memoirs Group, *From Our Lives: Memoirs, Life Stories, Episodes and Recollections* (Toronto: Mosaic Press, 1979).

95. Ibid., 2–4.

96. Ibid., 21, 23.

97. Ibid., 46, 48.

98. Ibid., 40.

99. Ibid., 123.

100. Paula J. Draper and Janice B. Karlinsky, "Abraham's Daughters: Women, Charity and Power in the Canadian Jewish Community," Jean Burnet (ed.), *Looking into My Sister's Eyes: An Exploration in Women's History* (Toronto: Multicultural History Society of Ontario, 1986), 77.

101. Ibid., 78–9.

102. Ruth A. Frager, "Uncloaking Vested Interests: Class, Ethnicity, and Gender in the Jewish Labour Movement in Toronto, 1900–1939" (York University, Ph.D. thesis, 1986), iv.

CHAPTER TEN

1. Benjamin G. Sack, *The History of the Jews in Canada* (Montreal: Harvest House, 1965), 218–20.

2. Leon Goldman, "History of Zionism in Canada," Arthur D. Hart (ed.), *The Jew in Canada* (Montreal: Canadian Jewish Publications Ltd., 1926), 291; *EJ*, XIV: 343, VIII: 1475.

3. Goldman, "History of Zionism in Canada," 291-2; Stephen Speisman, *The Jews of Toronto: A History to 1937* (Toronto: McClelland and Stewart, 1979), 201; Arthur A. Chiel, *The Jews in Manitoba: A Social History* (Toronto: University of Toronto Press, 1961), 154.

4. Stuart A. Cohen, *English Zionists and British Jews: The Communal Politics of Anglo-Jewry, 1895–1920* (Princeton: 1982), xi, 321–23.

5. Gideon Shimoni, *Jews and Zionism: The South African Experience (1910–1967)* (Capetown: Oxford University Press, 1980), 2.

6. See Yonathan Shapiro, *Leadership of the American Zionist Organization, 1897–1930* (Urbana: University of Illinois Press, 1971), 6.

7. Michael Brown, "Divergent Paths: Early Zionism in Canada and the United States," *JSS* 44, Spring 1982, 149–68.

8. Hart, *Jew in Canada*, 314.

9. Carman Miller, "Alexander Abraham de Sola," *DCB* XI: 253–55.

10. NAC, MG 29C 95, Clarence de Sola Papers, Microfilm Reel A913, Diary of Clarence Isaac de Sola.

11. University of London, Mocatta Library, Rabbi Dr. Moses Gaster papers.

12. Bernard Figler, *Lillian and Archie Freiman, Biographies* (Ottawa: Northern Printing and Lithographing Co., 1962) 202–03.

13. See "Early Zionism in Toronto," Louis Rasminsky (ed.), *Hadassah Jubilee Volume, Tenth Anniversary Toronto* (Toronto, 1927), 135–48, 174–78; Dov Joseph, interview with G. Tulchinsky, 2 Jan. 1980; Hart, *Jew in Canada*, 319.

14. Harry Gutkin, *Journey into Our Heritage* (Toronto: Lester & Orpen Dennys, 1980), 179; Hart, *Jew in Canada*, 318.

15. Goldman, "Zionism in Canada," 295.

16. Hart, *Jew in Canada*, 315–16.

17. Gutkin, *Journey into Our Heritage*, 179; Hart, *Jew in Canada*, 318.

18. CZA, KKL 5/359, "Federation of Zionist Societies of Canada, Financial Statements and Record of Zionist Achievement in Canada, Submitted to the Seventeenth Convention." [1921]

19. Louis Rosenberg, *Canada's Jews: A Social and Economic Study of the Jews in Canada* (Montreal: CJC. Bureau of Social and Economic Research, 1939), 308.

20. NAC, MG 28, U81, Zionist Organization of Canada, Vol. 5, 473–74.

21. CZA, A 119/200–02, de Sola to Nordau, 28 Feb. 1910.

22. CZA, Z2/39, Clarence de Sola to Zionistisches Centralbureau, 8 Nov. 1910.

23. CZA, Z1/244, Jacob de Haas to Theodore Herzl, 14 Apr. 1903.

24. NAC, MG 28, U81, Vol. 5, 94–95, Richard Gottheil to Clarence de Sola, March, 1899.

25. CZA, Z4/1405, Goldman to Levin, 17 Dec. 1919. When similar temporary co-operation of Canadian with American Zionists was undertaken during the Second World War, the Canadian leaders and officials were reluctant partners and, when conditions changed, immediately broke the ties.

26. CZA, Z4/1405, Goldman to Zionist Organization, Central Office, London, 25 Feb. 1920.

27. CZA, Z4/1405, Goldman to B. Goldberg, 24 Dec. 1919.

28. *JT*, 30 Sept. 1898.

29. Ibid. Zionism, the *Times* author argued, could easily arouse more antisemitism, because it was essentially unpatriotic.

30. NAC, MG 28, U81, Vol. 5, 19.

31. CZA, de Sola to de Haas, 12 Feb. 1903.

32. NAC, MG 28, U81, Vol. 5, 201.

33. *Maccabean*, 20 Jan. 1911.

34. CZA, KKL 1/20 (1907–1913); A. Fallick to de Sola, 18 Oct. 1908.

35. *Maccabean*, 20 Jan. 1911.

36. CZA, KKL 1/21, de Sola to the Chief Bureau of the Jewish National Fund, Cologne, 13 July 1908.

37. *Maccabean*, 20 Jan. 1911.

38. Yossi Katz, "The Plan and Efforts of the Jews of Winnipeg to Purchase Land and to Establish an Agricultural Settlement in Palestine before World War One," *CJHSJ* 5, No. 1, Spring 1981, 1–16.

39. CZA, Z4/18, undated and unsigned letter to Nahum Sokolff, London.

40. A letter from Col. C.S. MacInnes to General Officer Commanding, Military District No. 4, Montreal, P.K., 5 Mar. 1918. Quoted in Zachariah Kay, "A Note on Canada and the Formation of the Jewish Legion," *JSS* 29, No. 3, July 1967, 173.

41. Shabtai Teveth, "The 'Two Sons' in America: David Ben-Gurion, Yitchak Ben-Zvi, and the Formation of Hechalutz, 1915–1916," Jacob R. Marcus and Abraham J. Peck (ed.), *Studies in the American Jewish Experience* (Cincinnati: American Jewish Archives, 1981, 2 volumes.) II, 127–201, 144.

42. Quoted in ibid., 151.

43. Quoted in ibid., 164.

44. Izhak Ben-Zvi, *The Hebrew Battalion's Letters* (Jerusalem: Yad Izhak Ben-Zvi, 1969), 61–62.

45. Joseph Ben-Shlomo, "Jewish Legion," *EJ* X: 74.

46. Zachariah Kay, *Canada and Palestine: The Politics of Non-Commitment* (Jerusalem: Israel Universities Press, 1978), 41.

47. *KA*, 22 Dec. 1908.

48. For the history of the Poale Zion in Canada, see Simon Belkin's *Di Poale Zion Bavegung in Kanada: 1904–1920* (Montreal: Actions Committee of the Labour Zionist Movement in Canada, 1956). The Mizrachi movement was begun in Toronto in 1911 and spread to other parts of Canada. Bernard Figler, "Zionism in Canada," Raphael Patai (ed.), *An Encyclopedia of Zionism and Israel* (New York: Herzl Press–McGraw Hill, 1971, 2 volumes), I: 174–79, 175. A Mizrachi convention of delegates from across North America took place in Montreal in December 1919, *KA*, 5 Dec. 1919.

49. George G. Greene, "The Hadassah Organization in Canada," Rasminsky, *Hadassah Jubilee*, 136. See also Esther Waterman (ed.), *Golden Jubilee: Canadian Hadassah – WIZO 1917–1967* (Montreal: 1967), 30–31.

50. CZA, Z4/1402, Leon Goldman to Chaim Weizmann, 8 Apr. 1919.

51. Greene, "Hadassah," 145.

52. Greene, "The Hadassah Organization in Canada," Hart, *Jew in Canada*, 287.

53. Ibid., 285.

54. Dov Joseph interview with G. Tulchinsky, 2 Jan. 1980.

55. Moe Levitt, "The Federation of Young Judaea of Canada," Hart, *Jew in Canada*, 289.

56. On the general character of Zionist youth organizations, see the excellent analysis by Samuel Grand, "A History of Zionist Youth Organization in the United States to 1940" (Columbia University, Ph.D. thesis, 1958).

57. *CJC*, Nov. 1917.

58. Carl Berger, *The Sense of Power: Studies in Ideas of Canadian Imperialism, 1867–1914* (Toronto: University of Toronto Press, 1970), *passim*.

59. Rasminsky, *Hadassah Jubilee*, 3.

60. See Veronica Strong-Boag, *The Parliament of Women: The National Council of Women of Canada, 1893–1929* (Ottawa: National Museum of Man, Mercury Series, 1976, History Division Paper, No. 18).

61. Rasminsky, *Hadassah Jubilee*, 169.

CHAPTER ELEVEN

1. From "The Sweatshop," by Morris Rosenfeld, in Irving Howe and Eliezer Greenberg (eds.), *A Treasury of Yiddish Poetry* (New York: Holt Rinehart and Winston, 1969), 78.

2, *Journal of Commerce*, 23 Feb. 1906.

3. See Charles J. Stowell, *Studies in Trade Unionism in the Custom Tailoring Trade* (Bloomington, Illinois, 1913), Chapter 1.

4. NAC, MG 28, I, *The Tailor in America* (official organ of the Journeymen Tailors' Union), 265, Microfilm Reel M5277.

5. Gregory S. Kealey and Bryan D. Palmer, *Dreaming of What Might Be: The Knights of Labour in Ontario, 1880–1900* (Toronto: New Hogtown Press, 1987), 102–03, 138–39.

6. See Jacques Rouillard, "Les travailleurs juifs de la confection (1910-1980) *Labour/ Le Travailleur* 8/9, 1981/82, Spring, 253-259.

7. Jean Hamèlin, *Répertoire des Grèves dans la Province de Québec au dix-neuvième siècle* (Montréal: les Presses de l'école des hautes études commerciales, 1970), 165–66.

8. *Montreal Daily Star*, 7 Sept. 1900.

9. Ibid., 8 Sept. 1900.

10. Hamelin, *Répertoire des Grèves*, 165-166.

11. NAC, RG 27, Department of Labour, Vol. 301, File 37.

12. *La Presse*, 12 Mar., 11 Apr. 1904.

13. See *La Presse*, 11 Feb. to 20 Apr., 1910, Hart, *Jew in Canada*, 343.

14. *Montreal Star*, 7 Mar. 1904.

15. Ibid., 10 May 1904.

16. Ibid., 11 May 1904.

17. Ibid., 13 May 1904.

18. The UGWA participated in Socialist Labour Party meetings in Montreal as early as 1907. *Montreal Daily Star*, 11, 29 Apr. 1907. These representatives may well have been members of the Arbeiter Ring, a socialist group which was organized in Montreal in 1907 as the Meyer London Branch (No. 151) of the New York–based Arbeiter Ring; Meyer Semiatycki, "Communism in One Constituency: The Communist Party and Jewish Community of Montreal, with Particular reference to the Election of Fred Rose of Parliament in 1943 and 1945" (York University, unpublished paper, 1977), 17.

19. RG 27, Vol. 295, File 298.

20. *Montreal Star*, 31 Aug. 1907.

21. RG 27, Vol. 297, File 3199.

22. *Montreal Star*, 6, 13 Mar. 1908.

23. NAC, RG 27, Vol. 298, Files 1123; 3309; 3310; 3392; 3402; 3434.

24. Harry Gale, "The Jewish Labour Movement in Winnipeg," *JHSWC* 1, June 1970, 3.

25. Hart, *Jew in Canada, passim.*

26. Ibid., 339.

27. Montreal *Gazette*, 11 June 1912.

28. *Montreal Witness*, 29 May 1912.

29. *Montreal Star*, 6 June 1912.

30. Montreal *Gazette*, 18 May 1912.

31. *Montreal Star*, 13 June 1912.

32. Montreal *Gazette*, 11 June 1912.

33. *Montreal Witness*, 3 July 1912.

34. See Marcus L. Hansen and John B. Brebner, *The Mingling of the Canadian and American Peoples* (New Haven: Yale University Press, 1940), 217, 241, 262, which treats the interchange of population and the periodic migration of skilled workers to Canada.

35. *Gazette*, 11 June 1912.

36. Bernard Figler and David Rome, *Hananiah Meir Caiserman: A Biography* (Montreal: Northern Printing and Lithographing Co., 1962), 28; Rouillard, "Travailleurs Juifs," 254.

37. Ibid., 37.

38. "Labour Zionist Organization of Canada," Eli Gottesman (ed.), *Canadian Jewish Reference Book and Directory* (Toronto: 1963), 378.

39. Ibid., 39; See Morris Winchevsky, *Stories of the Struggle* (Chicago: 1908).

40. RG 27, Vol. 300, File 3509, newspaper clipping, n.d.

41. Ibid., *Ottawa Citizen*, n.d.

42. Simon Belkin, "Reuben Brainin's Memories," *Canadian Jewish Year Book* II (Montreal: 1940-41); Hart, *Jew in Canada*, 456.

43. During a very bitter and protracted strike against Vineberg & Co., in 1914, Brainin acted as chairman of an all-Jewish arbitration board which brought the dispute to an end. NAC, RG 27, Vol. 303, File 112, newspaper clipping, *Montreal Herald*, 8 Jan. 1914.

44. RG 27, Dept. of Labour, Strike files, Vol. 300, No. 3509, *Gazette* clipping, 4 July 1912.

45. Hubert S. Nelli, "Ethnic Group Assimilation: The Italian Experience," Kenneth T. Jackson and Stanley K. Schultz (eds.), *Cities in American History* (New York: Knopf, 1972), 199–215, 200.

46. See H. Noveck, *Fun Meine Yunge Yorn* (New York, 1957), 180–82.

47. See *Les Midinettes 1937–1962: Union des Ouvriers de la Robe* (Montreal: Bureau Conjoint, Montréal Union Internationale des Ouvriers du Vêtement pour Dames (FAT-CIO-CTC), 1962).

48. RG 27, Vol. 299, File 3455.

49. Ibid., File 3495.

50. Ibid., File 3455.

51. Daniel Hiebert, "Discontinuity and the Emergence of Flexible Production: Garment Production in Toronto, 1901–1931," *Economic Geography*, July 1990, 225.

52. Ibid., 242.

53. Interview with Max Enkin, Cambridge Clothing, 15 July 1976.

54. See J. Terry Copp, *The Anatomy of Poverty: The Condition of the Working Class in Montreal, 1897–1929* (Toronto: McClelland and Stewart, 1974), 140–141.

55. H. Trachtenberg, "The 1912 Lockout-Strike at the T. Eaton Company Limited, Toronto," (York University, Ph.D. research paper, Sept. 1973), 1.

56. RG 27, Vol. 301, File 8.

57. Ibid., File 26.

58. Ibid., File 37.

59. Ibid., Vol. 297, File 3221.

60. Lewis Levitzki Lorwin, *The Women's Garment Workers, A History of the International Ladies' Garment Workers Union*, (New York: B.W. Huebsch, 1925), 222, 587.

61. RG 27, Vol. 299, File 3439.

62. RG 27, Vol. 303, Files 9 and 25.

63. Henry Pelling, *American Labor* (Chicago: University of Chicago Press, 1960), 121.

64. New York office of the Amalgamated Clothing Workers of America, *Documentary History* 1914–16, 104.

65. Harold A. Logan, *Trade Unions in Canada* (Toronto: University of Toronto Press, 1948), 214.

66. *Montreal Joint Board A.C.W.A.: from Drudgery to Dignity 1915–1955* (Montreal, 1955), 12.

67. Logan, *Trade Unions in Canada*, 214.

68. RG 27, Vol. 304, Files 16, 17.

69. Ibid., File 15.

70. Ibid., Files 16, 18.

71. Ibid., File 19.

72. Ibid., File 18a; newspaper clipping, *Montreal Mail*, 22 Dec. 1916.

73. Ibid., Brownlee to Brown, 6 Jan. 1917.

74. Ibid., newspaper clipping Montreal *Gazette*, 16 Jan. 1917.

75. *Montreal Mail*, 22 Dec. 1916; Montreal *Gazette*, 5 Jan. 1917.

76. RG 27, Vol. 304, File 18A, newspaper clipping, *Montreal Star*, 5 Jan. 1919.

77. RG 27, Vol. 304, File 17 (35).

78. *La Presse*, 20 Feb. 1917.

79. David Brody, *Workers in Industrial America: Essays on the Twentieth Century Struggle* (New York: Oxford, 1980), viii.

80. See Documentary History, 1918–20, 98, for list of employers' complaints against the union.

81. Michael Bliss, *A Canadian Millionaire: the Business Life and Times of J.W. Flavelle* (Toronto: Macmillan, 1974).

82. Hirsh Wolofsky, *Journey of My Life*, (Montreal: Eagle Publishing Co., 1945), 80.

83. See *Amalgam 1918*, 88.

84. Mathew Josephson, *Sidney Hillman, Statesman of American Labor* (Garden City, New Jersey: Doubleday, 1952), 88.

85. See Robert H. Babcock, *Gompers in Canada: A Study in American Continentalism before the First World War* (Toronto: University of Toronto Press, 1974).

86. See Gregory S. Kealey, *Toronto Workers Respond to Industrial Capitalism, 1867–1892* (Toronto: University of Toronto Press, 1980), *passim*; Bryan D. Palmer, *A Culture in Conflict: Skilled Workers and Industrial Capitalism in Hamilton Ontario, 1860–1914* (Montreal: McGill-Queen's University Press, 1979), 243–44.

87. See Henry J. Tobias, *The Jewish Bund in Russia, from Its Origins to 1905* (Stanford, 1972).

88. *Documentary History, 1918–1920*, 94.
89. Ibid., 96.
90. Ibid., 97.
91. Ibid., 101.
92. Ibid., 101–02.
93. RG 27, Vol. 306, File 17 (35), Report to Dept. Lab., 27 Feb. 1917.
94. *Documentary History, 1918–1920*, 102.
95. *La Presse*, 2 Feb. 1917.
96. *Le Devoir*, 21 Feb. 1917.
97. Ibid., 22 Feb. 1917.
98. Ibid., 22 Jan., 12 Feb. 1917.
99. Ibid., 30 Jan. 1917.
100. Ibid., 9 Feb. 1917.
101. N. Maurice Davidson, "Montreal's Dominance of the Men's Fine Clothing Industry" (University of Western Ontario, M.A. thesis, 1969), 2–4.
102. *La Presse*, 3 Avril, 1903; 24 Mars 1908; 2 Aout, 1909; 11 Mai, 1912.
103. Miriam Waddington (comp.), *The Collected Poems of A.M. Klein* (Toronto: McGraw-Hill Ryerson, 1974), 272.
104. *KA*, 24 Dec. 1916; 11, 12, 13, 14, 18, 19, 21, 26, 30 Jan; 1, 2, 5, 6, 11 Feb. 1917.
105. Ibid., 11, 13 Jan. 1917: See *Documentary History, 1918–1920*, 90.
106. *KA*, 11 Feb. 1917.
107. Ibid., 15, 16 Feb. 1917.
108. See Irving Howe, *World of Our Fathers: The Journey of the East European Jews to America and the Life They Found and Made* (New York: Harcourt, Brace, Jovanovich, 1976).
109. See Wolofsky, *Journey of My Life*.
110. *KA*, 3 Jan. 1917.
111. J.D. Borthwick, *History and Biographical Gazeteer of Montreal to the Year 1892* (Montreal, 1892), 465–69.
112. See Mark Zborowski, Elizabeth Herzen, *Life is with People: The Culture of the Shtetl* (New York: Schocken Books, 1972).
113. See Semiatycki, "Communism in One Constituency."
114. *Montreal Daily Star*, 23, 27 June 1904.
115. Hart, *Jew in Canada*, 121–22, 125.
116. "In those days [pressers] were very religious middle-age Jews, with long beards most of them immigrants recently arrived from Europe . . . the manufacturers and the foreman thought that these people would not be interested in trade unionism and that with a little bit of fear and pressure, they could keep them from mixing up with active members of the Union. But they were mistaken." Dave Cohen, "The Story of the Pressers," *From Drudgery to Dignity*, 18.
117. *Montreal Daily Star*, 28 Aug., 3, 4 Sept. 1907, 9 April 1908.
118. Hart, *Jew in Canada*, 186.
119. *Documentary History, 1918*, 103.
120. M. Brecher, "Patterns of Accommodation in the Men's Garment Industry of Quebec, 1914–1954," W.D. Woods (ed.), *Patterns of Industrial Dispute Settlement in Five Canadian Industries* (McGill University Industrial Relations Centre, 1958), 100.

121. Louis Rosenberg, *Canada's Jews: A Social and Economic Study of the Jews in Canada* (Montreal: CJC. Bureau of Social and Economic Research, 1939), 176.

122. Rosenberg, *Canada's Jews,* 177.

123. Ezra Mendelsohn, *The Class Struggle in the Pale: The Formative Years of Jewish Workers' Movements in Tsarist Russia* (London: Cambridge University Press, 1970).

124. Linda Kealey, "Canadian Socialism and the Woman Question, 1900–1914," *Labour/Le Travail* 13 (Spring 1984), 81, 91, 94.

125. Donald Avery, *"Dangerous Foreigners": European Immigrant Workers and Labour Radicalism in Canada, 1896–1932* (Toronto: McClelland and Stewart, 1979), 75.

126. Ibid., 80.

127. Ibid., 82.

128. Ibid., 88.

129. Barbara Roberts, *Whence They Came: Deportation From Canada, 1900–1935* (Ottawa: University of Ottawa Press, 1988), 95.

CHAPTER TWELVE

1. Arnold Haultain, *Goldwin Smith, His Life and Opinions* (Toronto: McClelland & Goodchild, 1910), 68, 125, 146, 189, 206.

2. See Goldwin Smith, *Essays on Questions of the Day: Political and Social* (New York: Macmillan, 1893), 183–220, 263–308.

3. Goldwin Smith, "England's Abandonment of the Protectorate of Turkey," *Contemporary Review,* 31 Feb. 1878, 619.

4. Goldwin Smith, "The Jews. A Deferred Rejoinder," *Nineteenth Century,* Nov. 1882, 708–09.

5. See Jaroslav Petryshyn, *Peasants in the Promised Land: Canada and the Ukrainians, 1891–1914* (Toronto: James Lorimer Press, 1985), Chapter 7.

6. See James S. Woodsworth, *Strangers within Our Gates, Or Coming Canadians* (Toronto: The Missionary Society of the Methodist Church, Canada. The Young People's Forward Movement Dept., 1909), 111–159.

7. David J. Bercuson, *Confrontation at Winnipeg: Labour, Industrial Relations and the General Strike* (Montreal: McGill-Queen's Press, 1974), 126–27; Kenneth McNaught, *A Prophet in Politics: A Biography of J.S. Woodsworth* (Toronto: University of Toronto Press, 1959), 119, 135–36. Henry Trachtenberg, "The Winnipeg Jewish Community and Politics: The Interwar Years, 1919–1939," *Historical and Scientific Society of Manitoba,* Transactions, Ser. III, Nos. 34 and 35 (1977–78; 1978–79), 115–53, 119–20.

8. See W. Peter Ward, *White Canada Forever: Popular Attitudes and Public Policy toward Orientals in British Columbia* (Montreal: McGill-Queen's University Press, 1978), 197, *passim.*

9. Louis Rosenberg, *Canada's Jews: A Social and Economic Study of the Jews in Canada* (Montreal: CJC. Bureau of Social and Economic Research, 1939).

10. See Stephen A. Speisman, *The Jews of Toronto: A History to 1937* (Toronto: McClelland and Stewart, 1979), 67. See Gerald Tulchinsky, "Immigration and Charity in the Montreal Jewish Community to 1890," *Histoire Sociale–Social History* 16, No. 33 (November), 370–71.

11. See Simon I. Belkin, *Through Narrow Gates: A Review of Jewish Immigration, Colonization and*

Immigrant Aid Work in Canada (Montreal: CJC and Jewish Colonization Association, 1966), *passim*.

12. See John Zucchi, *The Italians in Toronto* (Montreal: McGill-Queen's University Press, 1989), and Anthony W. Rasporich, *For a Better Life: A History of the Croatians in Canada* (Toronto: McClelland and Stewart, 1982, Generations: A History of the Canadian Peoples).

13. Bernard Figler, *Biography of Sam Jacobs, Member of Parliament* (Ottawa: private, 1959); Speisman, *Jews of Toronto*, 251.

14. Todd M. Endelman, *The Jews of Georgian England, 1714–1830: Tradition and Change in a Liberal Society* (Philadelphia: JPSA, 1979), 86–87.

15. Haultain, *Goldwin Smith*, 85.

16. Goldwin Smith, *Reminiscences*, edited by Arnold Haultain (New York: Macmillan, 1910), 380; "England's Abandonment of the Protectorate of Turkey," *Contemporary Review* 31, Feb. 1878, 603–21.

17. Ibid., 619.

18. Goldwin Smith, "Can Jews Be Patriots?", *Nineteenth Century* 3, May 1878, 877.

19. Ibid., 884.

20. Ibid.

21. Jacob Katz, *From Prejudice to Destruction: Anti-Semitism 1870–1933* (Cambridge: Harvard University Press, 1980), 260–72.

22. Moses Zimmerman, "From Radicalism to Antisemitism," *Antisemitism through the Ages*, Shmuel Almog (ed.), (London: Pergamon Press, 1988, Vidal Sassoon International Center for the Study of Antisemitism, The Hebrew University of Jerusalem), 264.

23. "The Jews. A Deferred Rejoinder," *Nineteenth Century*, 707.

24. *The Bystander* 3, 1883, 250–52.

25. Queen's University. Goldwin Smith Papers. Laister to Smith, 12 Feb. 1882; "Many thanks for the cheque . . . the money is welcome and will help to get me a holiday this year . . .", Laister to Smith, 19 May 1882.

26. *The Bystander*, 3 July 1883, 251.

27. *Weekly Sun*, 29 July 1897.

28. Haultain, *Correspondence*, 462.

29. See *The Bystander*, 3 July 1883, 250–52.

30. "The Jews. A Deferred Rejoinder," 706.

31. *The Bystander*, 3 July 1883, 251.

32. Ibid., 251–52.

33. See Kenneth Bourne and D. Cameron Watt (General eds.), *British Documents on Foreign Affairs: Reports and Papers From the Mid-Nineteenth Century to the First World War, Series A, Russia, 1859–1914*; Dominic Lieven (ed.), *Russia, 1881–1905* (Washington: University Publications of America, 1983), 1–65; "The Jews. A Deferred Rejoinder," 692.

34. *The Bystander*, 1 Aug. 1880, 445–46.

35. *The Bystander*, 1 Mar. 1880, 156.

36. *Weekly Sun*, 15 July 1897.

37. *The Bystander*, 3 July 1883, 251.

38. "The Jews. A Deferred Rejoinder," 688–94; Goldwin Smith, "New Light on the Jewish Question," *North American Review* 153, Aug. 1891, Part 2, 129–43, 131.

39. Ibid., 133.
40. *Weekly Sun*, 27 Mar. 1907.
41. Goldwin Smith, "Is It Religious Persecution?", *The Independent* 60, 1906, 1474–78.
42. Ibid., 1476–77.
43. *The Week*, 24 Feb. 1894. If, as Smith suggested, the state should forbid the Jewish rite of circumcision because "it has nothing to do with religious opinion, nor in repressing it would religious liberty be infringed," then, Grant argued, the state would have the right to "forbid the Christian rite of baptism on the same grounds." However, "the law against it [circumcision] would be a dead letter. Their [the Jews'] respect for us would be gone forever, and our self-respect would go at the same time." As for Smith's demand that the Jew forget his allegiance to Zion and Jerusalem, Grant observed: "Why should he be obliged to forget the city that is bound up in his mind with everything that he esteems glorious in the past as well as eternally sacred? The Jew that forgets Jerusalem is not likely to be a better citizen of the country in which he lives." I am grateful to Dr. Barry Mack for this reference.
44. *The Week*, 18 Feb. 1897; *Farmer's Sun*, 18 May, 1 June, 28 Sept. 1904; See John Higham, *Strangers in the Land: Patterns of American Nativism, 1869–1925* (New York: Atheneum, 1975), Chapter 4.
45. *Weekly Sun*, 29 July 1897; 28 Aug. 1907.
46. Naomi Cohen, *Encounter With Emancipation: The German Jews in the United States, 1830–1914* (Philadelphia: JPSA, 1984), 278.
47. NAC. Mackenzie King Diary, 20 Feb. 1946. I am indebted to Professor Jack Granatstein for this reference.
48. *Morning Chronicle*, 20 Dec. 1878. In reporting this story, the *Chronicle* stated that one of these "Jews and Shavers" was employed by the Nova Scotia government, and another was appointed to the Provincial Legislative Council. I am grateful to Professor Ian McKay for this reference.
49. Phyllis M. Senese, "Antisemitic Dreyfusards: The Confused Western Canadian Press," unpublished paper accepted for publication in Alan T. Davies' forthcoming anthology, *Antisemitism in Canada: History and Interpretation* (Waterloo: Wilfrid Laurier University Press).
50. *Chronicle*, 8 Aug. 1903; *Halifax Herald*, 30 June 1904. I am grateful to Professor Ian McKay for these references.
51. Mariana Valverde, *The Age of Light, Soap, and Water: Moral Reform in English Canada, 1885–1925* (Toronto: McClelland and Stewart, 1991), 56.
52. Ibid., 106.
53. *Halifax Herald*, 10 June 1913.
54. Terence Craig, *Racial Attitudes in English Canadian Fiction 1905–1980* (Waterloo: Wilfrid Laurier University Press, 1987), 34.
55. Hilda Neatby, *Queen's University, Volume I 1841–1917, And Not To Yield*, Frederick W. Gibson and Roger Graham (eds.) (Montreal: McGill-Queen's University Press, 1978), 265.
56. *CJC*, 18 April 1919.
57. Ibid.
58. University of Toronto Archives, A67–0007, Arthur L. Smith to Godfrey J.H. Lloyd, 5 July 1911.

59. Ibid., Godfrey J.H. Lloyd to Falconer, 13 July 1911.

60. Ibid., James H. Mavor to Falconer, 20 July 1911.

61. A.I. Willinsky, *A Doctor's Memoirs* (Toronto: Macmillan, 1960), 25. He was forced to travel abroad in order to qualify, though by 1918 he became a department head at the Toronto Western Hospital.

62. Stanley B. Frost, *McGill University, For the Advancement of Learning* Vol. II, 1895–1971 (Montreal: McGill-Queen's University Press, 1980), 128.

63. Paul R. Dekar, "From Jewish Mission to Inner City Mission: The Scott Mission and Its Antecedents in Toronto, 1908 to 1964," John S. Moir and C.T. McIntire (eds.), *Canadian Protestant and Catholic Missions, 1820–1860s: Historical Essays in Honour of John Webster Grant* (New York: Peter Lang, 1988, Toronto Studies in Religion, Vol. 3), 247.

64. See Speisman, *Jews of Toronto*, Chapter 9.

65. Quoted in Dekar, "Jewish Mission," 248.

66. Ibid., 250.

67. Paul-André Linteau, René Durocher, Jean-Claude Robert, *Quebec: A History 1867–1929* (Toronto: James Lorimer, 1983), 44.

68. Ibid., 47.

69. M. Brown, "France, the Catholic Church, the French Canadians and Jews before 1914," (unpublished paper).

70. Ernest Nolte, *Three Faces of Fascism: Action Française, Italian Fascism, and National Socialism* (New York: New American Library, 1969), 77.

71. See Gordon N. Emery, "The Lord's Day Act of 1906 and the Sabbath Observance Question," J.M. Bumsted, ed., *Documentary Problems in Canadian History*, 2 volumes (Georgetown: Irwin Dorsey, 1968) II, 37-40.

72. Canada. House of Commons. Debates. 1906, 5637–8.

73. Pierre Anctil, *Le Devoir, les Juifs et l'Immigration, de Bourassa à Laurendeau* (Montreal: Institut Québécois de Recherche sur la Culture, 1988), 25.

74. *Le Devoir*, 25 Feb. 1913; 15 Apr. 1914.

75. Gordon N. Emery, "The Lord's Day Act of 1906 and the Sabbath Observance Question," Jack M. Bumsted, ed., *Documentary Problems in Canadian History: Post Confederation*, 2 volumes (Georgetown: Irwin Dorsey, 1968) II, 39.

76. *Le Devoir*, 29 Jan. 1913.

77. Ibid., 7 Feb. 1916.

78. Arthur D. Hart (ed.), *The Jew in Canada* (Montreal: Canadian Jewish Publications Ltd., 1926), 499–500.

79. CJCAM, William Nadler, "The Jewish–Protestant School Question," manuscript, 1925.

80. *JT*, 6 Dec. 1901.

81. Linteau *et al.*, *Quebec: A History*, 209.

82. In place of it they received a mark which was the average class mark of the Christian children. When they challenged the Protestant board on its stand, the Jewish defenders were tactless enough to make an issue of this mark by arguing that it was unfair since Jews would undoubtedly have done better than the class average. Even if this were true, to advance the argument in the highly charged atmosphere perhaps demonstrated that some Jews were not too clever after all.

83. Quoted in Nadler, "School Question," 9.

84. Maxwell Goldstein, "The Status of the Jew in the Schools of Canada," Hart, *Jew in Canada*, 497.

85. Quoted in Nadler, "School Question," 10.

86. Ibid.

87. *Statutes of Quebec*. 3 Edward vii, chapter 16.

88. Nadler, "School Question," 12.

89. Ibid.

90. Hart, *Jew in Canada*, 497.

91. Nadler, "School Question," 13.

92. Ibid.

93. *JT*, 30 July 1909.

94. Ibid., 2 Apr. 1905.

95. Ibid., 7 Jan. 1910.

96. Ibid., 12, 20 June 1913.

97. *KA*, 1 July 1913.

98. *JT*, 27 Aug. 1909.

99. *KA*, 12 Aug. 1913.

100. *JT*, 27 Aug. 1909.

101. David Rome, compiler, "The Plamondon Case and S.W. Jacobs," Part 1, CJCA, new series, No. 26 (Montreal: National Archives, CJC, 1982), 7–18.

102. *La Libre Parole*, 31 July, 1909.

103. Ibid., 30 Oct. 1909.

104. Ibid., 4 Dec. 1909.

105. Ibid., 1 Jan. 1910.

106. Ibid., 12 Feb. 1910.

107. Ibid., 26 Feb. 1910.

108. Ibid., 26 Mar. 1910.

109. Rome, "Plamondon," 14.

110. NAC, RG 13, CLXI, S. Glazer to A.D. Ellsworth, 29 Mar. 1910.

111. Cited in Rome, "Plamondon," 86.

112. *JT*, 30 May, 1913.

113. Ibid.

114. Shmuel Ettinger, "The Modern Period," H.H. Ben Sasson (ed.), *A History of the Jewish People* (Cambridge, Mass.: Harvard University Press, 1976), 887.

115. Ibid., 888.

116. *JT*, 11 July 1913.

117. *JT*, 27 June 1913.

118. See Rome, "The Plamondon Case and S.W. Jacobs," Part 2, Canadian Jewish Archives, new series, No. 27 (Montreal: National Archives, CJC, 1982).

119. *KA*, 14, 26 May 1913.

120. Ibid., 26, 27 Oct. 1913.

121. *JT*, 22 Oct. 1913.

122. Antonio Huot, *La Question Juive: Quelques Observations sur la Question de Meurtre Rituel* (Quebec: Editions de l'Action Sociale Catholique, 1914), 20.

CHAPTER THIRTEEN

1. Arthur D. Hart (ed.), *The Jew in Canada* (Montreal: Canadian Jewish Publications Ltd., 1926), 108.

2. Ibid., 87.

3. Ibid., 92.

4. Ibid., 126.

5. Ibid., 130.

6. Ibid., 161, 167.

7. Ibid., 186.

8. Ibid., 175.

9. Steven J. Zipperstein, *The Jews of Odessa: A Cultural History, 1794–1881* (Stanford: Stanford University Press, 1985), chapters 1 and 2.

10. Bernard Figler and David Rome, *Hananiah Meir Caiserman: A Biography* (Montreal: Northern Printing and Lithographing Co., 1962), 52; see also Shlomo Wiseman, "The History of the Jewish People's Schools of Montreal," Hart, *Jew in Canada*, 189–92.

11. Harvey H. Herstein, "The Growth of the Winnipeg Jewish Community and the Evolution of Its Educational Institutions," *Transactions of the Historical and Scientific Society of Manitoba*, Series III, No. 22, (1965–66) 27–66, 48.

12. Stephen A. Speisman, *The Jews of Toronto: A History to 1937* (Toronto: McClelland and Stewart, 1979), 176.

13. Ibid., 177.

14. Frances Swyripa, "The Ukrainians and Private Education," Manoly R. Lupul (ed.), *A Heritage in Transition: Essays in the History of Ukrainians in Canada* (Toronto: McClelland and Stewart, 1982, Generations: A History of Canada's Peoples), 244–280. See also N.F. Dreiszinger, *Struggle and Hope: The Hungarian-Canadian Experience* (Toronto: McClelland and Stewart, 1982, Generations: A History of Canada's Peoples), 122–23.

15. See Irving Howe, *World of our Fathers: The Journey of the East European Jews to America and the Life They Found and Made* (New York: Harcourt, Brace, Jovanovich, 1976), 202–04 on the New York Jewish parochial schools in the early 1900s, and Robert Weisbrot, *The Jews of Argentina: From the Inquisition to Perón* (Philadelphia: JPSA, 1979), 140–42.

16. L. Rosenberg, *Kanada: A Zamelbuch* (Toronto: Ferlag Vissen, 1919).

17. See Adam G. Fuerstenberg, "Faithful to a Dream: The Proletarian Tradition in Canadian Yiddish Poetry" (American Association for Professors of Yiddish. Washington. December, 1984.)

18. Ravitch, "Yiddish Culture in Canada," Eli Gottesman (ed.), *Canadian Jewish Reference Book and Directory* (Ottawa: Jewish Institute of Higher Research/Central Rabbinical Seminary of Canada, 1963), 78–79.

19. Simon I. Belkin, *Die Poale Zion Bavegung in Kanada: 1904–1920* (Montreal: Actions Committee of the Labour Zionist Movement in Canada, 1956), 162–63.

20. Ibid., 163.

21. Ibid., 132.

22. David Rome, *Early Documents in the Canadian Jewish Congress 1914–21* (Montreal: National Archives, CJC, 1974. Canadian Jewish Archives, New Series 20.1), 2.

23. Ibid., 3.

24. Ibid., 11.

25. *Congress Bulletin*, Apr. 1968, 2.

26. Simon I. Belkin, *Through Narrow Gates: A Review of Jewish Immigration, Colonization and Immi-grant Aid Work in Canada (1840–1940)* (Montreal: CJC. Bureau of Social and Economic Research, 1939), 100.

27. H.M. Caiserman, "The History of the First Canadian Jewish Congress," Hart, *Jew in Canada*, 465–82, 465.

28. Harry Gutkin, *Journey into Our Heritage* (Toronto: Lester & Orpen Dennys, 1980), 195.

29. Leon Goldman, "History of Zionism in Canada"; Hart, *Jew in Canada*, 360.

30. NAC, MG29C95, Diaries of Clarence de Sola, 16 Mar. 1919. (Microfilm reel A915).

31. Caiserman, "First Canadian Jewish Congress," 466.

32. Ibid.

33. *CJC*, 17 Sept. 1915.

34. *KA*, 13 Sept. 1915, translated and reprinted in *CJC*, 17 Sept. 1915.

35. *CJC*, 1 Oct. 1915.

36. Ibid., 8 Oct. 1915.

37. Ibid.

38. Ibid., 23 Oct. 1915.

39. Ibid., 29 Oct. 1915.

40. Ibid., 19 Nov. 1915.

41. Ibid.

42. Ibid.

43. Melvin I. Urofsky, *American Zionism from Herzl to the Holocaust* (New York: Doubleday, Anchor Books, 1976), 159–60.

44. Michael Brown, "Divergent Paths: Early Zionism in Canada and the United States," *JSS* 44, Spring, 1982, 149–68, 159.

45. Caiserman, "First Canadian Jewish Congress," 468.

46. *CJC*, 17 Jan. 1919.

47. Caiserman, "First Canadian Jewish Congress," 469.

48. Ibid., 476.

49. Ibid., 477.

50. *CJC*, 17 Jan. 1919.

51. Ibid., 31 Jan. 1919.

52. Ibid., 21 Feb. 1919.

53. Ibid., 21 Mar. 1919.

54. See J. Keith Johnson, *Canadian Directory of Parliament 1867–1967* (Ottawa: Public Archives of Canada, 1968), 289–90, and Bernard Figler, *Biography of Sam Jacobs, Member of Parliament* (Ottawa: private, 1959).

55. *CJC*, 18 Apr. 1919.

56. Ibid. 16 May 1919.

57. Belkin, *Through Narrow Gates*, 95.

58. Ibid.

59. Ibid., 102.

60. See Nora Levin, *The Jews in the Soviet Union Since 1917: Paradox of Survival*, 2 volumes (New York: New York University Press, 1990) I, 43.

61. *KA*, 28 Nov. 1919.

62. Ibid., 19 Nov. 1919.

63. Belkin, *Through Narrow Gates*, 95.

64. Caiserman, "First Canadian Jewish Congress," 479.

65. Ibid.

66. See Belkin, *Through Narrow Gates*, 102–04, and Joseph Kage, *With Faith and Thanksgiving: The Story of Two Hundred Years of Jewish Immigration and Immigrant Aid Work in Canada (1760–1960)* (Montreal: Eagle, 1962).

67. Caiserman, "First Canadian Jewish Congress," 478.

CONCLUSION

1. Simon Belkin, "Reuben Brainin's Memories," *Canadian Jewish Year Book* II (1940–41), 138.

2. Shari Cooper Friedman, "Between Two Worlds: The Works of J.I. Segal," Ira Robinson et al. (eds.), *An Everyday Miracle: Yiddish Culture in Montreal* (Montreal: Véhicule Press, 1990), 122.

3. Irving Howe and Eliezer Greenberg (eds.), *A Treasury of Yiddish Poetry* (New York: Holt, Rinehart and Winston, 1969), 156–157.

4. Ira Robinson, "'A letter from the Sabbath Queen': Rabbi Yudel Rosenberg Addresses Montreal Jewry," Ira Robinson et al., *An Everyday Miracle*, 101–14. On Rabbi Rosenberg see Leah Rosenberg, *The Errand Runner. Reflections of a Rabbi's Daughter* (Toronto: John Wiley, 1981).

5. Kerby A. Miller, *Emigrants and Exiles: Ireland and the Irish Exodus to North America* (New York: Oxford University Press, 1985).

Index